WE SHOWED BALTIMORE

WE SHOWED BALTIMORE

The Lacrosse Revolution of the 1970s
and Richie Moran's Big Red

Christian Swezey

Foreword by Bill Tierney

THREE HILLS

AN IMPRINT OF CORNELL UNIVERSITY PRESS ITHACA AND LONDON

First published 2022 by Cornell University Press
Printed in the United States of America

Library of Congress Cataloging-in-Publication Data

Names: Swezey, Christian, author. | Tierney, Bill (Lacrosse coach), writer of foreword.
Title: We showed Baltimore : the lacrosse revolution of the 1970s and Richie Moran's Big Red / Christian Swezey, foreword by Bill Tierney.
Description: Ithaca [New York] : Three Hills, an imprint of Cornell University Press, 2022. | Includes bibliographical references and index.
Identifiers: LCCN 2021041831 (print) | LCCN 2021041832 (ebook) | ISBN 9781501762826 (hardcover) | ISBN 9781501762833 (pdf) | ISBN 9781501762840 (epub)
Subjects: LCSH: Cornell University—Sports—History—20th century. | Lacrosse—History—20th century. | College sports—New York (State)—History—20th century.
Classification: LCC GV989 .S94 2022 (print) | LCC GV989 (ebook) | DDC 796.36/20904—dc23
LC record available at https://lccn.loc.gov/2021041831
LC ebook record available at https://lccn.loc.gov/2021041832

For William, Charlotte, Beatrice, Robert, and Walker

Contents

Foreword

April 4, 1970, was the first lacrosse game I ever played in. The freshman squad from Cortland State in central New York was matched against its counterpart from Siena College in the Albany area. As we went through our warm-up drills four inches of fresh snow were on the ground. Little did I know at the time that that day would launch me into my life's career, profession, and obsession. Those were more austere and, frankly, weightier times in collegiate lacrosse. Wooden sticks, hard leather gloves, battle-ready arm pads, and shoulder pads, and a helmet that felt like it weighed ten pounds—lacrosse players were armored and encumbered. Lacrosse players also lacked resources, and at Cortland everything was shared. (Freshman lacrosse jerseys, for example, were also our freshman football jerseys.) Then there were the sticks. My journey to Nedrow, New York, and the Onondaga Reservation in order to pick out my first real stick was my best field trip ever. I found a beauty made by hand by the Onondaga, and while believing firmly that this one-of-a-kind stick would last forever, I quickly learned how to repair the cat-gut-and-leather pocket as well as fix up the wooden handle.

Soon, though, the game began to change. The polymer heads manufactured by STX were a sensation, and the introduction of an NCAA lacrosse playoff was an exciting innovation. I recall that my best friend, Ray Rostan, and I made a short excursion to Ithaca in 1971, a mere half-hour from Cortland, to shop at the regionally renowned Cullen Sport Shop. We wanted to see what those new "plastic lacrosse sticks" were all about. We saw them, and we decided then and there that we wanted to join the new lacrosse wave. We both dropped $35, which seemed like a life savings at the time, and came back to Cortland happy men with the implements that would "make us great." Cornell had just won the first NCAA Division I championship and I, like many before and after me, became even more obsessed with our great game and its traditions, even as the game was changing rapidly. Of course, the national championship at the time was reserved for the few mainstays, and the thoughts of others crashing the party was farfetched. Hopkins, Maryland, Virginia, Navy, and now Cornell were the premier teams.

For the 1972 spring season I had my new but broken-in STX Super Attack Midfield (better known by the acronym SAM) stick in hand and my Cortland Red Dragons had what I still consider the greatest Division III team in the history of the game. The year after they won the national championship in 1971,

Cornell was defeated by us in a regular-season game, and riding on field success and a 13–1 overall record, Cortland was named the third seed in the tournament. We upset Navy in the opening, quarterfinal round and then played Virginia in the semis at home in front of one of the largest crowds in Cortland State athletic history. We lost that game to the Cavaliers, but it is a memory embedded in my mind.

From these years at Cortland I also have the distinct memory of Jack Emmer, our young head lacrosse coach. Even in college, I had the idea that I wanted to coach the game, and Emmer set a great example. I learned firsthand how to deal with the complexities of the game, establish successful strategies to handle young men on and off the field, and use motivational techniques. I looked to Emmer first, since I was on the field with him day in and day out, but I also had an eye out for the all-time great coaches. Richie Moran and his Cornell teams were the pinnacle of success. Buddy Beardmore at Maryland, along with Bob Scott and Henry Ciccarone at Johns Hopkins, and Richie were the men I looked up to and hoped to emulate. Richie's Cornell teams went on to win two more championships in 1976 and 1977 and just missed an amazing three-peat in 1978. The Cornell teams of that era broke up the lacrosse world of the 1960s, centered on Baltimore County, and in doing so showed that the beautiful game of lacrosse was not owned by a handful of prep schools and colleges. By the late 1970s I was coaching high-school lacrosse on Long Island at Great Neck South, not very far from Manhasset High School where Richie began his career. "Could I do the same as Richie had?" I constantly asked myself. I knew there was no reason I could not, if I tried hard enough.

My college coaching career started as head coach at Rochester Institute of Technology in 1982, continued with an assistant spot at Johns Hopkins from 1985 to 1987, and then culminated, beginning in 1988, with my first Division I head coaching job at Princeton. I cannot help but see significance in the fact that my last game at Hopkins (the 1987 national championship) and one of my first games at Princeton were against Cornell. My target, once I got to Princeton and set an Ivy League crown as a first goal, was clear. I had to get our Princeton program past the great Cornell programs and their great head coach, Richie Moran.

Syracuse's winning the NCAA title in 1983 opened people's eyes, and then we at Princeton went on a run of six championships between 1992–2001. The doors were opened, and some new teams started to believe they could achieve the ultimate goal. In 2009 I was offered the opportunity to help bring this level of lacrosse out west to the University of Denver. We were fortunate, in 2015, to be the first team west of the Appalachians to win the NCAA championship. In the decade between 2010 and 2019, Duke, Loyola, Denver, and Yale expanded the ranks of champions. As we look back fifty years, the growth of championship teams may have begun with Richie's 1971 championship.

Over the years there were many great battles between Richie and me, and I'm not sure these two Long Island–bred Irishmen were fond of one another as coaches. What I know for certain, however, is that Richie Moran's acumen as a coach and the example of his success at an Ivy League school drove me every day. I am thankful for Coach Moran more than he could ever know.

Bill Tierney
Denver, Colorado
March 2021

WE SHOWED BALTIMORE

PROLOGUE
1978, 2001, 1970

When halftime arrived in the 1978 NCAA semifinal, a little after 6 p.m. on a warm, early summer evening in Ithaca, New York, the lacrosse players from Cornell and Navy headed toward their locker rooms inside Schoellkopf Field. They walked with their backs to the small red scoreboard that read "Cornell 7, Visitors 3." The Big Red players, in white helmets, white jerseys, and red shorts, slipped past a large soccer goal that had been removed from the field of play. They entered the two-story, gray-stone, ivy-covered building housing the locker rooms and turned left. Navy, in blue-and-yellow helmets, mustard-yellow jerseys, and blue shorts, entered and turned right. The game drew ten thousand spectators, enough to fill the raised, concrete section of stands behind the team benches—popular because the seats were out of the sun—and several rows of the much larger "Crescent" oyster shell stands on the opposite side.

In recent years the fans, had come to expect successful Cornell lacrosse teams. The seniors on the 1978 team were a perfect example. As members of the freshman team in 1975, the final year before Ivy League freshmen were eligible for varsity lacrosse, they had won all ten of their games. In 1976, their first year on varsity, with many sophomores as contributors, the Big Red went 16–0 and won an NCAA championship. The following year, Cornell went 13–0 and claimed another NCAA championship. Entering the semifinals on May 20, 1978, the Big Red was 12–0. Officially the winning streak—the NCAA, the governing body for college sports, only counted varsity competition—was a record forty-one games. One member of the senior class says that when the freshman season, preseason scrimmages, and exhibitions against postcollegiate club teams were tallied, the seniors entered the semifinal having played sixty-four contests—and won all of them.[1]

Inside the locker room at halftime, the air was heavy and stuffy. With no air-conditioning, the only breeze came from a series of long, tall windows facing the playing field. Coach Richie Moran, in his lucky outfit of black slacks and white polo shirt with "Cornell Lacrosse" written on the left chest, and assistant Mike Waldvogel, wearing a polo shirt with red and white horizontal stripes and khaki shorts, reiterated the game plan.[2] The defenders were reminded to pay attention to Navy's three main threats: Number 17, sophomore Mike Buzzell, from the burgeoning lacrosse power West Genesee High outside Syracuse, was Navy's best passer. Number 11, classmate Brendan Schneck, a Long Island native, averaged more than three goals per game. And number 21, junior Mike Hannan, was another Long Island native who had scored six goals in the quarterfinal win over Army earlier in the week.

Cornell's offense was told to run its motion offense—or "circulation," in Moran's terminology—for high percentage shots. Navy's goalie, a junior from Towson, Maryland, named Jeff Johnson, had played well in the first half, with eleven saves, but Moran believed if the Big Red continued to run on offense, setting picks for each other, the shots would start to fall. Many lacrosse teams rely on one attackman to initiate the offense, almost like a quarterback or point guard. The previous year Cornell had arguably the best initiator in program history. Eamon McEneaney was 5'10", 150 pounds, fearless, and uncommonly unselfish. He had sixty-five assists as a sophomore and sixty-one as a junior before being called to shoot more as a senior in 1977, when he finished with forty-one goals and thirty-eight assists, while leading the team in penalties and finishing third in groundballs, the rough equivalent of a basketball rebound. McEneaney also provided fiery leadership. He had no hesitation in confronting a teammate—or even Moran and Waldvogel, when he thought something was amiss.

Without McEneaney, in 1978 the offense was more solid than spectacular. The leading scorer entering the Navy game was senior midfielder Bob Henrickson, also a starting wide receiver on the football team, with more assists than goals. Henrickson, 5'10", 170 pounds, was one of the best players in the nation despite missing Thursday practices for course work in his animal sciences major—he wanted to become a veterinarian. He was also a member of the popular Sigma Phi fraternity. The best shooter was senior Tom Marino, 5'8", 160 pounds, whose sidearm left-handed shot from ten yards and beyond was released with such velocity he often kicked his left leg behind him, like a pitcher in fast-pitch softball or a professional bowler. Marino, bright and personable, had earned money for tuition by serving as a tour guide for prospective Cornell students and their parents, though in 1978 he turned to more lucrative work as a bartender in two popular establishments in the Ithaca Commons.

McEneaney left a void on the offense—and an even bigger one in leadership. In the final seconds of the first half against Navy, senior defenseman Chris Kane, under no pressure from an opponent, threw a fancy, behind-the-back pass to a teammate. The ball instead went directly to a surprised Schneck, who passed to Buzzell for an easy goal. The sequence took place in front of the Navy bench, and the players on the sideline roared and pumped their fists. Kane made sure to keep his back to the Cornell sideline and slowly walked to goalkeeper John Griffin. "I said, 'Is Richie looking at me?'" Kane says now. "Griff said, 'Yeah, his eyes are popping out of his head.'"[3] It is impossible to think Kane would have tried the risky maneuver in such an important game if he had to answer to McEneaney.

The mood at halftime, despite Kane's misstep, was confident. Senior Frank Muehleman, a three-year starting defenseman, had held Schneck, his charge for the day, to no goals and no assists before the errant pass from Kane. Buzzell and Hannan had each scored once. "Navy was in great shape and seemed like they could run forever," Muehleman says now. "They could run and check, but they couldn't move the ball as fast as we could; our skills were too much for them."[4]

Cornell's players emerged for the second half, many of them stepping onto the hard, kelly green Poly-Turf wearing white leather, high-top basketball sneakers, provided free of charge by a sporting goods store in Ithaca, thanks to coupons from the Cornell athletic department.[5] One senior, a reserve defenseman named Vincent Shanley, had been on the freshman team in 1974 that lost two games. He left school for a year, then returned and rejoined the team for the 1976 season. On May 20, 1978, he was the only senior to have lost a game at Cornell.

These days at Schoellkopf Field, the kelly green, concrete-like playing surface of the 1970s is gone. The stadium now features state-of-the-art synthetic FieldTurf, installed in 2016.[6] A giant video screen has replaced the red scoreboard at the far end of the stadium. The small concrete stands behind the team benches, filled for the 1978 semifinal, have been removed. The "Crescent," a pale half-moon set of stands built to hold twenty thousand people at a time when Cornell was a football powerhouse, looks nearly identical, seemingly updated only by several coats of paint. The stadium was built in 1915 and named for an alumnus; the Crescent is its calling card. The oyster shell is visible from parts of downtown Ithaca, far below; from inside some of the dorm rooms at Ithaca College, several miles away on the south hill overlooking Cayuga Lake; and from the farms that run along the two-lane, serpentine Route 96, more than four miles to the west.

For decades Cornell played its home games at Lower Alumni Field, across Campus Road from Schoellkopf Field. It featured a grass playing surface that by midseason had often turned to mud or baked clay. There was one section of cramped, wooden bleachers, with seating for a few hundred people, and a scoreboard so small there was room only for "Cornell" and "Oppon'ts." In 1971 the university decided to use the land that included Lower Alumni Field for an academic building. At the same time, an alumnus named Joseph P. Routh, chairman of the Pittston Oil Company, donated the money to convert Schoellkopf Field from grass to artificial Poly-Turf.[7]

And in 1972, fresh from Cornell's victory in the first NCAA lacrosse championship game, the university moved home lacrosse games to Schoellkopf Field. The following season, after years of lobbying and cajoling and pleading by Moran, one of the sport's established powers, Navy, agreed to a four-year contract to play Cornell. Two years later Johns Hopkins, *the* lacrosse power, came to Ithaca. Photos from that day show Sections EF and EG, the prime real estate in the Crescent, completely full, with fans cascading into the sections below. The twelve thousand people there was the largest attendance ever to see a lacrosse game in Ithaca.

Those crowds were thrilled by a lithe 5'10" attackman who arrived at Cornell with shoulder-length red hair and a hand-me-down wooden stick, a gift from an older brother. At Sewanhaka High in Elmont, New York, and against the best competition on Long Island, McEneaney had used the stick to score 125 points as a junior and 83 more as a senior. Without a lacrosse stick in his hand, he was generous, popular, fun loving, and erudite. As a senior at Sewanhaka High, he ran for student government as a member of the "Birthday Party." In his campaign photo, published in the school newspaper, he wore overalls, a blue T-shirt, and a huge grin. McEneaney's bookcase at Cornell was stocked, and a scan of the titles showed his passion for poetry. Favorites included *Five Decades: Poems, 1925–1970*, by Pablo Neruda; *Explorations*, by William Butler Yeats; *1,000 Years of Irish Prose*, edited by Vivian Mercier and William Grace; and several books by the American poet Hilda Doolittle, known as "H.D."[8]

He especially loved Irish poetry and literature and the music of Van Morrison. Teammates and Moran recall the long bus trips to away games during which McEneaney would take the brown paper bag that had contained his Cornell-provided lunch, consisting of a sandwich, yellow bag of potato chips, bright red apple, and a cookie. McEneaney would empty the bag of its contents and scribble poems as the landscape blurred past his window.

On the field McEneaney was something different: uncompromising, frighteningly competitive, not afraid to hold his teammates and even his coaches to the same standard he held for himself. "When you practiced with Eamon it was full speed," says Keith Reitenbach, a Cornell teammate. "When he fed you the ball, you were supposed to catch it and score. If you didn't, it wasn't like, 'Oh, nice try.' Eamon would have never had any use for 'my bad.'"[9] Longtime friend Bruce

Arena, who coached McEneaney on the freshman team in 1974, recalls going to Ithaca's parks to play pickup basketball with McEneaney toward the end of his freshman year. "He lived with me in downtown Ithaca for the final month of school," Arena says now. "There were six or seven of us, and he was just one of the gang. And we'd go to play pickup basketball, and Eamon would get into a fight or two as well. There were games at Teagle gym on campus that could get pretty spirited. Eamon was maybe 5'10", 150 pounds, and he was getting in fights with everyone. . . . When he stepped outside the lines of a lacrosse field or the basketball court at noontime, he was a great person, a gentleman. But between the lines he was the most competitive person I've ever been around."[10]

Another set-to came when McEneaney was a senior, in 1977. In the locker room following a midweek lacrosse game against Yale in New Haven, Connecticut, he accused a teammate of having been lazy on the field. McEneaney accosted him and started a fight. The fight was quickly broken up, though his teammates recall the incident happened after a game Cornell won, 14–2. "I thought, 'Okay, this guy is certa-fucking-fiable,'" says Kane, one year younger than McEneaney. "Thing is, no one worked harder than him. He was a gifted athlete, but he worked his ass off, too. We were all thinking, 'Yeah, we're following this guy. Because he wants to win.'"[11] Added Reitenbach: "As with any family, you don't always like someone 24/7, but when it's 'us versus them,' you wanted to be part of Eamon's 'us.'"[12]

With McEneaney leading the way, Cornell won. In his first game on the freshman team, a 22–6 victory over North Country Community College on Schoellkopf Field, McEneaney scored seventeen points. By way of comparison, the NCAA single-game record—counting only varsity competition—entering 2022 was sixteen points. As a sophomore McEneaney was named first-team all-American, and the Big Red fell in the NCAA semifinals. He was named first-team all-American again in 1976 and 1977 as the Big Red won the national title both times. He won three letters in lacrosse and two in football as a wide receiver. He was invited to try out for the New York Jets following his senior year. His chances of making the team were hampered when, the night before tryouts, he badly sliced his hand while opening clams with a knife.[13]

McEneaney's athletic career was over, but he retained his competitive spirit. On February 26, 1993, he was working on the 105th floor of the north tower of the World Trade Center when, below ground level, terrorists detonated a 1,300-pound bomb. The skyscraper shook, then filled with smoke. Electricity went out. His coworkers were frantic in the darkness of the interior corridors and offices. McEneaney, a fire marshal, calmed everyone down. He told each of them to soak a paper towel in water or milk, then hold it to their face with one hand. With the other hand they were to grab onto a coworker. With that, more than four dozen

people formed a human chain and began a quarter-mile descent down 105 flights
of dark, smoke-filled stairs, from crippling fear to uncertainty to safety finally on
the street. McEneaney led from the front as if he were on his way down Sections
EF or EG at Schoellkopf Field—a favorite Moran punishment—and the worst
thing awaiting him was a weekend showdown with a 6'4" defenseman from Johns
Hopkins.[14] McEneaney later told his wife he had simply walked out of the building with friends.[15]

Years later, in late May 2001, McEneaney was back on a lacrosse field. At the
halftime of the NCAA title game between Syracuse and Princeton at Rutgers
Stadium in Piscataway, New Jersey, he took part in a ceremony honoring the
twenty-fifth anniversary of the 1976 national champions. McEneaney was holding an American flag as he walked to midfield with his teammates.[16] It was the last
time many of them saw him alive. McEneaney, still working on the 105th floor of
the north tower, was killed in the terror attacks of September 11, 2001. Married
and the father of four, he was forty-six years old. His funeral in New Canaan,
Connecticut, drew several thousand people. There was another memorial service
in Schoellkopf Field, in April 2002, after the final regular-season home game
between Cornell and Princeton. In his eulogy teammate Mike French recalled
McEneaney's playing days. "We laughed, we didn't have a care in the world," he
said that afternoon. "We were invincible, and Eamon was the heart and soul of
our team, our spirit."[17] These days, when two of his teammates are asked about
McEneaney, they remember him with gales of laughter. There are also long
pauses, because they are crying.

The coach who brought McEneaney, French, and dozens of others to Cornell
arrived on campus in the fall of 1968 from Elmont High on Long Island, never
having coached at the college level. Moran's first season included a rare three-
game losing streak. In his second season, 1970, the Big Red went undefeated.
Moran coached the Cornell lacrosse team until 1997, a twenty-nine-year span
that included fifteen Ivy League titles, either shared or won outright. Moran, now
in his mid-eighties, remains in Ithaca. He places phone calls to his former players every year on their birthday, singing to them in intentionally off-key notes,
before asking about their health, and their families, and their other teammates.[18]
Moran attends every Cornell home lacrosse game and travels to several away
contests each year.

At Schoellkopf Field he watches from a small unobtrusive booth at the far end
of the concrete press box, several stories above the playing field and across from
the Crescent. "I don't talk during games," Moran says, politely but firmly. He has
his rituals, and he has earned his right to them. Most home games he watches
alone, with Pat, his wife of sixty years, in the booth next door, separated by a

glass partition, with the doors to each booth remaining open. During the game they are mostly quiet. During breaks in the action, they discuss everything from the game to that evening's dinner menu, to which Catholic Mass they will attend that weekend, to which former players were in attendance at the pregame tailgate party. Early in the 2019 regular season finale against Princeton, an offensive player for the Tigers tries to muscle his way for a close shot on goal. The big voice that implores the Big Red defenders to "Push him out!" only slightly muffled by the plexiglass window, does not belong to the former coach but to his wife.

During a break in the action in the 2019 regular-season finale, Moran is asked about his first undefeated team, in 1970. The NCAA tournament, championed by Moran, that would shake the sport from its decades-long sedentary and insular existence, was still a year away. In 1970, for one last time, the US Intercollegiate Lacrosse Association would determine the national champion as voted on by coaches and administrators. Those voters had strong preferences. From 1936 to 1969, the same five teams won at least a share of all but two national titles. Known as the "Big Five," Army, Johns Hopkins, Maryland, Navy, and Virginia were the class of the collegiate game and, year in and year out, dominated the USILA-bestowed honors.

In 1970, however, there was only one undefeated team in the country: Moran's Cornell. Each of the Big Five had at least one loss. The USILA revealed its national champion, as it did every year, at the halftime of the annual North–South College All-Star game, the final game of the season, held that year in Lexington, Virginia. At halftime on the searingly hot, mid-June afternoon, the USILA announced tri-champions: Johns Hopkins, Navy, and Virginia. As Moran later told the *Washington Post*, of the twenty-two people tasked with selecting the 1970 national champion, only eight attended the vote and only two of them had seen Cornell play in person. "We felt we deserved a share of the national championship," Moran is quoted as saying. "Instead . . . we had to sit by helplessly."[19]

Nearly five decades later, a pause in play at Schoellkopf Field ignites Moran's reverie. He is watching Cornell trying to wrest a needed victory from the visiting Tigers. This is late April, and because it is Ithaca, it is snowing. Both teams are fighting for a spot in the Ivy League tournament, another advancement from the days of championship-by-backroom-vote. Moran is asked how he found out his team had not won at least a share of the 1970 title. Did he receive a report from the North–South game? "I was there," he says, adding that his role as an officer in the USILA required that he be in Lexington that day. Asked whether he remembers anything from the afternoon, he immediately sits bolt upright in his chair as if shocked by an electric current. He seems to have been transported to a press box in the Shenandoah Valley roasting under an early summer sun, where he watched as three coaches walked off a grass field, each holding part of a large silver trophy, congratulating each other, joking about who would have possession of it first.

Moran was the fourth coach, the outsider, undefeated and unrewarded, literally forced to watch the bonhomie from which he and his players had been excluded. Below there is a burst of a referee's whistle, offering a reminder of the current game, in snowy Ithaca, where the teams are breaking their huddles. The referees, bundled up like the sons of an overprotective mother, are back on the field. The time-out is ending, the moment almost gone, the ghosts flickering in Moran's eyes about to be extinguished by his compulsion to track the late-game play on the Schoellkopf turf. There is time for a final question. "Did you use it as motivation?" Moran's eyes remain locked on the field. He nods his head slightly and, eyebrows raised, answers in a voice barely above a whisper. "Oh, yes," he says.[20]

JUNE 13, 1970

That Saturday in Lexington, Virginia, dawned bright and blazingly hot. It did not take long for shirts to become damp with sweat, for ice cream to melt onto the napkins of adults and the fingers of children. Still, the small town of seven thousand people, nestled in the Shenandoah Valley, was busier than usual on June 13, 1970. That afternoon Lexington was hosting the twenty-ninth annual North–South College All-Star lacrosse game. And in 1970 the game was as important an event as lacrosse, a sport older than baseball, could muster. It was the culmination of four days that included the unveiling of the all-American teams and the naming of the national champion. "The showplace for lacrosse," says then-Cornell coach Richie Moran, "was the North–South game."[1]

The annual exhibition ostensibly featured the top fifty-two seniors from around the country, though in 1970, as in previous years, nearly two-thirds listed their hometowns as either Maryland or New York, primarily Long Island. (The next-best represented state in 1970 was New Jersey, with four participants.) It was of this period that Paul Attner wrote, in 1976 in the *Washington Post*, "Lacrosse once had an image of being a prep-school, rich-boy's sport, a label it deserved. . . . [Although lacrosse] has been adopted by public schools in the Baltimore and Long Island areas, and is growing steadily in other eastern regions, the old preppie tag still lingers."[2]

Maryland and New York had also combined to host almost every previous North–South game since the inception of the contest in 1940.[3] For the 1970 contest, however, the US Intercollegiate Lacrosse Association, the sport's governing body, sent the talent showcase for the first time to a location south of Maryland.

The USILA liked to send its premier event every so often to an area where lacrosse was either unknown—in 1952 the game was played in New York's famed Polo Grounds—or just starting to grow, such as the 1949 contest at Rensselaer Polytechnic Institute in Troy, New York.[4]

Lexington was in the latter category. Washington and Lee is one of the oldest colleges in the nation, established in 1749; the school had fielded lacrosse teams since the late 1930s. In 1970 the sport's main publication, the NCAA annual *Official Lacrosse Guide*, featured on its cover Washington and Lee senior defenseman Ned Coslett. That spring, the Generals enjoyed their best season to date, with eight victories in eleven games. Senior attackman Tom Groton, the team's leader with twenty-five goals, was selected to play in the North–South game on his home field.[5] The sport was generally on the upswing west of the Blue Ridge Mountains: That spring Virginia Military Institute, which shares Lexington in a grudging coexistence with Washington and Lee, for the first time fielded a club team.[6]

And for the North–South game Lexington rolled out the red carpet with festivities including a garden party, a golf outing, an "old-fashioned Virginia barbeque dinner" and a parade down Main Street.[7] Welcoming banners were hung, and some of the stores maintained window displays honoring specific players.[8] The players themselves were given free passes to the Fairfield Pool, ten miles from campus, and free rein of the school's student union building, complete with ping-pong, arcade games, pool tables, payphones, and foosball tables with small ashtrays behind each goal, ashtrays that, when students were on campus, filled up quickly with small, white, crushed cigarette butts.[9] Quietly, during breaks in the festivities, the six-person NCAA Lacrosse Tournament and Rules Committee, charged with shepherding in the first playoffs that the college sports governing body had approved for the following season, held its inaugural meetings in Lexington.

Virginia Governor Linwood Holton, Republican and W&L alum, bought the first ticket—$2.50 for him and any company he would bring with him, half-price for his children—in a ceremony photographed by the school.[10] "To my knowledge," said W&L coach Dick Szlasa in the lead-up, "this will be the biggest athletic attraction ever held in Lexington."[11] Lexington's rolling hills certainly were unfamiliar to lacrosse players and coaches. One attendee recalls being told that a North–South player from the Midwest had missed the first day of practice because he had gone to Lexington, Kentucky.[12]

Lacrosse was not well known in Lexington, Virginia. The town certainly knew the concept of North against South. In 1859 it was cadets from VMI who provided security for the hanging death of antislavery activist John Brown in Harpers Ferry, West Virginia, at the conflux of the Potomac and Shenandoah rivers. One of VMI's professors in the late 1850s was Stonewall Jackson, later a Confederate general in the Civil War. He is buried in Lexington, as is a better-known Confederate general, Robert E. Lee, whose name in 1970 in Lexington alone was affixed to the university, a hotel, a street, the historic Lee-Jackson House near campus, and an Episcopalian church.[13] Both the North–South game and the preliminary contest—pitting the top high-school seniors from Baltimore County against their counterparts from New Jersey and played hours before the college game—offered uncanny reminders. The North–South game included a midfielder from Syracuse University named Jeff Davis. The preliminary game featured a Baltimore County goalie named Jeb Stewart.[14] And fans walking to the game from Main Street in the historic downtown area would have passed the venerable hotel named for Lee, a six-story, red-brick building with a white lobby jutting into the sidewalk. A neon sign on the roof advertised "HOTEL" in giant capital letters and below and smaller, "Robert E. Lee"; individual air-conditioning units stuck halfway out many windows.

On the opposite side of the street was the Southern Inn restaurant with its distinctive T-shaped neon sign. A few doors down was McCrum's Drug Store, complete with a pharmacy and a large selection of magazines and newspapers, including the Wednesday-only Lexington News-Gazette. The lead editorial that week, titled "Welcome, All-Stars," urged the townspeople to attend the game even if they had never seen lacrosse. As if to reinforce the point, an adjoining story, nearly a full page in length, was titled "LACROSSE—Here's How It's Played."[15]

Closer to the campus was the State Theater, one of two movie theaters in town, and the Dutch Inn, popular among students a little worse for wear from a night of drinking because, as one W&L alum of the era recalls, it produced hamburgers within two minutes, day or night. Attendees walking along Main Street then arrived on campus, the scene dotted with red-brick buildings with translucent white trim set on lush, well-manicured lawns. To reach Wilson Field attendees crossed a narrow footbridge. The stadium held seating for seven thousand people—the town's entire population could fit inside.

Spectators who arrived early would have seen the warm-up, a blur of colors at once mystifying to the uninitiated. The North, practicing in the end zone at the southern end of the stadium, wore red jerseys with white numerals and white shorts. The South, sequestered at the other end, wore white jerseys with blue numerals and the same white shorts. The wood of both teams' lacrosse sticks seemed as if burnished with a deep suntan. The wide, webbed opening at the top from which the ball was caught and passed resembled a child's snowshoe. Locals more versed in warmer outdoor endeavors may have likened the sticks to fishnets affixed to the end of extra-long handles; the players themselves, throwing and catching with the heavy, odd-looking instruments, looked as if they were using brooms to shoo away a bird.

The heavy sticks had almost no pocket; the strings were taut catgut and leather—almost like an oversized tennis racket—and even the slightest of touches to the stick from an opponent could dislodge the ball. It was also hard to generate velocity on passes or shots because the ball so easily slipped out of the webbing. In that era fans often stood within a few yards of the action, even behind the goals, with little to no fear of being struck by a shot traveling at excessive speed. The ball traveled slowly enough for spectators, if needed, to simply duck out of the way.

Indeed, the lacrosse sticks in use in 1970 were essentially older than Washington and Lee University itself. In the early 1970s "the sticks we were using were basically the same as the [Native Americans] used in the 16th or 17th century," said former Syracuse coach Roy Simmons, Jr., in 1986. "All of them hand-carved—mostly by [Native Americans]—and there were too few sticks to go around. . . . Kids couldn't just walk into a sporting goods store and buy a lacrosse stick. And even if they could, the sticks were expensive and broke easily."[16]

The wooden stick was one piece. The entire apparatus would have to be replaced if there were damage to either the head or shaft. The webbing could be repaired, a laborious process best handled by an expert. Players of the era recall blocking off several hours to purchase a stick, in order to find one perfectly weighted and balanced in their hands. There was primarily one retailer selling them—Bacharach Rasin with its giant warehouse on 802 Gleneagles Court in Towson, Maryland, outside Baltimore. The sticks were made by hand on Native American reserves in Canada and arrived in batches every year in early spring, with Baltimore-area players receiving the word and racing to Towson to select the best possible stick and thus the pick of the litter. Once the sticks were gone, usually by April, there was no more inventory until the following year.

The one-piece sticks were also made specifically for right-handers and left-handers. In fact, it was this predicament that changed the sport forever. In the late 1960s four men in Baltimore—one of them a left-hander who could not find a left-handed stick—began working on a prototype for a plastic lacrosse stick. They started with the stick head and decided on a utilitarian design that would be the same for lefties and righties. The novel design was not yet in circulation. An attackman at the University of Virginia recalls the early attempt at a plastic head, one he used briefly in a game in 1969. "It was a piece of crap," Tom Duquette says now. All of the players in the 1970 North–South game used wooden sticks.[17]

If any players of the era could twirl the heavy one-piece wooden sticks with a measure of aplomb they could be found at Johns Hopkins. (The Baltimore school was such a power that the US Lacrosse Hall of Fame, initiated in 1957 and dedicated in 1966, was hosted on its campus.[18]) Between 1956 and 1970 Johns

Hopkins shot better than 28 percent once, and averaged more than eleven goals per game nine times in fifteen seasons.[19] Between 1960 and the recently completed 1970 season, the Blue Jays had three times scored more than twenty goals in a game. These offensive stats put the Blue Jays at the top of the college game, at a time when the "fastest game on two feet" was a bit slow and favored defenses.

On the grass of Wilson Field, the players completed their North (red) and South (white) uniforms with their college helmets, making the game look a little ragtag, like a summer pickup game. The helmets themselves were hard plastic and resembled a version of the winter hats with earflaps that are popular among hunters in cold climes. The lacrosse helmet adds one flourish, a full facemask similar to what offensive and defensive linemen wear in football. In later years players would refer to the model, also made by Bacharach Rasin, as "bucket helmets." The *Cornell Daily Sun*, the student paper, often referred to the team as "the guys walking around with birdcages on their heads." The most distinctive bucket on the field in Lexington belonged to number 13 in white. Warren Galvin, a graduate from Ohio State but a native of Long Island, wore the Buckeyes' helmet featuring a red top half and bill and a white bottom half. He looked like a woodpecker and stood out on the field. He also stood out because he was one of seven players from schools west of the Allegheny Mountains.

The South player wearing a white jersey with a blue "11" and some additional protective gear stood in front of what looked like a small guardhouse with a loose white net around the back. When asked, the curious were told that he was the goalie and he was in front of the goal. Number 11's name was Len Supko, from Brooklyn Park, Maryland, near Annapolis. On this day, he may have drawn stares. In his final college game, Supko continued his tradition of beginning his warm-up routine by stopping shots not with the head of his stick but with the shaft.[20] (Supko also continued a tradition of Navy goalies refusing to wear a chest protector, another sign of the low speeds at which the ball traveled.) However unorthodox—goalies used the same webbing to throw and catch and save shots as the other players—Supko believed the unusual routine improved his hand-eye coordination. There was method to the madness: At the all-American banquet in Washington and Lee's Evans Hall dining room the previous night, Supko, roughly a week removed from his graduation from the Naval Academy, had been named the best goalie in college lacrosse.

The sport's matrix became a little clearer as players moved through their warm-up routines and the spectators flipped through the game program, which cost fifty cents. Two other players on the South side of the field wore the same dark-blue helmet as Supko; they were his teammates from Navy. Fans may have checked the game program for confirmation; heavy, blue-and-white, forty pages long, the program featured lineups, small bios of each player, a full page of "Questions and Answers about Lacrosse" (including "What is lacrosse?" and "How many players on a side?"), and advertisements heavily tilted to Baltimore-based businesses.[21] The program confirmed that the trio of players with identical helmets hailed from Navy. Besides Supko, the one with the regular-sized wooden stick, jersey number 18, was a thin, smooth-running midfielder named Harry MacLaughlin, from Catonsville, Maryland. The third, number 32, with the longer wooden stick, was defenseman Greg Murphy, from McLean, Virginia. Thanks to his two years playing football at Navy, he had large biceps and tree trunk legs. One attendee likened him to the comic book hero "Incredible Hulk."[22]

Murphy had arrived in town two days earlier on his motorcycle. "A 650 Triumph," he says now, "riding through some of the most beautiful countryside in Virginia."[23] He did a quick turn through the player's living quarters for the weekend, a W&L dorm without air-conditioning though organizers did provide electric fans.[24] Murphy had spent four years at Navy's Bancroft Hall, also sans air-conditioning. That had been more than enough. He left campus and rode his motorcycle to the Robert E. Lee Hotel and its promise of a color TV and cool air. It was his final game and he was determined to go out in style. He looked ready as he went through his line drills.

MacLaughlin's father, a doctor, was sitting in the stands for pregame warm-ups when he noticed something amiss with his son. "I had food poisoning," Harry MacLaughlin says now.[25] Dr. MacLaughlin snuck onto the sideline to ask if his son was okay. No one asked him to leave so he spent the rest of the day watching his younger son's final game from as close as was physically possible. His older son, also an all-American lacrosse player at Navy, might have joined him on the field had he not been killed four years earlier in the Vietnam War.

Warm-ups on the other side of the grass field revealed the team in red also had talented players. Undefeated Cornell had three representatives: Defenseman Jeff Dean, tall, with heavy glasses, was enrolled in Cornell's six-year PhD program.[26] Midfielder Brooks Scholl was the son of a former Cornell football and baseball letter winner. And attackman Mark Webster's main sport at Ithaca High years earlier had been tennis. He also played for a local club lacrosse team and as a senior at Cornell scored thirty-five goals while not giving up on his tennis background; sometimes he would turn his stick around and use the tight backside to guide the ball into the goal from a teammate's pass, as if he were using a two-handed technique to return a serve in tennis.[27]

When the ball was on the ground number 21 could swoop in at full speed and pick it up without breaking stride. He was Tom Leanos of Hofstra, and at 5'7", 145 pounds, he was the smallest player on the field. He impressed both regulars and newcomers alike not only with his vacuum cleaner of a stick but also because he could throw and catch equally well as a righty and a lefty, an extreme rarity.

FIGURE 1.1.   Ithaca native Mark Webster, left, shown against Princeton at Lower Alumni Field in 1970, scored thirty-five goals as a senior at Cornell. Webster was one of three Big Red players selected for the 1970 North–South College All-Star game in Lexington, Virginia. (Photo courtesy Cornell Athletics)

Leanos, selected as an alternate, made the squad only after a midfielder from Harvard dropped out because his parents gave him, as a graduation present, a trip to Europe.[28] "I think it was [North assistant coach] Jerry Schmidt who picked me," Leanos says now. "He must have said, 'Get me that little groundball guy from Hofstra.'"[29]

Number 22 in a red jersey was tall and thin and wore a series of white, hard-plastic pads along his arms. When he took the field he looked like a knight called into action before his armor was completely in place. He was Pete Cramblet of Army, and he wore the West Point signature jet-black helmet. The previous night he had walked away with the national attackman-of-the-year and player-of-the-year awards. When warm-ups turned to firing the ball on goal, Cramblet shot the ball noticeably harder and faster than anyone else.[30] He was also the only one who could shoot underhand, almost like a golf swing.

Cramblet was the latest in a long line of Army players to appear in the North–South game. In 1952 an Army senior named Ray Austin, using a defenseman's six-foot stick to play attack, was selected to the game in New York's famed Polo

Grounds following a year in which he had scored fifty-two goals. In a 22–5 victory over Cornell, he scored ten goals, a total that, entering the 2022 season, remains a school record.[31] Ten years later Austin was an assistant coach at Army when the six-foot stick of senior defenseman Bob Fuellhart was ruined in a preseason scrimmage. Seeing how upset the player had become—breaking in a new wooden stick would take until at least midseason—Austin donated to Fuellhart his own six-foot stick, already perfectly broken in. Fuellhart used it to become a first-team all-American and the 1962 defenseman of the year. He earned a spot in the North–South game held at Rutgers University.[32]

"This would seem to be quite a rarity," wrote then-Army coach Jim "Ace" Adams, "for two players, in two opposite positions, ten years apart, utilizing the same stick to become outstanding players of their times."[33] In a postscript fitting for the era, Austin and Fuellhart shared one last similarity: both were killed in Vietnam.[34] US Army Col. Joseph Austin died March 19, 1967, when his plane was shot down during a combat mission. US Army Lt. Robert Fuellhart was killed in action on August 11, 1965; the same day, in Shamokin, Pennsylvania, his wife gave birth to their only child, a baby girl.[35]

The Vietnam War dominated college campuses and television screens across the country in 1970, and lacrosse was not given a respite in an era marked by anxiety and protest. Princeton entered the 1970 season having won, in the previous fourteen years, two national titles, the only times the title did not go to a Big Five member, and ten Ivy League championships. On May 7, 1970, little more than one month before the North–South contest, everything changed. In protest over the continuing Vietnam War and recent US military strikes in Cambodia, dozens of Princeton spring sports athletes quit their teams.[36] Among them was roughly half the lacrosse roster.[37] The school's athletic director supported the move. "One kid," said Ken Fairman, "says to our lacrosse coach, 'You told us not to play unless we have a 100 percent commitment, and I don't.'"[38] The exodus left the Tigers with sixteen players, roughly half the number needed to field a successful squad. The following day, the number was down to fifteen; the starting goalie had broken his collarbone in practice.[39] Princeton athletic administration officials and physical trainers met to discuss whether it was too much, physically, to ask such a small roster to participate in the three full games that remained in the season.

In any other season the final three games might have been canceled. But 1969–70 had not been a normal year. In December longtime Princeton coach Ferris Thomsen, sixty-two years old and already a member of the sport's Hall of Fame, announced that he would retire at season's end. He planned to move with his wife, Helen, to Holderness, New Hampshire, and devote his energy to the family's summer camp there. The idyllic plan was irreparably marred when, on February 13, Helen suffered a sudden stroke and died. The season began, and Princeton lost its first five games. Several weeks later it lost nearly half the roster in the strike.

The players who remained after May 7 were desperate to give Thomsen his final three games. Athletic officials relented. With the smaller roster, the scrappy Tigers lost all three games. Their final record of two wins, nine losses was their worst since 1945. Even with the losses, the final weeks of the 1970 season remain a point of pride among those who remained. "I still feel our lacrosse team did the right thing, completing the season for Coach Thomsen," says Peter Lips, a midfielder and team captain. "The conclusion of our lacrosse season will remain a very positive memory despite our awful record."[40]

Other lacrosse programs protested that first week in May 1970, albeit on a smaller scale. Dartmouth canceled its game against Holy Cross.[41] Brown played its contest against Cornell in Ithaca, New York, but staged a protest of its own— its players took the field that weekend wearing orange armbands with brown peace symbols.[42] Before the game a Bears sophomore midfielder named Jim Ria-noshek read a 135-word statement, according to one report, "voicing his squad's protest against the political and social events of the past week [and] asking for a moment's silence before the game."[43] Whether the Bears, who entered undefeated in Ivy League competition, were distracted by the week's events may never be known, but Cornell dominated play in a lopsided 20–6 victory.

Washington and Lee was seemingly in a world apart from those on the Atlantic seaboard. Its enrollment was fewer than 1,500 students, all of them male and all of them required to wear a coat and tie to class.[44] Its faculty featured 130 members, all but one of them male.[45] On other campuses students were staging sit-ins in administrative buildings and taking part in antiwar rallies. Washington and Lee students prepared for hosting the North–South game by designing both the cover for the game program and the promotional posters placed around town.[46] When the USILA selected Lexington as the site for the annual showcase, the committee might have been looking to the expanding future of the game. It also situated the North–South game in a collegiate post where protest and drugs were rumors.

The North–South game on June 13, 1970, began as all lacrosse games do, with a face-off. The referee placed the ball at the exact center of the midfield, and one player from each team crouched next to it. The field, for an instant, was the picture of order. On one side of the field, three red-shirted attackman stood next to three white-shirted defensemen with longer sticks; on the other side, three red-shirted defensemen stretched and jogged in place nervously behind the white-shirted attackmen. Both goalies did a series of quick calisthenics. Four North and South players flanked the face-off, two to each side and twenty yards away, leaning over like sprinters awaiting the starter's gun. The referee blew his shrill whistle, and order shifted into motion. The face-off men sprang into action like squirrels fighting over an acorn. Soon one team gained possession and play became not chaos but pattern and cycles.

The North, in red, scored the first goal, then the second and third. The South, much favored by the home crowd in Lexington, roared back thanks to goals from the midfielder in a white helmet with red patch-like stickers, and one in a white helmet with alternating light-blue-and-black stickers. They were, respectively, Reed Kaestner from Maryland and Charlie Coker from Johns Hopkins; playing on the same line as MacLaughlin, by the middle of the second quarter they had helped tie the game at 4.

The fans, many of whom were watching the sport for the first time, settled into the action. They were helped by play-by-play commentary from public address announcer John Wolf, in his first year at W&L law school.[47] "Shot and save," he said after one sequence in the second quarter, his voice echoing over the crowd. "Shot by Rich O'Leary, save by Lenny Supko." Supko then began the process of delivering the ball to his own offense though passes and running akin to a basketball team trying to break a pressure defense.

Those familiar with the sport's history may well have appreciated the perfect vistas of Wilson Field. The stadium had a steel-and-concrete pile of stands on one side and nothing on the other but a small scoreboard and, in the background, the football goalposts from the practice field. The unusual construction meant fans were staring not at another set of stands across from them but instead at an unspoiled, bucolic backdrop of thick, lush trees and grass, though on June 13, 1970, they would also have spied a white station wagon resting near the H-shaped goalposts on an adjacent football practice field.

The action picked up again just before halftime. The South led 6–5 when, seconds before intermission, number 22 in the black helmet—Cramblet—rifled a shot past the goalie to tie the game at 6. The crowd, having sat through the blistering early-summer heat, might have wanted to use halftime to find a little shade. Those who did so missed the denouement to the season, the announcement of the winner or winners of the Wingate Trophy as given to the sport's national champion and awarded every year at the halftime of the North–South game. The game program included a recap of the 1970 season: "Once again there was no clear-cut champion . . . and the committee was expected to announce a three-, and maybe even a four-way, tie for the national title."[48] The article noted Cornell's Ivy League title and added, "The Big Red thus may be named as part holder of the national title."[49]

When it came time for the unveiling of the Wingate trophy, three teams were honored. Undefeated Cornell was not one of them. Instead the award was shared by Johns Hopkins, Navy, and Virginia, each a member of the famed Big Five, the programs that, between 1936 and 1970, had won or shared all but two national titles. The three coaches gleefully accepted the trophy and debated who would take ownership of it first. (That determination was made by a coin toss.) Cornell coach Richie Moran watched sullenly from the press box.

Doug Tarring, a sophomore and reserve attackman for Virginia in 1970, recalls learning he had won a national title, the pinnacle of college sports, from a phone call at home in Baltimore. "There was no real ceremony," Tarring says now. "The North–South game was over, and we'd won, and it was like, 'Yay, we're national champions, whoop-de-doo.' There was no real way to celebrate. There may have been a ceremony at halftime of a football game in front of five hundred people, but that's it. The way they awarded the championship was just weird."[50]

On January 14, 1970, the National Collegiate Athletic Association (NCAA), the governing body for college athletics, agreed to initiate a postseason tournament for lacrosse, starting the next season. Prior to that, the NCAA offered postseason tournaments for twenty-five sports.[51] Lacrosse simply was not one of them. Instead, starting in 1934, the USILA's Championship Committee began determining national champions. Two years later the designation came with a tangible prize, the W. Wilson Wingate trophy, named for a Baltimore sportswriter and lacrosse enthusiast killed at the age of thirty-eight when a rifle accidentally discharged into his abdomen.[52] Wingate is credited with being the first to call lacrosse "the fastest game on two feet," and several weeks after his death, the University of Maryland became the first team to win the trophy named in his honor.[53] A ceremony was scheduled for June 19, 1936, during halftime of the exhibition between the college all-Americans and the Mount Washington post-collegiate club team at Johns Hopkins's Homewood Field, the earliest precursor to the North–South contest.[54] The first halftime ceremony began with the crowd of one thousand people rising to their feet in silence. Baltimore Mayor Howard Jackson presented the trophy to Rutgers coach Harry Rockafeller, head of the USILA. He in turn gave it to Maryland junior Charles Ellinger, a starting attackman and the team's best player. The crowd remained silent as a bugler played "Taps."[55] The surprisingly dirge-like ceremony augured what was to come for the trophy, how it was awarded—and, crucially, why it ended.

That the Terrapins won the first championship was not a surprise. At the time there were thirty-eight USILA members and nearly half—seventeen—hailed from either New York or Maryland.[56] With the USILA in charge of naming national champions, five teams came to the fore: Army, Johns Hopkins, Maryland, Navy, and Virginia. Starting in 1936, the Big Five dominated the sport's highest honors. That domination, in numbers, looked like this: In 1942 and 1953 Princeton was the lone winner of the Wingate trophy. And those were the only times in thirty-four years that a member of the Big Five did not win at least a share of the crown, if not claim it outright. The Big Five players were ever present atop the USILA all-American teams as well. From 1960 to 1970, there were 129 first-team all-Americans. All but twenty-seven came from the Big Five. Put another way, less than a half-dozen programs accounted for 79 percent of the first-teamers.

The USILA's oversight was much needed. In college lacrosse's early days championships were bestowed by several regional organizations. Cornell was named Intercollegiate Champions five times between 1902 and 1916. One title, in 1903, came after the Big Red had won only two of seven games. The Intercollegiate Champion was determined by the best record among the Ivy League. Even then, Cornell's 2–1 mark in league play was behind undefeated Harvard. The Crimson was deemed to have used an ineligible player, thus awarding the title to runner-up Big Red. It was emblematic of the sport's early days, which were not for the faint of heart. A cartoonist for the *Brooklyn Daily Eagle* in 1925 called lacrosse "a cross between football, basketball, hockey, prize fighting, wrestling and murder."

The Big Five schools also had very good players and coaches. Joe Finn, archivist for US Lacrosse and an Annapolis, Maryland, native, recalls attending games while a student at the University of Maryland in the late 1960s. He said the results of the Terrapins' early season games, against non–Big Five teams, were foregone conclusions. "The gap between the Big Five and everyone else was huge," says Finn. "When I was at Maryland they played all the good teams at the end of the year. It was almost like the NCAA tournament. The games at the beginning of the year, against the lesser lights, were hard to watch. Those teams were sloppy and not even remotely competitive."[57] Between 1936 and 1970, and against non–Big Five teams, the Terrapins won 199 games, lost 10, tied 1. Navy was similarly dominant against non–Big Five; in the same thirty-five seasons it won 188 games, lost 12, and tied 2. More pointedly, between 1960 and 1968 the Midshipmen did not lose to a non–Big Five team.

The issue was not so much the dominance of the Big Five but the exclusion of others. In the USILA's system, only eight teams, at most, were technically eligible to win the national title. The USILA grouped its teams in divisions named for some of the sport's luminaries, though the Ivy League retained its name. And the national champion in every year came from a group called the Miller Division, named for turn-of-the-century lacrosse player and official Cyrus Miller. Even when Princeton won the title, it did so as a member of the Miller Division, playing a dual schedule of opponents in the division and in the Ivy League. The Big Five clearly were atop the sport's summit. And the USILA committee gave them little incentive to share the spot.

Big Five coaches and athletic directors also were disinclined to invite outside competition. In 1957 there were two undefeated teams, Syracuse and Johns Hopkins. The Orange was led by midfielder Jim Brown, who scored forty-three goals in ten games and later became an NFL Hall of Fame running back. On the day of its season finale against Big Five member Army, the *Syracuse Post-Standard* tried to generate support for a one-game playoff. "A meeting between unbeaten teams from the north and south, which would be made possible by a Syracuse win [against Army], would be far more attractive than the annual North–South All-Star Game. . . . It could decide a real national champion."[58] Syracuse defeated Army, 8–6. But the plea for a decisive playoff fell on deaf ears. In 1957 the lone USILA national champion was Johns Hopkins.

Eleven years later, there again were two undefeated teams: Cornell and Johns Hopkins. Both of their seasons ended on the same Saturday in mid-May with a month until the North–South game. Cornell athletic director Robert J. Kane and coach Ned Harkness had an idea: They called Johns Hopkins officials and suggested a one-game playoff between the sport's two best teams.

The Big Red was 10–0 and no flash in the pan: In the previous three seasons it had won thirty-five of thirty-six games. Harkness was not the outsider that Syracuse coach Roy Simmons, Sr., had been in 1957; Harkness's father was a member of the US Lacrosse Hall of Fame. Yet Johns Hopkins demurred. There would be no playoff. Weeks later the Blue Jays were selected as the lone USILA national champion. "Not many people know we tried to schedule that one-game playoff," says Tom Harkness, a midfielder on the 1968 Cornell team and Ned's son. "Dad and Bob Kane were really upset when Hopkins said no. . . . Hopkins almost certainly had better personnel than we did. But we were in such good condition. We were running teams into the ground."[59]

The incidents reinforced the feeling that, in the Baltimore-centric USILA's watch, only the Big Five would ever receive the sport's highest honors. "I don't think we even thought about winning a national championship," says Bob Shaw, a starting midfielder on Cornell's undefeated team in 1970. "We just didn't think there was a chance a team from the North could win it. It just didn't happen. Our goals were to win the Ivy League and beat Syracuse."[60]

This is different from saying the USILA always pleased the Big Five. For one thing, for a championship with only seven or eight main contenders, the USILA opted to award it to multiple teams with alarming regularity. In its final years alone the USILA Championship Committee named co-champions in 1961 (Army and Navy); tri-champions in 1967 (Army, Navy, and Johns Hopkins); co-champions again in 1969 (Army and Johns Hopkins); and the following year, tri-champions (Army, Johns Hopkins, and Virginia). "College lacrosse is a marvelous sport at its best," wrote Bill Tanton in the *Evening Sun* toward the end of the 1970 season. "But at the administrative level there is no sport quite like lacrosse for creating frustrating situations. There is no other sport in which, annually, only a handful of teams can reasonably expect to win the national championship. And I mean a handful—like, four or five teams at most. Yet with so few legitimate contenders, and all of them situated within a few hundred miles of one another, lacrosse somehow manages to come up with more co-champions than any sport extant."[61]

In May 1970, as the USILA readied again to name tri-champions, officials decided to use a spur-of-the-moment postseason tournament to settle a three-way tie. But it was not in the college game. Instead the impromptu postseason was in Division II of the Maryland public-school lacrosse league; a playoff was used to break a three-way tie among Parkville, Milford Mill, and Woodlawn.[62] The *Baltimore Sun* story detailing the playoff appeared next to an article about Cornell's strong 1970 season though it was unlikely to finish with a national title.

In Lexington, as the three coaches figured out which of them would carry the silver loving cup trophy back to his campus, the day became far more comfortable; clouds rolled in, as did a bit of a breeze.[63] On the field the patterns of play remained the same—which is to say, a very even game with neither team able to pull away. The crowd was having fun. Late in the third quarter one of the long-stick defenders wearing the helmet with light-blue-and-black stickers—he must be from Johns Hopkins—galloped the length of the field and scored to tie the game at 7, then turned quietly and jogged back to his position with little celebration. He was Paul Weiss. The game program said he had never played lacrosse growing up near St. Louis, in Florissant, Missouri. Instead he picked it up in college as a way to stay in shape for football, where he was a starting running back for the Blue Jays.

Those who were seeing lacrosse for the first time may well have liked it; the sport seemed to lend itself to hyperbole among first-time viewers. In March 1971 Hobart and Ohio Wesleyan played a neutral-site game in Greensboro, North Carolina. The story in the next day's Greensboro *Daily News* compared lacrosse to "running the full length of a football field with an egg on a spoon while everyone else is hacking at your arms trying to make you drop it."[64] Weeks later, on May 6, 1971, Johns Hopkins and Navy, two of the sport's giants, moved their annual game to Houston, Texas, at the behest of a Johns Hopkins alumnus, who used the contest as a fundraiser for the city's famed Texas Heart Institute. Inside the cavernous Houston Astrodome, home of a major-league baseball and an NFL team, most in the crowd were seeing lacrosse for the first time. The game drew 18,459 fans, an NCAA record. One Houston sports columnist, himself new to the sport, went a little overboard in his enthusiasm: "Compared to lacrosse," he wrote, "baseball is dull, football is for girls, basketball has no fast break at all and hockey players should use two sticks."[65] No doubt, many in Wilson Field in Lexington felt the same way.

Early in the fourth quarter the North tied the game at 10 on a goal by Syracuse's Jeff Davis, whose name alone earned him a smattering of applause from the locals rooting for the South. With three minutes to play, and still tied at 10, Navy's MacLaughlin danced through the defense and took an eight-yard shot. It eluded goalie Mike Stanton of Yale and went in. It proved the winning score in the South's 11–10 victory.

On the surface MacLaughlin seemed to have nothing but Baltimore establishment bona fides—Maryland native, team captain at Navy of the Big Five. But he

FIGURE 1.2.   Navy's Harry MacLaughlin scored the winning goal in the 1970 North–South College All-Star Game in Lexington, Virginia. MacLaughlin also helped the Midshipmen to a share of the 1970 national title. (Photo courtesy Naval Academy Athletics)

had grown up on a farm in Catonsville. Just ten minutes outside the city, Catonsville was a world away from the city's private-school league. MacLaughlin and his older brother, Don, played at the public Catonsville High. At the family's home they used the side of a barn as a makeshift goal. Don, seven years older, played soccer and lacrosse at Navy, often with Harry in the stands. "I don't know how many games I missed," Harry says now. "But it wasn't many."[66] Don MacLaughlin took care of his younger brother, bringing him back lacrosse sticks, game-worn cleats, and jerseys discarded by his Navy teammates. "No eighteen-year-old wants his snot-nosed eleven-year-old kid brother around," Harry says now. "But still, he was very good to me. When he would bring his Navy teammates home and they would go up to the field and throw the lacrosse ball, they always brought me along."[67]

Don MacLaughlin graduated from the Naval Academy in 1963 as a first-team all-American lacrosse midfielder. Within weeks he was married to his high-school sweetheart and living in Jacksonville, Florida, where he had gained admission into the rigorous Navy pilot training program. His final stop before going to Vietnam was Norfolk, Virginia. The family traveled there to see him off.

On January 2, 1966, when Harry was a senior at Catonsville High, he came home from school—"I still took the school bus," he says somewhat sheepishly—and saw an unfamiliar black sedan in the driveway. It belonged to officials from the US Navy. The two men were delivering the news that Don MacLaughlin's plane had been shot down by enemy ground fire in Vietnam. He was missing in action. The next day Harry returned home from school and the car was there again. The officials had an update: the plane had been found. Lieutenant junior grade Don MacLaughlin's status had gone from "missing in action" to "killed in action."

Don's last letter to the family, written Christmas Eve, arrived after his death. He ended the letter this way: "I hope to God what I am doing now will help make the new year a peaceful one." He was twenty-four years old. The USILA's award for the top midfielder in lacrosse bears his name.

"My goal was to be as good as he was," says Harry, his voice shaky with emotion but his memory clear. "I was so young. I just wish I had gotten to know him as an adult."[68] He says he thought about becoming a Navy pilot like his brother; he had the grades to be accepted into the program. "But I could not follow that path," he says. "It would have killed my parents with worry."[69] He did, however, follow after his brother on the lacrosse field. The night before the North–South game, Harry MacLaughlin learned he had been named first-team all-American, just as his brother had been as a senior. The next day Navy officially won a share of the Wingate trophy, just as it had done when Don MacLaughlin was a senior.

And even though Army's Cramblet scored a game-high four goals, Harry MacLaughlin's winning goal and performance in the second half earned him game MVP. "I was so happy to see Harry get that award," says Greg Murphy, the Navy defenseman. "He and his brother represented everything that was good about Navy lacrosse."[70] Harry MacLaughlin walked off the field for the final time, joined by his father, holding an MVP plaque, the team captain of a national champion, saying one last goodbye to a sport handed to him by a beloved older brother.

A sign of changing times came in the hours before the 1970 North–South game. The preliminary contest, at 10:30 a.m. on Wilson Field, pitted a high-school all-star team from New Jersey against all-stars from Baltimore. It had originally been pitched and scheduled as Baltimore against all-stars from either Long Island or upstate New York.[71] But New York's high-school athletics did not permit players to take part in postseason games out of state, and a late change had to be made. Washington and Lee coach Dick Szlasa, scrambling for a replacement after having promised a game to the Baltimore County team, called a friend at the Peddie School in New Jersey named Dietrick E. O. van Schwerdtner. Could van Schwerdtner gather twenty or so New Jersey–based high-school lacrosse players and come to Lexington? It was expected to be a blowout, the sport's epicenter, Baltimore, against a country cousin. The experts looked to be right early on when, after six minutes, one team was ahead 5–0. But the experts were also proven wrong; it was New Jersey that had taken the lead. Maryland scrambled back but fell well short, and New Jersey won, 11–8.

George Martz of Columbia High School in Maplewood, New Jersey, finished with three goals and three assists, and David Hallock of Fair Lawn added two goals and two assists for the Jersey team. When the game ended, a feeding frenzy ensued. Published reports say Maryland coach Buddy Beardmore, head coach of the South all-stars in the college game and watching the high-school game before the main event, offered Martz and Hallock scholarships on the spot. Johns Hopkins coach Bob Scott, in Lexington as a USILA officer and ready to receive a share of the Wingate trophy, offered scholarships to two other New Jersey players, Michael Perez of Maplewood Lacrosse Club and Paul Edwards of Montclair.[72] "It was probably the most important day in schoolboy New Jersey lacrosse," wrote van Schwerdtner in 2007.[73]

In the late afternoon, after both all-star games ended, fans made their way back downtown. The players, not in any rush to leave the field after the final game in their college careers, talked with family and friends and teammates and opposing players milling around with their families and friends. Afternoon drifted to evening. Finally Wilson Field emptied, but the campus was not entirely quiet; barbeques and small tailgate parties dotted the landscape. The weekend had included the initial discussions for the first NCAA tournament, and it may have started to dawn on at least a few people that the sport might never again look as it did on the afternoon of June 13, 1970. When dusk descended on the small town, it did so like a heavy velvet curtain.

THE CLIMB BEGINS

Cornell's stellar won-loss record in the late 1960s and its undefeated season in 1970 was the result of a plan executed by dozens, but hatched by one man—Cornell athletic director Robert J. Kane. Kane cut an imposing figure: Tall, well dressed even when he came into his office on a rare day off, Kane was an Ithaca native who had graduated from Cornell in 1934. He had been a track and field star, and his Cornell record in the 200-meter dash stood for forty years.[1] In 1939, at the age of twenty-nine, Kane was named assistant athletic director.[2] Athletic director James Lynah became involved in the World War II effort, and Kane was named athletic director on an interim basis. In 1944 he was given the job permanently.[3]

In April 1977 he left to become president of the US Olympic Committee, tasked in part with preparing for the 1980 summer games in Moscow.[4] And it was he who oversaw the decision, at the request of President Jimmy Carter, to boycott the Olympics because of Soviet military intervention in Afghanistan. Kane was personally devastated, not least because he had been one of the few officials who steadfastly supported the US appearance at the games. "I had 537 athletes depending on me," he said in a 1989 interview. "And there wasn't anything I could do for them."[5]

At Cornell, Kane was more successful serving athletes. He oversaw national championships in four sports—hockey, men's lacrosse, polo, and rowing—and upgraded the facilities to the tune of $9.5 million.[6] "He was very intimidating," says Elli Harkness, who worked in the Cornell athletic department for more than four decades. "He had a vocabulary bar none. When I took his dictation, I had to keep a dictionary at my elbow for all the big words he used."[7]

Kane's vocabulary matched his outsized vision for Cornell lacrosse. He noted the success, relatively speaking, of Ivy League rival Princeton, the one non–Big Five school that proved a consistent foil to the sport's established powers. Princeton's undisputed national titles had come under coaches Bill Logan (1942) and Ferris Thomsen (1951). Both had played college lacrosse in Maryland, Logan at Johns Hopkins, and Thomsen at St. John's of Annapolis. Logan had also gone undefeated against Cornell; entering the 1962 season, Thomsen also had a perfect record against the Big Red. Princeton's success gave Kane an idea.

On February 6, 1962, Cornell announced the hiring of Bob Cullen as head lacrosse coach.[8] Though not reported at the time, Cullen's son says the hiring was the first time the school had made the position full time.[9] Cullen was then flying on the wings of a 15–1 record coaching the Cornell freshman team. The previous Cornell varsity coach, Ross H. (Jim) Smith, had left to become athletic director at Massachusetts Institute of Technology. The Boston school was not exactly an athletic powerhouse: Prior to his arrival MIT's only top-level national championships had come in fencing (1925) and coed dinghy sailing (ten times). [10] Kane made a second announcement that February night. He gave Cullen a full-time assistant—one with impressive credentials and, privately, the tag of "coach-in-waiting."[11] The assistant, Alphonse "Junior" Kelz, was a Baltimore native with something in common with Logan and Thomsen—he had played college lacrosse in the state of Maryland. (Cullen, on the other hand, was a member of the football and lacrosse teams at Hobart College, forty-five miles north of Cornell.)

Kelz graduated from St. Paul's School in Baltimore in 1957 and was recruited to the University of Maryland. He began with the freshman team, per eligibility rules. As a sophomore and junior he was academically ineligible for varsity competition, according to published reports. As a senior in 1961, he transferred to the University of Baltimore. And there, playing midfield, he scored thirty-seven goals and was named first-team all-American.[12] Kelz was working for the National Cash Register Company when Kane hired him.[13] By naming a coach and someone from the sport's epicenter, both full time, Kane had announced his intentions to the lacrosse world.

With Kane's blessing, ahead of the 1963 season Cullen and Kelz introduced winter conditioning and winter box lacrosse workouts that culminated with a box scrimmage against Rutgers.[14]

To prepare for the box lacrosse period—and the far more important spring season—the team held regular indoor practices during the early winter and once boasted a six-team intersquad league made up of the varsity and freshmen players, who were not eligible for varsity competition but remained part of the program nonetheless. The indoor games were played in Cornell's polo barns, on the southeast edge of campus. The accommodations were not fancy, but at least the players were inside and not subject to Ithaca's famously brutal winters. One drawback to the polo barns existed: Practice could not start until the players had cleared the surface of horse manure.

There were several other firsts under Cullen and Kelz. They began recruiting high-school players. Kelz, with his network of Baltimore contacts, took the lead. He and Cullen also hit the road to scout opposing teams in person. The work on the recruiting trail paid off within two years. In the spring of 1964 Kelz helped land the best goalie recruit in the Baltimore area, a Boys' Latin senior named Butch Hilliard, who had been named to the *Baltimore Sun*'s all-Scholastic team as a senior that spring.[15] In his final two years of high school, Hilliard's teams lost just one game. "To begin a turnaround you need a good goalie," says Terry Cullen, Bob's son and a Cornell assistant lacrosse coach in the early 1960s. "And [Hilliard] sure was a good one."[16]

Cornell's turnaround on the field did not happen overnight. In 1964 the team finished 3–7 overall and won only one of six Ivy League contests. The 1965 season began with a spring break trip to Maryland. The Big Red lost to the University of Baltimore, 13–12, then fell to the University of Maryland, 13–6. The contest against the Big Five member had not gone well; at halftime the Big Red trailed 9–2.[17] The Ivy opener was similarly chastening, a 15–5 loss to Yale in which Cornell junior Bruce Cohen, who had led the Ivy League in scoring the previous year, was injured in the opening minute.[18] Cohen remained in the game but was held scoreless and afterward needed six stitches to close a wound on his face.[19]

Cornell's program was headed in the right direction in the spring of 1965; Hilliard was set for a starring role on the freshman team and Cohen was showing immense promise. But the current team was winless in three games, and worse was to come.

On April 21, four days after the loss to Yale, a pair of Cornell lacrosse coaches joined a professor from the school's College of Agriculture and Life Sciences on a four-seat airplane piloted by the professor. They were flying to Boston to scout the Harvard–Brown midweek game.[20] The Big Red was to face Harvard in three days and Brown early the following month. Initially, Terry Cullen and his father were to be the two coaches on board. At the last minute, the son demurred— he had a graduate-school exam and wanted to stay home and study. His father remained home too.[21]

In their place went Kelz and volunteer assistant Michael Herriott, a first-team all-American the previous year at Dartmouth, where he had led the team to one of the three Ivy League titles it has ever won. Herriott had also won academic awards as a math major and was helping coach at Cornell while enrolled in graduate school. The forty-two-year-old pilot, William Genter, owned the red-and-white Piper Tri-Pacer aircraft. A native of Ithaca and a graduate of Ithaca High, Genter had been a professor at Cornell's school for animal husbandry for nineteen years and was part of Ithaca's East Hill Flying Club.[22]

The trio left Ithaca at noon and flew to Bedford, Massachusetts, then drove to Cambridge. They saw a great game: In an upset, Harvard scored the winning goal in the final thirty seconds for an 8–7 victory. The return leg of the journey was set to land at 9 p.m. at Tompkins County Airport in Ithaca.[23] Rain and heavy fog made flying difficult, and speeds were much slower than usual—officials later said there was a low ceiling and visibility was about one mile.[24]

The flight ran into trouble in Otsego County, New York, approximately ten miles from Cooperstown Airport. By 9:30 p.m., still eighty miles east of Ithaca, an eyewitness saw the plane circling a large field with its landing lights on. It circled a second time and came into the field low, then tried to lift off again when it struck the ground.[25] In 1965 Cooperstown Airport did not light its runways at night unless requested to do so well in advance by incoming pilots.[26] No request had come; Genter's plane was not expected. The ailing aircraft avoided a large cluster of houses but crashed nose-first into a muddy field.

Officers arrived to a grisly scene. The front of the plane, from the propeller to the windshield, was completely submerged in mud.[27] The cockpit was covered in blood, and the wreckage was so compacted that the bodies had to be removed by firefighters using hacksaws.[28] The mud in the field was too heavy for ambulances to drive onto the scene; the three bodies were removed instead by a horse-drawn wagon.[29] As the sun rose the following morning, it became clear that the trio had died in the otherwise picturesque setting of an apple orchard, right next to a stream.[30]

Baltimore native Herriott, twenty-two, was just starting on his career. He was living on Esty Street in downtown Ithaca, less than two miles from campus, and was on track to receive his master's degree in industrial statistics in 1966.[31] Kelz, twenty-six, was living at 134 Hawthorne Place on Ithaca's South Hill. At the time of his death, he and his wife were expecting the birth of their third child.[32] Genter was a member of the Kiwanis Club and the Salvation Army. He was survived by four children. The Civil Aeronautics Board later ruled that the plane had crashed after it ran out of fuel, and it attributed the accident "first to inadequate flight preparation, secondly to the attempt of the pilot, not rated to fly by instruments, to continue visual night flight in adverse weather."[33] Kelz's widow filed a civil lawsuit against both the East Hill Flying Club and Genter's estate; she was awarded $85,000. Herriott's family also filed a civil lawsuit against the flying club and Genter's estate; details of their settlement were not disclosed.[34]

On April 21 the coaching staff and families became concerned when the trio did not return as planned. After 10 p.m., anxious family members and friends gathered to keep vigil at Bob Cullen's house at 101 Elmwood Drive in the Belle Sherman neighborhood just south of Cornell's Collegetown. It was a little before midnight when officials began sharing the tragic news. Everyone in the Cullen house remained awake, too shocked and saddened to sleep. "Dad had called up Junior [Kelz] and Mike Herriott to go to the game, and they never came back," Terry Cullen says now. "It was very traumatic."[35]

The lights inside the house remained on. At 3 a.m. there was a knock at the door. The school's legendary hockey coach stood at the threshold with a message for the grief-stricken head lacrosse coach. "He said, 'Bob, you need time to bury your dead,'" remembers Terry Cullen. "'Don't worry about your team. I'll take care of them.'"[36]

Nevin J. Harkness—he directed his players and others to call him "Ned"—won two NCAA hockey titles at Cornell, the second of which, in 1969–70, went 29–0–0, the last team in Division I to go undefeated and untied in a season. But his family had a long history in lacrosse as well. His brother was head coach at Yale from 1949 to 1963 and his father, Bill "Pop" Harkness, is in the US Lacrosse Hall of Fame as a player and coach. Ned Harkness excelled in teaching lacrosse to newcomers, a trait particularly helpful in an era when few high schools sponsored the sport and many college players were picking it up for the first time.

Tom Harkness recalls being at the dinner table as a child and seeing father and grandfather talking lacrosse strategy using salt and pepper shakers as players. Ned Harkness also excelled in converting athletes more familiar with other sports into lacrosse players, something he could not do with hockey because of the ice skating skills needed. "Lacrosse was dad's favorite," says Tom Harkness. "The reason he loved it was because you could coach it. Hockey had techniques you could coach and certain ways to do things, but if you couldn't skate you were dead. . . . Lacrosse had so much more to do. Dad enjoyed the battle, he enjoyed the chess match."[37]

Ned Harkness arrived as hockey coach at Cornell in 1963, after fourteen seasons at Rensselaer Polytechnic Institute in Troy, New York. The highlight of his RPI years came in March 1954 as the Engineers reached the four-team NCAA hockey tournament in Colorado Springs, Colorado. In the semifinal round they defeated Michigan, 6–4. In the other semifinal, powerful Minnesota defeated Boston College, 14–1. (The thirteen-goal margin remains an NCAA hockey record.)[38] The Golden Gophers looked dominant in the semifinals; in the title game, Harkness's Engineers won in overtime, 5–4.

But Harkness's first national title at RPI was not in hockey. In 1952, with Harkness calling the shots for the lacrosse team, the Engineers went 10–0 and claimed a share of the Wingate trophy—split, predictably, with one of the Big Five, in this instance Virginia. Oddly, or perhaps appropriately, given its outsider sta-tus, RPI never received the actual trophy.[39] Then-Syracuse coach Roy Simmons, Sr., had prevailed upon Harkness and Virginia coach Robert Fuller to attend the North–South game and take part in the halftime trophy announcement. It had been determined that Virginia would receive the award for the first six months, then find a way to get it to RPI for the next six. From there, however, the stories diverge. Published reports say that the trophy was stolen just before the presenta-tion at the Polo Grounds and was not recovered. (Though hardly a chaotic scene, the crowd that afternoon was a disappointing three thousand people.) Harkness's son says his recollection, as well as that of an RPI player on the team, was that the trophy was recovered following the postgame confusion, spent six months with Virginia, and then went missing again. "RPI never got to have possession," says Tom Harkness now. "Dad's theory, and that of some of his players, was Virginia never wanted to share the trophy."[40]

A replica was made and awarded to the new champion, Princeton, at the North–South game in 1953 at Homewood Field in Baltimore. One thing is clear: RPI had never actually taken possession of the trophy it won.[41] And this affected the coach acutely. When he led RPI to the NCAA hockey title two years later, Harkness made a point of not letting the trophy leave his sight, and he made sure it came home to Troy with the team. One of the first congratulatory telegrams he received after winning the hockey title jokingly advised him "not to lose the trophy."[42]

Harkness also had the distinction of coaching before the largest crowd ever to watch a lacrosse game. In 1948 RPI was chosen—based on its 13–0, but still not championship-worthy, regular-season record—to represent the United States in a lacrosse exhibition as part of the summer Olympic Games in London. (Unde-feated Johns Hopkins was the sole recipient of the 1948 Wingate trophy.) Played at iconic Wembley Stadium, the exhibition drew at least sixty thousand fans, though some reports said the crowd was more than eighty-five thousand. The US and All-England stars played to a 5–5 tie.

Harkness, a proven winner in two sports, had rules that applied to hockey and lacrosse. He wanted players to be in constant motion. Anyone who stopped moving even for a few seconds risked being benched. There was such a premium on conditioning that four-mile runs before lacrosse practice were standard. Tom Harkness says his father's favorite adage was not about hockey but lacrosse: Don't stand around. You're killing the grass. "He always said the ball moves faster than you do," Tom Harkness recounts. "Same with the puck in hockey. He wanted people to pass and cut. Never stay in one spot. When your defender turns around to see where you are, you're gone."[43]

Ned Harkness showed this on his first day of practice with the Cornell lacrosse team in 1965. "I went out and said [to the players], 'I don't know you and you don't know me,'" Harkness recounted years later. "'But you're going to run more today than you ever have in your lifetime.'"[44]

Cornell, fighting through the emotion of losing two beloved members of the program, finished the 1965 season 4–7, going 4–4 once Harkness took charge. In its final game Cornell defeated its nemesis Princeton for the first time in thirty-three years. Harkness could be gruff—when evaluating one Cornell goalie, Harkness told his assistants, "If lacrosse had the red light that goes off after goals [as in hockey], our goalie would get sunburn."[45] But he knew and loved lacrosse, and the victory over Princeton, combined with Cullen's emotional state, meant that Harkness was becoming an appealing option to take over the program. After the season an emotionally spent Cullen asked Harkness if he would coach the team full time. Harkness agreed, and the plan received approval from Kane. "There is no finer lacrosse coach in the country" than Harkness, Cullen told the *Ithaca Journal* following the announcement. "Our lacrosse program should be greatly strengthened."[46] Terry Cullen, his son, was more succinct. "Ned Harkness," he says now, "was as good a coach as ever lived."[47]

The intervention was needed and appreciated. After the crash "Bob was so distraught," says Elli Harkness, who worked in the Cornell athletic department at the time. "You'd see him coming to check his mail and his face was down to his shoes."[48] Bob Cullen remained at Cornell as freshman lacrosse coach and lightweight football coach, holding the latter position for thirty-one years, until his death in 1996.

Ned Harkness made a few changes. He eliminated the previous tradition of using the weeklong spring break for scrimmages and early-season games in New Jersey or Baltimore. He replaced it with a twenty-three-hour (one-way) bus ride to Florida Atlantic University in Boca Raton. There, the team had twice dailey practices in balmy weather, escaping the bitter cold of upstate New York and the iffy weather of the mid-Atlantic. Cornell scrimmaged among themselves or, importantly, played exhibition games against Southern teams on the way home. Harkness also stopped scouting opponents in person. "His teams were going to outrun you and outwork you," remembers Tom Harkness. "He didn't feel he had to scout because he knew what he wanted to do. He wanted *you* to adjust to *him*."[49]

With Harkness at the helm, encouraging a newly aggressive and speedy style of play, Cornell was off and running. And Lower Alumni Field, site of home lacrosse games at the time, became a campus hot spot. The 1966 lacrosse team, according to the *Ithaca Journal*, "had basically the same personnel as last year's 4–7 outfit."[50] But they had a new coach, and a new era was dawning. One year after losing its first three games, the Big Red began 3–0, including a come-from-behind, 13–11 overtime win over a Yale team whose starting lineup included attackman Dick Pershing, the grandson of World War I hero General John "Black Jack" Pershing.

The Big Red ran its record to 6–0 leading to the game against Brown in Ithaca on May 7. And for the first time school officials gave Lower Alumni Field a public address announcer for a lacrosse game. The announcer was busy. In a contest that was high scoring for the era of wooden sticks, Cornell came back from a late three-goal deficit to win, 11–10. The good times continued. The ninth consecutive win—over visiting Hobart, 14–4—drew an overflow five thousand people to Lower Alumni Field. In the tenth win, Cornell outshot Syracuse 71–11 en route to a lopsided and unprecedentedly high-scoring 19–2 victory. Watching the Cornell–Syracuse game was Princeton coach Ferris Thomsen, already a member of the sport's hall of fame.[51] The Tigers entered 1966 having won nine consecutive Ivy League titles. To that point, the Big Red had yet to win any. (The league had incorporated lacrosse in 1956.) With Harkness running the show, Thomsen was taking Cornell seriously enough to scout in person.

He was right to be worried. On May 21 Cornell went on the road and defeated Princeton, 8–7, on a goal by Cohen with less than three minutes to play. Cornell had won all eleven of its games and, with that win over Princeton, secured at least a share of its first Ivy League title. Afterward, Thomsen told the *Ithaca Journal* it was the best Cornell team he had seen in his fifteen-year tenure.[52] He also said, in what must have been music to Kane's ears, the Big Red compared favorably to Army and Maryland, Big Five members who had beaten Princeton earlier in the year.[53]

Cornell's record-breaking season ended with a home game against Dartmouth (4–6, 1–4 Ivy League) on May 28, top of the Ivy League against the bottom. A festive day was planned, in the hopes of a victory as the clincher. The setting was Lower Alumni Field, located slightly behind and downhill from Lynah Rink, home of the successful hockey team, and directly behind Teagle Hall, which housed the athletic administration offices. A tall chain-link fence protected the windows of Teagle Hall from errant passes and shots.

Lower Alumni Field featured one small area of permanent stands, on the side of the field opposite the team benches. Other fans lined the field either standing or, if they had the foresight, sitting on picnic blankets. There was one scoreboard, hand operated and situated behind the team benches. It was so flimsy that, in the victory over Syracuse weeks earlier, a strong gust of wind had knocked it to the ground.[54] It was also so small that it had room for only three categories: "Cornell," "Oppon'ts," and "Period." There was no admission charge, and fans weren't necessarily entirely focused on the game. One local writer joked that to determine the attendance at a Cornell home lacrosse game, one should "count the beer cans and divide by three."[55]

On May 28, 1966, a cloudy, sixty-five-degree day, spectators stood three- and four-deep around the playing field in anticipation of an undefeated season and the school's first Ivy League lacrosse title. The crowd was estimated at six thousand people. It was Memorial Day weekend, and the lacrosse game was a welcome respite from the anxiety over the Vietnam War. The Big Red gave the overflow crowd something to celebrate with a 21–5 victory, Cohen leading the way with two goals and seven assists. The Big Red had its first undefeated season in nearly sixty years and its first Ivy League title in lacrosse. The team held its annual banquet immediately after the game. The festivities then were to move to the first-ever "lacrosse homecoming" party, held at the Sigma Chi fraternity house, a beautiful gray-stone mansion on the northwestern edge of the campus.

The statistics show the transformation. In 1965 Cohen led the team in goals and assists with twenty-eight and eleven, respectively. No other Cornell player finished with more than twelve goals or nine assists. In the first full year under Harkness, Cohen finished with thirty-six goals and twenty-six assists. He was also the program's first first-team all-American attackman in twenty-two years.

FIGURE 2.1. Cornell's Bruce Cohen, middle, plays defense in a 1966 game. The wooden sticks used in the 1960s had seen little to no change for decades. (Photo courtesy Cornell Athletics)

Junior Thomas Quaranto went from eleven goals to thirty; senior Thomas Peddy went from nine assists to eighteen; junior George Gould went from two goals to twenty-two; and Canadian Harry Orr, despite missing three games with injuries, went from two goals to sixteen. The defense featured the excellent Hilliard in goal; in his first season on varsity he finished with 163 saves and was named second-team all-Ivy and honorable mention all-American. Cohen, senior mid-fielder Doug Zirkle, and senior defender Bruce Mansdorf were first-team all-Ivy.

Accordingly, the Big Red had blown out a lot of teams in 1966. Cornell also proved it had learned how to win in competitive games, with one victory coming in overtime and three others in the final two-plus minutes of regulation. Harkness "seems to have instilled in those kids the same spirit his hockey teams have," an unnamed Cornell athletics follower told a local paper in 1966. "You're aware of their confidence. They really believe in themselves."[56]

Something else was starting to bloom. Though Harkness was raised in upstate New York and went to high school at the private Worcester Academy in Massachusetts, he was born in Ottawa. He did not become an American citizen until 1949, spending World War II in the Royal Canadian Air Force and flying thirty-nine combat missions in the European theater. His familiarity with Canada helped restart a modest tradition of Cornell's recruiting lacrosse players from that country.

In 1966 under Harkness, the Big Red had also won the Ivy League hockey title, and reports indicated that a National Hockey League team, believed to be the New York Rangers, had contacted Harkness about its coaching vacancy. Such success made the school even more attractive to recruits from Canada. Players from Canada have been part of Cornell's lacrosse program since its very first game, in 1898 against the University of Toronto in Ithaca. Then, lacrosse teams took the field with twelve players; in its very first game, Cornell's starting lineup featured five natives of Canada. It did not help; Toronto won, 10–3. But there was a long time when Canadian players were on few, if any, US college lacrosse rosters, including Cornell's. Ivy League varsity lacrosse in 1968 featured three players from Canada—one each on Cornell, Dartmouth, and Princeton. Cornell's freshman class of 1968 showed the new trend with four Canadian hockey-lacrosse dual-sport recruits.

Just as in hockey, lacrosse victories were not in short supply under Harkness. He followed his initial 12–0 record in 1966 with a 10–0 start the following year. The *Cornell Daily Sun*, the student newspaper, thrilled in the transformation. "Cornell was never a lacrosse school and it wasn't often an athlete came here for lacrosse alone," wrote Malcolm I. Ross in the May 19, 1967, edition. "Yet for some reason, which certainly isn't lacrosse breeding, Cornell has won . . . 24 straight games."[57] The season ended with a game against Princeton, with the Ivy League title on the line.

On Wednesday, May 17, 1967, three days before the game, Harkness approached assistant Terry Cullen with a question: Were teams required to list the first and last name of every player on the roster into the official scorebooks, the ones kept by Cornell and its opponent? Cullen researched it and returned with an answer: No, only the first name was necessary. "I didn't ask why he wanted me to look into it," Cullen says now, "because you didn't ask, 'Why?' to Ned Harkness."

That Wednesday afternoon, Orr, fresh off a standout season with the Cornell hockey team, joined the lacrosse team for practice for the first time in more than a year. Orr had played box lacrosse in his native Canada and, with the Big Red the previous year, had scored sixteen goals, mostly on extra-man offense. Harkness said nothing to Cullen nor the other coaches about Orr's appearance, likely because there were numerous questions about Orr's eligibility. Cullen says Orr had either already signed or was about to sign a professional hockey contract with the Syracuse Blazers of the Eastern Hockey League, and he also says he wasn't sure Orr was academically eligible either—never mind that Orr was not on the team roster.[58]

On Saturday, May 20, 1967, a crowd of six thousand fans packed into Lower Alumni Field for the showdown with rival Princeton. Harkness dutifully entered his roster into both the Cornell scorebook and the one maintained by Princeton, first names only, though Orr's first and last names were listed correctly in the game program. Early in the first quarter Princeton was called for a penalty. Orr entered with the extra-man offense and scored the opening goal. Minutes later, back on the field with the regular offense, Orr took an underhand shot from ten yards with such velocity that the *Ithaca Journal* reported the Princeton goalie barely moved as the ball went past him and into the net for a goal. Cornell led, 2–0.[59]

At this point, Thomsen checked the scorebook to see the goal scorer's identity and realized that Cornell had not entered last names in the scorebook. Between the first and second quarter he approached Cullen on the Cornell bench. "Ferris came over to me and asked, 'Who is number seven?'" Cullen says now. "I told him I don't know. I mean, I knew it was Harry, I recognized him, but Ned had never told me it was him. Then Ferris went over to Mr. Kane, and Mr. Kane called me over. 'Terry, who is number seven?' I told him I didn't know. 'How can you not know, you're an assistant coach on the team?' I told him I just didn't know. I lied to Ferris and Mr. Kane."[60] Thomsen stormed back to his team's sideline. And Princeton began its comeback. The Tigers led 6–4 midway through the fourth quarter when Orr scored again, his third goal of the game, but Princeton held on to win, 7–5. Before the postgame handshakes between the teams began, Cullen remembers Orr taking off his helmet and making a beeline for his car parked on Tower Road, then driving off. "I don't think," Cullen says now, "we ever saw him again."[61] Afterward, Harkness defended the decision. "He [Orr] came out for practice Wednesday, I asked him to come out," he told the *Ithaca Journal*, "thinking we might be able to give Princeton a little surprise."[62] The article noted that the move had not been publicized "and was a surprise to everyone." Thomsen had arrived in Ithaca expecting some sort of surprise, so much so that he took the unusual step of bringing the team manager, a freshman from Washington, DC, named Sandy Murdock, to Ithaca, the coach offering to pay for his hotel room and meals. "I was on the penalty clock," Murdock says now. "Coach Thomsen had reason to believe Coach Harkness ran a bad clock."

The following year Harkness and Cornell did not need any outside help. In 1968 the Big Red went 12–0, winning another Ivy League title. The slim chance of a USILA national title was spoiled by the refusal of Johns Hopkins to hold a one-game playoff. Harkness's three-year record against college competition was thirty-five wins, one loss. But coaching two sports full-time was draining the perfectionist. In 1967, for instance, Harkness led the Big Red to its first NCAA hockey title. The championship game was on March 18 at Onondaga County War Memorial in Syracuse, a 4–1 victory over Boston University. Less than twenty-four hours later Harkness was back in Ithaca on the lacrosse field—or more specifically, the indoor polo barn—running a preseason practice. Two days after that he was on the bus for the twenty-three-hour ride to Boca Raton, Florida, where he would begin a week of twice daily practices as part of lacrosse spring training.

His schedule was so busy it even influenced his son and daughter-in-law's wedding date. "He asked us to get married on January 13, [1968]," says Elli Harkness. "It was the only free Saturday he had."[63] Published reports say that Ned Harkness's days in the winter, when hockey was in midseason and lacrosse was preparing to begin, began at eight in the morning and ended around midnight. [64]

On November 1, 1966, Harkness hired an assistant, Jerry Schmidt, an all-American at Johns Hopkins, from his job as a teacher and coach at Baltimore's Calvert Hall School.[65] Schmidt had gained notoriety four years earlier when he became the first lacrosse player to make the cover of *Sports Illustrated*. At Cornell, Schmidt would do much of the administrative work. But he and Harkness, each with something of a hot temper, famously did not get along. Schmidt left Cornell after just one season and became head coach at Hobart. Some of his players at Hobart recall being told that Schmidt had been forced out by Harkness. Over in Geneva, less than fifty miles from Ithaca at the northern end of Seneca Lake, he built a very successful program and retained an immense dislike for Cornell for the rest of his career.

The answer for the new problem of filling the top assistant coach position came to Harkness in one of his rare losses, albeit an exhibition that did not count toward his record against college programs. On April 7, 1968, before two thousand fans on Lower Alumni Field, Cornell lost to the postcollegiate Long Island Athletic Club, 9–8. The next day's *Cornell Daily Sun* article noted, "It looks as though coach Ned Harkness has found a tremendous prospect."[66] The article was referring to attackman Mark Webster, then a little-used sophomore who scored three goals against LIAC. Someone else also caught Harkness's eye that afternoon—Richie Moran, the thirty-one-year old coach of LIAC. "It was a heated game," says Terry Cullen, then an assistant for Cornell. "During a dead ball one of the Long Island defenders absolutely ran over one of our guys. Ned was pretty tough on the sidelines, and Richie on the sideline was in a league of his own. They got into it pretty good."[67]

In the late 1960s Moran was not just the coach of LIAC. He was also the athletic director at Elmont High on Long Island, where he coached junior varsity football, varsity basketball, and varsity lacrosse. Each of the endeavors proved a success. In four seasons coaching JV football, Moran's teams went 27–5, including a nineteen-game winning streak.[68] His basketball teams went 82–35, with two league championships.[69]

But it was in lacrosse that Moran was quickly making his name. As a player at Sewanhaka High in Elmont, New York, Moran played midfield from 1954 to 1956, and his teams did not lose a game. At the University of Maryland, he was a member of the 1959 USILA national champions. After graduation in 1960, Moran spent six months with the US Marine Corps before starting his career as a high-school teacher and coach. His lacrosse teams at Manhasset High went 67–5 and won Long Island titles in 1963 and 1964.[70] He switched to Elmont High, where his teams went 29–3, including an undefeated season in 1967. And in 1968, weeks after the victory over Cornell, Long Island Athletic Club won the postcollegiate national championship.

Though Moran says he was happy coaching on Long Island, he had dropped a hint to Cornell alum Bruce Cohen, then playing for LIAC, that he might be interested in coaching football and lacrosse at the college level. Two months later, the 1968 North–South College All-Star game was held at Hofstra Stadium on Long Island. The night before the game, Moran hosted Harkness and longtime Harkness friend Jim Bishop for dinner. (Moran says now he believes the dinner was a way for Harkness to get to know him a little better.) Not long after the dinner, Moran was contacted by Kane, who asked whether he would be interested in interviewing for the job of assistant lacrosse coach.

The interview was at 8 a.m., and Moran, famously fastidious from his days in the Marines, arrived on time and with his shoes shined. The nattily attired Kane approved immediately. "I think it was my shoes," Moran says now, "that got me the job."[71] Moran indicated he would take the job only if he could also help out with Cornell's football program. By the time the job was offered and accepted, however, it was October 1968, too late for Moran to help on the gridiron that season. Still, Moran was now the lead assistant at Cornell, despite having never coached at the college level, and largely based on the run-in months earlier on Lower Alumni Field. In announcing the hire, Harkness called Moran "a splendid all-around coach who will prove a great asset to Cornell."[72]

Moran arrived at a university that was founded in 1865 by two men, Ezra Cornell, self-educated and a self-made millionaire, and Andrew Dickson White, a professor educated at Yale and in Europe.[73] Ezra Cornell's real estate, where he raised cattle and livestock, sprawled over three hundred acres. By the late 1960s and through the 1970s, the university campus had grown to 740 acres in the Finger Lakes region of central New York. In that era Cornell boasted an enrollment of roughly sixteen thousand students, approximately 4,700 of whom were enrolled in graduate school. Cornell also boasted 1,700 faculty members.[74] Students hailed from all fifty states and ninety foreign countries. By the end of the 1970s, the university libraries contained more than four million volumes. The Uris Library, used primarily by undergraduates, had study carrels for more than one thousand students.[75]

With lacrosse still several months away, Moran spent the winter of 1968–69 accompanying the Cornell hockey team on a handful of trips to road games, mostly to talk lacrosse with Harkness. On January 24, 1969, Moran joined the team on its trip to play Penn in Cherry Hill, New Jersey. He settled into his seat at the Cherry Hill Arena next to Phil Langan of the *Ithaca Journal*. Immediately Langan turned to Moran and said, "Congratulations." "I didn't know what he was talking about," Moran says now. "I just said, 'Thanks, I'm happy to be here.'"[76] The hockey team returned late that night following an easy 10–3 victory. The next morning Moran was awakened by a phone call. It was Kane. He asked whether Moran could be in Kane's office in an hour.

It was then, in the athletic director's office in Teagle Hall, that Moran was told there was good news and bad news. The bad news: The plans to have Moran help with the football team were being put on hold indefinitely. The good news: Moran was being offered the head coaching job in lacrosse for the 1969 season. Harkness no longer could continue coaching two sports.[77] "Bob Kane said, 'I know you want to coach football, but could you just think about being head lacrosse coach?'" Moran says now. "And I said, 'Let me think about it.'" Here, Moran pauses for one second. "Then I said, 'I'll take it.'"[78]

Moran, thirty-two years old, and Harkness had many similarities. Both espoused a lacrosse philosophy with influences from other sports—hockey for

Harkness, basketball for Moran. Both placed a heavy emphasis on physical conditioning: Moran, again, credits his time in the Marines with teaching him this
lesson. "They were both excellent coaches," Webster says, "but in different ways.
Ned was one of those scary, gruff guys. He wanted to run the other team into the
ground and wanted us to be in the best [physical] condition. He wanted to win at
any cost; losing was not an option. Quite frankly, as a sophomore playing for him,
I was scared to death of him. Richie was a little more cultured, if you will. And his
enthusiasm was contagious. He was more like a father figure."[79]

Both were also considered outsiders by the Baltimore establishment, despite
having at least some familiarity with it. Harkness's father had been inducted into
the US Lacrosse Hall of Fame in 1961.[80] Moran, though he grew up on Long
Island, had played collegiately at the University of Maryland, a member of the
Big Five. Yet, both learned fairly quickly that the Baltimore establishment would
not be giving Cornell lacrosse a helping hand. Harkness saw this when he was
shunned in his efforts for a one-game playoff with Johns Hopkins in 1968. Moran
experienced it repeatedly early on as he tried to add members of the Big Five to
his schedule.

Moran's arrival was good news in another sense. The freshmen recruited primarily by Schmidt were now eligible for varsity lacrosse—and they had reservations about playing for Harkness. Players of that era recall Harkness as frequently
being in a bad mood and focused almost entirely on hockey. Mickey Fenzel, a
reserve midfielder, recalled a game against visiting Harvard on April 12, 1969. It
was parents' weekend, and the game was played in the snow and mud of Lower
Alumni Field.[81] Cornell trailed at halftime, 4–1. The Big Red gathered in Lynah
Rink, and Harkness, either in his role of former lacrosse coach or manager of
Lynah Rink, delivered a diatribe. "He barely talked to us all year and then at
halftime he reamed us out," Fenzel recalls. "He said, 'You've got to get your asses
in gear!' I think it was the only time we saw him all year. It was the most bizarre
experience."[82] The pep talk, such as it was, did not help: Harvard won, 12–4. "If
Ned Harkness had still been the varsity coach I think a bunch of us would have
considered not playing for him," Fenzel says now. "The best thing Richie Moran
had going for him was he wasn't Ned fucking Harkness."[83]

But the main talk on campus the weekend of the Harvard loss was not the
lacrosse game, or the weather, or even parents' weekend. That Saturday marked
the beginning of the Willard Straight Hall takeover.

The standoff was precipitated by an event the previous night: A burning cross
was left outside Wari House, a cooperative for Black female Cornell students.[84]
The next day members of Cornell's Afro-American Society (AAS) occupied the
on-campus building "to protest Cornell's perceived racism, its judicial system
and its slow progress in establishing a black studies program."[85] Thus began the

takeover, one of many chapters in Cornell's combustible 1960s history. Soon after, white members of Delta Upsilon fraternity tried to retake the building and started a fistfight with the hundred or so AAS students. The fraternity brothers were removed from the scene, but the AAS students, fearing for their safety, armed themselves with guns. With that, police officers from all over New York State descended on the campus.[86] The standoff ended peacefully on Sunday night, but it had been a tense thirty-three hours.[87]

The entire campus was roiled with various protests in the late 1960s. One player recalled that in the spring of 1970, the unrest became such that Cornell offered a policy whereby students could take any class as pass/fail rather than for a letter grade. Later in 1970, upon returning from a road game against Yale, players learned that Fr. Daniel Berrigan, a Jesuit priest and antiwar protestor who was in hiding, was on campus and appearing at Barton Hall.[88] Fenzel recalls going to hear what Fr. Berrigan had to say.

Overall, however, the players tended to stay out of the protests, in part because they were busy with lacrosse, studies, and social events, but also because Moran, the former Marine, was not exactly enamored of the antiwar fervor. "I don't think Richie . . . had very positive feelings for the protestors," Fenzel says. "And I don't think many of us on the team talked with each other very much about the war."[89] Added Bob Rule, starting goalie in 1969: "There were protests and gatherings swirling around campus. The team was a mixture of supporters and nonsupporters of the war. . . . The moment you walked in the locker room you left your partisanship at the door."[90]

In May 1972 the campus was embroiled in more protests. This time students took over Carpenter Hall to rally against the Vietnam War. Unlike the Willard Straight Hall takeover, these demonstrations did not end peacefully; instead, the protestors were dispersed with tear gas.[91] The ramifications of the tumult on campus were felt for years afterward. And the success of the lacrosse team throughout the 1970s was a welcome distraction. "In 1969 there were students with rifles on campus," says Buck Briggs, a 1976 Cornell graduate. "Right before my freshman year Watergate had occurred. . . . It was a very ambiguous, unsettled time socially and politically. And I always felt Cornell had a very hands-off attitude during that period of time: 'If you don't burn anything down and don't cause any turmoil we'll let you do your own thing.' I'm not saying the lacrosse team was a safety blanket. But there's no question it was a very important thing to a lot of us in a time of a lot of ambiguity."[92]

The lacrosse team did not always find success in the tumultuous times. The loss to Harvard on the day of the Willard Straight Hall takeover in April 1969 was the first of three consecutive defeats. The last was to Schmidt's Hobart, 14–11. It was a difficult time for a program not accustomed to losing streaks. But Moran remained positive, and the Big Red rallied to finish 8–3 overall and shared the 1969 Ivy League title with Brown and Yale, both of whom Cornell had beaten that year.

In 1970 Cornell continued its challenge to the Big Five. Moran brought in an assistant coach, Mike Waldvogel, nicknamed "Bones" because he was, as Moran said, "skin and bones."[93] Waldvogel, just months removed from his own playing days as a defenseman at Cortland State, was the perfect foil to the head coach. Moran was a master motivator. Waldvogel was more practical, more analytical about on-field trends and issues and strengths and weaknesses. Waldvogel was also a free spirit off the field. Moran likened him to the actor Paul Newman, who used to enjoy driving sports cars in his free time. Waldvogel opted for hiking, riding his motorcycle, and mountain climbing. Moran says Waldvogel even rappelled up and down the facade of Schoellkopf Field.[94]

On the field, however, Waldvogel was focused and serious. His theory on defense: Most goals were scored only after three consecutive mistakes by the defense. "The third mistake was the goalie who should have made the save," says Keith Reitenbach, a midfielder from 1975 to 1978 who played under Moran and Waldvogel. "But the first two could have been anything from a player not getting back on defense to someone being late on a slide [a lacrosse version of a double-team]. He wanted to avoid three consecutive mistakes."[95] On the sideline Waldvogel held a clipboard and charted every goal the Big Red gave up and why, along with which players had been at fault, either by last name or jersey number. The mistakes were rarely pointed out during film sessions; Waldvogel didn't want to embarrass the players in front of the rest of the team. Instead, the mistake was corrected quietly, usually just between the player and Waldvogel. "He made sure you knew about it," Reitenbach says now.[96] Moran gave a lot of autonomy to Waldvogel, so much so that the defensive players realized Moran often blamed the coach, not the player, for on-field mistakes. "During practice we'd always tell Mike he better be nice to us," says Chris Kane, a defender from 1976 to 1978, "or we'd make a mistake and then Richie would yell at him, not us."[97]

Leading to the 1970 season, the coaches had the entire fall of 1969 to work with the team in order to improve on an Ivy League co-championship that, while impressive, did not bring Cornell to the attention of the coaches who named the USILA national champion. With Webster back on attack, the 1970 prospects looked very promising and gave Moran reason to think about contending with the likes of Navy, Maryland, Army, Johns Hopkins, and Virginia. An April 2 regular-season contest against Virginia in Charlottesville was set to be the perfect test.

The Big Red arrived in Charlottesville from its spring break trip down South on April 1. The next morning, hours before the game was set to begin, Moran recalls, he was awakened in his hotel room by a phone call and by a steady stream of rain outside. He was told that Virginia was canceling the game because of rain; its coaches were worried about ruining the grass playing surface so early in the season and had already told the referees, coming from Baltimore, not to make the three-hour trip. Moran was incandescent with anger. He offered to pay for the referees out of his own pocket if they would travel to Charlottesville in case the weather improved. Virginia said "no." Moran eyed the Virginia schedule and noticed it did not have a game the following weekend. He persuaded Harvard, Cornell's opponent that weekend, to move their contest to May and asked Virginia to travel to Ithaca. Again, the Cavaliers said "no." The game was canceled. To Moran and many of his players, it was another sign of disrespect from the Big Five.

The Big Red won its first eight games. The Baltimore media was unimpressed. The *Baltimore Sun* noted that Cornell's last Ivy League victory of the season, over Princeton on May 16, came with the Tigers using only fifteen players. For a game that relies on bursts of hard play from multiple shifts of midfielders, such a small roster meant that six exhausted midfielders were doing the work of nine or twelve. In Ferris Thomsen's final college game the Big Red defeated Princeton, its former nemesis, by a perfunctory 15–5 score. Afterward, Princeton captain Peter Lips recalled, Moran and Waldvogel, fully aware that it was Thomsen's swan song and that it had been a rough year for him, went into the Princeton locker room to congratulate the players on finishing the season for their legendary leader. The *Baltimore Sun* quoted Moran as saying that the Tigers' gutsy performance against Cornell in a 15–5 loss was "the athletic story of the year." The story concluded with this zinger: "The real story will be if Cornell is named as one of the recipients of the national crown."[98]

As if a harbinger, Moran's 1970 season, while undefeated on the field, literally limped to a conclusion. He watched the season finale against Syracuse on crutches; the previous week he had suffered a severe Achilles tendon injury to his right foot. The finale came on a wet, rainy afternoon at Lower Alumni Field. The Orangemen entered with a 7–2 record, having won seven games in a row. It was also the final game for legendary coach Roy Simmons, Sr.; he was retiring after thirty-five years, handing the job to his son, Roy Simmons, Jr. The Orangemen, eager to spoil Cornell's undefeated season and send their coach off on a high note, jumped to a 4–1 lead. But the Big Red battled back for an 11–7 victory before one thousand rain-soaked fans. Moran held out hope for recognition from the USILA. "My campaign for our ranking starts tonight," he said.[99]

Cornell held its postseason awards dinner immediately after the win over Syracuse. The guest speaker was Harkness, installed a month earlier as coach of the National Hockey League's Detroit Red Wings. On his return to Ithaca, he told Moran and the players, "You are the greatest Cornell lacrosse team ever."[100] That praise, and the Ivy League title they had clinched with a 20–6 victory over short-handed Brown, would be Cornell's only postseason team accolades. The Big Red had not won a national title since 1916. Entering the 1971 season, the drought was fifty-four years and counting.

BARBARIANS AT THE GATE

The Cornell lacrosse offices in 1971 were housed in Teagle Hall, a low-slung building clad in fieldstone in the collegiate gothic style, across Campus Road from Schoellkopf Field. The interior featured wood-paneled walls, exposed gray stone, and collegiate gothic archways; it looked more like a medieval chapel than a modern sports complex. Coach Richie Moran's office was on the main level, with a window overlooking massive Barton Hall and a cluster of trees. His visitors during the 1971 season may have noticed the bookshelf. The top shelf featured three small silver loving cups, each on a mahogany wood stand. They were the Ivy League championship trophies from 1968, 1969, and 1970. The rest of the space was empty. When asked, Moran said he was reserving the space for two things. One was another Ivy League trophy. The second, he quickly added, was the first NCAA tournament trophy.[1]

Cornell was on a quest to win the trophies with a roster unlike any other in the sport. It started with Moran, the fiery Long Island native. He began politicking for a postseason tournament almost as soon as he was named Cornell's head coach. His first team went 8–3 and would not have challenged for national honors, but Moran was not deterred. "It's a must," he told the Baltimore *Evening Sun* in 1969 regarding a postseason tournament. "Who's to say whether Ivy League lacrosse is better, or Southern lacrosse or Denver or anyplace else?"[2] His second season, in 1970, had ended with an undefeated record but no national title. "When we went undefeated and finished fourth Richie just exploded," said Pat Gallagher, a reserve attackman on that team.[3] Even though 1971 brought with it the inaugural NCAA playoff, Moran felt compelled to state his case. A few weeks before the tournament, he told *Sports Illustrated* that people in Baltimore "were brainwashed" into thinking there was no championship-caliber lacrosse outside the Big Five. "Nobody knows how good [Cornell] lacrosse is," Moran said in the article. "They need to be enlightened."[4]

All his talk led Cornell's players to realize that their coach was different from his collegiate colleagues. "Richie was a young, very brash, aggressive coach, which ran counter to what I remember of the 'Baltimore' coaches, who tended to be older and much more reserved," says Bob Rule, starting goalie in 1971. "Bob Scott at Johns Hopkins, Buddy Beardmore at Maryland, and Willis Bilderback at Navy were what I would call gentlemen coaches coaching a gentleman's game. . . . Up on Long Island we produced 'lunch pail' players who liked the rough hitting part of the game. And Richie represented one of the first major coaches who came from Long Island."[5] Says Dan Mackesey, starting goalie for Cornell in 1976 and 1977: "The lacrosse establishment in Baltimore was kind of floored by Richie. They kind of shook their heads at him. Richie was so ebullient but they perceived that as cocky. Most of them were reserved, and Richie was anything but reserved."[6]

Moran was the barbarian at lacrosse's gate, but he was not much of a revolutionary. He was and is a practicing Catholic, married to his college sweetheart, and the father of three children. Family and team events often included holding hands and singing "God Bless America." Moran's older brother had been killed in World War II, when Moran was seven years old, and the coach was patriotic about the country, as his players learned on May 16, 1970. That day, Cornell traveled to face short-handed Princeton. The bus was temporarily halted by an antiwar protest on Princeton's campus. As the demonstrators railed against the Vietnam War, an enraged Moran stood up in the bus and shouted out the window, "Stick it up your ass!"[7] The previous week, amid the antiwar protests, Moran had received permission to install a flagpole and an American flag at Lower Alumni Field.[8]

His reputation for being anathema to the Baltimore establishment was well earned. First was his sideline demeanor. The sport in that era was genteel, so much so that referees, in the rare instance they were spoken to directly, were to be addressed with the headmasterly title of "Sir." Many of the coaches born and raised in Baltimore, notably Bob Scott, wore neckties during games.[9] Moran's sideline attire was a frumpy concoction of black pants, white Cornell lacrosse polo shirt, and red sweatshirt with "CORNELL" in a white semicircle across the front.

As for speaking to referees, Moran barked instructions and commentary at them in the same way he did anyone else, with a mixture of charm, humor, and thinly veiled barbs. Moran had no use for the reserved, polite lacrosse world; he had games to win. The coach was so consumed by the action on the field that often, after games, he would quietly approach the team statistician and ask for the final score. "He knew whether we'd won or lost," says Kim Eike, also the team public-address announcer in the 1970s. "But he was so intense during the games he'd forget the score."[10]

Reflecting its coach, the Big Red offense for 1971 would be a little different from what was on offer with the Big Five. Senior Al Rimmer, a native of Toronto, was one of just two Canadian natives playing Ivy League lacrosse in 1971. (The other was a reserve midfielder at Dartmouth.) Rimmer was tall, rail-thin, and quiet, with smooth, sharp features and brownish-blonde hair. He arrived on campus as a hockey recruit who had never played outdoor lacrosse. He had, however, played the indoor version of the game popular in his native

FIGURE 3.1. Al Rimmer, far left, arrived at Cornell as a hockey recruit in the fall of 1967, and had never played outdoor lacrosse. By 1971, he was one of the top players in the Ivy League. (Photo courtesy Cornell Athletics)

Canada, and he tried the outdoor game, or "field lacrosse," at Cornell at the behest of Ned Harkness.

In many ways Rimmer was an unlikely candidate. He was slow afoot and almost exclusively left-handed. "When he ran," Moran recalls, "it looked like he was tiptoeing."[11] Teammates joked about how little power he put on the ball when he shot. "I don't think [his shot] could break a plane of glass," says teammate Mickey Fenzel.[12] Rimmer's stick was famously temperamental. On the 1970 spring break trip to Gainesville, Florida, Moran sought to teach Rimmer a new shooting technique. The coach went through the mechanics of the conventional overhand shot; it resembled a farmer tossing a bale of hay over his shoulder. Moran was a midfielder on Maryland's 1959 national-title squad and an honorable mention all-American the following year; he was no neophyte. To demonstrate the shooting motion further he grabbed Rimmer's stick and launched an overhand shot on goal. The ball sailed forty yards over the cage, out of the field and into the nearby tennis courts, where two University of Florida female students, in mid-match, saw it and scurried for cover, shoulders hunched, tennis rackets covering their heads.[13]

Where Rimmer excelled was his accuracy. His shots and passes were inch-perfect. He had also mastered the art, popular in Canada but unheard-of elsewhere, of the stick fake. He could throw goalies off balance by using his shooting motion, then pulling the stick back—with the ball still in the pocket—and firing a shot at a completely different location. In 1971, relying on that skill shooting close to the cage, Rimmer was set to be a starter on attack; he was coming off a season in which he led Cornell in scoring, with nineteen goals and a team-high thirty-two assists. He was also indirectly given the highest of compliments from Moran. In lacrosse, to encourage shots on goal, the rules stipulate that the team with a player closest to the ball when it crosses the end line retains possession. A longtime Moran axiom was, when the offense won the race to the end line and was given the ball to restart play, the best offensive player had to be the one in possession when the referees allowed play to resume. And in 1971 that player was Rimmer.

The Canadian was one of two starters on Cornell's attack in 1971 who had not played high school lacrosse. The other was junior Frank Davis, 5'9", 170 pounds, and a full-blooded member of the Tuscarora Native American nation thanks to his mother—the tribe took into account only maternal bloodlines. His fair skin and reddish-brown hair came from his father's Welsh-Irish roots. His parents had met on the Tuscarora Reservation in Sanborn, New York, near Buffalo, after the elder Davis had accompanied his father, a Baptist minister doing missionary work. Frank Davis defines the relationship by borrowing lyrics from a popular 1968 Dusty Springfield song. "My father," he says with a smile, "was the son of a preacher man."[14]

The Tuscarora place a heavy emphasis on lacrosse, both physically and spiritually, though they almost exclusively play indoor box lacrosse. Davis began playing box lacrosse at the age of three and hardly ever stopped. Davis joined the Tuscarora teams in their youth league games in nearby Ontario, Canada, not far from where Rimmer was playing. The sport had helped Davis navigate the sadness after his father was killed in a car accident when Davis was a sophomore in high school. In the 1960s and 1970s the Tuscarora also were among the tribes who created wooden lacrosse sticks, and Davis learned how to make them—and, crucially, how to repair them when they broke.

When it came time for college, Davis says he chose Cornell over Bucknell and Cortland State. He had no intention of playing college lacrosse. While being an excellent student and box lacrosse player, Davis was recruited by college swimming teams as a one-meter diver.[15] When Davis arrived in Ithaca in the fall of 1968, he did so with a spot on Cornell's swimming team. He says he planned to rekindle his love for lacrosse only in the summers and only in the Tuscarora's competitive box leagues. That is where things stood when, one day in the fall of his freshman year, he happened to look out the window of his room in what was then called University Hall No. 4 Dormitory, an all-male building on the West Campus. Below were several students with lacrosse sticks. Davis raced down the stairs and ran to them. The sport's adherents in those days were used to any number of ignorant queries: "What sport is that?" or "What are you doing with those crab nets/snow shoes/fish nets?" Davis came up with the one question the group—which turned out to be the recruited freshmen lacrosse players—could not possibly have been expecting. "I asked them," Davis says now, "'Is there a lacrosse team at this school?' They looked at me like I was crazy."[16]

Davis's upbringing in the indoor game meant he knew almost nothing about the outdoor game. He made Cornell's freshman team and wound up as a starter on attack. As a sophomore in 1970, he finished with fifteen goals and eleven assists and even started two games when Mark Webster was injured. Davis became well known among his teammates for being able to fix their wooden sticks—he was so skilled that he took the field with an ambidextrous wooden stick he had made himself. When Moran wanted to run an isolation play for Davis—allowing Davis to take a shot by having his teammates clear out of his way—the coach found an unusual way to get his message across. Rather than using the accepted methods of designating a code word or name of a specific play, the clue for his teammates to accede to Davis came when Moran lifted his fingers to his lips, let out a trademark shrill whistle, clapped his hands twice and yelled, "Make it happen, Frankie!"[17]

The third starter on attack was slated to be junior Glen Mueller, a Long Island native fresh off a stint as a reserve forward on the basketball team. At 6'3", 220 pounds, Mueller was the most physically imposing of the group and considered by many of his teammates to be the lacrosse team's best athlete. "He easily could have played football at Cornell, as a tight end," Rule says now. "He had hands like magnets."

The promising attack unit would be joined by a starting midfield, or first midfield line, that was more solid than spectacular. An exception was junior Bob Shaw, whose thirty-two goals the previous year were second only to all-American Webster. Shaw hailed from Lafayette, New York, outside Syracuse, and had attended Lafayette High, which drew heavily from the nearby Onondaga Reservation. Roughly half of Shaw's teammates were Native American, and Shaw credits their influence for teaching him the skills that made him, in 1971 terms, a complete iconoclast. "I was one of maybe two people in college lacrosse who shot sidearm and underhand," Shaw says now. "I picked up ground balls with one hand. Other coaches would yell at me. Richie encouraged it."[18]

The son of a professor at Syracuse—his father was chair of the physical education department—Shaw was Lafayette High's valedictorian. On the field his career ended with Lafayette's lacrosse teams on a forty-two-game winning streak. Yet the only schools to recruit him were Syracuse and Cornell. He chose Red over Orange because, as he says, "I loved my father but didn't want to see him every day."[19] His high-school teammates who excelled either went to Army, Hobart, Syracuse or, in some cases, didn't attend college at all. Solidly built at 6'1", 190 pounds, Shaw was the most feared outside shooter. Those shots from ten yards or so are the ones a defense usually gives up because they are low percentage. Not so in Shaw's case. In particular his sidearm shot left the stick like a rocket. In the wooden-stick era shooting the ball with a lot of velocity was basically unheard-of. Nowhere was this fact more obvious than at Brown University. One of the goals at Aldrich-Dexter Field on the edge of campus butted up against the backyards of the giant houses along tony Stimson Avenue in East Providence; errant shots went careering against the facades of private homes, gabled windows acting like targets in a shooting gallery. But in the wooden-stick era this situation did not raise any alarms because none were necessary. The houses were safe.

At Cornell spectators at Lower Alumni Field were allowed to stand within a few feet of the playing surface, held back only by a long, thin rope suspended from waist-high posts. "Lower Alumni Field had almost no seating," says Jules Sieburgh, a 1971 Cornell alumnus and regular attendee at lacrosse games at the time. "People lined the side of the field and stood behind the goals. And it wasn't really a big deal since, unlike today, the ball didn't go very fast. Except when Bob Shaw was shooting. The ball really moved. It could be dangerous and, in hindsight, I'm amazed no one was injured. It's a good thing his shot usually went in the goal."[20] The starters alongside Shaw in midfield were senior Mickey Fenzel, the only Baltimore native in the starting offensive rotation and the best defender of the group, and junior Bill Molloy, a Long Island native known for his work on defense and ground balls.

The offense featured recruits from hockey, swimming, and basketball. Cornell's starting defense featured a pair of starters from the football team, senior John Burnap and junior Bill Ellis. Burnap, 6'4", 200 pounds, was a tight end and, in the football team's on-field huddles between plays in 1970, he stood next to star running back Ed Marinaro. Burnap had not played high-school lacrosse in Pelham, New York, roughly fifteen miles from Manhattan. He only tried out for the freshman team at Cornell because his older brother, a former Cornell football player, had urged him to avoid, at all costs, the drudgery of spring football practices.[21] Burnap entered 1971 as Cornell's top defender, strong and physical. He was set to guard the opposing team's best passer.

Ellis lived a dual existence, a native of central New York, who had learned lacrosse in the Baltimore private-school league. Ellis's father, a college football referee, was on the same crew as the athletic director at McDonogh School, a boarding school in Owings Mills. Ellis arrived at the school as a ninth grader, primarily to play football. His freshman English teacher talked Ellis into giving lacrosse a try, in part because the teacher had played lacrosse at Princeton and needed athletes on the freshman team he was coaching.[22] In Baltimore Ellis was playing high-school games before hundreds of spectators, with daily in-season coverage in the *Baltimore Sun*. At home, in Auburn, New York, forty miles from Ithaca, "none of my friends knew what lacrosse was," Ellis says. "They were all about baseball."[23] At 6'2", 210 pounds, Ellis was quick and, unlike Burnap, had played top-level lacrosse for years. He would be tasked with defending the opposing team's best goal scorer. The third starter was junior Russ Greene, a Long Island native, who was moving into the starting lineup after having been the top reserve as a sophomore.

Cornell's starting offense and defense may have lacked pedigree. That was not a problem with the goalkeepers. Junior Bucky Gunts was highly regarded from his time at Friends School in Baltimore's private-school league. And in 1970 Moran and assistant Mike Waldvogel had asked him to trade in his goalie's stick, with the much wider head, for the model used by midfielders. Gunts was too good an athlete and too intelligent about the game to be on the sideline, and there was no chance he would beat out either of the goalies ahead of him.

Senior Bob Rule had grown up outside Boston and excelled as a hockey goaltender. As a sophomore at Natick High in 1965 he was named the team's most valuable player. That summer his father's job transferred him to New York City, and the family settled in Manhasset, which did not offer hockey. It did, however, offer lacrosse, and Rule's friends who played the sport noted the two goalies on varsity the previous year had both graduated. With that, Rule threw himself into lacrosse as a high-school junior, working all winter with assistant coach Renzie Lamb, fielding countless shots either outside, weather permitting, or inside the school gymnasium. The first lacrosse game Rule ever saw was the first one in which he played, a 4–3 victory over Freeport in 1967. The following year, as a senior, Rule helped the Indians win all eighteen of their games. When Rule arrived at Cornell the success continued. He played on the freshman team in 1968. As a sophomore he was the starting goalie on the team that shared the Ivy League crown with Yale. In the fall of 1969 and on something of a whim, he tried out for Cornell's hockey team. Rule made the roster as a backup goalie and the team went 29–0–0 and won the NCAA title. He was earmarked for a leading role in lacrosse in 1970.

Then fate, in the person of Bob Buhmann, intervened. Buhmann looked like the prototypical lacrosse player. At 5'11", 180 pounds, he had good size, complimented by cat-quick reflexes; he excelled in the clearing game, whereby the defensive team, once it gains possession, attempts to move the ball to the offensive end. With his long black hair and high cheekbones he had more than a passing resemblance to the actor Warren Beatty. But Buhmann also had a health issue not immediately obvious from watching him play. During his senior year at MacArthur High School in Levittown in 1967, he had received a diagnosis of epilepsy. It caused him to miss part of that season and also meant he could not legally drive a car or drink alcohol. (The drinking age at the time was eighteen years old.) Even today, it is extremely rare for a college athlete to play with epilepsy, despite all the medical advances, let alone five decades ago.

The diagnosis scared many college coaches. Buhmann was largely ignored in the recruiting process and enrolled at Nassau Community College on Long Island. In two years there, he led the Lions to thirty-two victories in thirty-four games and two junior-college national championships.[24] Even after proving himself as the star goalie on the best junior-college team in the nation, Buhmann received only tepid interest from Division I programs. He told friends that his offers came from two schools. On his recruiting trip to the University of Massachusetts, he was told the team already had a starting goalie, one year older, and Buhmann would be the backup for at least one season.[25]

Moran, the Long Island native, had been tipped off by his many contacts about Buhmann. His offer was even less appealing than the one from U-Mass—not only did Cornell already have a starting goalie, he would be in Buhmann's class. In the end Buhmann picked the Ithaca school, facing the prospect of never being a starter in college, after he was offered free tuition because his medical condition meant that he qualified as a disabled student.[26] Buhmann's high school friends were pleased he had landed on his feet. "No one else wanted him," says Ira Hochstadt, a high-school teammate of Buhmann, who was a star defenseman at Maryland. "And Richie was smart enough to pick him up."[27]

The two goalies were a study in contrasts.

Rule, with his cherubic looks, portly build, and sharp wit, looked and acted less like an all-American goalie and more like a favored uncle. Teammates teased him for his rotund physique. Officially listed as 5'10", 195 pounds, he says now that he was heavier than that. Rule jokingly called himself "a pachyderm."[28] Assistant coach Mike Waldvogel, somewhat less diplomatically, says of Rule, "He couldn't run for shit."[29] On the field Rule was parental, authoritative, and unhurried. He surveyed the scene dispassionately and never seemed ruffled, even on the rare occasions when he gave up a goal. He was also fiercely competitive. His nickname, playing off both his last name and his somewhat aloof demeanor, was "Ruler."

Buhmann was a puppy dog on the field: excitable, emotional, constantly on the move. Fans couldn't take their eyes off him. True to his mercurial character, Buhmann tended to play up or down to the competition. During games against the elite men's club teams that dotted college schedules at the time, Buhmann could look like the best goalie in the country, making saves that even Rule would not have. In practice, when the thermometer dipped into the thirties and twenties and unforgiving winds whipped around Lower Alumni Field, a bundled-up and disinterested Buhmann could struggle to make any saves at all.

Rule excelled on stopping low shots—a remnant from his days as a hockey goalie—but could struggle on high shots to his right. Buhmann, with his quick hands, ate high shots for lunch but struggled going low. Both were good in the clearing game but again as complete opposites. Rule preferred a quick pass for defensemen to do the clearing—more than one former teammate suggested Rule's tendency to be overweight may have contributed to his preference not to run up the field to quarterback clears. Buhmann, fast and fearless, liked to bring the ball up the field himself.

The two also cut different paths off the field. Buhmann, handsome and happy-go-lucky, had an encyclopedic knowledge of music and a record collection to match. But as a transfer student he was two years behind the others in making friends at Cornell and, with his medical condition, was forbidden from drinking. "He still had fun," says Fenzel, who declined to elaborate.[30] Several teammates came from Long Island, but most were from Suffolk County in the south; Buhmann came from Nassau County in the north and thus was not part of the clique. Meantime, Rule and several teammates—including Shaw and Mueller—were members of the popular Sigma Phi Epsilon fraternity. Rule, a teetotaler, was a famous conversationalist, bright and alert, with a contagious laugh.

In the undefeated 1970 season, Moran and Waldvogel did what they could to appease both. Rule and Buhmann played roughly the same amount—Rule played in twenty-three quarters, Buhmann in twenty-one.[31] Their final statistics were fairly close. In lacrosse, a save percentage above .600 is considered good. Both goalies blew that out of the water. Buhmann had sixty-five saves and gave up thirty goals, with a save percentage of .684. Rule was even better—he finished with ninety saves and twenty-nine goals-against, for a .756 save percentage.

One thing Rule and Buhmann had in common: neither liked being told the day of the game whether he would be the starter. So for 1971 Moran and Wald-vogel determined to use only one main goalie. Because both candidates were left-handed, there was no strategic advantage to be gained by playing one and then the other in the same game—whereas a righty-lefty platoon would cause the offense to recalibrate. Rule stopped low shots with aplomb, while Buhmann excelled on shots above his shoulders. Those strengths, too, canceled each other out.

The decision came down to one factor: Who was the best at stopping the ball. "Rule looked big and fat," Waldvogel says now. "But his hand-eye coordination and his play on the field were just phenomenal. And he was ultra-competitive."[32] As for Buhmann, "he had 'it' in games but he didn't always have 'it' in practice. He wasn't always focused on stopping everything. He definitely was a little loosey-goosey."[33]

To begin the 1971 season the coaches made two decisions: They named Rule the starting goalie and gave Buhmann a defenseman's longstick. They were asking Buhmann to use his athleticism and switch to defense. The coaches' decision turned an already frosty relationship between Rule and Buhmann into a deep freeze. "Let's just say," Fenzel says, "they didn't hang out together much off the field."[34] Hochstadt is even more to the point. "They hated each other," he says.[35]

Cornell began preparing for the 1971 season several months before it began. There were the fall workouts and the conditioning typical of college programs. But there was also the small matter of trying to find a locale in which to spend spring break and escape Ithaca's famously brutal weather. In previous years the team had traveled to Florida—namely Boca Raton and Gainesville. The visits had been extremely beneficial but financially expensive.[36] So Moran decided to spend spring break in less costly Raleigh, North Carolina, which would offer both warm weather and the chance to scrimmage teams from the area, including growing programs at Duke and the University of North Carolina. Raleigh at the time was a small city, with a population of about 122,000 people, one-quarter of what it is today.

The team paid its own way with a series of fundraisers. The most successful came just before Thanksgiving break in Cornell's Barton Hall, the dingy, grimy, yet oddly charming multipurpose airplane hangar of a basketball arena. Moran orga-nized a basketball exhibition between the Harlem Globetrotters—complete with

Meadowlark Lemon and Curly Neal—against their foils du jour, the New Jersey Reds.[37] Tickets were four dollars for reserved seats, three dollars for general admission, with one dollar taken off for children under twelve. Proceeds went toward the trip. The game drew fifty-two hundred spectators and was a financial success.

Moran also cut costs where he could. Players slept four in a double room or two in a single room. The tradition was to walk into the hotel room and immediately go to each mattress, one player removing it and placing it on the floor as his bed, the other claiming the box spring to sleep on.[38] Moran and Waldvogel were so meticulous that, during the season, they often posted the following day's practice plan before the players had left the locker room after finishing that day's session. (The coaches placed their postings on the bulletin board outside the Schoellkopf Field home locker room, along with scouting reports, newspaper clippings, and the hand-tallied ground ball statistics from Scotty Johndrew, a member of the Ag School faculty. Players checked the bulletin so often, Moran said, "it was like the Bible.")

Not surprisingly, given everything at stake in the 1971 season, with the nascent NCAA tournament, the trip to Raleigh featured an ambitious, detailed itinerary: Thursday, March 25—depart Ithaca; March 26—practice twice at North Carolina State; March 27—scrimmage the University of North Carolina in Chapel Hill; March 28—two practices on the grass fields at North Carolina State; March 29—morning practice at North Carolina State, then a scrimmage against Duke in Durham; March 30—two practices at North Carolina State; March 31—morning practice at North Carolina State, then board the bus for the trip to Charlottesville for the season opener against Virginia on April 1. It was Cornell's first game against a member of the Big Five in six years.

Rooms in Raleigh were reserved at the College Inn, a two-story, L-shaped edifice of red brick with a white roof across the street from a main entrance to North Carolina State University.[39] The Cornell players were looking ahead to luxury on the cheap.

On March 25 players and coaches ate dinner in an on-campus cafeteria in Ithaca and boarded the team bus at 7 p.m. The route included a long run south along the somewhat new Interstate 81, then onto Interstate 95 into North Carolina. Driving through the night, Moran believed, would help the players sleep and make the time go faster. There were two drivers keeping a rotation, one driving, the other sleeping. One of the drivers was named Cal but the players nicknamed him "Cannonball." "He drove like a maniac," says Burnap.[40] Moran, if he thought the trip was running behind schedule, was famous for trying to speed things along. "He'd often ask the drivers, 'Is this as fast as the bus can go?'" Rule says. "'You seem like a good driver, I bet you could get it to go just a little faster.'"

Six hundred miles to the south, the team's destination of Raleigh welcomed a surprise visitor: snow. It had begun the previous day, with weather forecasters saying it would not last long. Instead it continued throughout the afternoon and into the evening, bringing the Tar Heel state to a halt. Even without the snow things had stopped as the region hunkered down for the televised college basketball game between Duke against North Carolina in the National Invitation Tournament semifinals in Madison Square Garden. (North Carolina won, 73–67.) While basketball holidays were common, snow days were out of the ordinary. By the following morning several inches of snow had fallen; school children were given the day off, and the icy roads led to a series of accidents, at least one of them deadly.[41]

Cornell's coaches and players pulled into Raleigh a haggard bunch, their trip having been delayed six hours by the surprise weather; they had navigated the untreated roads slowly and carefully despite Cannonball Cal's penchant for speed. That day in Ithaca temperatures reached the mid-40s; the following day it was in the 50s. In Raleigh the Saturday scrimmage against North Carolina was canceled because of the bad weather. By Sunday, though playing and practicing outdoors on the precious full field was still impossible, more seasonal weather returned, and Moran began making plans.

First he held an indoor practice at Reynolds Coliseum, home of North Carolina State's nationally ranked basketball team. The Wolfpack's season had ended two weeks earlier with a loss in the ACC tournament. Still, several basketball players had been at Reynolds Coliseum for a workout, and they sat in the stands to watch Cornell's lacrosse practice. They saw a Moran special: The Cornell players dropped their sticks and began running, then stretching, then more running, then more stretching. At one point one of the basketball players shouted, "Do you guys do anything but exercise?"[42]

Cornell's itinerary changed: Monday, scrimmage Duke and Rensselaer Polytechnic Institute in Durham; Tuesday, scrimmage North Carolina in Chapel Hill; Wednesday, a quick practice, then a situational scrimmage against the Tar Heels, then depart for Charlottesville. Thursday, April 1, the Big Red was still slated to face the top-ranked Cavaliers. The Big Red won the scrimmage against North Carolina, 14–5.[43] It was the least impressive showing in Raleigh. One day earlier the Big Red had defeated RPI, 25–2, inspiring the *Ithaca Journal* to say that it was "more target practice than game situation."[44] The Big Red's other preseason contest, against Duke, was a rare shutout in which Rule in particular was outstanding in goal. The Big Red boarded the bus to Charlottesville having looked good in scrimmages, but lacking game practice.

The trip to Raleigh was not all bad. The scrimmage against RPI drew several onlookers who cheered wildly for the Big Red. Afterward, the group congratulated a handful of Cornell's players. Moran noticed the exchange and asked his players if they knew the onlookers. No, they said, stifling smiles, and only years later did they reveal that the spectators had become Cornell fans after meeting a handful of the players who had, the previous night, snuck out to a local bar after curfew.[45]

As the Big Red left Raleigh and made a roughly three-hour trip north to Charlottesville, many Baltimore-based lacrosse fans and officials made a roughly three-hour trip south to the same location. The group included the head of the USILA's All-American Selection Committee and even a sportswriter from the *Baltimore Sun*. The Big Red and Moran had complained the loudest and longest about the USILA method for awarding the national championship. And the Baltimore establishment wanted to see what all the fuss out of Ithaca was about. It had already been an unusual year in Baltimore—and not just because the NCAA tournament had rendered moot the USILA method of selecting a champion. Johns Hopkins, one of the Big Five and the defending national tri-champion, had lost its season opener. Not only that, it had been soundly beaten, at home, by underdog Yale. The *Baltimore Sun* reported after the 8–4 victory that "the Yale locker room . . . was like the Super Bowl. Champagne flowed and players were hooting and hollering and slapping one another on the back."[46]

The Cornell–Virginia game on April 1 was set for 1 p.m. The weather was clear and bright—sixty-five degrees, with a warm, soft breeze.[47] There was no chance for the game to be canceled, as the previous year's had been (controversially). Cornell's team bus dropped the players at the University Hall Field, next to the school's white-domed basketball arena. Virginia's players were on the grass field going through warm-ups. In 1971 those drills featured something different from any other high school, college, or men's club team— many of the Cavaliers were using sticks with plastic heads.[48]

The idea for plastic heads had been percolating since the early 1960s. Dick Tucker, a lacrosse all-American at Johns Hopkins, was the vice president of William T. Burnett & Co., a plastics manufacturer in South Baltimore.[49] He came up with the idea for a plastic lacrosse stick head and enlisted three friends and former lacrosse players to help—Bill Crawford, Joseph Sollers, and Roland Fracalossi. Product testing, such as it was, took place in an era with little oversight. In the spring of 1969, the men gave a prototype to Joe Cowan, a senior at Johns Hopkins and all-American attackman. On May 3, during the late stages of a 20–5 victory over Rutgers at Homewood Field, Cowan traded in his one-piece wooden stick for one with the plastic head. "He went in the game, twirled it around a little and scored a couple goals," says Wick Sollers, the son of one of the four inventors.

"He then handed it back to Dad and said, 'Yeah, I like that.' All this I'm sure was highly illegal. I mean, the stick hadn't even been approved yet."[50]

Months later, in the fall of 1969, Tom Duquette, a Baltimore native and graduate of Gilman School, enrolled at the University of Virginia as a recruited lacrosse player. For the 1970 season he used a wooden stick, but his backup was one of the STX prototypes, given to him by Crawford, a former lacrosse player at Virginia. "It was a piece of crap," Duquette says now. "It was just a plastic triangle with strings on top of a broomstick. I used it in the second half of the Carolina game and it was terrible, but it was a first step."[51]

On April 21, 1970, the US government approved patent no. 3,507,495: the plastic lacrosse stick head. When Duquette went home over Thanksgiving in 1970 he saw an ad from STX saying it was seeking candidates who knew how to string a lacrosse stick. Duquette answered the ad and, over Christmas, began working for the company. The feedback from the prototypes had been returned, and the stick head was now improved. "Bad weather wreaked havoc with the wooden sticks," Duquette says now. "The catgut strings would become like a bag. STX was starting to experiment with synthetics. The other thing was, no two wooden sticks were alike. Each one had a different balance. With STX, every stick was symmetrical and perfectly balanced."[52]

To address how to improve play in wet weather, the developers settled on stringing the new heads with a nylon called "cord no. 3," whose primary use was in Venetian blinds.[53] "It was more forgiving in wet weather," Duquette says. "It had a filament inside it, and then it was woven in casing material. It was ideal."[54] In 1971 the USILA Rules Committee narrowly approved the use of the plastic stick head at the college level.[55] Duquette brought several plastic stick heads, affixed atop wooden shafts, for his teammates for the 1971 season. He estimates that, at most, half the college players, primarily those who played offense, owned a plastic stick head.[56] Defensemen preferred the heavier wooden sticks because they were more effective when throwing checks. "They were like a club you could hit opponents with," Duquette says.[57]

Virginia's equipment did not escape the notice of Cornell's players, several of whom recalled not having seen a plastic stick before. "We were asking, 'What are those?'" said Gunts. "I don't think we had ever really seen one before. We were proud of our wooden sticks, we had Frank Davis who could string them for us. I remember thinking Virginia's plastic sticks weren't really fair."[58] Ellis, the starting defenseman, said he, too, had never seen a plastic stick head before April 1, 1971.

Virginia took the field on April 1 ranked number 1 in the *Baltimore Sun* and coming off an easy 18–2 victory over another Ivy League team, Princeton. The Big Red entered ranked number 6 in the *Sun* and having had its preseason practices in Raleigh significantly truncated by the surprise snow.[59] The Cavaliers took the field looking very much the establishment, with nine starters from Baltimore and one from Long Island, all of whom had played high-school lacrosse. Among the starters was a freshman midfielder named Doug Cooper from Boys' Latin in Baltimore. Cornell's freshmen, barred by Ivy League rules from competing in varsity sports, were back in Ithaca.

The game on the grass surface in Charlottesville began. After fifty-one seconds the Cavaliers took the lead, on a goal by Jay Connor, a native of Towson, Maryland. Virginia was dominating Shaw on face-offs and took eleven more shots in the quarter. None got past Rule, who ended the quarter with six saves and offset a Big Red offense that did not score. In the second quarter Virginia continued its onslaught. This time it found a way past Rule, thanks to goals from Cooper, Connor, and junior Pete Eldridge, an Annapolis native, to lead 4–0. Rimmer answered for Cornell before Cooper scored again for a 5–1 halftime lead. In the first half Virginia had outshot Cornell 25–8.

One minute into the third quarter Virginia led 6–1 following a goal by junior Bobby Proutt, a graduate of Baltimore's Gilman School. Less than a minute later it was 7–1, following a goal by Cooper off a flashy behind-the-back pass from Jim Ulman, from Perry Hall High outside Baltimore. Ten seconds later the Cavaliers scored again, with Long Island native Rick Beach's goal off an assist from Cooper on another breakaway, for an 8–1 lead. Moran had politicked for his team the previous year to be included in postseason honors; he also had pushed hard for the NCAA tournament. It looked like Cornell was not ready to be counted among the Big Five.

Two goals by Cornell's Gallagher, a 5'6" reserve attackman, were sandwiched around a goal by Rimmer to cut the deficit to 8–4 late in the third quarter. The Cavaliers had another breakaway from Connor. This time Rule made the save and cleared the ball. Soon after, Rimmer scored to cut the deficit to 8–5. Early in the fourth quarter Rimmer struck again to make it 8–6, then again for 8–7 and, with nine minutes to play, Davis scored to tie the game at 8. The game went into seesaw mode, Connor scoring for Virginia, Rimmer answering for Cornell. Finally, with less than two minutes to play and the contest tied at 9, Davis and his homemade stick were called for a one-minute slashing penalty. Duquette scored on the extra-man chance with 1:11 to play for a one-goal lead. Cornell had two chances at ground balls late to gain possession and possibly tie the game but missed both of them. The Cavaliers held on, 10–9.

Despite the loss, the reasons for Cornell's optimism were everywhere. In the brave new world of the NCAA tournament, the loss was less a death knell and more a building block. It gave Cornell confidence that it could play with the best; once the postseason tournament arrived, its players knew anything could happen. Rule finished with seventeen saves. Rimmer's accuracy was as advertised—his six goals came on seven shots.

The following day the Big Red traveled to Baltimore for a 7 p.m. scrimmage against the Baltimore Lacrosse Club at Norris Field. In a driving rainstorm Cornell won, 13–8, thanks to four goals from Shaw and three more from Mueller.[60] The team then boarded the bus and arrived in Ithaca at 6 a.m. But the bus was a little heavier on the way home. Before the scrimmage in Baltimore, Moran added an item to the itinerary: a visit to Bacharach Rasin. There each player was permitted to pick one stick with a plastic head, purchased by Moran.[61] (Each stick cost $20.50, or around $135 today.[62]) The next day, Sunday, the *Baltimore Sun* published its weekly top 10 rankings. Virginia remained number one. Cornell was fifth.[63]

Cornell returned home and won its next eight games, against Cortland State, Harvard, Syracuse, Pennsylvania, Colgate, Yale, Brown, and Dartmouth. Moran's team entered its regular season finale against Princeton with an eight-game winning streak, ranked number five in the *Sun* poll, and casting an eye toward a berth in the eight-team NCAA tournament.

NCAA tournament organizers were working behind the scenes, putting the finishing touches on the inaugural event. In announcing the playoff, the college sports governing body also established the NCAA Lacrosse Rules and Tournament Committee and installed as its head a forty-one-year-old former US Marine who had been president of the USILA and was currently lacrosse coach at tiny Union College in Schenectady, New York.[64] Bruce Allison cut an imposing figure physically, a fit 6', 210 pounds, with a crew cut and black, Clark Kent–style glasses. In other ways he was less Clark Kent and more Superman. At the time of his death in 2013, at the age of eighty-three, Allison was a member of eight athletic halls of fame, both as an administrator and an athlete.

Allison graduated from Penn Yan Academy, located at the north end of Keuka Lake in central New York, in 1947, having won varsity letters in football, basketball, baseball, and track and field; he was considered one of the best athletes in school history.[65] He spent four years in the Marines, based primarily in Camp Lejeune, North Carolina, and eventually enrolled as an undergraduate at Cortland State in the fall of 1951. There Allison was a starting lineman in football and a starting defender in lacrosse. He also helped coach both teams and still managed to graduate magna cum laude.

After teaching at a high school in Pennsylvania for a year, Allison turned to coaching. At Union College his lacrosse teams had punched above their weight, including a 12–2 victory over Syracuse in 1966. In the spring of 1970, he and his committee—featuring representatives from Air Force, Denison, Penn State,

Stevens Tech, and Washington College in Maryland—began their work to plan the first NCAA tournament for the following spring, with Washington College as the only representative with even a remote relationship to the Baltimore establishment.[66]

Other signs of change in the sport were impossible to miss. In May 1970 *Sports Illustrated* ran a story on the growth of lacrosse on Long Island. The headline ran: "They're Not Going to Like It in Maryland."[67] The story noted that within a five-mile radius of Hofstra University there were five thousand boys playing lacrosse.[68] When asked subsequently how many were playing the sport within five miles of Johns Hopkins in 1970, the historian for the US Lacrosse Hall of Fame answers quickly. "About a thousand at most," says Joe Finn.[69]

Johns Hopkins coach Bob Scott had sounded the alarm about Cornell and Moran. "He has real good Long Island contacts, and he'll get the boys he wants on the Island," Scott told the *Baltimore Sun*. "I don't know whether Baltimore people realize it or not, but the population on Long Island has grown so that there are over 100 high schools out there now. Sixty of them play lacrosse. We have about 35 high schools playing lacrosse in Maryland."[70]

Sports Illustrated asked former Princeton coach Ferris Thomsen whether the better high-school players could be found in Baltimore or Long Island. Thomsen was a Baltimore native and had coached at both Gilman School and McDonogh School before taking the job at Princeton. In answering, he cited the toughness of the typical Long Island player and the sheer number of Long Islanders playing the sport. "Maryland won't like hearing this," he finished, "but the Island passed them five years ago."[71] The *Sports Illustrated* article also noted that Hofstra played its home games at night, a time slot reserved primarily for professional teams, and that Hofstra Stadium had a brand new $400,000 artificial-turf surface, purchased with funds from the New York Jets pro football team, which used Hofstra for its preseason training. (Jets players called the new astroturf "the plastic fantastic.") And the turf field was busy: In the spring and summer of 1969, Hofstra Stadium, at all age levels, hosted 111 lacrosse games.[72]

Roughly one month after the *Sports Illustrated* article, on the weekend of June 12–14, 1970, the Lacrosse NCAA Rules and Tournament Committee met for the first time in Lexington, Virginia, during breaks in the North–South festivities.[73] The sport's long road to the NCAA tournament had officially begun. The six men compiled recommendations that would grow to sixty pages and were to be delivered to the NCAA executive committee in its annual meeting in Seattle in August, 1970.[74] Among the suggestions was the schedule for the eight-team, single-elimination tournament and the location for the neutral-site championship game. Allison went to great lengths to point out to the lacrosse community that the final decision belonged to the NCAA—and with good reason: He was about to deliver a hammer blow to the Baltimore establishment.[75]

The first recommendation was a location for the neutral-site championship game. Just weeks after the *Sports Illustrated* article extolling Long Island's lacrosse bona fides, the group argued that Hofstra University be the host. "Long Island is a highly active lacrosse area," Allison told the *New York Times* a week after the initial meetings. "Playing a championship game there should arouse a great deal of interest."[76] For all of Hofstra's advancements, the sport's biggest crowds, hands down, were found in the Big Five. The record attendance at a college lacrosse game had been set on May 31, 1969, when 16,056 fans attended Army's 14–4 victory over Navy in Annapolis, Maryland.[77] Navy–Maryland and Johns Hopkins–Maryland also reliably drew at least ten thousand fans.[78] With Allison touting the Hofstra site, he seemed to be claiming that Long Island spectator numbers would eclipse Homewood Field.

Even Hofstra's artificial-turf surface was outside the Big Five realm, as each of the sport's powers played home games on a grass surface. In lacrosse, grass leads to slower game action and accentuates the danger of bounce shots, or shots that hit the ground before reaching the goal, like a bowler's delivery in the sport of cricket. Bounce shots were effective on grass because even the most skilled goalie could be fooled by a shot that is misdirected by a clump of dirt. Artificial turf negated bounce shots simply because there are no divots at which to aim; the ball's bounces are predictable and easy for an experienced goalkeeper to read and thus to save. The surface also allowed for a generally faster pace of play.

The recommendation of a title game on Long Island would have been music to Moran's ears. He had used Hofstra Stadium as a home field while coaching the Long Island Athletic Club in 1967 and 1968. Moreover, as noted, artificial turf helped accentuate a player's athleticism, his speed and strength. In 1971 few in the sport could match the speed and strength of a Cornell squad whose starting lineup included two varsity football players and a varsity basketball player.

In discussing dates for the tournament, and keeping in mind the opportunity to provide financial benefits to the NCAA, Allison and his committee recommended that the tournament be played over three Saturdays, with the first round completed by May 22; the semifinals by May 29; and the title game on June 5, keeping the North–South game in its traditional slot of the second weekend in June. The schedule completely disrupted the late-season traditions of the sport's major players. Army, Navy, and Maryland had each slated regular-season games on May 22, including the Navy–Maryland contest, one of the sport's biggest rivalries. (Cornell also had a game scheduled for May 22, against Dartmouth; the teams quietly rescheduled for May 11.)[79] The June 5 date given for the NCAA title game also featured the Army–Navy game in Annapolis.

Navy officials said the gate receipts from home games against Maryland and Army often combined to reach $40,000.[80] Now the NCAA was asking Navy to reschedule—or not play at all—its two biggest and most lucrative contests. In angering Navy, Allison had poked a Big Five member, and in the 1960s Navy was *the* member of this elite club. From 1960 to 1967, the Midshipmen won or shared every USILA national championship. They also turned the trick in 1970, a run of nine titles in eleven seasons that has not been equaled. In the 1960s Navy also won a then–NCAA record of thirty-three consecutive games. The domination was such that, between 1960 and 1970, Navy gave up ten or more goals to a college opponent just nine times. In that span opponents averaged fewer than five goals per game. Following a victory over previously undefeated Maryland in 1965, one flummoxed Terrapins player told reporters, "I don't think Navy is ever going to lose another lacrosse game."[81]

Overseeing the success was coach Willis "Bill" Bilderback, to whom winning lacrosse was nothing new. He became the Navy varsity coach having directed the academy's plebe, or freshman, team for eleven years. Those squads had finished undefeated six times. Bilderback's teams were a mixture of skilled offensive players and fast, strong, aggressive defenders—many of whom had never played lacrosse before arriving at the academy, where they were typically recruited from the school's successful football program. "He understood a basic theory of

FIGURE 3.2. Navy Coach Willis "Bill" Bilderback is carried off the field following a season-ending victory over Army in 1964. Under Bilderback, the Midshipmen won nine national titles in eleven seasons. (Photo courtesy Naval Academy Athletics)

lacrosse that still exists today," says Greg Murphy, the Defenseman of the Year in 1970, who had been recruited to Navy from McLean, Virginia, to play football. "If you have the best athletes, you will be the best team." Bilderback knew ironclad, intimidating defenses translated to a formidable won-loss record. His success at Navy was clear proof of the wisdom of his approach.

Bilderback was seething with anger over the nascent NCAA tournament.[82] But he waited until he was sure the Midshipmen would be in the running for a berth before going public. As the calendar turned to May, the dam burst. On May 6, 1971, as Cornell was preparing to face Brown in an ex post facto Ivy League title game, the *Baltimore Sun* ran a screamer of a headline: "Navy, Army May Skip NCAA Tournament." Columnist Jack Chevalier wrote under the attention-grabbing words, "At this point, it's probable Army and Navy will decline with regret when invitations are issued next Monday."[83] Bilderback is quoted as saying, "It's very hard to find a conclusion. I think the service academies will act together, though. The Board of Control will make a decision in the next few days and that will be it." Bilderback wasn't done. "I've discussed [the inaugural tournament] so much it makes me mad just to talk about it," he said. "It was planned wrong and organized wrong. We were left hanging as if we didn't belong to the group. . . . It's very easy for the small schools to say, 'Let Army and Navy abandon all traditions and make 100 changes.' But would they bend in a similar situation?"[84]

Bilderback offered the NCAA a counterproposal: Keep the quarterfinals and semifinals on the same dates; keep Army–Navy on June 5; and move the title game to June 12. The offer was rejected. The immediate problem was that most schools would be nearly one month into summer vacation by the time of Bilderback's proposed title game. Moreover, June 12 was already reserved for the North–South game, and attendance there was mandatory for many coaches and administrators.

Chevalier's column described the bottom line for the Baltimore establishment. "An eight-team NCAA tournament," the columnist wrote, "sounds like a fine reward for clubs like Towson State, Washington & Lee, Hofstra, the Ivy League champ, the New England champ, etc. But among the big boys, a simple [one-game] playoff . . . would be good enough to settle things in most seasons."[85] The delineation between "Ivy League champ" and "big boys" may well have caught the eye of the Cornell players and coaches as they read copies of the day-late paper in Uris Library. It was not a misprint. Bilderback himself later echoed the call for a tournament for smaller schools and a one-game "bowl game" playoff among the Big Five to determine the "true" national champion.[86]

Two nights before Cornell played its final home game, against Princeton on May 15, Sigma Phi Epsilon fraternity held a mixer at its mammoth red-brick house with a gray slate roof and ivy climbing up the walls, on the south edge of campus, near Willard Straight Hall. Among the attendees were a freshman from Manhasset, New York, named Alice Brown and her close friend Shelley Cosgrove, a freshman from Pittsburgh. Brown and Cornell goalie Bob Rule, a member of Sigma Phi, had been friends in high school, and they renewed their acquaintance at the mixer. But Rule also spoke with Cosgrove, and the direction of Cornell's season changed because of it.

Rule started a conversation and decided to try to impress Cosgrove. "She knew nothing about sports," he says now. "And I was being pretty arrogant. I told her during the Princeton game I was going to run down the field and take a shot on goal."[87] Shelley, now married and living on the East Coast, has a different recollection. "I thought Bob was really nice," she said in an email. "Growing up in Pittsburgh I had never been to a lacrosse game before. I knew that Cornell was good in both lacrosse and hockey and Bob played goalie on both teams. But pre-game bragging isn't something I remember. Bob was humble as I recall."[88] Their differing recollections aside, Rule's confidence in his team's chances on Saturday were well founded. The Big Red, unbeaten since the opening loss to Virginia, also entered having won fifteen consecutive Ivy League contests dating from 1969. The Tigers, former scourge of the Big Five, entered with one victory in eleven games under rookie coach Art Robinson. Cornell would win the Ivy League title with a victory—and this time the prize came with a berth and a likely home game in the inaugural NCAA eight-team tournament.

Rule had reason to be confident. He entered the regular season finale giving up 3.3 goals per game. He had also seen off the challenge of Buhmann, who played sparingly in 1971, starting only three games, all of them midweek encounters, instead of the marquee matchups on weekends that featured Rule. (One of Buhmann's starts came against a Colgate squad with only fourteen players—and played in a snowstorm. Buhmann faced eleven shots in an 18–1 victory.)

Saturday, May 15, arrived and with it came the best weather of the season—a sunny afternoon with temperatures in the seventies. An overflow crowd, including Brown and Cosgrove, filled the meager bleachers at Lower Alumni Field and ringed the dust-and-grass playing surface, standing six- and seven-deep, including behind both goals. The crowd was estimated at three thousand people. Even the normally staid *Ithaca Journal* stated, "Saturday was a day for . . . beer-drinking fans and enjoyment."[89]

The proceedings did not begin as planned when, after twenty-nine seconds, Rule gave up a goal. From there, however, he made eleven consecutive saves and, with Rimmer leading the offense, the Big Red jumped to a 10–1 lead early in the second quarter. Following his twentieth save late in the first half, Rule made a calculation. He knew the NCAA playoffs started the following Saturday, and the

Big Red still had a Tuesday regular-season contest against Hobart. Rule believed, correctly, that his time in goal was about to be over for the day; and knowing he had yet to make good on his boast to the two girls at the mixer, and already in possession of the ball, he made a dash toward the Princeton goal.

Rule reached as far as midfield when he realized that taking a shot on goal was probably not in anyone's best interests, including his own. As he turned to pass the ball to a teammate, and with no Princeton player nearby, Rule's right knee twisted in the wrong direction, and he heard a small "pop."[90] Rule completed the pass, then collapsed on the field. He says he was later told that he looked like "a hippo had been shot and went down in a cloud of dust."[91] The goalie who had given up an unheard-of 3.3 goals per game in Ivy League play was unable to walk off the field and had to be lifted off by teammates.

Cosgrove says she "vaguely" recalls Rule being injured.[92] Moran says now he was not worried about Rule's injury, largely because he had faith in Buhmann.[93] Rule did not know the extent of the injury, but later said that it would be years before he revealed to Moran that he had taken off down the field on his mad dash to impress a girl.[94]

The immediate plan was for Rule to be taken to the school's Sage Infirmary on the South Campus. There was no ambulance at Lower Alumni Field, so Rule and team trainer Alf Eckman improvised. Rule was carried to Eckman's two-seater sports car, which would transport the best goalie in college lacrosse to the infirmary.[95] By this point, just about halftime, the crowd was at least ten people deep around Lower Alumni Field, and the festivities had been in high gear for hours. Navigating the crowd was virtually impossible; every few steps Rule and Eckman were stopped by a well-wisher or Sigma Phi fraternity brother, or they had to circumvent a group not paying attention. Moreover, because Rule could not bend his knee, he did not fit in Eckman's car. In the end he was loaded on the back of the two-seater car in the luggage rack. "Alf had to drive about four miles an hour or I would have fallen off," Rule says now. "He kept turning around asking me, 'Bob, are you okay? Are you okay?' When we were going through the crowd everyone was drinking. It was insane."[96]

As Rule headed toward the infirmary, Buhmann trotted onto the field. Staked to a 10–1 lead against Princeton, Buhmann did not have trouble in what was a 21–6 victory. He was in goal again three days later when the Big Red ended the regular season against Hobart on Tuesday, May 18. The Big Red had to endure both an eighty-five-degree afternoon and a fired-up Hobart team and its fans in Geneva. The game featured twenty-five penalties and was close into the fourth quarter before the Big Red pulled away. To say the Big Red fought its way out of Boswell Field was almost literally true, for the final quarter featured a shoving match between Creighton and Cornell reserve midfielder Jim Skeen. Later in the quarter Ellis nearly came to blows with Hobart freshman attackman Rick Gilbert; each received a rare three-minute penalty.

Buhmann played the entire game in goal. He finished with fifteen saves in a 14–8 victory. The *Ithaca Journal* noted that Rule was expected back for the NCAA first-round game four days later.[97] So did Cornell's in-house sports information director Ben Mintz, who wrote in his official game notes, "Sr goalie Bob Rule . . . retired in 2nd per. vs. Princeton last Sat. with knee ailment after stopping 11x12 shots but is expected to be in nets" for the NCAA tournament.[98]

THE FIRST NCAA TOURNAMENT

Cornell's suddenly turbulent turn of fortune due to Bob Rule's injury was nothing compared to the trouble facing Bruce Allison and the NCAA Lacrosse Tournament and Rules Committee. On Sunday, May 9, 1971, the day after Cornell's 12–4 victory over Brown that effectively decided the Ivy League championship, and two weeks before the start of the NCAA tournament, the committee held a conference call. Allison told reporters that the call would be used to determine the eight teams in the tournament and also first-round game sites and times and the semifinal sites and times.

At the NCAA's direction, the field of tournament contenders was broken down into a handful of districts, or regions. District One, for instance, was for New England, District Two featured New York and New Jersey, and District Three, the most competitive, featured the mid-Atlantic. Given lacrosse's unique geography, with a heavy emphasis on the East Coast, the committee grouped together the Midwest, Southwest and Far West—Districts Four, Five, Six, Seven, and Eight—into one classification. Thus the eight-team field would be consist of the top team in District One, District Two, District Three, and Districts Four through Eight. The remaining four spots would be determined on an at-large basis.

On May 10 it was revealed that the committee had selected, rather than all eight participants, only a preliminary five. They were Brown, the top seed and automatic qualifier in District One; Army, the top seed and automatic qualifier in District Two; Cornell, the putative Ivy League champion, as an at-large from District Two; Virginia, the top seed and automatic qualifier in the ultra-competitive District Three;

and Navy, an at-large selection from District Three. All five teams still had several regular-season games remaining. It's unclear what would have happened had Cornell, for instance, lost any of its final three games. The committee also announced a pair of first-round matchups—Brown at Cornell and Virginia at Navy.

There was an immediate negative reaction—not surprising, given so much of the regular season was still to be played. Brown and Virginia threatened to turn down their bids if the sites were not reversed so they could host.[1] To make their case, the schools used the NCAA's own terminology against it. Brown believed it deserved a home game because it was an "automatic qualifier" whereas Cornell was an "at-large" selection. The argument was not a great one, not least because Cornell had won the aforementioned head-to-head meeting and was also on its way to being the champion of the league that included Brown. But the use of the automatic qualifier to establish priority highlighted the disorder that reigned over the proceedings.

And Virginia had a much more solid bone to pick. Like Brown, it was an automatic qualifier whereas Navy was an at-large. Moreover, the undefeated Cavaliers had won the head-to-head meeting with the Midshipmen. And, perhaps most crucially, Virginia was the top-ranked team in the influential weekly *Baltimore Sun* poll. It was beyond impossible to demand that the Cavaliers travel to Annapolis for a first-round game.

Because of the protests, the locations remained unsettled when the NCAA committee scheduled another conference call for Sunday, May 16, only six days before the quarterfinal games. Topics for that meeting included settling the impasse on the first-round locations and determining the final three participants. During the second call the committee prevailed upon Brown to accept its road game against Cornell for Saturday at 2 p.m. As of Monday morning, May 17, five days before the start of the inaugural NCAA lacrosse tournament, that was the only first-round game with a site, time, and location.[2]

Navy and Virginia knew they were playing each other but remained at loggerheads over the date and location. Air Force and Maryland were added to the field as, respectively, an automatic bid from Districts Four through Eight and an at-large. They were set to play each other in College Park, Maryland, though the date and time were unknown, thanks to the uncertainty over Navy's regular-season game against Maryland (both schools were insisting on playing). And Army still had no first-round opponent; the committee had neglected to determine the final team in the field. That decision, they said, was coming.

The ramshackle nature of the selections did not escape the notice of the Baltimore establishment. The day after the second conference call, the *Baltimore Sun* ran a story under the headline "Confusion Hits Stick Tourney." It made reference to the "poorly run tournament" and noted that if Navy agreed to change its contest against Maryland and host Virginia on Saturday in the playoffs, the profits from the more advantageous weekend contest would go not to Navy but to the NCAA.[3] The story also included a remark from Cornell officials saying that if it defeated Brown, it was expecting to host a semifinal.

Later on Monday the eight-team field was completed when Hofstra was added as Army's first-round opponent. Yet this, too, created rancor. The Flying Dutchmen (with a 9–3 record) were chosen over Towson State (13–1), Washington and Lee (11–2), Denison (10–2), and Cortland State (11–1, with its only loss to Cornell). Though Hofstra had a good team, there was a strong sense that their cause had been helped immeasurably because the school was hosting the title game: their presence in the tournament might boost ticket sales and visibility on Long Island for the championship contest. In the *Baltimore Sun* rankings released earlier in the day, both Towson State (ranked seventh) and Washington and Lee (ninth) were ahead of the tenth-ranked Flying Dutchmen.[4]

It is uncertain how close Navy came to boycotting the inaugural NCAA tournament. What is known is that officials at Army played no small role in convincing Navy that it would be in the best interests of both programs to be flexible and participate. "The financial situation was rough on Navy," Army coach Al Pisano said soon after the inaugural tournament. "That's why they wanted out. But my boys wanted to prove they are number one in the country. It was a borderline decision by the two athletic directors [at Army and Navy]. I favored the tournament because I think the service academies might hurt their own recruiting if they didn't compete for a national title."[5] And so, on the afternoon of May 17, Allison held a conference call of a different kind. From his office in Schenectady, he dialed Charlottesville and then Annapolis. On the line were Virginia athletic director Gene Corrigan and Navy athletic director Capt. J. O. Coppedge, US Navy. The set-up of the first NCAA lacrosse tournament would be decided just five days before the initial set of games.

Allison held a coin in one hand. He tossed it and asked Corrigan to call heads or tails. Corrigan called it correctly, and Navy accepted a quarterfinal road game against Virginia.[6] Navy also announced that it would play its regular-season game against Maryland the following Tuesday.[7] That meant that Navy and Maryland would play a regular-season game *after* they had played their initial NCAA tournament games. And academy officials announced the Army–Navy game in Annapolis would be pushed back one day, to June 6, with the Naval Academy graduation happening three days later. "No doubt about it," wrote Reid Detchon in the *Evening Sun* on May 18, 1971, "Navy came out on the short side of the NCAA lacrosse controversy."[8]

All the shuffling left an enormous issue on the horizon: If Army and Navy reached the title game—and some in the sport expected them to—they would be playing twice in twenty-four hours in locations 250 miles apart. Given Bilder-back's disdain for the NCAA tournament and his reverence for tradition, there was speculation that he would play a team of reserves for the NCAA game and saved his starters for Army–Navy. Tournament organizers and its supporters like Moran were hoping they would not find out.

May 22 arrived, and with it came a new horizon for the sport. Four locations were set to host the first NCAA lacrosse tournament games: College Park; Charlottes-ville; Ithaca; and West Point. Each of the games was to start at 2 p.m. The *Balti-more Sun* began its story on the morning of the games with this: "The somewhat controversial and confusing NCAA tournament begins this afternoon. . . . The tourney has drawn criticism because of the first-round pairings and is confus-ing, especially to Navy and Maryland fans, because the tournament will be held during the regular season. Navy has two games left on its regular schedule and Maryland, one."[9]

The Terrapins were facing undefeated Air Force, in just its fourth year fielding a team.[10] The Falcons entered the NCAA tournament having given up fifty-six goals in fourteen games, an average of four goals, an impressive number even in the lower scoring wooden-stick era. The codicil: The impressive record had largely come against barely established collegiate and postcollegiate West Coast programs like UCLA, Stanford, Colorado College, Colorado University, Colo-rado State, Los Angeles Lacrosse Club, and Orange County Lacrosse Club.[11] Still, the Falcons were ranked sixth in the *Sun* poll, one spot behind Maryland.[12]

The Air Force offense featured a native of Plainview, New York, on Long Island, named Mike Kaczmarski. A 5'9", 160-pound sophomore, he entered the tournament with a team-high thirty goals. He also was the only member of the ten-player starting lineup to have played the sport in high school. In all, the sixty-one-member roster featured players from twenty-three states, including three players from Iowa.[13] The Falcons arrived in College Park on Thursday, stayed at the Holiday Inn about three miles north of campus on Route 1, and held a prac-tice inside Byrd Stadium the day before the first-round game.[14] The setting was a familiar one to Air Force coach Jim Keating. He had been the leading scorer for Maryland in 1955 and 1956 before joining the Air Force. By 1971 he had risen to the rank of major and, once the season ended, was set to leave for a six-month deployment as a pilot in Vietnam.[15]

The Vietnam War also factored into the first-round matchup between Hofstra and second-ranked Army inside Michie Stadium. Taking the field for Army that afternoon was a senior attackman from Levittown, New York, named Tom Cafaro. He was big for the position, 6'2", 195 pounds, and had been considered the best high-school player on Long Island as a senior in 1967. Playing for MacArthur

High with Cornell's Bob Buhmann and Maryland's Ira Hochstadt, Cafaro finished that year with ninety-one points but was overlooked by four-fifths of the Big Five. He drew the attention of Army after a former Army assistant coach, who had recently taken a job as a teacher at Suffern High in Rockland County, New York, saw Cafaro in action and alerted his friends at West Point.

Cafaro says he chose Army for practical reasons: "I wasn't really looking to go to West Point. But my father was a policeman," he says now, "and we didn't have a lot of money."[16] West Point Cadets do not pay tuition so Cafaro went despite, not because of, the Vietnam War. "If they wanted me to go Vietnam I would have gone," he says now. "But I also think anyone who wants to go to war is a little silly. . . . We were lucky, we were the first or second class that didn't have to go, though some guys obviously did."[17] Cafaro took the field on May 22, leading Army in goals, with thirty-nine, and assists, with twenty-six.

Navy's Bilderback reportedly said during the season, "Take away Cafaro and you've got a mediocre team."[18] Opponents tried their best to deal with Cafaro. The previous year, Hobart's coaches decided to use two goalies at the same time. Though highly unusual, the tactic is legal as long as only one player uses the larger goalie stick. For Hobart, backup goalie Rusty Bergen, a lefty, used the regular equipment and Dave Creighton, a righty, joined him in the cage with a midfielder's stick. In front of the goalies the Statesmen played a 2–3 zone defense. Decades later, Cafaro remained nonplussed. "I just tried to shoot between the goalies," he says. "If you shoot at one of them he will save it, but shooting between them, they have to decide who's going to get it."[19] Cafaro finished with his seemingly requisite six goals in a 13–4 victory. One year later Army entered the postseason having won all eight of its games against college competition, though it would not play Navy for another couple of weeks. Cafaro was using a stick with a plastic head, the only player on the Army roster to do so. Weeks before the 1971 season, one of the owners of the Bacharach Rasin store asked him to give the new equipment a try. Cafaro said it was his backup stick until his wooden stick was broken midway through the season, and he switched to the plastic model full time. "It was more accurate than the wood heads," he says now. "I just got used to it and used it the rest of the season and into the playoffs."[20]

A crowd of ten thousand people was expected inside Scott Stadium in Charlottesville for the pick of the quarterfinals, third-ranked Navy against top-ranked Virginia. The Cavaliers, along with Army, were the last major teams undefeated against college competition. Under the previous system, where the USILA determined national champions, Virginia would have clinched at least a share of the Wingate trophy; Army would have clinched a share of the title with a victory over Navy. In the new world of the NCAA tournament, however, both the Cadets and the Cavaliers were three victories short of a championship. Virginia's players had one claim to fame—they were the only ones in the tournament field widely using the plastic-stick heads.[21] Northern teams like Cornell and Brown, opponents in the fourth NCAA first-round contest, owned plastic sticks, but almost none were used in games.

On May 22, 1971, in Ithaca, temperatures were in the mid-sixties with a slight breeze when Cornell, ranked fourth by the *Sun*, and Brown, ranked eighth, took the field for warm-ups.[22] School officials, expecting a big crowd, had installed temporary bleachers for two thousand people on the east side of Lower Alumni Field, the side behind the team benches. Along with the permanent bleachers on the opposite side, there was seating for about three thousand, plus enough standing room for hundreds more. At the behest of the NCAA, Cornell charged admission for a lacrosse game for the first time in decades, two dollars for adults, one dollar for children fourteen and under, with the majority of the proceeds going to the college sports governing body. The game was broadcast on the radio, WHCU 97.3 FM, starting with a pregame show at 1:50 p.m. hosted by Jay Levine, who also did the play-by-play.

Brown entered with a school-record eleven victories. Crease attackman Bob Scalise, a senior from Long Island, entered with forty-four goals, an incredibly high number in the wooden-stick era. It was no fluke: The previous year he had scored forty-seven. A few weeks before the NCAA tournament, Scalise had gone on a tear that rewrote the record books. On May 3, in a 16–3 victory over Dartmouth in Hanover, New Hampshire, he tied a then–Ivy League record by scoring seven goals. Three days later, in a 19–6 victory over the University of Connecticut in Storrs, Scalise scored eleven goals; at the start of the 2021 season that feat remains tied for an NCAA single-game record. In the regular season, in a 12–4 loss to Cornell, however, he had been hounded all afternoon by Bill Ellis, and scored none.

Starting goalie Bob Rule's status for the first-round game may have been in question elsewhere but not in Ithaca. He had received treatment for his right knee all week, and when Cornell took the field for warm-ups, Rule was in goal, facing practice shots from assistant Mike Waldvogel, looking no different except for the extra bulk indicating a knee brace hidden under his customary red sweatpants. The game started, Brown earning the first possession. The Bears took a shot that Rule saved but did not completely control. The rebound fell right to Scalise who dumped it into the net for a 1–0 lead. On Brown's next possession the lead became 2–0 after a goal by Dean Rollins, a senior captain like Scalise. On its third possession, a shot from a Brown player hit Rule in his ailing right knee. "I saw the shot," says Ellis. "And I turned to start our clear when I heard Bob screaming in agony."[23] The game stopped; Rule was helped off the field. In came Buhmann, wearing white shorts and high white socks. He jumped around like a boxer in his corner before the bell rings, full of nervous energy. On the sideline Waldvogel remembers thinking that Buhmann played his best in the biggest games. And suddenly the backup goalie found himself in the biggest game in program history.

The Big Red battled back to tie the game at 2, on goals from reserve attackman Pat Gallagher and star midfielder Bob Shaw. By then, Rule's injury was not Cornell's only problem. Brown coach Cliff Stevenson, after reviewing the past two blowout losses in the series, by a combined 33–10, adjusted his game plan. Specifically, he decided that Rimmer was the Cornell player to stop. Every time Rimmer made a move to the goal, an extra defender—and sometimes two—swarmed to him as if attracted by a magnet. With this new scheme Rimmer was held without a goal or an assist in the first quarter, then again in the second. Even with Rule out of the game and Rimmer out of sorts, the Big Red led 5–4 at halftime. It extended the lead to 9–5 starting the fourth quarter, though it did so without help from Rimmer, who was held scoreless again in the third.

In the fourth quarter, the Bears woke up. Reserve midfielder Joe Dougherty scored to close the deficit to 9–6. It became 9–7 after Rollins scored on a low-angle shot from the right crease. And midway through the fourth quarter it was 9–8 following a goal on a bounce shot from the left by Rupert Scofield. Brown then had possession following Scofield's goal with a chance to tie the game. But the Big Red forced a turnover and began a fast break. Rollins succeeded in stopping the transition but only because he went offside to do so and was called for the penalty. Seven minutes remained. Brown had the momentum but Cornell had something almost as valuable: Because Rollins had committed an infraction Brown would, for thirty seconds, be forced to play with only five players on defense against a full complement of six for Cornell on offense.

Moran called his special extra-man play, a basketball-type motion offensive set focused on creating an open shot in the middle of the thirty-five-yard-long restraining box, also called the offensive box, for Shaw, or something closer for crease attackman Gallagher. Seconds into the sequence, a Brown defender tipped a pass, and the ball was loose on the dusty grass field. Another Brown player left his spot in the zone defense to attempt to corral it. If he succeeded and the Bears cleared the ball, the penalty would be released under the rules of the day and the dangerous Scalise would have another chance to the tie the game. But the defender overran the ball and a Cornell player picked it up, then exploited the open space left by the gambling defender. He fired a quick pass to midfielder Bill Molloy, and as Brown's defense scrambled to recover, Molloy spotted Gallagher all alone in front of the crease. The left-handed Gallagher caught the pass, shot over goalie Doug Spiro's shoulder and into the net, then ran into Molloy's arms. The Big Red led 10–8 with six minutes and forty seconds to play.

The Bears had a handful of possessions trailing 10–8 but three ended in turnovers, a fourth resulted in a wild off-balance shot that actually beat Buhmann but hit the goalpost and bounced away. Another shot also hit the goalpost, and Cornell held on to win by two goals. There was no immediate word on Rule but it seemed certain that he was unlikely to play again in 1971. Meantime, Rimmer had been held scoreless by Brown's perfectly executed plan. "Everywhere I looked there were sticks and bodies," he told the *Ithaca Journal*. "It seemed like sometimes they had three men on me."[24] Two weeks later, on Hofstra's steamy artificial turf, Maryland would not devote as much care to stopping Rimmer—and would pay dearly for the mistake.

Though the Big Red had won, the first NCAA tournament game had been far from perfect. The extra bleachers were almost completely superfluous; attendance at Lower Alumni Field was 2,500. Even the *Ithaca Journal* called the crowd "somewhat disappointing."[25] (The small crowd may well have been because of the admission charge. Another factor may have been the recent blowout victories that Cornell had recorded in the series.) The final minutes were played with a white Labrador dog running on the field, the referees unable to shoo it away. It had been a ragged day and perhaps not what Allison, in attendance after driving the roughly 160 miles due west from his home near Schenectady, had dreamed.

But Moran was all smiles. As the players undressed in the Schoellkopf Field locker room, Moran walked among them, grabbing shoulders and slapping bare backs. Having been informed that Army had advanced to the semifinals with a 19–3 victory over Hofstra, he told his players over and over, "What's next week? The long gray line, baby."[26] The other winners were Maryland, which defeated Air Force, 10–1, before a crowd of 2,200, far smaller than the ten thousand that its athletic department officials had been expecting. Virginia also drew a smaller than expected crowd, 6,500 spectators, for its game with Navy, won by Navy, 11–7. The semifinals were set, Maryland against Navy and Cornell against Army. Neither game, however, had an agreed-upon location. And Navy and Maryland were still set to meet in the regular season.

The day after the first-round games, Cornell sports information director Ben Mintz sat in his office in Teagle Hall and did some research. The Big Red had never defeated Army in fifteen tries; they were 0–11 against Navy; and 1–4–1 against the Terrapins, with the lone win coming fifty years earlier. The other three semifinalists were card-carrying members of the Big Five against whom the Big Red was a combined 1–30–1. Now, to win the school's first national title since 1916, Cornell would have to beat the Big Five twice in seven days. The three remaining teams were part of the cabal that had won or shared all but two titles since the Wingate trophy originated thirty-four years prior. Mintz showed his work to Moran, who loved being the underdog.

The Big Red believed it would host the semifinal, but Army held the trump card: A bigger and better venue for a larger crowd and more money for the NCAA. Army was also the higher-seeded team. In the first-round victory over Hofstra, Cafaro had scored four goals and added four assists. He entered the semifinals with seventy-two points. Army's second-leading scorer, senior Rich Enners, had forty-six. Cornell's plan to stop Cafaro was simple—put senior John Burnap on him and tell everyone else to get out of the way. The matchup would pit the player eventually named defender of the year against the one named attackman of the year.

There were two sidelights to the main Cafaro-Burnap matchup. One involved Cafaro and Buhmann. The best player in the college game and the backup goalie thrust into the spotlight had known each other since birth. The elder Messrs. Buhmann and Cafaro were New York City police officers, stationed in the same precinct in the Bronx and later assigned as partners to the same patrol car.[27] Both families later moved, within months of each other, from the Bronx to Seaford, New York, on Long Island; they lived a half mile apart.[28] They were such close friends that, to cut down on costs, the families shared a car for grocery shopping and other errands. Buhmann and Cafaro attended Douglas MacArthur High, and as seniors in the 1967 yearbook, their headshots, grouped alphabetically, were within centimeters of each other.

The second sidelight began a little after noon, two hours before the opening face-off, when a helicopter landed near the academy's parade ground and out stepped President Richard Nixon. He had arrived to preside over the Saturday ceremonial parade of Cadets before delivering a speech to the entire student body, all three thousand of them—or at least those not preparing for lacrosse—plus several thousand onlookers. The title of the speech, fittingly for both events on campus that day, was "Hope for a New Era."[29] In it, the president said that the seeds were being planted so that "a new era of world peace will come true," a reference to ending the Vietnam War. He also told the assembled Cadets that they would be "America's peace-time soldiers," adding "at least we have the end of the American role [in Vietnam] clearly in sight."[30] His remarks ended at 2 p.m. By then, both teams were warming up on the sunny, clear afternoon. Temperatures were in the low eighties with no humidity. "Picture-postcard weather," wrote the *Ithaca Journal*.[31] Cornell wore its all-white uniforms—shorts, jerseys, and helmets. Army wore all black—helmets, shorts, and jerseys with "West Point" written in a semicircle across the front.

Fans arrived in the impressive, thirty-thousand-seat Michie Stadium and were greeted with a giant scoreboard advertising the world-famous Zodiac Watch Company. The simple four-page game program was printed on gray heavy card stock with black typeface and information on front and back. It included rosters, starting lineups, NCAA playoff notes, and a recap of both teams' seasons to date. This final section highlighted how close the game was likely to be. The Black Knights and Big Red had played four common opponents, and the comparative scores were telling. Against Yale, Army won 12–5, Cornell 12–4; against Syracuse, Army won, 17–8 and Cornell by 17–9; and they both beat Hobart, Army by 13–8, Cornell by 14–8. Only Princeton was something of an outlier. Both teams won easily, Army by 15–3, Cornell by 21–6. The scores portended two very evenly matched teams.

Dozens of Cadets, still wearing the ceremonial dress uniforms of gray tops, white sash, and white pants, dribbled into the stadium—the NCAA, in a moment of generosity, had waived the admission fee for cadets. Around fifteen hundred Cornell fans, many dressed in white shirts, sat behind the team bench in the east stands, the section of the stadium with its back to Lusk Reservoir. WHCU-FM and Jay Levine again broadcast the game, sharing airtime with reports from the Ithaca College baseball team's trip to the NCAA Tournament East Region in Virginia Beach, Virginia.

The game started at 2:15 p.m. In the first two minutes Cafaro scored. Two minutes later Cornell answered on a goal by Frank Davis, assisted by Glen Mueller. By the end of the first quarter, Cafaro and his stick with its plastic head already accounted for two goals and one assist. But Cornell's constant motion offense, originated during Moran's days as a high-school basketball coach, was creating high-percentage shots. (In the Cornell playbook Moran's motion offense was called "circulation.") Most lacrosse teams in that era employed a crease attackman and then five players around him; the focus was to get the ball to the player on the crease for a shot or pass. Cornell eschewed the crease attackman and instead relied on all six players in a circle, constantly moving. Each had the green light to pass and shoot.[32] Army's defense entered, giving up 6.8 goals. By the end of the first quarter, the Big Red led 7–4. In the second quarter Army scored four in a row to lead 8–7. Cornell battled back and led 11–10 at halftime, a total that would have been a rather high-scoring complete game in the wooden-stick era. Cafaro, in the first half, had four goals and three assists.

By the end of the third quarter, Cafaro had accounted for six goals and three assists, but Cornell led, 13–12. Early in the fourth quarter Army senior Ron Liss, midfielder and face-off specialist, scored twice in ten seconds to give the Black Knights a 14–13 lead. Army retained possession again, and seconds later Buhmann was hopping up and down in pain; in a battle for a loose ball, he was jostled from behind by an Army player and had twisted his right knee. The referees stopped the contest for Buhmann's injury. Rule was in attendance but unavailable to play with his own knee injury. On the sideline the coaches told Gunts to find a chest protector and prepare to enter the game as the goalie, a position he had not played since his days on the freshman team two years earlier. But during the break in action, Buhmann shook off the injury.

The Big Red scored consecutive goals from Davis and Rimmer for a 15–14 lead with six minutes and fifty-six seconds to play. Cafaro answered for Army to tie the game again, this time at fifteen. (It was the fiftieth goal of the year for Cafaro, still a school record.) Fenzel scored for Cornell; Liss answered for Army, and the game was tied again, at sixteen, with about four minutes to play.

Even with Cafaro playing the game of his life, Cornell junior Bob Shaw may have been the best player on the field. Nicknamed "Bobo," Shaw to that point had accounted for two goals, one assist, and eighteen ground balls, roughly three times an above-average haul of loose balls. Moran, sensing that Shaw was playing the game of his life, decided to run the first midfield unit—Shaw, Fenzel, and Molloy—into the ground. He would make the inaugural NCAA title game with them or not make it at all. "I've never been so tired during a game," Shaw said later. "Every time I'd come to the sideline and try to catch my breath, I'd hear Richie yell, 'Bobo, you're up!'"[33]

Tied at sixteen, with about two minutes and thirty seconds to play, the Big Red had possession. The Cadets were well aware of Shaw's rocket sidearm right-handed shot and defended him accordingly. Shaw, partly from exhaustion and partly to throw a changeup, took a weak, left-handed shot from ten yards. It eluded senior goalie Greg Doepke and went into the net; Cornell led, 17–16, with two minutes, seven seconds to play. Army won the ensuing face-off. The threat of another goal by the record-setting Cafaro loomed. Before Cafaro received possession, a second-string midfielder from Cornell named Jim Skeen, from public Lansdowne High outside Baltimore, stuck his wooden stick high in the air and intercepted an Army pass. Four Army players desperately converged on him; still, Skeen managed to clear the ball. It went like a bauble into the sticks of Rimmer and then Shaw, and they took turns running out the clock. "With two minutes left I remember thinking, 'Hang onto it, hang onto it,'" Ellis said. "The way Army was scoring I didn't want them to get the ball back."[34] Moran agreed. "Without that [interception]," Moran said, "we were in trouble."[35]

With the Cornell fans rising to their feet, the clock ran out. Cornell was headed to the NCAA championship, 17–16 victory in tow. Davis, with his homemade wooden stick, finished with four goals. Rimmer finished with four goals and two assists. One week earlier, Brown had labeled Rimmer as the player to stop, and their constant double-teams held him without a goal or assist. Army did not face Cornell in the regular season, and Pisano believed that Cornell's biggest threat was junior Glen Mueller, the Long Island native and sixth man on Cornell's basketball team. He deployed Don MacLaren, the lone senior defenseman, to guard

Mueller. That left Davis and Rimmer facing a pair of inexperienced sophomores, matchups they exploited again and again. "Glen was a good player," Cafaro says now. "But no way was Rimmer not the number one guy. That was a mistake by our coaches."[36]

What decided the game may well have been Cornell's conditioning, all the running and exercise that were hallmarks of Moran's system. Army was well known for dominating teams in the third and fourth quarters with its superior conditioning. On May 29 Army and Cornell each scored two goals in the third quarter and four goals in the fourth. The Big Red quite literally had matched Army stride for stride, when other teams faltered due to fatigue.

The game had featured eight ties and six lead changes, and an exciting time in general for the sport. "Lacrosse fans of the world unite!" wrote Fred Yahn. "Your cause celebre—your dream game—was played here Saturday. If there were ever a game to convince skeptics that lacrosse is here to stay, not with its political fraternity of the past but with a new generation of plucky athletes that don't stop running until the final gun bangs, it was played here."[37]

Cornell's players, celebrating the first win over Army in school history and a berth in the title game, threw their sticks in the air and ran around hugging each other. Some local teenagers, perhaps miffed that their preferred team had lost, snuck onto the field and, in the mayhem, walked off with several of the prized wooden sticks.[38] They managed to leave the stadium with the contraband, but military security stopped them before they left the academy grounds, recovered the sticks, and within a day or two, had sent them back to Ithaca. But a miscommunication meant the equipment was left sitting in the Cornell security office well into the summer. Several players, including Mickey Fenzel, a starting midfielder, were forced to play the national championship game with sticks that were far from broken in.

In the other semifinal, Navy met Maryland for the second time in five days. The teams had stuck to their regular-season meeting in Annapolis on Tuesday, May 25, after the first round of the NCAA tournament had been completed. With both teams knowing the far more important rematch was on the horizon, the Midshipmen won an anticlimactic 10–5 decision. The expected crowd of ten thousand did not materialize; the midweek matinee combined with the rematch just days later led to a paltry crowd of around two thousand. "I would have much rather played last Saturday," Bilderback told reporters afterward.

The fans who stayed away may have considered the regular-season meeting a dress rehearsal. Maryland coach Buddy Beardmore deemed it a warning. Following the loss, just days before the first NCAA tournament semifinal in the sport's history, he overhauled his entire offense, moving junior John Kaestner, the team's leading scorer, from attack to midfield. Kaestner's spot on attack was given to Eric

Nachlas, a 5'6", 140-pound senior, who, two years earlier, had been cut from the team because then-coach John "Hezzie" Howard considered Nachlas too small.[39] Nachlas did not try out for the team in 1970, Beardmore's first year, and did so in 1971 with few expectations on his part; he had produced little on the field. He entered the semifinals with three goals, having played sparingly.

Before a crowd of eighty-three hundred at Byrd Stadium—the Terrapins hosting because their athletic director correctly called heads on a conference call to determine the site with Allison and the snakebitten Coppedge—Maryland jumped to a 7–1 lead. Navy stormed back, and early in the fourth quarter the game was tied at seven. Minutes later Nachlas scored to give Maryland an 8–7 lead. He repeated the feat fifty-one seconds later. Those goals from the surprise starter on attack wound up being the final scores in Maryland's 9–7 victory. Howard was watching the game from the stands with *Baltimore Sun* columnist Bill Tanton. After the second goal Howard could not contain himself. He stood, slapped the writer on the back, and exclaimed, "Beardmore is a genius!"[40]

Cornell had dispatched one Big Five team. One remained. Moran was going to leave nothing to chance. He dipped into his deep reservoir of lacrosse associates and phoned George Rehorn, a Sewanhaka High alumnus living in Annapolis. Rehorn had not only played lacrosse for Maryland in the early 1960s, he had also seen the 1971 team play four times. Rehorn filed copious notes on his alma mater and sent them to Moran. Another Long Island contact, Pisano, gave Moran a jewel—the game film from Army's 16–7 victory over Maryland on May 1. Waldvogel, the defensive coordinator, took out a yellow legal-sized notepad and watched the film several times. He compiled pages of notes on Maryland's starting attack and even more on its top midfield units. He added further details on the Terrapins' offensive schemes, defense, goalies, face-off unit, and preferred clearing techniques. "Our scouting report," says Moran, "was a book."[41]

The work on scouting Maryland was well underway. One problem remained: In Ithaca the lacrosse team had no place to practice. The grass surface at Lower Alumni Field had become dusty and hard baked in the sun, and Moran considered it unusable.[42] Schoellkopf Field was off-limits again because workers had begun setting up the stage and chairs for Cornell's graduation on June 7. (It is a problem that exists to this day when the lacrosse team has a deep run in the playoffs.)[43] So for the two days of practice before departing for Long Island, and the biggest lacrosse game in program history, the Big Red lacrosse team settled on the outfield grass of the baseball stadium, which had been unused following the team's final game on May 23 against Syracuse.[44] In the practices that week Moran was harder on his team than usual, telling them they were going to get blown out by Maryland, saying he sensed they were pleased with having made the NCAA tournament title game; he accused them of not being interested in actually winning the title. "He got after us pretty good," Gallagher said.[45]

Proper practice facility or no, Cornell was putting its time to good use. Moran noted that the Terrapins, after the lopsided loss to Army, had switched their starting goalie. The job went to Baltimore native Bill Reilly, a hulking 6', 210 pounds who was also a reserve linebacker on the football team. To simulate Reilly, who was physically bigger than almost any goalie Cornell had seen in 1971, Moran used one of the goalies from the freshman team. Like Reilly, Alan Lampert weighed more than two hundred pounds and shared the football background.[46] When practice turned to six-on-six play, shooting attackman and midfielders found a mobile, bulky wall between them and the back of the goal, just as they would see at Hofstra Stadium.

While Moran and Waldvogel were conducting practices on the lush baseball stadium outfield grass, Beardmore and his staff spent the early part of the week putting the final touches on the team's annual postseason banquet, held Tuesday, June 1. In the scramble of the first-ever NCAA tournament, Beardmore had neglected to shift the date of the banquet, which in past years had always been immediately after the final regular-season game. (Moran, months earlier, had moved Cornell's end-of-season banquet to the fall, to coincide with football homecoming.) It was a surprising oversight from Beardmore, who had been battling to change the culture since his arrival in College Park. The Terrapins, under Howard, became what one player called "very laissez faire."[47] "Hezzie and [assistant] Rennie Smith would hang out during practice smoking cigars," said Kaestner. "The week before my first varsity game [in 1969] against North Carolina, practice consisted of two-on-two field hockey games, playing with our lacrosse sticks. It was Hezzie and me against all comers."[48]

During his stints at the University of Virginia and Hobart, Beardmore was known for his disciplined approach, his fashion sense, and as he had shown in the NCAA semifinals, his being unafraid to tinker with the starting lineup. With jet-black hair and angular features, Beardmore had more than a passing resemblance to the actor Harry Dean Stanton. On the sideline Beardmore was impeccably dressed, often in a short-sleeved shirt with a flyaway collar, matching colored bellbottom pants and a white belt with white leather shoes. "When they hired Beardmore, I said, 'You mean that maniac who always wears a white Sansabelt? That's horrible,'" Kaestner remembers. "And the guys on the team were saying, 'No, no, you don't get it. We're going to be really good now.'"[49]

Beardmore brought much-needed discipline to a program that, in recent years, had lagged behind the other Big Five members. If a player's locker was messy, he would find a one-word note from Beardmore: Steps. It meant the player was to run the steps of Byrd Stadium as punishment until his locker was clean. Beardmore wanted players picking up ground balls with two hands on the stick, not one. Those who demurred were benched. And he insisted that every team huddle ended with the words, "Be the best!" "He wanted you to believe in being the best you could be," Kaestner says. "Be the best you can be. I bought in. I knew we were going to be good."[50] In 1971 the Terrapins entered the title game with a record of nine wins and four losses in all competitions. No matter the quality of the Terrapins, just one year earlier they, like Cornell, would not have been in consideration by the USILA for any honors whatsoever. Now they were playing for the sport's largest prize.

Maryland's offense featured senior Tom Cleaver, a prolific crease attackman, who entered with forty-five goals. The Long Island native had transferred following one year as Cafaro's running mate at Army. Kaestner entered with twenty-eight goals and thirty-eight assists. His move to midfield boosted a unit with only one other member, senior Dan Furman, having reached double figures in goals; Furman entered the title game with fourteen. It also meant Kaestner would play half the game—midfielder lines play on a rotation. He still believes the change was a bad one. "Buddy wanted to mix it up," Kaestner says. "But the attack should have been asked to get the midfield more involved rather than moving people to the midfield."[51]

The answer to Maryland's scoring issues may have been the freshman who, one year earlier, was starring on offense for East Meadow High just three miles from Hofstra. Richie Bautz had led the Jets to a Long Island championship as a sophomore in 1968 and a South Shore championship the following year.[52] East Meadow did not fare as well in his senior year of 1970—it lost in the South Shore semifinals, though it was through no fault of Bautz, who finished the year with fifty-four goals.[53] At 6'4", 195 pounds, Bautz had also starred in basketball at East Meadow; one of the top scorers on Long Island, he averaged nearly twenty points per game as a senior. He was such a good athlete that before signing with Maryland, he coaxed a promise from Beardmore: He would attend Maryland only if he could receive a tryout with the school's basketball team. In those days, much like the Ivy League, the Atlantic Coast Conference banned freshmen from varsity basketball competition.

Maryland's freshman basketball team in 1970–71 featured Tom McMillen, a 6'11" center from Mansfield, Pennsylvania, who averaged fifty points per game in high school and chose Maryland after receiving more than two hundred scholarship offers. Also on the team was Len Elmore, a 6'9" forward whose Power Memorial High, a small Catholic school on West 61st Street in Manhattan, was considered the best in the nation. Bautz not only made the team, he was a starter and averaged more than seven points per game for a squad that went undefeated.[54]

In lacrosse Bautz had played attack and midfield in high school, but by the time the first title game rolled around, he was not playing either position. A few weeks earlier Beardmore, the famous tinkerer, had given Bautz a longstick and moved him to defense. Beardmore originally moved Reilly to defense, but the football linebacker, by his own admission, struggled and was placed back at goalie.[55] Bautz was an excellent athlete and uncompromising character, tough and intimidating and coming off a winter competing with and against several future NBA players and more than holding his own. "Richie Bautz was the biggest, baddest guy on the block," says John Danowski, a high-school teammate two years younger.[56] So it is not hard to see Beardmore's logic in making the move. More questionable was how Bautz would be deployed on June 5, 1971, at Hofstra Stadium.

Maryland and Cornell both held their first practices on the artificial turf at Hofstra Stadium on Thursday, June 3. Maryland went in the morning, Cornell in the afternoon. Before the Big Red took the field, one of its players handed Moran a sheet of paper he had found on the sideline. It was Maryland's scouting report. Moran threw it away without reading it, though he did note one thing: "It was less than two pages," he said.[57] Indeed, Maryland's players remember being unfamiliar with their championship game opponent. "We were expecting to play Army," says Kaestner. "They had beaten us handily, and we wanted another crack at them. We didn't know Cornell. They were up north, we didn't see them."[58] Beardmore himself intimated as much earlier in the week, in a *Baltimore Sun* story that would not have escaped the Cornell coaches and several players, who read the paper daily during lacrosse season. "I really can't say what we will do against them as yet," Beardmore was quoted in a story on June 2. "We scouted them against Army and they showed they can put the ball in the net. . . . But I've been kind of busy getting our awards banquet out of the way and getting ready to leave for Hofstra."[59]

Maryland was also unfamiliar with Hofstra's artificial-turf playing surface, as its regular-season and playoff games had all been on grass. "We hear it is pretty much a different ball game on that surface," Beardmore was quoted as saying in the *Sun* article on June 2. "After we get used to the new surface we'll decide what we are going to do."[60] Cornell, meantime, had played at Hofstra Stadium less than two months earlier, in a scrimmage against the Long Island Athletic Club on April 10. Moran had coached at least two dozen games at the stadium in his time with LIAC. He likely knew the surface better than any coach outside Hofstra's Howdy Myers and his staff.

Maryland stayed at the tony Island Inn in Westport, five miles from Hofstra Stadium. It featured a swimming pool, restaurant and cocktail lounge; the rooms were wood paneled with air-conditioning, color TVs, and private terraces. It also proved popular among those who were gathering for Saturday's Belmont Stakes, the third leg of horse racing's Triple Crown, which was being held the same day as the lacrosse title game. (Hofstra Stadium and Elmont Park are less than seven miles apart.) The Belmont Stakes was set to be a little more high profile than in recent years because Venezuelan-born Canonero II, winner of the Kentucky Derby and the Preakness Stakes, was going for the Triple Crown. A crowd of seventy thousand spectators was expected at Elmont Park racetrack, with millions more following on the CBS radio and television networks. The Island Inn was a popular destination.[61] Moran opted for something a little more Spartan. He housed his team at the Holiday Inn in Plainview, thirteen miles from the stadium and far from the horse racing fans. "I didn't want to be near all the distractions," Moran said later.[62]

Waldvogel and Moran's game plan designated Kaestner as the number one threat. He had played midfield for only one game, yet the Big Red was prepared: When Kaestner was in the midfield, he was to be guarded by Fenzel, backup stick and all. When Kaestner switched to attack, he would be shadowed by Burnap. For Cleaver, the prolific crease attackman, the Big Red would use Ellis. The third starting longstick, junior Russ Greene, would guard junior Dave Dempsey.

Maryland's defensive matchups were not as clear-cut. The Big Red starting attack, just like Maryland's starting defense, included a Long Island native who also played basketball in college. Mueller, rawboned, 6'3", and 195 pounds, was a part-time starting forward on the Cornell basketball team. Mueller's father was a successful high-school basketball coach on Long Island and had been the inspiration for the 1970s TV drama *The White Shadow*. The show starred Ken Howard, who had played basketball for Fritz Mueller at Manhasset High. The natural matchup of Bautz against Mueller, basketball player against basketball player, Long Island native against Long Island native, would have been a classic, especially for the hometown fans. Cornell's other starters on attack were the Canadian Rimmer, who entered the title game as the program's all-time leading scorer; and the Native American Davis, a rare ambidextrous shooter and feeder. Yet Beardmore and his assistants believed Mueller was the main threat on offense even though he entered fourth on the team in points, behind his two line mates and Shaw. ("I think it was because Glen was from Long Island," says Shaw, "and he was the only guy they'd ever heard of.")[63] Beardmore assigned senior Ira Hochstadt, the team's best defender, to guard Mueller. Doug Mayer, the number two defender, drew Davis. The star-crossed Bautz, who had played defense for only a matter of weeks, was asked to stop Rimmer, whose unusual Canadian box lacrosse skills had confounded some of the sport's best defenders, let alone a complete newcomer.

The first NCAA championship lacrosse game was broadcast on live television in one market—Baltimore. The decision was made for WBAL-TV, the city's NBC affiliate, to preempt the network's offering of the *Major League Baseball Game of the Week*, the St. Louis Cardinals against the Cincinnati Reds. The decision was made in part by Gunts's father, an executive at the network. Longtime sports anchor Vince Bagli provided play-by-play, and Fred Smith, an all-American defenseman at Johns Hopkins, handled color commentary.[64] Gunts's father arranged for the broadcast to feature full-color cameras rather than less expensive black-and-white ones. Fans in Ithaca tuned into the game on WHCU's FM and AM stations, with play-by-play from Levine and color from former Cornell varsity coach Bob Cullen.[65] *Sports Illustrated* and the Associated Press were among the outlets covering the event. The day before the game, the *Ithaca Journal* published driving directions from Ithaca to Hempstead, New York, courtesy of the Finger Lakes Auto Club. The morning of the game, the *New York Times* headline read, "Lacrosse to Decide No. 1. . . on the Field."[66] The *Washington Post* trumpeted, "'Big 5' Outsider Challenges Maryland."[67] The New York *Daily News* called the title game "an off-beat sports attraction."[68] Among television, radio, and the major-market newspapers sending writers to cover the championship, the contest generated far more publicity than the North–South game had ever done.

Speaking for many in the Baltimore area, on the morning of the title game Hymy Cohen wrote in the *Annapolis Capital* that the inaugural NCAA playoff "left a great deal to be desired."[69] The *Baltimore Sun* did not have articles about the championship game in its Thursday or Friday editions. Still, the championship game had arrived, whether the Baltimore establishment liked it or not.

The day was clear and bright in Hempstead, with temperatures in the low eighties. Hofstra Stadium, with a capacity of seventy-five hundred, had seating on three sides. The north end zone, instead of seats, had a scoreboard, a cluster of trees, and if one were seated high enough, a peak of the ribbon-like Hempstead Turnpike behind the stadium. The other end zone featured a pair of bleacher sections that on June 5 were about half full. The main stands, on the west side of the stadium, featured the press box and a large section of permanent seating; these reserved seats for the NCAA final cost three dollars, and the sections were almost full. Below, on the field level, were the benches for both teams. For those in the press box side of the stadium, Maryland was on the right, Cornell on the left.

The stadium's east side, opposite the press box and team benches, had individual sections of bleachers running the length of the field. The bleachers in the middle were taller than at either end. The south end of the bleachers revealed a cluster of thick trees and some of the ranch houses that ringed the outside of the campus.

Separating the fans from the playing field was an eight-lane cinder track, dark gray with running lanes in clumpy white chalk. The lime-green AstroTurf playing surface had the faint outline of football hashmarks, but there was nothing in either end zone or in the circle at midfield from which the face-offs originate play to designate it as an NCAA championship, let alone the first of its kind. The only sign the game was an NCAA championship was on the sideline, between the two benches and behind the small table at which the scorekeepers and statisticians were seated. There, a billboard, roughly three feet high, featured the gold NCAA logo on one side and on the other the letters "ncaa" in yellow inside a black circle.

When warm-ups began at 1 p.m., an hour before game time, Rule was wearing his white number 15 jersey and red sweatpants and throwing long passes with his goalie's stick. It was purely ceremonial. Moran had considered inserting Rule if Cornell had a large enough lead, but the goalie otherwise was unavailable. Gunts had spent the week in practice playing goalie; he still retained his spot on the third midfield line but was prepared to switch should Buhmann's ailing knee require it. Buhmann took the field in his traditional shorts and knee-high white socks in his white number 11 jersey. His right knee was wrapped with a beige covering, a remnant from the previous week's injury in the second half against Army. Knowing Buhmann's penchant for saving high shots but struggling on low ones, Waldvogel's warm-ups focused on low shots, and Buhmann bent down easily and made save after save, tossing the ball back to the assistant coach after each one.

In the stands opposite the press box, four players from nearby East Meadow High moved into their seats, third row from the field, having paid face value—two dollars—for each ticket. "We were lacrosse rats," says Danowski, a high-school all-American midfielder at East Meadow. "We went to lacrosse games all the time. . . . I remember looking around, and it was a good crowd but I was disappointed the stadium wasn't full. I thought for a game like this it should be full. In those days there was no tailgating. It was, 'Let's go to the game.' We were there to watch the game."[70] Also in the stands was a pair of twins from nearby Lynbrook High, juniors and both standouts on the lacrosse team. Watching the game, Harmon Levine rooted for Maryland and its up-tempo approach. His brother rooted for the Ivy League team and became fascinated with Moran's style on the sideline. Jonathan Levine decided on the spot to apply to Cornell and seek an opportunity to play there.[71]

Behind one of the goals, on the edge of the AstroTurf on the field level, Tom Leanos also prepared to watch. Leanos, a Baltimore native, had been one of the top players on Hofstra as a senior in 1970 and played in the North–South game. He remained on Long Island to finish his undergraduate degree; to earn a little money, he was working with the school's facilities management. One of his jobs was to clear pebbles and other debris out of the AstroTurf. He planned to watch the first NCAA title game despite having a clear idea who would be victorious. And it wasn't the Ivy Leaguers. "I fully expected Maryland to win," Leanos says. "I wasn't sure it was going to be all that close."[72]

In Ithaca a high-school sophomore named Dan Mackesey was painting the basement of his neighbor's house on Iroquois Drive when, at 1:50 p.m. sharp, he switched the radio to WHCU, in time for the pregame show. Mackesey was rooting for the Big Red because his father worked at the university and four older brothers had either gone to Cornell or were currently enrolled there. At Ithaca High, Mackesey had just picked up lacrosse and was playing goalie, the same position at which he excelled for the school's soccer and hockey teams.

Back on Long Island, it was nearly 2 p.m., and warm-ups were over. The game was set to begin. Maryland wore red jerseys with white numbers and red shorts with white piping; Cornell wore white jerseys with red numbers and white shorts with red piping. They were reverse photographic images, the program with nine Wingate trophies and a fully paid member in the illustrious Big Five against the outsiders, geographically and otherwise, who hadn't won a national title since 1916. Both teams took the field. As the referees readied for the opening face-off, the matchups took shape on the field. Kaestner, though set to play primarily as a midfielder, began the game on attack. Standing next to him, well prepared by Waldvogel, was Burnap. On the other end of the field, Cornell's Rimmer looked a little different. The night before the title game someone had broken into Cornell's locker room at Hofstra Stadium and stolen a few items, including Rimmer's black game cleats. So he took the field wearing a pair of white Chuck Taylor canvas high-top sneakers. Years later he revealed that they belonged to Cornell's trainer.[73]

Standing next to Rimmer, practically towering over him, was Bautz. Brown's coaches had designated Rimmer as the player to stop, held him scoreless, and nearly pulled off an upset. Army and now Maryland had decided against treading that same path. On the sideline both Moran and Waldvogel smiled. "We thought their matchups would be a little different," Moran said after the game.[74] Specifically, Cornell's coaches believed Rimmer would be guarded by junior Doug Mayer, the Long Island native and former Maryland football player who had held Cafaro in check for much of the Maryland–Army game in the film they had dissected.[75] Fans at Hofstra Stadium may have been surprised by the matchup as well, for in the eight-page, blue-and-white game program—cost, twenty-five cents—next to Bautz's name was the erroneous letter "A," for attack. "Seeing Richie move from attack to defense," says Danowski, "was so strange."[76]

The Terrapins won the opening face-off and worked the ball to Kaestner. Burnap, one week after guarding a player who finished with seven goals and three assists, stripped Kaestner of the ball. Cornell gained possession and cleared to its offensive end. The Big Red completed a few passes and the ball went to Rimmer. The star attackman, on the left wing, ran up the field; Bautz, an attentive dance partner, followed suit, but thinking he knew where Rimmer was headed, he went one step further. That was all Rimmer needed. He spun, leaving Bautz behind, went to the tip of the crease and fired a left-handed bounce shot. It eluded Reilly for a 1–0 lead. Fifty-nine seconds had elapsed.

Soon after, Fenzel, using Shaw's backup stick, was called for a one-minute penalty. Sixteen seconds later the game was tied after a goal from Cleaver, Maryland's outstanding shooter, assisted by Kaestner. The Terrapins were on the scoreboard thanks to their two most dangerous offensive players. Fenzel scored on a close shot for a 2–1 lead; Maryland's Steven Demzcuk scored to tie the game. Cornell took a 3–2 lead on a goal on a long bounce shot from reserve midfielder Bob Wagner, a senior from Newtown, Pennsylvania. His previous main contribution had been on the long trip to Raleigh weeks earlier, during spring break. Late at night the team bus pulled over alongside the highway so Cannonball Cal and Moran could investigate a noise in the engine. Several players took the opportunity to stretch their legs, the only light coming from the flashlight that Moran directed to the hood of the vehicle. Suddenly, from the woods a few yards away, a loud noise startled the group; Moran turned the flashlight to see a giant figure with wild hair and sharp teeth emerge. The coach screamed and dropped the flashlight. At this, Wagner removed his Wolfman Halloween mask and smiled.[77]

The Big Red led 3–2 late in the first quarter when Rimmer scored in a settled six-on-six situation, then again on extra-man for a 5–2 lead. Early in the second quarter Cornell's Craig Bollinger, a reserve midfielder, began a fast break. He passed to the program's all-time leading scorer; Rimmer, barely bringing the ball into his stick, immediately took a twisting shot that went past Reilly's shoulder and snuck under the top of the crossbar for a 6–2 lead. It was after this goal that the Maryland's goalie and defenders began to hang their heads. "We just couldn't handle Rimmer," Hochstadt said later.[78]

The next goal, Cornell's seventh, was even more chastening. Davis scored on a sequence that began with two bounce passes on the artificial turf involving Davis and Rimmer, the box players who had executed dozens and dozens of bounce passes in the indoor game. The Maryland players were card-carrying members of the Big Five and the Baltimore establishment. But on the artificial turf of Hofstra Stadium, in the first NCAA tournament championship game, the establishment darlings were starting to sense that they were out of their element. "We'd never seen a box [lacrosse] player," says Kaestner. "Then Rimmer comes out wearing Chuck Taylors and we couldn't stop him. . . . And I can still see those bounce passes on the carpet. We'd never seen those either. We'd never even played on a carpet before."[79]

It was still early in the second quarter and plenty of time remained, but Beardmore was scrambling. After the seventh goal, he tore up the defensive game plan and told Mayer to guard Rimmer—the matchup that Moran and Waldvogel had anticipated.[80] Maryland's offense increased its urgency against Buhmann. Its skilled shooters tended to aim for the top corners of the goal rather than relying on bounce shots, which on artificial turf were not as effective since they were easier for the goalie to read. Here, fate dealt the Big Red a good hand. Buhmann excelled at stopping high shots, and the low shots with which he struggled were effectively neutered by the artificial turf.

Early in the second quarter, trailing 7–2, Maryland's Cleaver found himself twelve yards from the goal, in the middle of the field, and having momentarily lost Ellis. Cleaver instead was matched up against short stick Bruce Teague, an offensive midfielder. Shots from the middle of the restraining box are most

FIGURE 4.1.   Glen Mueller drives to the goal against a Maryland defender in the inaugural NCAA lacrosse title game at Hofstra Stadium in 1971. Note Mueller's wooden stick; by the following year, plastic stick heads would become far more prevalent. (Photo courtesy Cornell Sports Information)

effective because the player has the entire goal at which to shoot. And Maryland's leading goal scorer did not pass up the golden opportunity: He unleashed a shot with such velocity in his follow-through that he kicked his leg, almost like a professional bowler after releasing a certain strike. Buhmann simply knelt to his left and stopped the ball, then threw a perfect outlet pass to Teague to start a fast break. Even though it did not result in a goal—a shot from the right wing by Davis bounced off the goalpost—the sequence began with Maryland's best shooter having a good shot and ended with Cornell nearly scoring another goal. Indeed, after Davis's shot a confused Reilly looked behind him, the universal signal that a goalie believes a goal has been scored.

Still trailing 7–2, on Maryland's next possession the ball went to Kaestner, again from near the middle of the restraining box. The Baltimore native and second-generation lacrosse star unleashed a bounce shot from about ten yards. Buhmann stopped the ball almost nonchalantly. In the final minutes the teams exchanged goals, Gunts scoring for the Big Red, Dempsey answering for Maryland. At halftime the Big Red led 8–3, and Buhmann had made twelve saves. The teams headed off the field to the locker rooms at the same time and in the same direction. They were in very different moods.

If the first NCAA lacrosse title game included a halftime show, it has been lost to history. The eight-page game program makes no mention of one, nor do any of the game accounts. The unveiling of the all-American teams remained under the purview of the USILA and would not be revealed until the following week's North–South game, held at Tufts University in Boston. The all-American lists may not have been complete anyway, for there still remained both the NCAA final and one regular-season game, Army–Navy in Annapolis one day later. The only activity on the field at halftime seemed to be Bagli, in a mustard-yellow blazer, and Smith, in a black Johns Hopkins blazer, doing first-half analysis for the WBAL audience.

In the third quarter the Terrapins began shooting more quickly, trying to make up the five-goal deficit. They took fourteen shots in the fifteen-minute quarter. Only one escaped Buhmann, a shot from Cleaver midway through the quarter. It narrowed the deficit to 9–4. It became 10–4 following another goal from Rimmer, his fifth of the day. At the start of the fourth quarter, the Terrapins finally began to click. Goals from Nachlas and Larry Hubbard, a reserve midfielder, decreased the deficit to 10–6. The Terrapins then had a fast break, which was stopped after a Cornell player appeared to throw a check at the helmet of the Maryland player in possession. If spotted by the referees, that would have been a one-minute penalty called "slashing." The referees did not throw a penalty flag. Beardmore raced onto the field to complain but was sent back to the sideline. Soon after, on a fast break in the other direction, Rimmer scored his sixth goal, assisted by Burnap. The defender who primarily guarded Kaestner had just equaled Kaestner's scoring output for the day. Maryland's momentum had fizzled.

Leading 11–6 with six minutes to play, Cornell began to focus on controlling the ball to run out the clock. It held possession for minutes at a time, completing passes, playing a version of the children's game keep-away. The Big Red controlled the ball, by one account, for nearly five minutes before Shaw, with forty-one seconds left, scored into a virtually empty net for a 12–6 lead. Moran then began calling each of the starters out of the game, first Davis, then Rimmer, then Shaw, each one mobbed by teammates when he reached the sideline. When the game ended, the 12–6 victory cemented in history, the majority of the Cornell players ran to Buhmann. He had made twenty-two saves, at least six on point-blank efforts where the huge advantage is to the shooter. Following one such save, a writer in the press box noted Buhmann's near season-long backup status. "Rule," he said, "must be incredible."[81]

Dozens of Cornell fans poured onto the artificial turf. After the impromptu celebrations there was a formal gathering near midfield. Mintz, the sports information director, was the first one to hand the NCAA lacrosse tournament trophy, dark-brown wood with a gold panel in the middle, to Moran. The coach stopped for an interview with Smith, the Johns Hopkins alumnus, whose black jacket and tie made him look as if he were attending a funeral. As the interview continued, Moran's voice became an unusual mixture of elation and irritation. "Do you think we showed Baltimore something?" he asked archly. "Do you think they'll rank us as high as third?"[82] More and more people joined the on-field celebration where Cornell's bench had been during the game. Moran could barely take two steps without being greeted by a well-wisher, shaking hands, nodding in appreciation at the kind words being bestowed upon him.

The joyful Cornell contingent moved from the field to the concrete locker room, where junior Harry Nicolaides, a reserve defenseman from Baltimore, had snuck in several bottles of champagne. The players doused each other and Moran with champagne and Miller High Life beer, to the obvious dismay of NCAA representatives. The players and alumni moved to Meadowbrook Bill's, a simple Formica bar across the street from the stadium; it had been a favorite of New York Jets quarterback Joe Namath during the team's annual summer training camp at Hofstra.

The day belonged to all those in Cornell red, all of the former and current players, and everyone who had played the sport but not won a championship for being outside the Miller Division, outside the Baltimore establishment. Several former Cornell players attended the game and snuck into the postgame celebrations. "We had more talent on the 1970 team," says Burnap. "We could have won the title then, too."[83] Says Rule: "The seniors in 1970 still say their team was better than '71. And they went undefeated, so I don't argue with them."[84] An editorial in the *Ithaca Journal*'s editions two days after the game revisited recent history as well. "P.S. Now that the myth of Army–Navy–Johns Hopkins–Maryland–Virginia superiority has been broken," the story concluded, "perhaps the NCAA can have a revote on the national champions of 1970, 1966, and possibly 1968. All were unbeaten Big Red seasons, but Cornell was lucky to get a No. 4 or No. 5 ranking from the 'experts.' This year it was rated No. 5 throughout the campaign."[85]

But mostly the afternoon belonged to Moran. Decades after the first title game, on a rainy Sunday in New York City, the writer who covered the contest for *Sports Illustrated* put down his crossword puzzle to share his recollections. He did not recall Rimmer, who finished with six goals and months later was married to his college girlfriend and living back in Toronto. Nor did Peter Carry remember Buhmann or Davis and his homemade stick. "I have a vague recollection of their names but no mental image of any of them," Carry says. "But I can still see Moran, a kind of short round guy with kind of a motor mouth and red face racing up and down Cornell's sideline."[86]

The title game was played just a few miles from where Moran grew up in Elmont. Many family members attended, but his mother was unable to do so.[87] After the game Moran was given a ride to his mother's house, NCAA trophy in tow. Moran had lost his father during his junior year in college, but his mother remained in the home where they had raised their eight children. Moran brought the trophy inside. His mother kissed the trophy, then kissed her son.[88] From there Moran and his friends went for a quick bite to eat at their favorite spot, the Waltz Inn in Stewart Manor, where patrons looked away from the small black-and-white TV showing the Belmont Stakes—Pass Catcher, a long shot with 8–1 odds, pulled away to defeat the thirteen-horse field that included Canonero II—to greet Moran, the native son, and to kiss the NCAA trophy as if they were venerating the crucifix at nearby St. Anne's Catholic Church on Good Friday. "Everyone there had also been at the game," Moran says now. "They took the trophy and passed it around the bar."[89] Moran then traveled with the trophy to the party celebrating the Bar Mitzvah of the son of his close friend Matt Levine. He brought the trophy inside with him. After a few minutes at the Levine reception, he joined the celebration at crowded, cramped, and sweaty Meadowbrook Bill's, still toting the trophy like a proud father parading his newborn child.

The events of June 5, 1971, lingered with several players. Bautz never again played for Maryland. Soon after the title game he transferred to Hofstra, and when the Flying Dutchmen reached the NCAA tournament in 1974, they did so with Bautz as one of their top offensive midfielders. Bautz later became a decorated detective with the Nassau County police force before a knee injury forced him to retire in 1996. On November 25, 2002, while walking to meet friends for dinner, Bautz was struck by a car and killed in a hit-and-run accident on the Hempstead Turnpike at Merrick Avenue, just one and a half miles from Hofstra Stadium.[90]

The day also lingered for Buhmann. After the game he was asked if his twenty-two-save performance had been his best. "It sure was my best," he answered. "But then again I didn't get to play many games."[91] "Bob Buhmann wasn't able to drive because of epilepsy," says Buck Briggs, a Cornell graduate and longtime friend. "So you can't trust him behind the wheel of an automobile. But in the biggest game of his life, and in the ultimate quick-twitch position in the world of sports, he finished with twenty-two saves. Maybe you can figure that out because I can't."[92] The day before the 1971 North–South game at Tufts University, Rule learned he had been named first-team all-American. But Buhmann's late-season heroics earned him a spot as an honorable mention all-American. In the sport's long history, it was one of only two times that two goalies from the same team was each named an all-American. (The other was Princeton in 1955.)

The relationship between Rule and Buhmann remained, in Rule's words, "cordial. We were certainly not friends."[93] Rule began a professional career as a teacher and assistant lacrosse coach at Manhasset High, his alma mater. The busy schedule and time commitment left him unable to attend team reunions and other functions.

But after Rule retired as an assistant lacrosse coach, he attended a reunion of the 1971 team in 2011. Buhmann, a frequent visitor to Cornell, was there as well. "I just had this hint I should say something," Rule said. "I walked over to him and said, 'I was scared to death of you. You made me work so hard because I knew how good you were.' And he said, 'I felt the same way about you.' From then on we became great friends."[94] Buhmann, the music aficionado, brought Rule to concerts, Neil Young, Paul Revere and the Raiders. "Stuff I would never have done on my own," Rule says. They took trips together. And in August 2014, when Buhmann was diagnosed with an inoperable brain tumor and given weeks to live, it was Rule and Mueller who brought him from Long Island to San Diego, California, to see his new grandchild. "I went to pick him up and he looked awful," Rule says now. "He was swollen from steroids [to treat cancer] and could barely walk. I told him, 'I don't think you can go.' He said, 'I don't care what the doctors say, I am going to see my grandchildren. . . . It was a tough trip, but seeing him with his two grandchildren made it totally worth it.'" Says Briggs, a mutual friend, "The trip could have killed him, he was in such bad shape. But Bob and Glen took really good care of him."

Three months later, on December 13, 2014, Buhmann died in hospice care, Rule and Briggs having arrived at the hospital a few minutes too late. He was sixty-four years old. Buhmann's memorial service featured stories about his two children, two grandchildren, dozens of friends, and his twenty-two saves on June 5, 1971. It also gave Rule a chance to reflect on his friendship, one he found before it was too late. About the trip to California, and giving a friend a last chance to visit family, Rule smiles. "It's something you'd do for a teammate," he says.[95]

FALLING SHORT

In the winter of 1962, Cornell athletic director Bob Kane believed that Cornell could climb to the top of the college lacrosse world. It took less than ten years to prove him correct. Kane was in attendance at Hofstra University for the first NCAA title game and was among the dozens who congratulated coach Richie Moran and the players afterward. The accomplishment went far beyond the athletic department. The weekend of the title game, back in Ithaca, Cornell's board of trustees was holding its annual meeting. The notes from the meeting, published in the *Cornell Chronicle*, began with congratulations to the lacrosse team.

Kane was so moved that, weeks later, he wrote a letter to backup goalie Bob Buhmann. "Dear Bob," began the typed correspondence, dated July 9, 1971, addressed to the backup goalie's home in Seaford, New York, "I guess I spoke to you at Hempstead and I hope everybody else on our wonderful lacrosse team to tell you how great you were in that final game, and I just want to restate it now. It was a thrilling and well deserved victory over Maryland and a well deserved prize with it: the National Collegiate Championship, the first legitimate one in the history of the game. You and your teammates, and your coach, Richie, were terrific. I'm proud of you all."[1]

Moran himself was no less pleased. As the school year was about to start in Ithaca, three months after the title game, he told the *Cornell Daily Sun* newspaper, "We still haven't come down to earth."[2]

Cornell's work toward defending its NCAA title began in the fall, in Ithaca's crisp fall air and against a backdrop of leaves in various shades of red, yellow, orange, and brown. Cornell had instituted annual fall workouts in 1947 when coach Ray Van Orman was released from his duties as the junior varsity football coach to hold practices "because of the tremendous growth of interest in the sport [of lacrosse] by the student body," wrote the *Cornell Daily Sun* in 1947. "As a result of this fall training session Coach Van Orman hopes to build a team that will better last season's dismal record and perhaps rival the top teams in the East."[3] Around that time other programs, including Army, Yale, and RPI, were holding fall lacrosse workouts.[4] Rutgers had held fall workouts as early as 1924.[5] Syracuse instituted fall practices two years later.[6] It is not clear when the Big Five programs instituted autumn practices. One thing was certain: By the fall of 1971, and the start of the NCAA tournament, lacrosse was becoming a year-round sport, the focus of a player's attention, and not just a way to stay in shape for another sport.

At Cornell, generally speaking, the fall practices were held three times each week over five weeks, and the training culminated with a scrimmage against another college program. In the fall of 1971, the opponent was Fairleigh Dickinson, which had ended the previous season ranked number 16 in the nation. Before the page turned completely from the national championship season, however, there was one last celebration. The annual team banquet, rescheduled by Moran so it would not conflict with NCAA tournament preparation, was held amid the fall practices on October 9 at the Sheraton Motor Inn, a couple miles from Schoellkopf Field and closest to the Ithaca Tompkins regional airport. The whole campus was in a festive mood. That afternoon the undefeated football team was hosting Princeton in the Ivy League opener, and the weather cooperated—to a certain extent. The morning's heavy rains relented just in time for the 2 p.m. kickoff, replaced by overcast skies and temperatures in the high fifties—perfect conditions for football and other outdoor activities.[7] "We had a tailgate party before the game, for everyone who had come into town," Moran says.[8] Cornell football won, 19–8, thanks to 144 yards rushing and one touchdown from senior Ed Marinaro.

Venerable Schoellkopf Field looked a little different. Weeks earlier, in time for the football season opener, the grass playing surface had been replaced by artificial Poly-Turf. One rumor making the rounds: Marinaro had been the second-leading rusher in the nation the previous year, and the switch in playing surface was done to help his chances to win the Heisman trophy. The real reason was less interesting. The university had simply designated Lower Alumni Field to be used for new academic buildings, and Kane had solicited a donation from an alumnus to pay for the Poly-Turf because it was better suited to withstand the increase in practices and games headed to Schoellkopf Field.[9]

On the night of October 9, the lacrosse banquet was sold out, with more than 250 people having bought tickets for a room with a capacity of 225.[10] One pleasant surprise was evident from a quick scan of the attendees: the large number of players from the title team who remained on the roster. The leading scorer, Al Rimmer, had been a senior, as had both goalies, Buhmann and Bob Rule. (Rule, also a member of the 1969–1970 NCAA hockey champions, is believed to be the first athlete in college sports history to win two NCAA team titles.) The Big Red had back the second-, third-, fourth-, fifth- and sixth-leading scorers, plus two-thirds of the starting defense. Also on the roster was a midfielder named Bruce Arena, a junior and transfer from Nassau Community College, who was an outstanding outside shooter, good athlete, and could also take face-offs. There was confidence that Cornell in 1972 might be even better than the previous year's national champions.

The offense and defense were set. The situation with the goalkeeper was more tenuous. Senior Bucky Gunts was playing the position regularly for the first time since he started for the freshman team in 1969, which went undefeated in nine games.[11] There were no questions about his ability. The graduate of Friends School was highly regarded in Baltimore's powerful private-school league and finished his senior year as an honorable mention all-Maryland Scholastic Association pick in the *Baltimore Sun*.[12] At Cornell, Buhmann's arrival from Nassau Community College bumped Gunts into the midfield and man-down defense for two years.

Gunts had grown up in a house that's now part of the campus at Friends School, so he never was far from the school's lacrosse goals and open fields. "But shooting with a goalie's stick is no fun," he says, "so I'd bring a midfielder's stick and shoot with that."[13] The extra stick work had come in handy in the spring of 1971. In the NCAA tournament semifinal against Army, he scored his first goal of the season, then added two more in the championship game against Maryland. Now Gunts finally had his chance to be the starting goalie. And he was expecting to play a lot, because sophomore Alan Lampert, whose star turn had come in the practices leading to the NCAA title game, was the only other goalkeeper on the roster. Moran and Waldvogel welcomed three goalies onto campus that fall as part of the freshman class, including a highly touted recruit from Levittown, New York, named Joe D'Amelio. They would, per Ivy League rules, spend the year with their classmates on the freshman team.

For the Fairleigh Dickinson scrimmage, Moran and Waldvogel decided to give Gunts as much playing time as possible to help him acclimate to the position. On October 23 inside Schoellkopf Field, the Big Red jumped to an 8–1 lead, effectively deciding the outcome. Gunts remained in the game for more work. The Big Red led 10–3 early in the third quarter when Gunts, who to that point had made nine saves, collapsed to the new Poly-Turf; he had injured his right knee. He left the scrimmage and was replaced by Lampert. "I don't think anyone thought it was too serious," Gunts says now. "I had never had a serious injury in my life."[14] Moran, too, told reporters after the scrimmage that the injury did not look as if it would require surgery.[15] After Gunts left, the goalie play dropped noticeably when Lampert gave up four goals, while making only two saves. The Big Red won, 21–7, and the account in Monday's *Ithaca Journal* began with Cornell's first lacrosse game on the new surface before addressing the main personnel issue: "Moran was pleased with his fall sessions although figuring out his goalie situation may give him some sleepless nights during the Winter months before practice resumes."[16]

Still, the offense looked unstoppable. Mueller finished with six goals and two assists, Gallagher added three goals and three assists, and Shaw finished with two goals and three assists. And that was without Arena, who spent the fall with Cornell's soccer team as its starting goalkeeper. Two days after the scrimmage came the bad news: Doctors said Gunts had torn cartilage in his knee. Their remedy was to put his leg in a cast for six weeks, assuring him it would come off in time for the preseason workouts and he would be healthy to make the trip in mid-March to North Carolina for a series of scrimmages. Gunts accepted the diagnosis and continued to lift weights with the team, working on his upper body while his right leg remained in heavy plaster.[17]

In Baltimore, following the first NCAA championship, the recriminations were even greater than the celebrations in Ithaca. The day after the NCAA championship, Army and Navy met in what had been the jewel of the lacrosse season. Now even the *Baltimore Sun* acknowledged the rivalry's also-ran status with its game-day headline: "Army and Navy Stickmen Meet Today in 'Ordinary' Game."[18] Army won, 7–4, before a crowd of ten thousand, large by the sport's standards—and bigger than the first NCAA title game had drawn—but more than six thousand people short of the attendance for their previous meeting in Annapolis two years earlier. "The whole thing, playing the day after the title game, was odd," says Steve Soroka, Navy's starting goalie that day.[19] The Baltimore establishment was waking up to the fact that the brash Moran, championing his team and "Northern" lacrosse in general like a boxing promoter, had been correct all along. "What's going on in lacrosse?" wrote *Baltimore Sun* columnist Bill Tanton one week after the title game. "Are the Yankees just plain better than we Rebels? With just one game remaining in the season, the North–South Club All-Star Game [at Homewood Field] Saturday night, it would certainly appear that way. . . . It used to be that Maryland was considered the top spawning ground for talent. Obviously, that is no longer the case."[20] Tanton was not alone in his thoughts on the sport's new dawn. "The NCAA Lacrosse Tournament," wrote *Baltimore Sun* columnist Jack Chevalier soon after the title game, "a fragile experiment that nearly collapsed a month ago, today ranks as an athletic reality with an interesting past and a promising future. It is like an infant who has just spoken his first word. It'll never shut up again."[21]

The Baltimore establishment had a couple arrows left in its traditionalist quiver. One was revealed in the week leading to the NCAA championship game when Army and Navy announced their decision to permit freshmen to play varsity lacrosse, effective for the 1972 season.[22] Johns Hopkins said it, too, planned to make freshmen eligible for varsity competition starting in 1972.[23] The other members of the Big Five, Maryland and Virginia, already permitted freshmen on varsity. Maintaining a freshman team, as Cornell and the rest of the Ivy League were required to do, had some benefits. It especially helped newcomers to the sport; they could learn the intricacies of lacrosse and receive ample playing time outside the spotlight of varsity competition. Cornell's championship roster in 1971 had twelve players who had never played the sport before college.[24]

But forbidding freshmen from playing varsity was becoming a problem. While benefiting some players, there is no question that at least a few of the freshmen at Cornell were talented enough to help the varsity team immediately. Many top recruits had played games like the Long Island championship, which drew several thousand fans to Hofstra Stadium. On the freshman team their opponents would include not Ivy League or Big Five opponents but Corning Community College (twice) and Farmingdale A&T. For the upper-echelon of experienced high-school players, competing at the freshman level was a step down and could turn players away from considering an Ivy League program, which already operated, athletically speaking, at a deficit because they did not offer scholarships.

Freshmen were appearing on an increasing number of varsity lacrosse rosters. The NCAA tournament, far from perfect in its first year, was set to become a mainstay on the sport's calendar. Yet the sport's biggest change for the 1972 season and beyond was neither of these.

Joe Finn settled into his seat at Byrd Stadium for a game between Maryland and Johns Hopkins during the 1972 season. The day marked his return to the sport following three years in the US Army. It was a beautiful, sunny, eighty-degree Saturday afternoon. But something was different. Cavernous Byrd Stadium had not changed, nor had the team uniforms—the Terrapins in red jerseys, red shorts, and white bucket helmets with alternating red-and-white stickers, the Blue Jays in light-blue jerseys, white shorts, and light-blue-and-white helmets. Squinting in the Maryland sunlight to make sure his eyes had not gone bad, Finn, watching his first lacrosse game in three years, finally arrived at his conclusion. "It hit me like a ton of bricks," he says. "They were using plastic sticks."[25]

In 1970 the polymer heads atop the wooden shafts had been nowhere in sight at the illustrious North–South game in Lexington, Virginia. Two years later they were everywhere. The plastic stick head, for the first time, was symmetrical; lefties and righties could use the same stick.[26] Once the plastic head came to the fore, other changes to make the sport quicker and less cumbersome were bound to follow. For 1972, however, the plastic stick heads were the only cosmetic change. The sport's helmets remained like overturned buckets, and the puffy lacrosse gloves resembled those worn by arctic explorers. But to Finn, in the stands at Byrd Stadium, the heads made the game look completely different. "You could notice right away how they [the plastic sticks] were changing the game," says Finn. "They were lighter, they were easier to handle, easier to throw and catch with, easier to shoot. They were far more accurate. They helped speed up the game and increased scoring. But the biggest thing about the plastic sticks was you could mass-produce them. . . . The wooden sticks, no two sticks were the same. That wasn't a problem with the plastic sticks."[27]

Tom Duquette, who played attack for Virginia in the early 1970s and parlayed his summer job with STX into introducing the new wares to his college teammates, recalls a very swift demise for the handcrafted, expensive, and hard-to-find wooden stick. "In the spring of 1970 it was all wooden sticks," Duquette says now. "In 1971 my guess is it was 50–50 wooden sticks and plastic sticks. . . . But by 1972 the plastic sticks had really started to take over. The game really started to be transformed by the plastic sticks. Part of the boom in lacrosse is directly related to the availability of sticks. And there's no way the Native Americans could have kept up with the supply of sticks that is needed today."[28]

Finn agrees, citing the 1967 fire at the Chisholm Lacrosse Manufacturing Company in Cornwall, Ontario. The firm was then credited with making 97 percent of the world's lacrosse sticks, all of them wooden.[29] The blaze to the uninsured building—built in 1930, it was dilapidated to the point that even the owner likened it to a massive shack—destroyed everything inside. Even though eight thousand hickory splits, later to be turned into sticks, were drying outside and thus were saved, it took several months and $100,000 in loans to get the company up and running again.[30] Losing such a large chunk of inventory was a disaster both for Chisholm Lacrosse Manufacturing and the sport. "I remember going into Bacharach Rasin to buy my stick" in 1969 before joining the Army, Finn says. "It was a big warehouse and normally the walls were covered with sticks. This time there were maybe two dozen sticks in the entire store. I was stunned. I think that was a wake-up call to people in the game to find a way to mass produce the sticks."[31]

The plastic stick heads were made by STX, a Baltimore company, and produced by the William T. Burnett plastics factory in South Baltimore. Tom Myrick, later a team captain at Johns Hopkins, recalls being given a tour of the Burnett factory in the early 1970s. On one side workers were making plastic lacrosse stick heads; on the other they were making pink hair curlers for women.[32]

In the fall of 1971, STX sent its catalogs advertising the new stick heads far and wide. One reached Ed Danowski, Jr., the head coach at Seaford High on Long Island. Younger brother John, a junior and standout at East Meadow High, was flipping through the catalog when he spied the stick heads. He and four team-mates—Dave Devine, John Hiller, Rich Werner, and John Green—immediately pooled their money and ordered five sticks. "I'm going to say it was November," John Danowski says now. "When the sticks arrived, I called my friends and they came over and we played catch in the streets. We thought it was unbelievable. We took to the plastic sticks pretty quick."[33] One reason, Danowski says, is because they actually owned the sticks. The wooden models provided by East Meadow High had to be returned at the end of the season, thereby precluding any offsea-son workouts and a chance to improve stick skills.[34]

The new technology was met with skepticism in some corners from those who adored the wooden sticks. Jeff Wagner, a face-off specialist for Brown in 1972, recalled practices when the plastic sticks had begun to gain footing even with the so-called northern teams, and the reaction of Brown's legendary coach, Cliff Stevenson. "Every time one of those guys with a plastic stick dropped a pass," Wagner says now, "coach Stevenson would shake his head and say, 'Those damn plastic sticks.'"[35] Frank Davis, who in 1972 was a senior and starting attackman at Cornell, said the main attraction of the wooden sticks was at the very core of the sport's roots. "I liked the wooden stick because everything came from nature," Davis says now. "The use of nylon and man-made artificial materials made the stick lighter, and it did a lot better in bad weather. It wouldn't stretch out like the leather pocket. . . . It's just my tradition, being born Native American, to want to use our own sticks."[36] The Native Americans also used natural elements to create their lacrosse balls, which were made of leather.[37]

On Long Island in the spring of 1972, a junior at Sewanhaka High was using a wooden stick given to him by his older brother. With that stick, Eamon McEne-aney scored 125 points in nineteen games, eighteen of them victories. "I, myself, preferred the pocket three-quarters of the way up the side wall," McEneaney wrote, years later, of his wooden stick, "where with one neat cradle, I could find my pocket and let fly with one of the truest and purest of flights. . . . The great love affair of the wooden stick, for those of us lucky enough to have played with one is no less than the love we have for the game itself. . . . When I look at the great game of my childhood and I dream of the ancient fathers and the great spirits of the game of lacrosse, I see them barefoot, in buckskin, on fields that stretch as far as the eye can see and they are cradling their imperfect sticks."[38]

Moran, the iconoclast who brought the sport into the modern era by advocating for the NCAA tournament, strikes a traditionalist tone when he says that to this day he prefers wooden sticks. Yet the events of 1972 would provide a final, fatal blow to the sport's quirky, romanticized, and ancient wooden sticks.

On March 18, 1972, the Cornell lacrosse team left Ithaca for its spring break trip to North Carolina, with another packed schedule. The Big Red would scrimmage the University of North Carolina twice and Duke once. There were also a couple rounds of twice daily practices.[39] One year after having its plans wrecked by the surprise snowstorm in Raleigh, the Big Red found nearby Chapel Hill, North Carolina, far more to its liking; temperatures were in the sixties and seventies. The team stayed in Chapel Hill from Saturday, March 19, to Tuesday, March 22, then boarded the bus and headed to Long Island for another packed itinerary: Wednesday, March 23, light practice at Hofstra; Thursday, March 24, season-opening afternoon game against the Flying Dutchmen, NCAA tournament participants the previous year; Friday, March 25, practice at Hofstra; Saturday, March 26, game against Adelphi, a squad praised by Hofstra coach Howdy Myers and a bit of fresh competition for the Big Red, in Garden City.[40] Immediately after the game Cornell would return to Ithaca. Gunts was on the bus, having worn the cast according to the doctor's instructions, and he was ready to be the starting goalie. Lampert, the backup goalie, was not on the bus; he had left the team soon after the fall scrimmage. "We were very positive going into 1972," Gunts says now. "We lost a lot of really good guys, but we had a good nucleus. . . . And I know they were counting on me in goal. I was the only goalie on the roster."[41]

In the weeks between the end of the fall season and the spring break trip to North Carolina, Waldvogel and Moran asked for volunteers to play goalie as Gunts's backup. Three players stepped forward. Jim Nowak was a junior who had previously played midfield and, before that, defense. Nowak had never played goalie. Nor had senior Bob Cali, a converted midfielder. The third volunteer, sophomore Perry Jacobs, was a standout high-school tennis player who had never previously played lacrosse.[42] "They were good athletes," Moran says now. "And they did a lot of training with Mike to get ready."[43]

The question of goalies did not appear to concern those outside the program. Cornell looked so formidable that it entered the year ranked number 1 by the *Baltimore Sun*. Back on attack were two returning starters, Davis (twenty-nine goals, twenty-one assists in 1971) and Mueller (seventeen goals, seventeen assists). They were joined by senior Pat Gallagher (fifteen goals), who had scored the clinching goal midway through the fourth quarter of the NCAA quarterfinal win over Brown. The midfield returned seniors Shaw (twenty-three goals, eighteen assists) and Bill Molloy (nine goals, twelve assists). They were joined by senior Craig

Bollinger, promoted from the second line. The defense had back two starters, Ellis and a senior named Russ Greene. The third starter was a junior from Baltimore named Brooks Bradley, who had wanted to quit the team the previous season because he was unhappy about his lack of playing time.[44] Moran talked him out of it. "He said quitting becomes a habit," Bradley says now. "If you quit once you do it more and more."[45] Bradley stuck with it and was the only nonsenior in the starting lineup for the 1972 opener. The first game took place on March 23 against Hofstra.

Gunts started in goal. The game began and Gunts made his first save, then about two minutes into the contest, took an awkward step and fell to the ground. He had reinjured his right knee and left the game.[46] At any of the Big Five schools, his replacement could have been a freshman. But this was Cornell of the Ivy League, and D'Amelio and his classmates were back in Ithaca, practicing with former varsity coach Bob Cullen in preparation for their season opener April 12 against North Country Community College.[47]

So the answer for the sudden vacancy in net, barely two minutes into the season opener, was Nowak, the converted midfielder. Hofstra, with a slow, patient offense, played into Cornell's hands somewhat by not immediately testing the new goalie. After the first quarter the game was tied at one; at halftime it was tied at two. Only in the third quarter did Cornell finally break free thanks to two extra-man goals by newcomer Bruce Arena and a third extra-man score by Shaw, the nonpareil outside shooter. But that was it for the offense; the defense led the way for a 5–3 victory. Nowak finished with nine saves.

The final leg of the spring break trip was much closer to what a top-ranked team should look like. On Saturday, March 25, Gunts again was out of the lineup, and with Nowak starting in goal, Cornell smashed Adelphi, 12–3. Davis finished with three goals and Nowak made eighteen saves, including thirteen in the fourth quarter. The team left Long Island after the game and returned to Ithaca around midnight. On Monday, Gunts was sent to the doctor for an examination on his troublesome right knee. It was then that they learned the extent of the injury: Gunts had torn the ligaments in his knee, aggravating the injury from the fall scrimmage. Essentially, Gunts's kneecap could pop out of place at any moment; besides being extremely painful, this also meant that he would need at least two weeks to recover.[48] The initial treatment of being in a cast for six weeks, which Gunts had followed, had not aided the healing process at all.[49]

Gunts says it was the right diagnosis but the wrong treatment. "All that happened to my leg after I got out of the cast," he says, "is my leg muscles had atrophied."[50] Had Gunts been told surgery was an option in the fall, he would have had the procedure and almost certainly would have been ready for the season, or at least most of it.[51] Instead, the medical advice given to Gunts meant that he had essentially wasted precious weeks between the initial injury and the start of the season. Cornell woke up on March 27 with a 2–0 record and the following options for its goalie position: Either Gunts could undergo immediate surgery and miss the season, or he could wait until the knee improved, then try and play as much as the pain and swelling allowed. The only full-time goalie on the Cornell lacrosse team's roster opted for the latter. "My memory of that season," Ellis says, "is how hard Bucky worked to rehab his knee and get back on the field as quickly as he could. He was constantly working on his knee. We all felt bad for him."[52]

As the team processed the news about its starting goalie, Cornell, still ranked number 1 in the *Sun,* prepared for its home opener on April 1 against fifth-ranked Navy.[53] For the first time Cornell would be playing a lacrosse game on Schoellkopf Field. University officials put in place their "ticket wickets," the red wooden ticket-selling stations that looked like London phone booths. Their presence meant that there would be an admission fee, one dollar in this case, marking the first time that Cornell had charged admission for a regular-season lacrosse game.[54]

Almost as rare as lacrosse inside Schoellkopf Field was a visit from one of the Big Five. The Midshipmen, unbeaten against Cornell in eleven tries, were making their first trip to Ithaca in twenty-six years. It is believed that Navy coach Bill Bilderback scheduled the games with Cornell to address his team's penchant for not playing well early in the season. A game against the defending NCAA champions would hold his team's attention throughout the off-season.[55] Bilderback was against the NCAA tournament format, but he was not naive about its existence, and the game against Cornell certainly would boost his team's profile one year after the Midshipmen had been forced to play both of its NCAA contests on the road. He and Moran agreed to a four-year deal, with each team receiving two home games.[56]

For Moran, the game against Navy was the culmination of a plan on which he had been working since arriving at Cornell. "We've approached West Point for the last five years," Moran told the *Baltimore Sun* in 1970, "and almost had Army on the schedule last season when they had an open date. But that open date was on the day we opened our Ivy League season and Army picked up Hobart on a home-and-home basis."[57] It would not have improved Moran's mood when he saw the score from that first Army–Hobart game in 1969; the Cadets, targeted with antiwar jeering and taunting from Hobart students, responded with a 29–2 victory in which Army coach Ace Adams, angered by the reception his team had received, played his starters almost the entire game so as to run up the score.[58] Moran knew Cornell would have given the Cadets far tougher competition.

FIGURE 5.1. In 1972, for the first time, Schoellkopf Field hosted Cornell's men's lacrosse home games. The stadium was built in 1915, and its calling card is the Crescent stands, shown here in 1975 in a game against Johns Hopkins. (Photo courtesy Cornell Sports Information)

Navy's players boarded the team bus to Ithaca, having already lost to Maryland, 12–10, in a game moved from mid-May to early March to accommodate the NCAA tournament schedule. When Navy took the field that day, its players were pelted with empty beer cans and subjected to antiwar jeers from Maryland students sitting in the front row of Byrd Stadium.[59] Such treatment was not exactly rare for Army and Navy during the height of the Vietnam War. In 1971 the Midshipmen had defeated Harvard, 8–3, in a contest that featured twenty-seven penalties. In one sequence a Navy starting attackman scored a goal, then absorbed a late hit from a Harvard defender that left him with a broken jaw; he missed all but the very end of the season.[60] "It was a cheap shot," Soroka says now.[61] After the game, two Navy players said they had been called "fascist pigs," among other names, by the Harvard players.[62] "We remember these things when we play Ivy League teams," midfielder Billy Kordis later told the *Baltimore Sun*.[63]

As if Navy needed extra motivation to face Cornell, the *Baltimore Sun* said the Midshipmen were in a "must-win" situation to have any chance of a berth in the NCAA tournament. This must have been news to Moran, who was happy to portray the Big Red as the underdog. "The last time we played Navy we lost 24–5 here and 25–4 in Annapolis," he told the *Cornell Daily Sun*. "Think we ought to show up Saturday?"[64] The coach's bravado was not as evident behind closed doors. The injury to Gunts had left Moran and Waldvogel scrambling. They worked with Cali and Nowak nonstop, to the point, Moran told reporters, that "Jim Nowak and Bob Cali have had about nine years of experience in this week's practice."[65]

April 1 arrived clear and bright, though chilly. The temperatures briefly reached fifty degrees before dipping into the thirty-degree range for the 2 p.m. start, and snow was piled on the sideline. "I remember the bus ride to Ithaca," says Soroka. "It was long, and the closer we got to Ithaca, the more and more snow we saw."[66]

People in Ithaca were finally seeing in person the Navy coach and the program that had won eight consecutive national titles in the 1960s. A crowd of four thousand people made their way inside Schoellkopf Field, most of them choosing the Crescent stands where they sat in the bright early-spring sunlight. Top-ranked Cornell, its fifteen-game winning streak in tow, took the field in its all-white uniforms and helmets. Fifth-ranked Navy wore its dark-blue jerseys with matching shorts and helmets. Very few players on either team were using the plastic stick heads.[67] Navy was playing for the third time in as many years on artificial turf, the other occasions being a 1970 victory on the road against Hofstra and a 1971 win over Johns Hopkins inside the Houston Astrodome. Soroka recalls liking the artificial surface because it was easy to read where the ball was going on bounce shots. "You could short-hop the ball, like what they do in baseball," Soroka says. "There were no real surprises."[68]

For Cornell, Nowak began the game in goal. By the end of the first quarter, he had given up three goals and was benched.[69] By halftime Cali had given up four goals, and with the Big Red trailing 7–4, Moran changed goalies again, putting Nowak back in the game for the third quarter.[70] The Midshipmen kept going, and by the end of the quarter, the game was no longer in doubt: Navy led 12–5. The Big Red, in the final minutes, rallied, but Navy held on for a 12–9 win. "I was very happy to beat Cornell up there" in Ithaca, Bilderback told the *Annapolis Capital*.[71] Said Moran, "Our goalies are learning by experience where to position themselves and to be on the ball at all times. Navy got four or five goals it shouldn't have had."[72]

Things improved slightly for Cornell in a midweek game against Fairleigh Dickinson, a 14–2 victory in windy Ithaca. Arena finished with four goals. Cali was the starting goalie and, after giving up a score in the first seventeen seconds, settled down and gave up only one more goal the rest of the day. The bigger central New York sports news that day came from Watkins Glen, roughly forty miles west of Ithaca. Officials at the Watkins Glen International race track announced that daredevil Evel Knievel's scheduled appearance in mid-May was postponed after he sustained an injury while jumping a motorcycle, at seventy miles an hour, over fifteen parked cars inside San Francisco's Cow Palace Arena.[73] Knievel cleared all fifteen cars, but on landing he flew over the handlebars of the motorcycle and sustained a broken ankle and blood clots in his leg. "I bounced all the way to the parking lot," he told the *Detroit Free Press* from his hospital bed.[74]

Things looked even better for the Big Red the following game: a 17–7 victory over visiting (and perennial also-ran) Dartmouth, in which Gallagher finished with an Ivy League–record seven assists. The headline from the game story in the *Ithaca Journal* looked both backward and forward: "Gallagher-Fed Redmen Romp Over Dartmouth; Cortland Duel Next."

It was an allusion to Tuesday's game between the Big Red and Cortland State. The Red Dragons were something of a surprise. They were unranked in the initial *Baltimore Sun* poll, and their preseason trip to the Heroes Invitational Lacrosse Tournament outside Baltimore in early April included a lopsided 17–5 loss to Virginia. The Cavaliers actually defeated Cortland State coach Jack Emmer twice that weekend; the twenty-seven-year-old former standout defender at Rutgers also played for the Long Island Athletic Club, which was included in the eight-team extravaganza. LIAC, too, lost to Virginia, 11–9, with the winning margin coming on a pair of extra-man goals scored after two penalties called on Emmer.[75] "I'm just so glad to beat these guys," Virginia's Pete Eldredge, the tournament's most valuable player, said of LIAC after the game. "They had a keg of beer at the motel, and they were giving us so much [grief]—like why did they come down here, there's no competition."[76] The Cavaliers, ranked number 1 in the *Sun*, looked to be stiff competition in 1972.[77]

Slow start aside, the Dragons had been pointing to 1972 ever since they were passed over, despite an 11–1 record, for the final berth in the inaugural NCAA tournament. The lacrosse team's new motto—"Avenge the Screw in '72"—was included in the school's 1972 yearbook four times, including once on a full page.[78] When the school's publicity department released a preseason preview of the lacrosse team, the snub was mentioned in the opening paragraph. "The team waited for an NCAA bid to the season. It never came. That team was miffed, to stay the least," read the release.[79] Cortland State's big ambitions belied its small-school status. The Dragons offered no athletic scholarships, had no full-time sports information director, and in every sport except lacrosse, they competed in the small-schools division, now called NCAA Division III.[80] Cortland State's football team, for instance, in the fall of 1971 faced similarly sized programs like Ithaca College, Indiana of Pennsylvania, C. W. Post, and SUNY-Brockport.[81] Other colleges in the small-schools division, like Johns Hopkins, Hobart, and Washington and Lee, popped on the radar of major lacrosse, but overall it was fairly rare.

Cortland State's optimism for 1972 was largely based on its prolific offense. Almost every key contributor was back, including the four attackmen Emmer liked to use at the same time, with one entering the offense as a midfielder and leaving once the Dragons went on defense. Paul Wehrum, crease attackman, scored thirty-eight goals as a sophomore and forty-six more as a junior. Also a star defensive back on the football team, in lacrosse Wehrum wore blue sweatpants for every game, home and away, regardless of the weather. It was an unusual choice not least because Cortland State's colors were red and white. And he played with a stick just a shade shorter than a defenseman's six-foot longstick—and far longer than the one used by attackmen and midfielders, which was closer to four feet. Wehrum believed the semi-longstick gave him a better ability to catch passes that otherwise might have gone over his head. Opposing goalies also noted that it gave them fits, as Wehrum, working the ride against clearing strategies of opponents, knocked down more than his share of outlet passes, sort of like an over-tall basketball player blocking shots. "Wehrum was as tough a kid as I ever coached," says Emmer. "But it wasn't pretty. Not only did he wear the ugly sweats, but he also had the longer-than-usual stick. Not pretty but for him, very effective."[82] Not for nothing was Wehrum's campus nickname "Wild Man."

Ken McEwan was the quarterback; he was back after finishing the previous year with a school-record forty-two assists. Bert Severns had finished 1971 with twenty-two goals and thirty-two assists, one of the program's first players to reach fifty points in a season. A native of the Syracuse suburb of Baldwinsville, he was the only one of the group not from Long Island.

The last member of Emmer's four-headed attack, John Eberenz, was the smallest of the quartet—he was listed at 5'6", 145 pounds. He had a beard, a thick mustache, and a mane of long black hair down to the middle of his chest that made him look like a member of the famed Allman Brothers rock-and-roll band. "His hair length," wrote Reid Detchon in the *Evening Sun* in the 1972 season, "may equal that of the entire Army team."[83] As a freshman on varsity in 1969, Eberenz's fifty-one goals nearly broke a school record and placed him among the best in the nation. As a sophomore he scored none—he had dropped out of school, only to return as a junior, when he scored thirty-three goals. "Johnny Eberenz was a very clever attackman," Emmer says. "He was a great shooter and sneaky quick. He didn't look the part with very long hair, and opponents didn't give him the respect he deserved."[84]

Cortland State and Cornell were around twenty miles apart. The cultures of the respective lacrosse teams were vastly different. Cortland State featured several players with long hair and Wehrum's strange choice of game attire, and their jerseys had the players' last names on the back. At Cornell, the 1972 team photo shows no players with beards or moustaches and only a handful with anything approaching shoulder-length hair. Cornell, like the New York Yankees, opted for no names.

On April 12, Cornell and Cortland State, differences aside, were set to play a classic. But on April 11, Emmer postponed the game. He said that Cortland State's grass College Field playing surface had been soaked by recent rains and was not usable.[85] The announcement sent Moran to the phone to call Emmer—the two knew each other from their days with LIAC. Cornell's coaches knew that the meat of the schedule—the Ivy League contests—was coming up, and Moran wanted to play Cortland State before those contests began. Their phone conversations were nearly as intense as the game promised to be. Moran told Emmer that the weather in Ithaca, only seventeen miles away, was just fine.[86] Emmer countered by saying that Colgate, another upstate New York school, had called off its game against Hartwick for the next day, citing too much rain on its grass field.[87] Moran offered to keep the game on April 12 and move it to the artificial turf of Schoellkopf Field.[88] Emmer demurred, saying he didn't want to lose the home game.

And so it went. Emmer suggested moving the game to May 1; Moran said no—the Big Red would be coming off its contest against improved Yale two days earlier, which was expected to be a taxing afternoon. Moran then countered with May 2. Emmer said no—his team was scheduled to play Hobart the next day, and he didn't want to go back to back.[89] Then there was the behind-the-scenes intrigue. An Ithaca journalist traveled to Cortland State on the day of the scheduled game and reported that he found only one small puddle on the field.[90]

Had Cornell defeated Navy it's possible that the Cortland State game would not have been played. The loss, however, meant that the Big Red needed a victory against a top opponent; and the Dragons, following a surprise 9–7 victory over Army, had jumped to number 6 in the *Baltimore Sun* poll. The Big Red, following the loss to Navy, was ranked fifth. (Virginia was ranked number 1.) In short, both teams needed a chance to impress the NCAA tournament selection committee. So they reached a compromise, with the unexpected help of Jerry Schmidt and Hobart. Cornell and Cortland State would play May 2, with the Cortland State–Hobart game moved back one day to May 4. But Moran remained flummoxed. "It seems to me," he told the *Ithaca Journal*, in remarks later reprinted by the *Cortland Standard*, "that Cortland State should take care of its fields a little better. This is a heck of a way to do business."[91]

Both teams looked impressive in the weeks between the April 12 cancellation and the rescheduled contest and entered May 2, a Tuesday, with identical 8–1 records. Cornell won all four of its intervening games, including blowout victories over supposedly improved Yale, 16–1, and Syracuse, 21–3. Cortland State lost to Hofstra, 5–4, but its victories included romps over Colgate, 23–0, and

SUNY Brockport, 21–1. Finally, May 2 arrived. At stake was upstate New York supremacy—and for the winner, an almost certain berth in the NCAA tournament. The loser would be firmly on the bubble and waiting to receive an at-large invitation to the eight-team postseason.

Cornell's team bus took its usual route north along two-lane Route 13, making a right-hand turn at the A&W Root Beer drive-in restaurant—"Home of the Burger Family"—then another right turn a couple miles down the road into the College Field parking lots. Davis, the three-year starting attackman, had not arrived by the designated time, and Moran left without him, handing a starting spot on attack to senior Art Fried. Despite the Tuesday afternoon date, an overflow crowd of four thousand attended, making the environment less a barebones stadium and more a bear pit. College Field's seating was filled and in some parts of the sidelines, fans stood eight or ten deep. "There were no ropes around the field, and the crowd was right on top of us," Ellis says.[92] (The previous year, Cornell had won, 13–5, but the crowd at Lower Alumni Field was heavily tilted to the Red Dragons. "Cortland took the off-the-field drinking contest by about 3,000 beer cans," noted the *Cornell Daily Sun*.)[93]

Cortland State's game plan was focused almost entirely on exploiting Cornell's inexperienced goalie—in this case Cali, who had moved ahead of Nowak into the starting lineup. Wehrum was tasked with making the outlet pass as difficult as possible.[94] Emmer also believed that Cali would struggle on College Field's natural grass surface, and he told his players to shoot bounce shots because Cali, having played almost all of his games on artificial turf, was used to bounce shots that were more predictable.[95] Emmer believed the craggy grass, torn up by use during football and lacrosse seasons, would result in erratic bounces.

Cortland State wore white jerseys with the player's last name on the back, along with red shorts and plain white helmets. Cornell wore its red jerseys and shorts and white helmets. Cornell took the grass field ranked third in the *Baltimore Sun*—the Red Dragons, after the loss to Hofstra, were outside the top ten and also receiving votes—and with the swagger of a defending national champion. The Big Red had also never lost to Cortland State in seventeen games. At the end of the first quarter, the Big Red led 5–0, and Davis, having received a ride from a friend, made his way onto the sideline. Less than two minutes into the second quarter Cornell led 6–0 following a goal by Mueller, his third of the afternoon.

But there were worries. Arena, not only an excellent dodger and outside shooter but also the main face-off specialist, was on the bench with a shoulder injury.[96] And Cortland State, spurred on by deafening support from the student body, slowly made its way into the game. At halftime the Big Red lead was cut to 7–3. In the third quarter the game was halted briefly when a Cortland State fan parachuted onto the field and landed on the playing surface.[97] "The crowd went nuts," Ellis says.[98] Arena, still injured, remained on the sidelines, and the Red Dragons upped the tempo, winning face-offs and gaining repeated possessions. Cornell began to struggle. Davis had entered the game in the second quarter, still with a chance to continue his streak of thirty-four consecutive games with at least one point. He had yet to score in the third quarter when he had a wide-open shot with only goalie Pete Graham to beat. Uncharacteristically, Davis shot the ball right into Graham's stick. At the end of the third quarter, Cornell still led, but it was a tight 7–5 contest.

By then, the trainers had told Moran that Arena's left shoulder injury was serious enough that he would not be permitted to return to the game. And Cortland State continued to dominate face-offs. Moreover, Cortland State's Wehrum-led ride, the lacrosse equivalent of a full-court press in basketball, where the defensive team makes it as hard as possible for the offensive team to bring the ball across midfield, was giving the defending champions major problems. In the third quarter the Big Red was successful in clearing the ball only four times out of eight.

Given repeated possessions, the four-man Red Dragons attack went to work. Four minutes into the fourth quarter Wehrum scored, assisted by McEwan, to make the score 7–6; Cortland State fans responded by lighting cherry bombs and throwing them onto the field, causing cackles of explosions and a brief stoppage in play.[99] Roughly one minute later, with acrid smoke still hanging in the air, McEwan's unassisted goal tied the game at seven. Thirty-one seconds later the Red Dragons had their first lead, on a goal by Severns, assisted by Eberenz. The crowd and the players on the sideline went into such a tizzy that Emmer and assistant Chuck Winters turned their backs on the game and asked the crowd to move off the playing field.[100]

The score remained at 8–7 until midway through the fourth quarter when Cali made a save and attempted a clear. He successfully fired an outlet pass to Skeen, the experienced senior, a calm and steady hand whose big play had saved the victory over Army in the NCAA semifinals the previous year. But McEwan ran at Skeen with such fervor that Skeen lost possession about ten yards from the goal.[101] McEwan picked up the loose ball and raced in on Cali. The player who had set a school record for assists and had been in the starting lineup for three years had a one-on-one with a goalie who had effectively played the position for little more than five weeks. McEwan made no mistake, scoring past Cali to give the Red Dragons a 9–7 lead.

Once again Emmer and Winters were forced to turn their backs to the game and motion wildly for the crowd ranged around the field to stop encroaching on the playing surface. But they need not have worried. "With the period only half-gone," wrote Fred Yahn in the next day's *Ithaca Journal*, "it was evident the

[Big] Red was a beaten team."[102] The players on Cortland State's sideline also grew wild, jumping up and down as the belief that they were finally going to beat Cornell and take a major step toward the NCAA tournament looked more like a certainty. On the field Eberenz scored a pair of goals, twenty-one seconds apart, and suddenly the Red Dragons led 11–7 with seven minutes to play. McEwan and Eberenz scored two more goals, the seventh and eighth consecutive goals of the fourth quarter for Cortland State, for a 13–7 lead. The Big Red was stuck on seven goals for more than twenty-two minutes. In the second half the team went 1 for 25 shooting.

The Dragons won, 14–8. As the game ended, Cortland State's fans stampeded onto the field. The moment was captured in the *Didascaleion*, Cortland State's yearbook, under the caption "Cortland is the Big RED."[103] Cornell's players left the field to catcalls. "Are you sure," one Dragons fan gloated, "that's the Cornell varsity?"[104] As the students departed the field, they continued their homemade chant of "N-C-A-A Alllll the Way!" Cortland State had a big game against Hobart two days later, but that didn't entirely curtail the celebration. "The madness of beating the defending national champion," says Bill Tierney, a reserve attackman on Cortland State's 1972 squad, "it was a big deal."[105]

After storming the field many of the students repaired to one of the town's several taverns, including The Mug on Main Street (where a bartender ceremoniously updated the lacrosse schedule poster behind the bar with the final score of every game as it ended); or The Red Dragon (whose logo was a fire-breathing dragon wearing a Cortland State football uniform and whose exposed brick bar included a pay phone); or The Tavern (with its wood paneling, numerous draft beer specials, and offer of "Cold 6 Packs To Go"). The screaming of the Cortland faithful would be ringing in the Cornell players' ears for hours.

Cortland State's merciless approach was represented by the Wehrum-led attack and its work in hampering Cornell's efforts to go from defense to offense. Most lacrosse teams clear the ball about 75 percent of the time. In the second half on May 2, the Big Red was successful on only eight of seventeen (47 percent). In the fourth quarter it was two for nine (22 percent). With "Wild Man" Wehrum leading the way, and spurred by the ferocious fan support, Cornell faded badly down the stretch. Davis finished without a goal or an assist. "It was one of those days," Ellis said later, "where nothing went right."[106]

The entire afternoon made Cornell look very establishment and Cortland State look very much the underdog that Cornell had been eleven months earlier, in the NCAA title game. After that contest Maryland coach Buddy Beardmore had said that Cornell won in part because it was hungrier. On May 2, 1972, in another vitally important contest, there was no question which team was hungrier. And it was not Cornell.

Three games remained for the Big Red—Princeton, Hobart, and Brown. The NCAA tournament criteria had shifted a little to feature only two automatic bids. With the Cortland State loss, Cornell's shot at the automatic bid from District One-Two, which included New York, was gone. But an at-large was still in play assuming the Big Red won out. Doing so would clinch another Ivy League title, not to mention that the Big Red expected to receive some benefit of the doubt since it had won the tournament the previous year.

Days before the eight teams were unveiled, Bruce Allison, again the head of the NCAA tournament selection committee, hinted that there would be controversy. "There's no question there's going to be some hurt feelings again this year," he told the *Ithaca Journal* on May 6, the day of the Cornell–Princeton game.[107] He added, somewhat pointedly, "Three losses would pretty much eliminate any team."[108] The Big Red, with eight wins and, more glaringly, two losses, had been warned.

Princeton entered Finney Field on May 6 below .500 but gave visiting Cornell all it could handle. The Big Red didn't take its first lead until a goal by Shaw off a bounce shot with eight seconds left to play. It was the final score in Cornell's 9–8 victory, but Arena remained sidelined with his shoulder injury, and his play, as shown by his indefinite absence, had been the spark of the offense. Cali made only one save in the first half but was excellent in the second half and finished with fourteen. "We're just an average, good lacrosse team—we have to scrap for everything we do," Moran told the *Ithaca Journal* afterward.[109] Cornell had navigated the first of three hurdles to keep alive its NCAA tournament hopes. The second came on a rainy, chilly Tuesday afternoon at Schoellkopf Field.

Coming off the Princeton win, Cornell was ranked number 8 in the USILA poll, and the goalie dilemma finally started to trend positively, as Gunts was feeling well enough to play in a reserve role. Hobart, the Big Red's next opponent, had no such questions with its goalie position. Its starter was mongoose-quick senior Dave Creighton. Growing up in Baltimore, Creighton had supplemented his speed with tutorials on shot-stopping by none other than Jerry Schmidt when the two were at Calvert Hall High, Creighton as a student and Schmidt as coach. Schmidt would bring the goalies into the school's dimly lit gymnasium before morning classes and fire shots at them with his cannon of a left-handed release.[110] When Creighton arrived at Hobart, he learned that Schmidt had continued the tradition, this time in the even murkier lighting of a Hobart athletic center squash court.[111] When the Statesmen arrived at Schoellkopf Field on May 9, goalie play would be a strength.

The Statesmen (10–1) were ranked number 11 in the USILA poll and had plenty of offensive firepower. Sophomore Rick Gilbert, a starting attackman, was among the national scoring leaders.[112] He was one of the first lacrosse stars of famed West Genesee High, outside Syracuse. Gilbert's high-school teammate, B. J. O'Hara, one year younger, started alongside him on attack at Hobart. O'Hara had cemented a spot in the starting lineup with his accurate shooting. He arrived on campus having been named the first high-school lacrosse all-American in West Genesee High's history.[113]

In a sign of the sport's tenuous journey into playoff competition, Hobart was also in the running for both of college lacrosse's postseason tournaments. One year after the inaugural NCAA playoff, the USILA got into the act with an eight-team tournament for small schools.[114] Hobart had already been offered a spot in the inaugural USILA tournament; Schmidt had not accepted the bid, preferring instead to wait and see whether the team would be invited to the NCAA playoffs, which were primarily for larger schools but actually open to anyone deemed worthy of a spot. (Cortland State in 1972 would also have qualified for both tournaments, had it not been obvious after the Cornell win that it was headed for the NCAA tournament.)[115]

Hobart and Cornell met on a gray afternoon, with temperatures in the forties and a slight drizzle making the Poly-Turf slippery. Arena played briefly before being removed by trainers, his shoulder injury still not healed. The Big Red led 3–2 at the end of the first quarter, 7–4 at halftime, and 9–8 after three quarters. Hobart junior Don Aleksiewicz, a reserve midfielder whose last name led to the nickname "A to Z," may have been the best athlete on the field. A running back on Hobart's football team, the previous fall he had rushed for 1,616 yards and nineteen touchdowns in nine games. (News outlets in upstate New York called him "the Ed Marinaro of Division II football.") He entered Schoellkopf Field having scored one goal all year. With the score tied at nine, he showed his prowess in lacrosse, a sport he first played at Hobart while staying in shape for football. Making an off-ball cut toward the Cornell goal, Aleksiewicz sent an inch-perfect pass from Gilbert past Cali for a 10–9 lead. Schmidt, whose immense dislike of Cornell was well known, raced onto the field to hug Gilbert and then Aleksiewicz.[116] But coaches are not allowed on the field during the game—and the referees nearly called Schmidt for an unsportsmanlike-conduct penalty.[117] If Schmidt thought "A to Z" had won the game right then, he was proven wrong with less than four minutes to play when Mueller answered for Cornell to tie the game at ten.

That is where things stood when, in the final minute, Aleksiewicz intercepted a pass near midfield and raced forty yards on a 5-on-3 fast break. All around him were proven offensive players: Gilbert, who finished the year with 122 points, still a school record; O'Hara, an excellent finisher en route to forty-seven goals as a freshman; and junior Kevin McLean, who entered the game with twenty-five goals. Aleksiewicz, he of the two goals in 1972, spurned them all. As he drove closer and closer to the goal, it became clear that he was not going to pass the ball to anyone. The game was riding on his stick. Finally, he readied to shoot. Cali guessed low; Aleksiewicz shot high, and as the ball went past Cali and into the goal, Ellis, trying to make a play, ran into the goal and knocked it to the ground.[118] Terry Cullen, the former Hobart two-sport athlete and current Cornell employee, was one of the two game referees. On the sideline, Moran believed the physical goal was knocked to the ground before the ball had gone in, which would have signified no goal. Schmidt argued that the ball was in the goal before Ellis had run into it.[119] "We had a big discussion on whether the goal should count," Cullen says. "Richie and Schmidty were like oil and water on the lacrosse field, and they were screaming and yelling at each other. But the other referee and I decided the ball was in the goal before the goal had been knocked over and the goal counted."[120] Hobart led, 11–10.

Thirteen seconds remained, enough time remained for Cornell to win a face-off and generate a shot on the excellent Creighton, who to that point had made fifteen saves. But the best face-off specialist, Arena, remained sidelined. Hobart's A. J. Russo won the all-important face-off, and the Statesmen ran out the clock. Immediately after the game, dozens of Hobart students and alumni stormed the Schoellkopf Field turf. Most made a beeline for Schmidt, knowing what the victory meant for him. "Fantastic, just fantastic," he repeated over and over.[121] Hobart athletic director Bill Stiles, following the congratulations, began working the phones. The Statesmen had a game against Penn State scheduled for May 20, which coincided with the first round of the NCAA tournament. Stiles called State College, Pennsylvania, to see whether the game could be moved.[122]

An hour after the game, Cullen and the other game's referee, Ray Morey, stopped by the Lehigh Valley House at 801 West Buffalo Street for a beer. The restaurant, founded in 1897 near Ithaca's railroad station, was about two miles from Schoellkopf Field. Soon, a bus pulled into the parking lot, and out stepped Schmidt and the Hobart lacrosse team; they were stopping for dinner before heading back to Geneva. "And ten minutes later Richie comes in for a beer," Cullen says now. "I turned to Ray and said, 'This ought to be good.'"[123] Hobart's team was seated in the dining room next to the bar, but soon Schmidt stepped out of the room and saw Moran. "And they began arguing," Cullen says. "Richie kept saying, 'I was the biggest jerk today during the game, I'm buying your beer.' And Jerry was saying, 'No, I was a bigger jerk to you. Sit down, I'm buying.' The four of us sat there and had a friendly beer after one of the most tumultuous games I ever saw."[124]

Aleksiewicz scored only two more goals the rest of his lacrosse career. Almost exactly one year after the win over Cornell, Aleksiewicz, then a senior at Hobart, was ruled ineligible; days earlier and with the blessing of school officials he had signed a contract with the Ottawa Rough Riders of the Canadian Football League. Aleksiewicz finished his football career at Hobart with eight school records. He finished his lacrosse career at Hobart with eight goals. When he died unexpectedly in 2014, at the age of sixty-two, leaving behind a wife and two children, teammates and school officials recalled his tryouts with the CFL, the NFL's Washington Redskins and San Diego Chargers, and the Philadelphia Bell of the World Football League. They also mentioned his two goals against Cornell. "The legend of 'A to Z' was born, not just by an accumulation of gaudy statistics, but the fact that they occurred in big moments," football and lacrosse teammate Bob Raleigh said in Hobart's obituary for Aleksiewicz. "The famous 13 seconds versus Cornell is a prime example."[125]

The NCAA tournament pairings were to be announced Sunday night, May 14. In a sign of organizational progress, the announcement would come after teams had completed their regular seasons. For Cornell, the final regular-season game came on May 13 at Schoellkopf Field against Brown. The Big Red entered with nine wins in twelve games; with a victory over the Bears, it would clinch a fifth consecutive Ivy League title. Among the crowd of one thousand that afternoon were scouts from the University of Maryland lacrosse program; they were in attendance to prepare a scouting report should the Terrapins face Cornell in the postseason.[126] But the mood among the Cornell players and assistant coaches was somber following the loss to Hobart. Local media reported as if Cornell had little chance at the postseason.

The regular-season finale arrived on a perfect spring day, sunny, with temperatures in the eighties. Cali remained the starting goalie, but Gunts was regaining strength in his knee and had even played the final thirteen seconds against Hobart, inserted into the game after "A to Z"'s second, winning goal. Against Brown, Cornell led 7–4 late in the second quarter when Gunts entered the game.[127] The Bears closed to 8–6 early in the third quarter before Cornell pulled away for a 14–7 victory. Shaw finished with three goals on only four shots; in one sequence in the fourth quarter, he won a face-off to himself, went down the field, and scored without giving up possession.[128] Gunts finished with six saves and helped calm the clearing game after Cornell, with Cali in the game, had six failed clears in the first quarter alone.[129] Davis, playing perhaps his best game of the year, scored four goals; Mueller scored three; Bill Molloy had two goals and two assists; and Gallagher finished with one goal and five assists. The Big Red made its final arguments for why it deserved inclusion in the eight-team NCAA tournament.

Moran had been told that the teams that made the tournament would be informed by 6:30 p.m. Sunday. Moran waited Sunday night for a call from Allison or another member of the NCAA Rules and Tournament Committee. No phone call came. By 8 p.m., Moran believed his team had not in fact been chosen, but he was still expecting a call with an explanation as to why the defending NCAA champion and current Ivy League champion was not considered one of the best eight teams in the nation. Again, no phone call came.

On Monday morning the seedings were released. Cornell, with a 10–3 record, was not in the field. Nor was any team from the Ivy League. (It would be the first of only four times that the tournament did not feature a team from the Ivy League.) Among those chosen in 1972 were all of the Big Five, including Virginia, which had struggled after its early-season success and sported a modest 8–4 record; tiny Washington and Lee, which had ended the season with a loss to Virginia; and Rutgers, which was unranked in the influential *Baltimore Sun* poll released the same day the seedings were announced.[130] The Big Red was ranked number 8 in that poll and, with Gunts back in the lineup, finally was starting to resemble the team that began the season ranked number 1.[131] "If we had gotten into the tournament," Davis says now, "we would have gotten our shit together and played better."[132]

The *Evening Sun* asked Moran for comment. The fiery coach was happy to oblige. "I would give more respect to a dying rat than they gave this team," Moran said of the NCAA Rules and Tournament Committee.[133] He later added that lacrosse was "a small world with a lot of small people and a lot of small thinking. . . . We played a quarter against Cortland that was pitiful and four minutes against Hobart that was pitiful. So 20 minutes of pitiful lacrosse is going to cost us the tournament. It's a bitter pill to take." He also took aim at one of the participants. "Which Ivy League team," he asked, "could Washington and Lee beat?"[134]

The players on the 1972 Cornell team believe there may have been some animus toward Moran that played into the nonselection. "We were Ivy League champions and defending NCAA champions," Gallagher says now. "It wasn't like we were 5–5. I remember thinking after we beat Brown at home that it was good enough to get us in. It still doesn't seem right. . . . I think it was Baltimore getting back at us. I really do. After the 1970 season Richie was aggressively critical of the Baltimore establishment."[135] Upon hearing the news that Cornell had not made the tournament, the senior Gallagher headed for the Fall Creek House, a bar in Ithaca popular with the school's hockey players. There he drank beers and commiserated with Arena and midfielder Steve Lucas, both juniors.[136]

Cornell was angry, but so was Hobart. The Statesmen had won fourteen of fifteen games, including the hastily rescheduled contest on May 17 with Penn State, and were ranked number 6 in the *Baltimore Sun* poll released that morning. No matter—there was no space for the team from Geneva either, and they accepted a berth in the smaller USILA tournament. Allison, who had run a far better selection process in 1972, took the criticism in stride. "There's always going to be a lot of displeased people," he told the *Ithaca Journal*. "That's just the way it's going to be."[137] But the season would have ramifications for Cornell far beyond the NCAA tournament snub. "After 1972," Waldvogel says, "Richie always made sure he had at least two goalies."[138]

Cortland State was the NCAA tournament's lone representative from upstate New York; it was given a first-round road game against Navy. The other contests featured Army against Virginia in Charlottesville, Rutgers against Maryland in College Park, and Washington and Lee against Johns Hopkins in Baltimore. The Red Dragons arrived in Bowie, Maryland, on May 19, the day before the game against Navy, and held a practice inside Navy-Marine Corps Memorial Stadium. They may have had an inkling that their time on the sport's biggest stages, at least in the postseason, was limited.

In 1972 there were 111 colleges fielding men's lacrosse.[139] All of them were technically eligible for the NCAA tournament, a far cry from when only eight teams were eligible to win the Wingate trophy. The arrival of the USILA tournament was a good news–bad news scenario: The eight-team, single elimination tournament was made up of schools that competed in small-college sports in everything but lacrosse, which did not distinguish between small-college and major-college classifications. The expectation was that the NCAA would take the tournament over following a two-year experimental phase.[140]

And once the NCAA took the "college division" tournament over, schools like Hobart, Washington and Lee, and Cortland State would have to choose either to move all of their programs to the University Division for lacrosse to compete for the larger title, or transfer their lacrosse program to the small-college division and compete for that championship. Cortland State had not yet addressed the issue publicly. But a school with no athletic scholarships could hardly be expected to upgrade all its athletics just for lacrosse, especially when the team's regular-season schedule would remain largely unchanged.

The day of the Cortland State–Navy game was overcast, with bursts of rain. As the national anthem was set to begin, a sparse crowd at Navy-Marine Corps Memorial Stadium rose to its feet. There were only a handful of Cortland State fans in the stands, but as the national anthem started, a burst of noise came from the stadium's north parking lot.[141] In came five buses, including one yellow school bus and a trail of cars, most with the royal-blue background and mustard-yellow writing of New York state license plates. "The kids were hanging out of the windows," Emmer says. "It was during the anthem and I think some people thought it was disrespectful, but I don't think the kids knew the anthem was being played."[142] Tierney remembered the moment as well. "It was during the Vietnam war. Every one of the Cortland fans had hair down to [their shoulders]. . . . It was just mayhem. Here we are at the US Naval Academy, and here comes a bunch of war-protesting freaks."[143]

Estimates put the total number of Cortland State students at more than five hundred, each having paid three dollars for a game ticket and driven five hours one way.[144] As the game began, the students raced down the stadium's grass hill in the south end zone and took their spots in the stands behind the team bench. The school's enrollment in 1972 was 5,092, meaning, including the lacrosse team, more than 10 percent of its students were at the game. They announced their presence with a non-stop "Gooooo, Cortland, go!" As rain pounded the stadium—one writer said it was, at times, hard to see the field from the press box—Navy jumped to a 4–0 lead.[145] The Red Dragons had come back from an even greater deficit against Cornell and did not panic. Soon the game was tied at four.

The Midshipmen replied with another spurt to take an 8–4 lead. Again, Cortland State rallied and closed to 9–8 with one minute and twelve seconds to play. Navy, however, was on extra-man following a Cortland State penalty. Holding the ball for the entire one-minute penalty would effectively have left Cortland State with just twelve seconds to try to gain possession, then to try to tie the game. But a Navy player, in possession and suddenly wide open near the goal, took a shot. Graham made the save; fifty seconds remained. In the rules of the time, a penalty was released if the short-handed team was able to get the ball past midfield. And Graham made a decision.

At 6'1", 225 pounds, Graham was the heaviest player on Cortland State's team.[146] He was also a tremendous athlete—he had been a standout football linebacker at Corning East High, where his first game as varsity lacrosse goalie ended with a rare shutout victory.[147] Rather than risking a pass in the torrential rain, Graham called his own number and began to race down the muddy field. He set one foot over the midfield line, and as he did so, Emmer called timeout. Forty-five seconds remained and the penalty had been released, though Cortland State still trailed 9–8. During the timeout the rain-soaked students continued their "Gooooo, Cortland, go!" Emmer set up a play to give his team the best chance to score in a six-on-six situation.

Following the timeout the Red Dragons took the field with their unique four-attackman grouping. The ball went behind the goal, and Severns began jogging slowly with possession. In an instant, however, he quickened his step just as Eberenz, ten yards in front of the goal, made a quick cut after two teammates legally impeded the player guarding him. Severns threw a pass and Eberenz, wide open, caught the ball, and scored to tie the game with thirty seconds left. The Cortland State contingent cheered wildly. The game went into overtime, which under the rules at the time was two four-minute periods. If the game was tied after that, it would go to sudden-death.

Both four-minute periods elapsed, with the game still tied. In sudden-death overtime, the game was decided when Navy senior goalie Steve Soroka, in possession, was being chased by Wehrum and his extra-long attackman's stick. In the wet weather Soroka's pass was an errant one, right to Severns, who ran toward the empty goal, and scored from point-blank range for a 10–9 victory.[148] The *Cortland Standard* had a picture of the postgame scene—hundreds of students racing from all angles onto the field faster than the players on the sideline.[149] The Red Dragons' attack had accounted for nine goals, and the students had accounted for more than half the announced 1,105 in attendance. "More than 500 Cortland State lacrosse fanatics traveled 280 miles today," wrote the *Washington Post*, "to spend the afternoon standing in the rain. Barring symptoms of pneumonia there were no regrets."[150] "Their lusty cheers," began the account of the game in the *Capital*, "undoubtedly played an important role in the performance of their club."[151] For the second year in a row, upstarts from central New York, wearing red, had left a mark in the NCAA tournament.

The first-round games spit out the following semifinal matchups: On May 27 in Baltimore, Johns Hopkins would face Maryland. On the same date the other semifinal would be between Virginia of the Big Five and Cortland State, whose players were eligible only for the "Little All-American" team and whose program featured no athletic scholarships, no sports information director, and a head coach only twenty-seven years old. The Cavaliers had benefited from a first-round home game despite being lower seeded. On May 20, Michie Stadium in West Point was not available for lacrosse because of a concert featuring the Supremes, Stevie Wonder, and the Ike and Tina Turner Revue, with proceeds going to sickle-cell anemia research.[152] The NCAA determined that Virginia should not host again and awarded the game to the Red Dragons. Cortland, New York, population 19,621, was set to host one of the biggest lacrosse games in the school's history.

Except that the semifinal was set for Saturday, May 27, the same day as Cortland State's graduation. The other bad news: Workers had already moved many of the bleachers from College Field into nearby Lusk Field House, the site of the commencement. The school addressed the first problem by moving graduation back one hour, to 3 p.m., in order to accommodate the 11 a.m. lacrosse game. "I always laugh about that," Emmer says. "Cortland had its priorities straight—it moved graduation for the lacrosse game."[153] Officials wrangled bleachers from everywhere they could think—including nearby Homer High—to get College Field's capacity to five thousand. The huge semifinal against Virginia would have been enough to swamp the small college town, as would the graduation ceremony. Taken together, they promised to make May 27 a memorable day.

Virginia received a taste of the chaos on Friday, the day before the game. It flew to central New York, one of the rare times the Cavaliers did not drive to a contest, arriving in Syracuse on Friday morning, then taking a bus to Cortland.[154] Their walk-through at College Field hours later was another rarity; hundreds of Cortland State students, having found out what time Virginia would practice, had arrived to watch the visitors and heckle them. Virginia goalie Rodney Rullman, a freshman from Long Island, began taking warm-up shots from an assistant coach. Every one he saved was met with boos from the students. The shots that went in were cheered. The Cavaliers then broke down to one-on-one drills and the same thing happened: Attackmen who were stripped of the ball were jeered, defenders who gave up a goal were chastised. "It was fun," says Doug Tarring, an attackman for Virginia, "but it also added fuel to our fire."[155] From there the Cavaliers drove thirty-three miles to their hotel in Syracuse; in Cortland, with graduation and the big game, there simply were no hotel rooms available.

Game day arrived warm and bright in central New York. The 11 a.m. start, early by the sport's standards, did not slow down the fans. A local bar called The Huddle at 103 Main Street, roughly one mile from the stadium, opened at 10 a.m. and ran a special of draft beers for ten cents each.[156] By the time Virginia's team bus arrived, Cortland State students had adorned College Field with several hand-painted signs. One suggested making graduation the halftime entertainment for the lacrosse game. The largest sign, several feet high, was placed on top of a nearby building that resembled an airplane hangar. It said, "What does Cortland eat?" then answered its own question in even larger letters: "VIRGINIA HAM!"[157] Another giant sign, plastered on the roof of a building overlooking College Field, simply stated, "Cortland State is No. 1." When asked about the pregame atmosphere, Tarring says, "I wouldn't say cocktail hour had started early," then his voice trails off and he doesn't finish the sentence.[158]

The Red Dragons entered ranked number 5 in the USILA poll, one spot ahead of the Cavaliers. Their offense had scored a school-record 223 goals, an average of 14.8 per game.[159] "We're basically a fast-break team," Emmer told reporters before the game. "And that's been the key to our success all year."[160] The Red Dragons, boosted by the fan support, entered College Field wearing white home jerseys with the player's last name on the back, red shorts, and white-and-red bucket helmets; Virginia wore orange jerseys, blue shorts, and blue-and-orange bucket helmets. Both teams had at least a sprinkling of plastic stick heads; Wehrum and Severns retained wooden sticks, as did many defenders on both teams. But most of the rest of the offensive players on both teams had switched to the more modern equipment.

The crowd was immense. Those driving to the lacrosse game were forced to park in a lot off Route 281 and take a shuttle bus to College Field because the parking lot was claimed for commencement.[161] Cortland State's bleachers for five thousand fans were not nearly enough; the overflow crowd was reported as close to seven thousand, with fans ringing the field four and five deep. The Associated Press reported that it was the largest crowd for a sporting event in the history of the school, founded in 1868 as Cortland Normal School.[162] Fans were given a yellow, four-page game program with rosters, season results for both teams, and on the cover a copy of the bracket showing Cortland State in the semifinals.

The game began promptly at 11 a.m. Cortland State's Sal Taormina, a senior from Long Island using a plastic stick, won the face-off against Virginia sophomore Greg Montgomery, and the Red Dragons went to work.[163] Virginia's skilled defense was ready for the four-attackman look and everything else. Cortland State failed to score for the first nine minutes. The Red Dragons' defense, led by a javelin-thin senior named Jack McGetrick, who doubled as the starting goalie on the soccer team, was equally formidable, and the Cavaliers too failed to score. Following a shot and save late in the first quarter, Graham controlled the ball and, just as he had in the final seconds against Navy, began a mad dash up the field. He crossed midfield and kept going. Twenty-five yards from Virginia's goal he finally drew the attention of a defenseman. Graham passed to Wehrum, who scored the game's opening goal, sending the crowd into raptures.[164]

Montgomery won the ensuing faceoff, and a pair of Virginia's several Baltimore natives, Jim Ulman and Jay Connor, combined for a goal scored by Ulman to tie the game. Montgomery won the ensuing face-off, and thirty-seven seconds later Connor scored again to give the Cavaliers a 2–1 lead.[165] Montgomery won the next face-off as well. The crowd began to grow quiet.[166] The quarter ended with the Cavaliers leading 2–1. When the second quarter began, Montgomery won the initial face-off. Suddenly the Cavaliers, with their skilled stick work and plastic sticks, were finding holes in Cortland State's defense as goals came from Eldredge and Duquette for a 4–1 lead. At the other end of the field, despite playing up-tempo and aggressive all season, Emmer had decided that his team, physically smaller than the Cavaliers, should use a more patient approach.[167] The physical contrast could be seen when Eberenz, at 5'6", 145 pounds, and McEwan, at 5'8", 150 pounds, stood next to towering Virginia defenders Big Boo Smith and Bruce Mangels. It could also be seen in Montgomery, 6', 190 pounds and a member of Virginia's football team.

At halftime the Cavaliers led 7–2, and Montgomery had won ten of eleven face-offs. The Red Dragons, so used to playing up-tempo, were unable to create havoc against Virginia's athletic, skilled defensemen, partly because the game plan called for a slower pace and partly because the Cavaliers, thanks to the face-offs, were dominating possession. The third quarter began. Virginia scored four more goals to balloon its lead to 11–2. Eberenz and Wehrum eventually answered for the Red Dragons, but the damage was done. The Cavaliers lollygagged in the fourth quarter, playing several substitutes en route to a 14–7 victory.

Afterward, as Cortland State's players showered in a silent locker room, Emmer gave interviews outside it, speaking in hushed tones as if he were the proctor of a high school's final exam. Emmer congratulated Virginia and was complimentary of its athleticism, while expressing disappointment in the out-come. The Cortland State yearbook weighed in as well: "Crowds collected on the field and spirits were high. The game began with confident Cortland crowds and progressed with increasing doubt. Something was wrong. The faceoffs, the field, the heat, the nervousness, everything was blamed."[168] These days, Emmer believes he knows the answer: He is disappointed in himself for his choice of game plan, for his decision not to play the usual up-tempo style. "I tried to slow the ball down, and in retrospect it wasn't the thing to do," Emmer says. "Our guys weren't accustomed to that."[169]

It's possible the Cavaliers would have won regardless. Their prowess was shown best by Montgomery, the face-off specialist. The Cavaliers dominated in face-offs, 20–5, shots, 59–31, and groundballs, 80–41. One of the team's few players from upstate New York, Montgomery had followed his older brother from Watertown to Charlottesville. Scott Montgomery played lacrosse and foot-ball for the Cavaliers before graduating in 1968. Three weeks later he was dead, the result of a single-car accident in upstate New York. His younger brother, returning to his native New York, was ready to play the game of his life. Cortland State and its throaty fan support did not have a monopoly on motivation.

Cortland State never again played in the NCAA's tournament for major-college teams. In 1973 the Red Dragons, shorn of their senior-heavy lineup, failed to reach the NCAA tournament, but landed in the USILA college divi-sion postseason. Before the 1974 season, the NCAA, as expected, took over the USILA tournament designated for smaller schools. Part of the reason was that the lacrosse tournament for larger universities was, according to published reports, the only one of the organization's seventeen postseason endeavors to turn a profit in its first two years of existence.[170] The tournaments were renamed the Division I men's lacrosse tournament and, for smaller teams, the Division II tournament.[171] Cortland State's officials opted to have lacrosse compete for the Division II crown, essentially the same level as its other sports programs, rather than moving all its programs to the larger classification to accommodate lacrosse. (Johns Hopkins and Washington and Lee received waivers from the

NCAA to participate in the Division I tournament. It is unclear whether Cortland State ever applied for one.)

But the events of 1971–72 were not to be forgotten. That year the entire campus seemed to have been sprinkled with magic, beginning in the fall of 1971, when ninety-seven candidates tried out for more than thirty spots for the lacrosse team. On March 19, 1972, Lusk Field House, adjacent to College Field, hosted a concert by the Beach Boys, still near the height of their dizzying popularity of the 1960s. In April was the lacrosse victory over Army and former Cortland State coach Al Pisano. May brought the first-ever victory over Cornell, the NCAA tournament win over Navy, and then hosting the NCAA semifinal before the largest crowd in the school's athletic history.

With thirty seconds remaining in the game against Virginia, the outcome long since decided, the fans began serenading the head coach with a happy chant of "Emm-MER! Emm-MER!" The season was over but it had been a lot of fun. "Seldom has student interest in a single sport been as great as it was for lacrosse on the Cortland campus in May," wrote the *Cortland Standard* after the season. "The large crowds were only part of the picture. Lacrosse fever was evident in bumper stickers, booster buttons, and signs hanging outside the Moffett Center."[172] When the game clock finally hit 0:00, the Cortland State fans gave both teams a standing ovation. "They were shaking our hands and cheering us after the game," Tarring says. "They were even handing us beers."[173]

THE ESTABLISHMENT STRIKES BACK

The 1972 NCAA championship game pitted Johns Hopkins against Virginia, in College Park, Maryland. With it, ostensibly, came a return to normalcy for the sport's Baltimore establishment. Before a crowd of seven thousand fans, and on the Big Five's preferred natural-grass surface, the Cavaliers won, 13–12, thanks to a goal by Pete Eldredge with four minutes to play. One year earlier the NCAA title game had been played on artificial turf, and the offensive star had been from Canada. Eldredge hailed from Annapolis and had played in Baltimore's prestigious private school league, for Severn School.

But the sport's brave new world was on display even in a title game between teams loaded with Baltimore natives and played in the establishment's backyard. Virginia, with four losses in the regular season, would not have had a chance at a national title in the days of the USILA voting just two years earlier. Instead, the Cavaliers entered the NCAA tournament with an unsightly won-loss record but also plenty of confidence. When asked his thoughts on his team, coach Glenn Thiel sounded fairly bullish. "I knew we would get in it," Thiel said after the title game, "and I knew we had a good chance of winning it."[1] *Evening Sun* columnist Bill Tanton noticed the trend as well. "A lot of lacrosse people are concerned about the fact that the first two NCAA lacrosse tournaments produced the wrong champions," he wrote soon after the 1972 title game. "Virginia had the best team in the regular season last year and should have been the champ but was bounced in the first round of the playoffs. This year Hopkins and Maryland had much better seasons than Virginia, but all that matters is who wins the playoffs."[2]

The other trend was that for the first time every goal, assist, and save in the NCAA title game was made by players using sticks with plastic heads. The previous year every goal, assist, and save in the title game had been made by players using wooden sticks. The new equipment, virtually unknown two years earlier, was now everywhere. "By the end of 1972," says Jeff Wagner, a face-off specialist for Brown and later an employee for Brine, a sporting goods manufacturer, "I think it was 90 percent done. The plastic sticks had taken over. There were still some guys whose favorite stick was wood, and they didn't change right away. But otherwise it was over in a year and a half."[3] Wagner recalls bringing four or five wooden sticks to every game because his sticks often broke during face-offs. "That wasn't an issue with the plastic sticks," he says now. "They didn't break. Well, they could break, but if they did, you just replaced the head with another that was the exact same."[4]

Two companies were creating the plastic stick heads: The leader was STX, based in Baltimore; the other was Brine Sporting Goods, founded by William H. Brine in 1922 and based in Boston. Brine owned several storefronts in and around the city and also delivered sporting goods to the New England prep schools, becoming an ex post facto exclusive provider for almost all of their athletic equipment.[5] Because most of those schools played lacrosse, Brine began selling wooden sticks, lacrosse gloves, and lacrosse balls. Already familiar with lacrosse, the company set out to improve it. In the mid-1960s William H. Brine's two grown sons, Bill and his younger brother Peter, developed a metal mold for a plastic lacrosse stick head while working in the company warehouse in Milford, around forty miles west of Boston. They held off on producing the head because they considered the plastic composites of that era either too soft or too rigid.[6]

But in 1971, with the STX plastic head growing in popularity and having been approved for use by the NCAA, Brine released its own plastic head with a composite developed by DuPont Plastic. In late 1971 Brine placed advertisements in the *Annapolis Capital*. "Don't buy until you see ours!" read one ad in December 1971, with a giant photo of the plastic stick head and, later, a reference to the partnership with DuPont.[7] Another, in the *Capital* in March 1972, read: "Here is the stick you have been waiting for!! Strong, stiff, light, rugged, but inexpensive. We have invested thousands of dollars in development and mold costs and ten years of research to bring you the best lacrosse stick ever made."[8]

The initial Brine heads, mostly purchased by high-school and college players in New England, were heavier and more rigid than the STX models, and the company lagged behind in visibility, sales, and quality.[9] But the Brine brothers believed their stick would improve if they identified the right version of plastic—one lighter and stronger than anything currently on the market. As Brine released its initial, imperfect heads, Bill Brine, an engineer, continued mining his contacts at the DuPont labs in Chestnut Run, Delaware, for any word on a plastic that would better fit what he was looking for.

A national champion with four losses, and the rise of plastic lacrosse stick heads, were shocks to the system. Another was on its way. On June 13, 1972, just days after Virginia's victory in the NCAA championship, Navy coach Willis "Bill" Bilderback announced his retirement from a career that included winning eight consecutive national titles in the 1960s.[10] "I feel there comes a time to turn it in," he said on the day he retired. "I owe it to myself and my wife. The last few years have taken too much out of my life and I felt the strain very much this last season."[11] Bilderback, sixty-four, retired on the same day as his longtime assistant, Buster Phipps. The pair had seen the sport's new horizon and did not care for what the future held. Phipps's son recalls the decision was made soon after the NCAA tournament loss to Cortland State nearly one month earlier. "My father was upset there were more Cortland State fans at the game than Navy fans," says Wilson Phipps. "He felt it was time to go. He and Bildy were sort of stuck at the hip, and I think they both decided together it was time. . . . My recollection is with the Vietnam War it was tougher to get things done and to get kids interested. Kids were changing. Also my father and Bildy were not proponents of the NCAA tournament."[12]

Bilderback's players say they were saddened by the announcement. "He was a calm, soft-spoken, grandfatherly type of guy," says Steve Soroka, the starting goalie on Bilderback's final Navy team. "He never really raised his voice or demeaned you or called you a knucklehead. He guided us, he demonstrated things to us, he held us accountable but was in no way vindictive. I'm not sure I knew he wasn't in favor of the NCAA tournament, but I'm also not surprised. He was a pretty old-school guy."[13]

The establishment—the Big Five, the USILA, and the attitudes of the sports columnists at the *Baltimore Sun*—was changing at a rapid pace. There even was growing acceptance, or at least acknowledgement, of Moran and Cornell. In 1973 the Big Red was among the eight teams selected for the three-day Hero's Invitational Lacrosse Tournament (HILT), held in late March in the Baltimore suburbs of Catonsville and Towson. Its cosponsors were the *Baltimore Sun* and Hero's Lacrosse Inc., which operated youth leagues in the state of Maryland and a summer league for collegiate players.[14] The HILT games technically were exhibitions, and it was a prestigious field that included the postcollegiate club champion Carling Lacrosse Club of Baltimore; NCAA champion Virginia; USILA small-college champion Hobart; plus Cornell, Maryland, Washington and Lee, Towson State, and Brown.[15] Tickets were available only as all-session passes, seven dollars for adults, four dollars for children.[16]

With the Hero's Invitational as a scrimmage springboard, the Big Red would open the season on March 31 against the Big Five's Navy in Annapolis, in the second year of the four-year, home-and-home contract. The opener in Ithaca one week later was against Johns Hopkins, which was playing the Big Red for the first time since 1940 and, remarkably, doing so on the artificial turf of Schoellkopf Field.

But the early-season attention came at a time when the talent in Cornell's program was at a low ebb. Nine starters from the previous imperfect season were gone. The only returning was senior defenseman Brooks Bradley. He spent the summer of 1972 in Ocean City, Maryland, where his opportunities to play lacrosse were virtually nonexistent. Instead, during the day he worked construction and at night he lifted weights in a local gym.[17] He emerged from the summer a fine physical specimen at 6'2", 210 pounds of solid muscle. The wisdom of his workouts became clear when he happened to run into Moran and his family in Ocean City. "His wife was from Maryland, and they'd sometimes go to Ocean City," Bradley says now. "He saw me and said, 'What the hell have you been doing?' I think he was impressed."[18]

Leading the offense was senior midfielder Bruce Arena, who had registered twenty-three goals and seven assists the previous year, despite missing a handful of games with a shoulder injury. Arena would carry the offense, but those around Cornell were not worried. "Bruce Arena doesn't get the credit he deserves as a lacrosse player," Terry Cullen said later. "He was fantastic." The Big Red also had available several members of the previous year's freshman team, which had won ten of eleven games. The offense had looked crisp in the fall workouts, which culminated in a 14–3 scrimmage victory over Rutgers on October 22 on the Poly-Turf of Schoellkopf Field.[19] The defense featured Bradley and, after the previous year's debacle, three full-time goalkeepers. The starting job came down to a highly recruited sophomore named Joe D'Amelio, the starter on the 1972 freshman team, and junior transfer Mike Emmerich, the starter for Nassau Community College when it won the 1972 junior-college national title.[20]

But leading to the regular season, Moran sounded more guarded than optimistic. When asked by the *Ithaca Journal* about the team's prospects for 1973 he did not mention anything about the assembled talent. "If the workouts and attendance are any indication we've got the best team unity I've seen for a while," he said.[21] Two weeks later he gave this verdict to the *Cornell Daily Sun*: "We're lean and green, but tough and mean."[22] Moran later estimated of the sixteen main offensive players, thirteen had never played a varsity game.[23] The dearth of options on offense was such that Arena was being groomed to play first midfield, to be the main face-off specialist, and Moran and Waldvogel were considering using him on attack when he was not in the game in either of the other capacities.[24] Such a workload was unusual at a time when midfielders, tasked to play both offense and defense, rarely played more than one-third of a game. Arena was on track to play forty minutes each contest.

Cornell's program was not without talent. Moran was making strides in recruiting top players. "I don't like to call it recruiting," Moran says. "I called it 'recommending.' Recruiting has a connotation of free tuition. We don't have scholarships."[25] Moran's criteria for identifying high-school lacrosse players to attend Cornell went far beyond their performance on the lacrosse field and in the classroom. Moran says he was looking primarily for two- or three-sport athletes. "We always thought they were more coordinated and, with that athletic experience, could diagnose something in lacrosse and come up with a solution," Moran says now. "For instance, someone who has had to take two free throws in the final seconds of a close basketball game would know something about pressure."[26]

Moran relied heavily on the octopus-like tentacles of his scouts, friends, and trusted sources in the lacrosse world, all of whom knew the type of players that Cornell wanted. And in the mid-1970s those sources helped him land him the nucleus of the teams that would transform the sport. The practice fields in Ithaca for the 1973 season featured several players who were ineligible for the varsity but would have, if eligible, changed the team's chances immeasurably. Attackman Jim Trenz, a native of Oceanside, New York, was a transfer from Penn State. As a sophomore the previous year with the Nittany Lions, he led the nation in scoring with seventy points, on forty-two goals and twenty-eight assists. After the season Trenz arrived at Cornell in part because, as one Penn State program member at the time says, "We just didn't have anything to put around him." After deciding to leave State College, Trenz was not permitted to have any contact with Moran or Waldvogel—it was forbidden under NCAA rules. His transfer was done largely through his high-school guidance counselor, even though Trenz was two years removed from Oceanside High.[27] Trenz also was, per NCAA rules, not eligible to play for Cornell in 1973, following his transfer. His only contact with the team would be in practice. Trenz spent the season practicing with the Big Red and, on weekends, playing for the Long Island Athletic Club.

The freshman class included a pair of Long Island attackmen who looked immensely talented, Billy Marino and Jonathan Levine. Marino was the son of a former professional baseball player; his father had played for the New York Yankees farm system in the 1950s before leaving for military service during the Korean War.[28] Billy and his brother Tom, two years younger, played baseball growing up. One afternoon Billy, then a sophomore at Massapequa High, arrived home carrying a wooden lacrosse stick. "Dad looked at him," says Tom Marino, "and said, 'What the hell is that?'"[29] The brothers immediately shifted to lacrosse, finding it the perfect vehicle for their compact builds and abundance of speed.

Two years after picking up the sport, Billy Marino was named a high-school all-American and arrived at Cornell to play lacrosse and football, as a running back. In the spring of 1973, he was one of the fastest players in Cornell's lacrosse program. Coaches believed Marino was the rare athlete who could, if needed, have played all sixty minutes of a game.[30] "He was 'the guy,'" says Buck Briggs, a 1976 Cornell alumnus. "Good-looking, history major, dating one of the most beautiful girls in school, and a great lacrosse player."[31]

Levine, Marino's Long Island compatriot, was a left-hander from Lynbrook High. Tall and thin with long dark hair and bookish black eyeglasses that he wore during games, Levine may not have looked like a star lacrosse player. But he graduated from Lynbrook as its all-time leader in assists and points while receiving a lacrosse education from then-coach, and future NCAA and professional coach, Tony Seaman. Levine's specialty was an accurate shot from the right wing, ten or twelve yards from the goal.

Moran had already assembled this impressive group of young or ineligible players when, in the spring of 1972, he received a call from Jim Bishop, a longtime friend of former Cornell coach Ned Harkness. At the time, Bishop and Harkness were both working in the front office of the National Hockey League's Detroit Red Wings, Harkness as general manager and Bishop as vice president. Yet Bishop remained enamored of Canadian amateur sports, especially lacrosse, and he mentioned to Moran that he knew of a talented prospect from St. Catherine's, Ontario, who had just finished Canada's thirteenth grade of high school.[32] Like Al Rimmer and Frank Davis, starting attackmen on the 1971 NCAA title team, Mike French had not played much, if any, outdoor lacrosse. Moreover, neither of his parents had even finished high school, let alone attended college. Indeed, in the spring of 1972, at the time of Bishop's call to Moran, French was on the waiting list for a lucrative and secure job at the General Motors plant in St. Catherine's.[33]

French's best friend was a football quarterback and lacrosse star at nearby Ithaca College, and Bishop thought there was a chance that French would eschew the General Motors job for a chance to attend college and play lacrosse. Moran agreed to host French on a weekend recruiting trip, arranging for him to stay at the Sigma Phi fraternity house, where he befriended several lacrosse players. French arrived in Ithaca as a strapping 6'2" teenager with fairly long red hair. Moran pulled out all the stops, taking the prospect the first night to dinner at Joe's Italian Restaurant on Buffalo Street in downtown Ithaca.[34] "I was from a town of about five hundred people," French says now. "Back there we had 'minute steaks,' which were glorified hamburgers. I thought that was steak. The first night Richie took me out for a real steak, and I thought wow, this is pretty good."[35] The next night Moran took French out for a seafood dinner at the Sylvan Hills Restaurant, at 1749 Slaterville Road on the eastern edge of Ithaca.[36]

(Moran joked that his main memory of the weekend is of French's rapacious appetite.)[37] By the end of the trip, sufficiently impressed with Ithaca's dining options and the Cornell lacrosse program, French agreed to Moran's request to take the Scholastic Aptitude Test (SAT) one more time to improve his chances of gaining admission to Cornell. In the summer of 1972, French received his acceptance letter, with a caveat: His full grant-in-aid would cover Cornell's tuition but, for other expenses, he would have to wash dishes at a fraternity house.[38] French took his name off the waiting list at General Motors. "I was really close" to working for GM, French says. "Where I was from, you graduated from high school and college wasn't stressed as much. . . . My visit to Cornell, I had never seen a town of more than five hundred people. I just consider it all very, very good luck."[39]

French arrived for the first day of fall practice, freshmen and varsity working out together, and made an immediate impression with his wooden stick. "He was moving the stick like I'd never seen anybody move a stick," Levine says now. "He was faking the goalie, faking high and shooting low, flipping the ball behind his back. I thought, 'What the hell did I get myself into?'"[40] Glen Mueller, helping coach the 1973 freshman team while in graduate school, recalls the workout as well. "The first time I saw Mike French," he says, "I thought to myself, 'That's a bigger, stronger Rimmer.'"[41]

But French was using his stick from indoor lacrosse; it was several inches too small for the NCAA's regulations. Cornell's coaches gave him a new stick, with a plastic head, legal for the outdoor game. "I had never used a plastic stick," French says.[42] Two days later he used it at his first practice and couldn't even throw and catch.[43] Teammates, including Levine, stayed behind after practice to give him some pointers. The season on the freshman team would hinder Moran and the Cornell varsity. It appeared set to help French.

Cornell's future was taking shape, especially on the freshman squad, in the spring of 1973. The present moment for the varsity was another matter. The Big Red entered the season ranked number 8 in the initial USILA poll, meaning that it was expected, barely, to qualify for the eight-team NCAA tournament. On March 16, the start of a week-long spring break, the Big Red departed Ithaca for several days of workouts in Raleigh and Chapel Hill, North Carolina, then traveled to Baltimore for the HILT. The scrimmages featured twelve-minute quarters and no face-offs after goals, only at the start of each quarter. The previous season had ended with an angry Moran asking the *Baltimore Sun* rhetorically, "Who in the Ivy League could Washington and Lee beat?" Ten months later, and likely not in a coincidence, a tournament cosponsored by the *Sun* featured a first-round game between the Big Red and the Generals. The rite of passage, the invitation to the

Hero's tournament, appeared to have been turned into a challenge to Cornell's claim to be a lacrosse power.

Dick Szlasa had left Washington and Lee over the summer to replace Bilderback as Navy's head coach. Szlasa left behind an arguably better group of players. Among them was junior Skeet Chadwick, coming off his first year as the Generals' starting goalkeeper. He arrived in Lexington having led Towson High to back-to-back Baltimore County championships in 1969 and 1970. Junior midfielder Ted Bauer, from Gilman School, was the spitting image of rock star Mick Fleetwood, with his lanky 6'5" frame, long blonde hair, and dark moustache. Bauer's howitzer of a high, hard outside shot was delivered from a plastic stick head that was navy blue and white, matching W&L's colors. (Chadwick and Bauer, and almost every other Washington and Lee player in 1973, were using sticks with plastic heads.) Their coach was Jack Emmer, fresh off having taken Cortland State to the NCAA semifinals. The announcement naming him as Szlasa's replacement was released on Emmer's wedding day.[44] For the 1973 season the young coach had another excellent team at his disposal.

The Big Red took the field on March 23 at Catonsville Community College, fifteen miles south of Baltimore, and jumped to a 5–2 lead. Then the offense stalled, and the Generals came back. The contest turned into a nail-biter. The scrimmage was tied at six in sudden-death overtime when Bauer eschewed his hard outside shot and instead sent a sharp bounce shot past goalie Mike Emmerich.[45] Bauer's winning goal set off a wild celebration on the W&L sideline.[46] Cornell's Emmerich had made eighteen saves but the Big Red offense, after jumping to the early lead, had done almost nothing. "Our attack went sour," Moran told reporters after the game, "after we were able to do what we wanted early in the game and our defense didn't do too much."[47] It was the first varsity action for several Cornell players, but Moran was in no mood to use inexperience as an excuse. "We can't keep using that as a reason for our mistakes," he said. "When it comes game time we should be ready to play."[48]

The Big Red rebounded the next day, March 24, to defeat Hobart, 6–2, also at Catonsville Community College. Cornell's offense, in roughly one hundred minutes, had managed just twelve goals. The Big Red headed back to the Finger Lakes region with a lot of work ahead and having slipped to number 9 in the USILA rankings. Next up were back-to-back contests against a pair of Big Five members, Navy in Annapolis and Johns Hopkins in Ithaca. Despite its considerable strides in recent years, the Big Red had never beaten either program.

On Friday, March 30, the Big Red boarded a bus and drove more than three hundred miles to Annapolis.[49] On board was Arena, though he was questionable to play, thanks to an injury to his left knee that he had suffered in practice that week. The Midshipmen were ranked number 4 in the USILA poll, and Szlasa retained Bilderback's preference for using football players in lacrosse. Among the starting defensemen were linebacker Chuck Voith and offensive lineman John Pilli. Saturday, March 31, was a chilly, wet afternoon, and the grass field at Navy-Marine Corps Memorial Stadium quickly grew muddy, hardly ideal conditions for the offensive game. In 1973 neither Cornell nor Navy had the personnel to press the attack anyhow, even though Arena took the field with his left knee heavily wrapped and played the entire game at either attack or midfield. At the end of the first quarter, the game was tied at one. At halftime the score was knotted at two. With two minutes to play in the game, Navy had taken a 4–3 lead when Arena gained possession in the defensive end, sprinted the length of the field, and scored unassisted to tie the game with one minute and fifty-nine seconds remaining.

Arena won the ensuing face-off, and the Big Red appeared set to take a shot on goal before time expired, but turned the ball over with fifty-five seconds to play. Moran prepared to turn the game over to the defense to try to force overtime. In particular, senior Steve Sanford, a defensive midfielder, had shadowed Navy's Bill Kordis for the first three-plus quarters and held him without a goal or assist. In lacrosse any ball that travels out of bounds can be followed by a horn, signifying a stoppage in play to allow both teams to substitute, a rule similar to basketball. Lacrosse also only allows substitutes to enter and exit through a substitution box, a twenty-yard rectangle between both team benches.

In Annapolis, following the Cornell turnover, no horn sounded, but Navy sent Kordis into the game. Moran and Waldvogel did not notice right away; when they did, they requested a horn so Sanford could enter and defend Kordis. The request was denied. As a surprised Moran asked, again, for a horn and another stoppage to match Navy's substitutions, the play resumed and the Midshipmen moved the ball downfield. Two Cornell players stepped onto the field, assuming the horn was imminent.[50] Sanford stood next to the coaches, waiting to be recognized to take the field. Amid the confusion Kordis collected a pass from a teammate and scored for a 5–4 lead with forty seconds to play.

Following the goal, play finally stopped. Moran continued his arguments on the sideline. One of the two referees threw a penalty flag, then huddled with the other official. Following their conference came the verdict: Citing the Cornell players who had walked onto the field anticipating the stoppage in play, the penalty was on Cornell for having too many men on the field. The goal was good. Moran sprinted onto the muddy field and came within inches of the referees.[51] "Moran spent at least five minutes arguing with officials," wrote the *Baltimore Sun*.[52] The *Ithaca Journal*, riffing on Red Barber, called it "a five-minute rhubarb."[53] Following the lengthy appeal from Moran, the referees held another quick discussion. They emerged giving the signal for a goal in lacrosse, the same as a touchdown in football, with both arms upstretched. Navy led 5–4. Forty seconds remained, enough time for Cornell to win a face-off and try to force overtime with a goal, but the Midshipmen won the ensuing draw and ran out the clock.

Moran, in the locker room, told reporters that he was filing an official protest with the USILA. "I'm not upset because we lost," he said, "but it's the principle of the thing. They substituted on a dead ball and we tried to do the same. . . . I don't know when we will hear the results. I hope by Monday or Tuesday. We don't have a very good team this year and something like this is a heartbreaker for the kids, who played so well."[54] Moran's anger was met with a shrug of the shoulders from the Baltimore establishment. The *Capital* of Annapolis called the scenario "by no means unusual, although unfortunate. The action is so fast that many times the official at the table, responsible for substitution, does not see the players trying to get into the game."[55] Following the loss, the Big Red actually moved up one spot in the USILA coaches' rankings, to number 8, but fell out of the *Baltimore Sun*'s top 10 and into the "also receiving votes" section.[56]

The following week Johns Hopkins, ranked second in both polls, arrived in Ithaca. It was a cool, overcast Saturday afternoon, with temperatures in the low fifties. A crowd of five thousand people, mostly seated in the Crescent stands, watched the Blue Jays jump to leads of 3–0 and then 8–1 on their way to a 17–8 victory. Perhaps the only highlight for the home team, such as it was, came when Bradley hit a Johns Hopkins player so hard, albeit legally, that the player left the field spitting blood.[57] One week after falling to 0–13 all-time against Navy, the Big Red fell to 0–8–1 against Johns Hopkins. The success of 1971 seemed a very distant mirage.

The Big Red next was to begin play on the terra firma of Ivy League competition with a contest against Brown on April 14 in Providence, Rhode Island. Cornell entered having won twenty-two consecutive conference games and five consecutive Ivy championships. And before a crowd of thirty-five hundred that packed Brown's tiny Aldrich-Dexter Field, with its grass playing surface and two sets of permanent bleachers, both streaks were in jeopardy almost immediately. By the end of the first quarter, Brown led 5–0. At halftime it was 9–1. It was 10–3 in the fourth quarter when Bradley put a hard check on one of Brown's players during a loose ball near the scorer's table. No penalty was called, but Bears sophomore Chris Brown, watching from the sideline, took exception to what he thought was a cheap shot. He left the team's bench, ripped off Bradley's helmet, and a bench-clearing fight ensued. Bradley disputes the tag of cheap shot. "I never tried to hurt anyone," he says now. "I hit hard but I also hit clean."[58] When order resumed, Chris Brown was given a rare three-minute penalty. Cornell, with extra-man specialist Arena hampered by shoulder and knee injuries, made no headway. The final goal instead came from Brown all-American Steph Russo. The Bears, for so long Cornell's foil in Ivy League play, won handily, 11–3.

Two days later, in the early afternoon of Monday, April 16, there were celebrations around the Cornell athletic department when Jon Anderson, Cornell class of 1971, won the seventy-seventh running of the Boston Marathon, in a time of 2 hours, 16 minutes, 3 seconds.[59] The lacrosse team was at the opposite end of the spectrum. That morning, when the USILA released its rankings, Cornell had dropped to number 14. In the *Baltimore Sun* poll released the same day, the Big Red did not receive a single vote.[60]

Moran remained optimistic. In an interview with the *Cornell Daily Sun* before the midweek game on April 18 against Syracuse, he succinctly said, "We are not an 0–3 team."[61] The next day the Big Red won its first game, 12–3, over the unranked Orangemen on Manley Field. Still, the Big Red had needed seventy-five shots to tally twelve goals, and even former Syracuse coach Roy Simmons, Sr., watching from the sideline, noticed the difference in this Cornell team. After the game he told Moran, "You just don't have the shooters that you used to."[62] While undeniably true, behind the scenes the Big Red was amassing a formidable offense for the future. On the same day that the varsity recorded its first victory of the season, the freshman team, also playing on the Syracuse campus, in a game that started one hour later, defeated Syracuse's freshman team in a rare shutout, 29–0. The Cubs, as the freshman team was known, took seventy-one shots; Levine and Burr Anderson, from Ithaca High, each scored four goals.

It was the latest in a series of successes for the Cubs. They began their season on Long Island on March 23, the night before the varsity's scrimmage against Washington and Lee. The Cubs trailed Farmingdale Community College by one goal with twenty seconds left when Levine scored, off an assist by French, to send the game to sudden-death overtime. There, French scored, assisted by Levine, for a 14–13 victory. A 15–7 loss to powerful Nassau Community College followed, though the Cubs had fared better than the Rutgers varsity; in a scrimmage a week earlier the Scarlet Knights were shut out, 8–0. The blowout victory over Syracuse gave the freshmen five wins in six games. The leading scorers were Levine, French, and Billy Marino.

On Sunday, April 8, while the Cornell varsity was digesting its resounding loss of the previous day to Johns Hopkins, the New York *Daily News* ran a nearly full-page story on page twenty-eight under the headline "Big Macs Chew Up Sewanhaka Foes."[63] Featured was a three-column photo of one of the Macs, junior attackman Fran McAleavey, scoring a goal with his wooden stick in a 17–1 victory over Baldwin High. The other Mac, not pictured but also using a wooden stick, was senior attackman Eamon McEneaney. The pair had led the Indians to victories in twenty-three of twenty-four games from the previous season. Winning lacrosse games was nothing new at Sewanhaka. The school, located in the Floral Park section of Long Island, opened in 1929 and first fielded a lacrosse team nine years later. Between 1948 and 1957, the Indians won ninety-one consecutive games, a national high-school record. The coach during the winning streak, Bill Ritch, was still on the sidelines in 1973. He was fifty-five years old, a physical education and driver's education teacher, and he still spoke with a slight lisp, still wore during games a baseball hat in Sewanhaka's colors, purple with a gold S. The only changes were the wisps of white hair protruding from under the hat and the fact that, in the winter of 1972, Ritch had been elected to the US Lacrosse Hall of Fame.

Two years earlier, Ritch had considered leaving high-school coaching. In the spring of 1970, as the offense averaged fewer than six goals per game and the Indians struggled through a rare losing season, a frustrated Ritch openly said that he was looking for a college coaching job.[64] "The high school situation is not as good as it used to be," Ritch was quoted telling *Newsday* during the 1970 season. "You know—with drinking and smoking and marijuana, the whole bit. You just don't have as many good kids as there were. A lot of kids grow long hair and mustaches and are wearing hippie clothes. They're more concerned with their appearance than with being athletes."[65]

Months later, in the fall of 1970, McEneaney enrolled at Sewanhaka. The youngest of seven from a middle-class family, McEneaney began playing lacrosse in the seventh grade at Sanford Junior High in Elmont, using a wooden stick given to him by older brother Blayney. The two also shared a December 23 birthday, ten years apart. Soon after McEneaney picked up the sport, Ritch began hearing about McEneaney's prowess in lacrosse and football. (Moran, himself a Sewanhaka alumnus who had played for Ritch, received his first reports on McEneaney when the star player was in eighth grade.) Sewanhaka was a three-year vocational public school with an enrollment of about eighteen hundred students, many training to be auto mechanics or learning other trades.[66] McEneaney arrived as a sophomore in 1970–71, having attended Sanford Junior High through ninth grade.

In lacrosse McEneaney became a rarity, a sophomore who made Sewanhaka's varsity team. Even more rare was that for the season opener he cracked the starting lineup. "Long Island lacrosse was so competitive," says John Danowski, an all-American that spring at East Meadow High. "On our team, we had third-line and fourth-line midfielders who became all-Americans in college. You just didn't make the starting lineup as a sophomore. If you did, you were the best of the best."[67]

Yet Ritch had plans for McEneaney even beyond being a starter. In the 1971 opener McEneaney was joined on attack by two seniors who were close friends.

Midway through the first quarter it was obvious that the seniors were passing only to each other and not to the newcomer. On the sideline Ritch grew more and more perturbed. Finally he called out, "Get the ball to McEneaney! Get the ball to McEneaney!" The seniors threw the ball to the skinny sophomore with the large wooden stick and bushy red hair popping out under his white helmet. "Eamon finally got the ball, made two moves and scored," says Frank Muehleman, in attendance that day. "He got the ball again, made two moves and scored. Got the ball [a third time], made two moves and scored. It was clear he was going to be a player. . . . He was just so quick. He could lose his defender in one step."[68] In the 1971 season the Indians won fourteen of eighteen games but lost in an early round of the Nassau County playoffs.

The following season, when McEneaney was a junior, the Indians traveled to Baltimore to face Boys' Latin in a rare intersectional game between one of the top teams on Long Island and a top program in Maryland. On April 1, 1972, "cars were parked a half-mile away because people wanted to come see this kid," says Jay Sindler, a Baltimore native who attended the game. "The bowl at Boys' Latin was full just because it was Eamon."[69] McEneaney finished with three goals and one assist in a 10–8 victory.[70] One of McEneaney's family members was introduced to his prowess weeks later, in a setting far from the lacrosse field. Kevin McEneaney had moved out of the family home and was living in Brooklyn. On an early-spring day in 1972 he was inside Snooky's Pub, on Seventh Avenue in Park Slope. "The bartender had played lacrosse at Rutgers, and he said a bunch of his buddies were going to Sewanhaka games just to watch Eamon," Kevin McEneaney says now. "I thought I had some scoop, so I called home and asked my brothers if they knew Eamon had become pretty good in lacrosse. They said, 'Well, yeah, we know. He's kind of a phenom.'"[71] The Indians entered the 1972 Nassau County championship game against East Meadow at Hofstra Stadium with an 18–0 record and having defeated the Jets twice in the regular season. In the title game at Hofstra Stadium, Danowski and East Meadow pulled off an 11–9 upset.[72] "I still don't know how we did it," Danowski said later.[73] McEneaney finished the year with eighty-three assists and 125 points, both single-season records in the iconic Sewanhaka program. He was also named a high school all-American, and Ritch was named Nassau County coach of the year. If Ritch was still looking for a job coaching in college, he kept it to himself.

In the summer and fall of 1972, as McEneaney entered his senior year, college lacrosse coaches were regular visitors to the McEneaney family home at 7 Francis Court in Elmont. Among the regulars were Maryland, Penn State, and Navy, with Moran also receiving updates from Ritch and his other Long Island sources. McEneaney cut a similarly impressive path in Sewanhaka's crowded hallways. "Eamon was a mythical figure," says Sewanhaka alumnus Sal Paolantonio, two years younger. "When he walked through the halls with his lacrosse teammates, there was literally a parting of the sea. He was treated with total awe and reverence. But he wasn't aloof. He was just so good at what he did with a lacrosse stick, we all just thought of him as different from the rest of us. He was, literally, Eric Clapton with that stick, a virtuoso. And that's the way he was treated. Like a rock star."[74]

Sewanhaka High was filled with students from lower- and middle-class backgrounds, for whom a four-year college experience was either unappealing or impossible. Alongside McEneaney's senior photo in the 1973 *Totem* yearbook are classmates who listed their future plans as beauticians, air-conditioner technicians, auto mechanics, secretaries, legal secretaries, and executive secretaries; only a handful said they planned to attend college. "It was a rough-and-tumble school," Moran says now. (One Cornell teammate says that when the team bus pulled out of the Brown Stadium parking lot following the 1976 NCAA title game, there was laughter when McEneaney pointed out two of his high-school friends, overserved from alcohol, getting into a fistfight with each other.) McEneaney's star teammate, attackman Fran McAleavey, one year younger, scored seventy-three goals as a high-school junior (many assisted by McEneaney), scored 190 in his career, and never played Division I college lacrosse.

Against this backdrop Moran urged Ritch to tell McEneaney to take the toughest possible classes at Sewanhaka, ones that would look better on an application and transcript to Cornell. In the fall of 1972, Moran invited McEneaney to Ithaca on a recruiting trip. McEneaney agreed. On Friday, December 1, 1972, McEneaney traveled alone by bus to Ithaca and arrived in the early evening at the Greyhound Bus Terminal at 710 West State Street. He walked more than two miles to Cornell's campus and then to Moran's office at Teagle Hall. The lights were off, and the door was locked.

McEneaney used the pay phone outside Teagle Hall to call Moran's house on Oakwood Lane, in the northwest section of Ithaca, four miles from campus. Moran was just sitting down to dinner and was surprised to receive the call. His surprise turned to shock when he realized what had happened: McEneaney had arrived one week early.[75] Moran quickly arranged for Bruce Arena and reserve defenseman Jay Gallagher, both Long Island natives and members of the Sigma Alpha Epsilon fraternity, to head to Teagle Hall and pick up McEneaney. He asked them to take McEneaney to dinner at the Statler Hotel on campus.[76]

On Saturday morning, the front page of the *Ithaca Journal* blared the headline, "Vietnam Settlement Possible Next Week"; the story reported that a cease-fire in the years-long conflict was being negotiated in Paris. In Ithaca Moran and McEneaney met for a tour of the campus.[77] It was a cold, brisk morning, with temperatures near freezing, and small mounds of snow ringed the campus.

Moran and McEneaney began with a quickly arranged meeting with Dr. Leonard Feddema, dean of the College of Agriculture and Life Sciences, fortuitously available on such short notice.[78] Prior to joining the "ag school," Feddema had spent eight years in admissions at Cornell.[79] His voice, respected and knowledgeable, would be an important one if McEneaney were to successfully steer through the admissions process. McEneaney, star lacrosse player and starting football quarterback, still only seventeen years old, surprised both Moran and Feddema when he pulled out some of his writing samples; he and Feddema began discussing writing and poetry, comparing notes on favorite authors and poets and their own writing techniques.[80]

From there, Moran took the star recruit to see the campus, including Sage Chapel, the libraries, and several scenic overlooks, before returning him to Gallagher for the afternoon.[81] Gallagher took McEneaney to Barton Hall, where they played pickup basketball before going back to the SAE house, which was hosting a party that night, complete with live music.[82] That afternoon, Arena was busy with the Cornell soccer team—in an NCAA quarterfinal against Harvard on Schoellkopf Field, with the snow piled on the sidelines, Arena was the starting goalie as the Big Red won, 2–0, to reach the NCAA semifinals in Miami later that month.[83] Arena rejoined the group for the party at the SAE house. Late in the evening he had to leave. "I told Jay, 'Make sure you don't get him into a fight,'" Arena said.[84]

After Arena left, McEneaney began dancing with a young woman who just happened to be the girlfriend of an SAE brother, a former Cornell baseball player who had no idea, or didn't care, that McEneaney was one of the top recruits in lacrosse history. The fraternity brother, several inches taller, fifty pounds heavier, and considerably more agitated, confronted McEneaney. The two exchanged words, then began fighting. It ended quickly, and McEneaney received the worst of it. He wound up being taken by Gallagher to Sage Infirmary. Because McEneaney was not enrolled at Cornell, in order to receive the necessary seven stiches over his eye he had to borrow a different SAE brother's student ID and pretend to be the student, rather than reveal that he was the best lacrosse recruit in the nation.[85]

The next morning Arena met with Gallagher and McEneaney. "Eamon had a black eye," Arena says, "and he might have been missing a tooth too. But he was smiling. He said, 'This place is the greatest place in the world.' . . . He wanted to go to Cornell. He was not a stellar student in high school, by any means. Being at Cornell really opened his eyes, and he became a good student."[86] The first order of business was to get McEneaney out of town before Moran saw the results of the fistfight. Gallagher and Arena drove McEneaney to the Greyhound station early in the morning. Later, Arena and Gallagher told the coaches that they very much liked McEneaney. Feddema, too, told Moran that the writing samples had convinced him that McEneaney could handle the rigors of an Ivy League education.[87] Maryland reportedly had offered McEneaney a full scholarship, and in College Park he could play for the varsity immediately. At Cornell, not only would he play for the freshman team for one year, he'd have to maintain an on-campus job to help with the tuition, while also working over the summer to earn money for tuition and other expenses. Still, McEneaney put in his application to Cornell.

In late March 1972, McEneaney was back in Ithaca, this time with the Sewanhaka High lacrosse team. The Indians had been selected, with Corning East, Ithaca, and Manhasset, to take part in the four-team Ithaca Lacrosse Invitational sponsored by Ithaca High. The two Long Island powers would take on the two Central New York teams on back-to-back days, March 30 and 31, on Schoellkopf Field. Manhasset was one of the most storied programs on Long Island and by then had churned out dozens of college lacrosse players, including Cornell's Bob Rule and Glen Mueller and Syracuse's Jim Brown. Ithaca High's program was in its first couple years of existence and was coached by Tom Harkness, Ned's son and a midfielder on the undefeated Cornell team in 1968.

Corning East began its program in 1967 under Joe Corcoran, a World War II veteran and star box lacrosse player. By the start of the 1973 season, Corning East had won two league titles and a region title. Corning is about forty miles southwest of Ithaca along Route 15, and Corcoran and Moran had struck up a friendship long before the tournament on Schoellkopf Field. Among their discussions in 1973 was the four-team tournament hosted on Cornell's campus. "Coach Moran had told my father Sewanhaka had the best high-school player in the country," says Terry Corcoran, then a sophomore and starter on attack for Corning East. "It didn't take long to figure out who he was talking about."[88] At 4:15 p.m. on Friday, March 30, McEneaney took the Schoellkopf Field artificial turf as Sewanhaka faced Corning East. The game was tied at one, two, three, and four before Sewanhaka pulled away for a 9–6 victory. McEneaney finished with four goals and three assists, and McAleavey added four goals.[89] At 2 p.m. the following day, under cloudy skies with temperatures in the fifties, McEneaney was once again on the artificial turf, wearing his purple number 12 jersey, still using the same wooden stick as in his varsity debut two years earlier, to face Ithaca High.

After five minutes the Indians led 5–0.[90] By the end of the quarter, it was 7–0, and McEneaney had accumulated two goals and three assists.[91] By the middle of the third quarter, it was 14–0, and McEneaney, with three goals and six assists, was on the sideline, his services no longer needed in what became a 15–1 victory.[92] "He was just different from everybody else out there," recalls Tom Harkness.[93] Added his wife Elli, who attended the game: "He looked like a scrawny little thing but he sure could play. I couldn't believe how good he was. His passes were pinpoint accurate."[94] Also making their Schoellkopf Field debuts that day were Sewanhaka reserve defenders Muehleman and Greg Raschdorf and Manhasset starting midfielder Bob Henrickson, all of whom would later play for Cornell. Henrickson's Manhasset team went undefeated in the weekend, with a 7–1 victory over Corning East and an 11–3 win over Ithaca High. Goalkeeper Dan Mackesey, from Ithaca High, was not playing that weekend. He was in the same class as McEneaney at Cornell, but was actually one year older; for the 1972–73 school year he had already graduated high school and was spending the year studying abroad.

Following the showing in Ithaca, McEneaney continued his tear through high-school lacrosse, attracting attention the entire time. Early in the 1973 season, an attackman at Massapequa High named Michael O'Neill suffered a season-ending ankle injury. Excused from some practices, he used his afternoons to travel around Long Island and watch the best high-school and college players to pick up tips. Invariably he would head toward wherever Sewanhaka was playing and sit behind the goal at which McEneaney was working.[95] Sewanhaka High was a blue-collar, middle-class school, drawing from neighboring communities because of its vocational programs. Many students, including Paolantonio, had after-school jobs. Four-plus decades later, however, Paolantonio has a confession. "We all skipped work," Paolantonio says now, "to watch Eamon play."[96]

It was not just high-school students who were enamored of McEneaney. When Kevin McEneaney, on the advice of the bartender at Snooky's Pub, attended one of Eamon's games, a regular season victory over East Meadow, he was struck by what happened afterward: "Eamon had all these kids following him around." One of McEneaney's future teammates at Cornell recalls, years after their playing days, running into a man in Connecticut who said he and a half-dozen friends had found their way to several of McEneaney's games at Sewanhaka. "Eamon didn't know who the guys were," says Chris Kane. "They told me they were just a group of guys who would follow Sewanhaka around to see Eamon play. He was like a cult figure. I mean, these were grown men."[97]

McEneaney apparently paid little attention to the adulation. Ritch became famous for installing box lacrosse–type practices in the off-season, where players would gather at an outdoor tennis court and play pickup lacrosse for hours. Often, McEneaney was the first to arrive, and he took it upon himself to shovel the snow to the side so the games could commence.[98] And he had a fun side to him, with his quick smile and love of music and practical jokes. In Sewanhaka's 1973 yearbook McEneaney listed his future occupation as "clergy."[99]

Yet the fun stopped whenever the game started. "It's kind of hard to describe him," Moran says now. "Number one, he was a different person when he put a helmet on. A different part of him came out. Not that he was vicious. Without a helmet on he was kind, gentle, with a huge smile. He loved people, he loved his teammates. But on the field he would do everything possible to help his team win."[100] McEneaney would greet an opponent's mistake with cackles of laughter. While awaiting a face-off McEneaney sometimes would say "tick . . . tick . . . tick," into the ear of the defender guarding him. When the defender finally asked what McEneaney was saying, he would respond, "I'm a bomb, and I'm about to go off on you."[101] When a goal or assist inevitably followed, McEneaney would scream, "It's explosion time!"[102] The palaver made McEneaney something of a marked man on the field, where his quickness would come in handy to avoid the retribution that was headed his way, especially from defensemen who still played with heavy wooden sticks that could cause serious physical harm. "He could really take you out of your game," Muehleman says now. "He could force defensemen to become more emotional than they wanted to be."[103]

The race to win the hotshot recruit from Sewanhaka suggested that it would define the trajectory of college lacrosse for the mid-1970s. And it was not a secret. "I am thoroughly convinced," says Sindler, a midfielder for Washington and Lee's NCAA tournament teams from 1975–1977, "that Eamon McEneaney could have been on any of the top five teams in the nation, and they would have won at least two national titles."[104]

As the calendar turned to late April, the Cornell varsity lacrosse team began improving. With three losses in three weeks, the NCAA tournament was almost surely out of reach. But self-respect was a strong motivation. Following the loss to Brown, the Big Red reeled off eight consecutive victories. Among them was a 9–8 win over Penn in late April in a game that lasted five overtimes—or seventy-nine minutes and twenty seconds—far longer than the regulation sixty minutes. Arena, twice sidelined with a shoulder injury, snuck into the game and scored the winning goal.[105] The *Ithaca Journal* account began with this: "Jumping up and down like the little kid that got the toy train under the Christmas tree, Cornell lacrosse coach Richie Moran raced up and down Schoellkopf Field Saturday afternoon, hugging every redshirted Cornellian he could find. His exuberance frothed over into the Cornell dressing room, where he couldn't shake enough hands."[106] Moran had not lost his fighting spirit, nor had his players. Around this time, McEneaney was admitted to Cornell's class of 1977.

The Big Red, with eight wins and three losses, did not win the Ivy League title; it went to Brown. At the end of the regular season, Cornell found itself ranked number 10 by the USILA and number 9 by the *Baltimore Sun*. Once again Cornell was left out of the eight-team NCAA tournament. Unlike 1972, this year Moran heaped no aspersions on any of the teams qualifying for the tournament. Cornell had no argument. Maryland entered as the number 1 seed following its 17–4 victory over Johns Hopkins in the regular-season finale for both teams. Ivy League champion Brown, with ten victories in eleven games, was seeded number 8 and faced the Terrapins in an NCAA first-round game in College Park.

Emmer's Washington and Lee entered the regular-season finale against Virginia on May 13 in Lexington undefeated in twelve games and ranked number 4 by the USILA. In another sign of the sport's unsure footing with its new postseason arrangements, the Generals still had no idea whether they would be named to the NCAA tournament or the smaller USILA College Division postseason. Against the Cavaliers, before a near-capacity crowd on a sunny, perfect spring afternoon at Wilson Field, Ted Bauer scored six goals, and Skeet Chadwick added twenty-three saves as the Generals won, 15–11. The victory gave Washington and Lee a first-round home game in the NCAA tournament against Navy. (The University of Baltimore received the USILA College Division bid that had been earmarked for W&L.) On the other side of the NCAA tournament bracket, number 2 Johns Hopkins hosted Army, and number 3 Hofstra hosted Virginia.

The first-round games were held May 19. In Baltimore the big news that afternoon was Kentucky Derby winner Secretariat's appearance at the Preakness Stakes, the second leg of horse racing's Triple Crown. A record sixty-one thousand fans watched Secretariat win by two and a half lengths. Five miles to the south, Johns Hopkins drew only twelve hundred fans for its 11–4 victory over the Cadets at Homewood Field. Maryland hammered Brown, 17–8, and Virginia upset Hofstra, 12–5.

Washington and Lee, facing former coach Dick Szlasa, went to overtime against Navy, then into sudden-death overtime tied at twelve. Sixteen seconds later the game was over when W&L's Chip Tompkins fired a shot from ten yards that eluded Navy goalie Ray Finnegan and went into the goal. W&L students stormed the field in celebration. For the second consecutive year Emmer had taken one of the sport's smallest programs into the NCAA tournament and defeated Navy of the Big Five. The fun ended the following week when Maryland defeated the Generals, 17–8, in College Park. The Terrapins then had a rematch against Johns Hopkins in the NCAA title game at Franklin Field in Philadelphia. Before a record 7,117 fans—the third consecutive year that attendance had gone up in the title game—the Blue Jays used a much different strategy from the one they employed in the thirteen-goal regular-season loss in College Park.

For the title game, the Blue Jays won the opening face-off, then held the ball without making a move to the goal. After four minutes, the anxious fans began slow clapping, a sign of impatience, mixed with disrespect. After six minutes the Blue Jays finally began to spring into action—and then led 1–0, following a goal by junior Mike Perez, who had been discovered by the Johns Hopkins coaches while playing for the New Jersey all-Stars before the 1970 North–South college game in Lexington, Virginia. The Blue Jays took a 2–0 lead on a goal from junior Rick Kowalchuck before the Terrapins answered.

Johns Hopkins continued its stall for much of the warm, sunny afternoon. The Blue Jays led 9–7 with less than five minutes remaining in the game, before goals from junior Doug Radebaugh and freshman Frank Urso tied the game and sent it to overtime. In overtime, Urso took a shot with no sight of the goal, but it went past goalie Les Matthews, and the Terrapins had won their first NCAA title, 10–9. "I saw that the goalie was screened so I shot it," Urso said later. "I figured, I couldn't see him so he couldn't see me."[107] Few freshmen would take a shot without being able to see the goal in sudden-death overtime of an NCAA title game. But Urso was no ordinary freshman; *Sports Illustrated* called him "the mustachioed manchild." Days later, before the North–South game in Princeton, New Jersey, Urso was named a first-team all-American, one of the first freshmen in decades to receive the designation.

By the time the North–South game began on June 9, in Princeton, Moran had learned that McEneaney would enroll at Cornell for the fall. McEneaney later said that when he told Maryland's coaches of his decision, adding that he planned to win a national title at Cornell, they laughed at him.[108] The moment stuck with McEneaney for years afterward. Already ultracompetitive, and grateful to have been accepted at Cornell—he had repeated the phrase "this is the greatest place in the world" several times during and after his recruiting trip—the Maryland coaches had unwittingly gift-wrapped an extra layer of motivation.

After the North–South game, Moran headed to Long Island to attend Sewanhaka's season-ending lacrosse banquet. The Indians had again fallen in the Nassau County playoffs, again to East Meadow, but McEneaney had been named high-school all-American for a second time and finished his career with 139 goals and 152 assists, in only three years, all in the lower-scoring wooden-stick era. On the early summer afternoon in 1973, Moran caught a ride to Long Island with Kim Eike, the Cornell lacrosse statistician and public-address announcer who had attended the North–South game and was headed to his parents' home in Fairfield, Connecticut. During the drive, Moran revealed his hopes for McEneaney. "He said to me on the 'QT,'" Eike said later, "'With Eamon we'll win three national titles. He's that good.'"[109]

ASSEMBLING THE PIECES

On September 28, 1973, sixty of the top lacrosse players in the nation were warming up under the lights on a warm Friday evening at Homewood Field in Baltimore. Half were college players and wore white jerseys and white shorts, the other half were the best postcollegiate club players wearing blue jerseys and white shorts. They were about to take part in a venture called "The Lacrosse Superstar Game," organized by local attorney and former Maryland defenseman Joe Harlan, thirty-one, who also gave himself a roster spot with the postcollegians.[1]

The game was a vehicle to raise some of the $80,000 needed to send a US national team to the 1974 World Lacrosse Tournament, to be held from June 30 to July 4 in Melbourne, Australia.[2] The evening was something of a success; it did not raise all the needed funds, but it drew 4,182 fans to Homewood Field on a Friday night in the middle of football season.[3] The college team, which included Maryland sophomore Frank Urso, won, 15–11.[4] Jimmy Trenz, a senior at Cornell, finished with three goals and one assist and was named most valuable player.[5] Trenz had yet to play for the Big Red after transferring from Penn State and sitting out one year, per NCAA rules, but he clearly had made an impression on coach Richie Moran and staff—he took the field in Baltimore having been named a Cornell tri-captain for the 1974 season.[6]

A major lacrosse game in the fall was not the only aspect that made the venture foreign to the lacrosse establishment. It also made apparent just how many of the sport's top players were using the new lacrosse sticks, with the plastic head and synthetic webbing. *Sports Illustrated* covered the game and began with a look at the change in equipment. "Up until 1970 all serious lacrosse players used wooden sticks handmade by Onondaga Indians in upstate New York," wrote Bill Gilbert in the magazine's October 8 editions. "No two sticks were identical, their quality varied considerably and they broke easily. Once a piece broke, the stick was useless and had to be replaced. A new stick cost 20-some dollars. Furthermore, there was only one retail outlet anywhere that specialized in top-grade one-of-a-kind lacrosse sticks—the Bacharach Rasin Company of Baltimore."[7]

The article noted that in the 1974 season, not long after the plastic stick heads had become widely available, about 85 percent of college players would be using the new sticks with synthetic heads and webbing. "They were cheaper, more durable and since they were standardized they could be repaired by replacing broken parts with new ones," Gilbert wrote. "Finally, they came in a variety of bright colors and patterns included a tie-dyed one—the [Native Americans] had stuck to hickory. Lacrosse purists grumbled the new sticks were a corruption and abomination, and no self-respecting player would use them. That prediction proved false."[8]

The transformation of the sport's equipment was not done. Prior to the start of the 1974 season, the NCAA approved lacrosse stick shafts made of aluminum. Suddenly the sticks were becoming lighter, stronger, less expensive, more accurate, and easier to use. Among the stick manufacturers, Brine still trailed Baltimore-based competitor STX. The Brine brothers, from their outpost in western Massachusetts, far away from the Baltimore establishment in more than just geography, continued to believe they could improve upon the new lacrosse stick technology. In 1974 Brine introduced its Superlight stick head. While it came in bright neon colors that made it popular among youth players and was an improvement on Brine's earlier efforts, the head was still not exactly what the Brine brothers wanted, and their product remained squarely behind STX in quality and sales. Bill and Peter Brine remained convinced that a better plastic composite would come along.[9]

Improvements were coming for the goalkeeper's stick as well. Given the nature of the position, goalie stick heads are allowed to be larger than other positions; the NCAA permitted goalie stick heads to be twelve inches across the top, roughly double offensive and defensive sticks. For STX, goalie stick heads were nothing more than a larger version of the heads made for attack and defense, retaining the triangular shape. Bob Rule, first-team all-American goalie at Cornell in 1971, saw a problem with that design. "I wanted the biggest damn stick you could use," Rule says now. "The rules said the goalie's stick could be twelve inches across but did not specify the shape it could take."[10] In 1974, drawing inspiration from the oversized spatulas used by restaurants to move pizzas in and out of ovens, Rule designed a goalkeeper stick head with a circular shape while retaining the required twelve inches across the top. "My stick was still twelve inches at the top," he said, "but I was able to make the circumference much bigger."[11] Rule presented the goalie stick head and another prototypes to the NCAA rules committee. In an era where there was no limit on how many longsticks could be on the field, Rule had also designed a stick with an aluminum shaft that acted like an umbrella; with the click of a button it could change from a shortstick to a longstick and back again as needed. "People started screaming, 'What the hell is this?'" Rule says now. "They refused it because they said it would change the complexion of the game."[12] But the NCAA committee approved his design for the goalie stick head. He sold the idea to Brine, which called the stick the BRG, short for Bob Rule Goalie.[13] The emerging lacrosse sticks had drawn inspiration from venetian blinds for the plastic head's strings and now a pizza spatula for its new goalie stick design.

The other major change in the sport in the 1970s, the advent of the NCAA tournament, was proving to be less revolutionary. Cornell had won the initial playoff in 1971. Since then, every champion and runner-up had come from the Big Five, and the Big Red, after its initial success, had not qualified for the tournament again. Cornell, and the rest of the non–Big Five teams, were on the outside looking in. The year 1974 did not appear to signify a departure. The USILA preseason poll, compiled primarily by coaches, had as its top three teams Maryland, Johns Hopkins, and Virginia, in that order. Washington and Lee and Cornell followed, with Navy ranked number 6. Four of the Big Five remained very much in the championship hunt. Only Army, ranked number 11 in the preseason, seemed out of the picture. But new names were starting to appear in the rankings. Merely having the rankings made public each week was a step forward, given Moran's complaints less than four years earlier regarding the secrecy of the 1970 championship-by-backroom-vote. Geographical outliers dotted the 1974 USILA preseason rankings: number 14 North Carolina, Ohio's Bowling Green at number 15, and Air Force, ranked number 16.

The *Baltimore Sun* preseason rankings, with a heavy emphasis on Baltimore-area voters, were less geographically diverse. The top four were, in order, Maryland, Johns Hopkins, Navy, and Virginia. Cornell was outside the top ten, in the "also receiving votes" category. Despite the *Sun*'s projection, the 1974 season held promise for Moran. Five of the top six scorers from the previous year were back. That included senior attackmen Chris Murison and Michael Cunningham, who in 1973 had tied for the team lead in goals, with nineteen. In Moran's twenty-nine seasons at Cornell, the team-high nineteen goals was tied for the lowest mark. Murison's team-leading thirty points was the lowest in Moran's tenure.

Moran always preferred to give seniors the first shot at playing time. So in the fall of 1973, while Trenz and French had cemented spots on the starting attack, sophomore Jon Levine, leading goal scorer for the freshman team in 1973 while playing attack, had been moved to midfield. "I was like a chicken with my head cut off," Levine says now. "I don't have the body to play midfield and I didn't know how to play midfield."[14] After three practices, the coaches reached the same conclusion and moved Levine back to attack.

But the leading goal scorer on the previous year's freshman team was sixth on the depth chart, behind Trenz, sophomore Mike French, and the returning players. Levine caught one break. On extra-man offenses, most coaches want at least two left-handed players to play on the same side and give balance to the formation. Because Levine is left-handed, he earned a spot on the extra-man offense, which had only one other left-handed player, Trenz. For the fall scrimmage against the University of Massachusetts, on October 27, 1973, at Schoellkopf Field, Trenz and French both scored four goals in a 12–8 victory.[15] Levine, in his first varsity action, added three assists, all on extra-man plays and all on goals by Trenz.

FIGURE 7.1. Cornell's Jon Levine was a three-year starter on attack but nearly didn't make it into the lineup at all following a mistake before the season opener in 1974. (Photo courtesy Cornell Athletics)

The defense featured junior transfer Dave Devine, an all-American the previous year for Nassau Community College, who emerged, after only a few weeks, as the number one defenseman at Cornell. The second defensive starter, senior Andy Siminerio, was enrolled in Cornell's engineering program and already planning to be back in Ithaca for graduate school in 1975. Gallagher, a cocaptain and Garden City native, was the biggest of the trio, at 6'4", 200 pounds. Gallagher earned the nickname "Big Galls," to differentiate him from former teammate Pat Gallagher, 5'6", 140 pounds, and two years older, who was known as "Little Galls."

Starting in mid-February, and with an eye toward the season opener on March 23 against Adelphi, Moran put the team through rigorous workouts, many of them held outdoors despite temperatures that barely reached twenty degrees. Moran held an intrasquad scrimmage inside Schoellkopf Field on March 2, 1974, three weeks before the season opener. "The scrimmage will be at noon on Schoellkopf," noted Joe Glajch in the *Ithaca Journal*, "for any fans who wish to brave the weather."[16] The week of the opener in mid-March, the starting lineup on offense was taking shape. The starting attack was set, and included none of the returners, with the first unit identified as varsity newcomers Trenz, French, and Levine. The first midfield was dotted with new faces too, with sophomores Bill Marino and Bob Mitchell, both up from the freshman team, joining senior Steve Sanford, the only returner from the previous year's offense. The other leading scorers from 1973 were either on the bench or no longer on the team. Marino was the best offensive player and best athlete. Mitchell, an Ithaca native, was a solid defender and offensive threat. Sanford was, by far, the best defender of the group. A native of Baldwinsville, New York, he had originally enrolled at Princeton, then transferred to Cornell after one year to study veterinary medicine. His nickname, "Farmer," came from the time he spent as a child at his grandparents' farm in Stamford, Vermont. He accentuated the moniker by driving around the Cornell campus in a red pickup truck that he affectionately called "Little Richie," complete with a lacrosse trophy serving as the hood ornament.[17]

Sanford had taken a slight dig at Moran with the name of his vehicle, but the coach was instrumental in his life. After Sanford died suddenly in 2017 at the age of sixty-four, a successful veterinarian in Vermont, his obituary noted that Sanford maintained a list of sayings he had learned from Moran: "Always call your mother on Mother's Day, then go to church and the library." "Big Red is the only gum there is!" "When you are thinking of someone, call them, otherwise they'll never know." "Enthusiasm is contagious." "Never burn a bridge, someday you might want to go back." "Stay a little bit hungry. It's great to be the underdog." "The value of game preparation." "Sometimes it's best to turn the other cheek and walk away." "There's no such thing as a bad day, it's just some are better than others." "It's great to be here."[18]

The season opener on March 23, 1974, arrived with temperatures in the high forties and mounds of snow ringing the sidelines of Schoellkopf Field. Cornell's new-look offense was set to make its debut. The game against Adelphi had a 2 p.m. start time. Players were told to arrive at Schoellkopf Field by noon. Levine was not there at noon, or 12:15, or 12:30. His teammates had already eaten their pregame meal and were on the artificial turf warming up by the time he arrived at 12:45, having overslept.[19] Moran, the former Marine, punctual to a fault, was not impressed and let the sophomore attackman know it.

Moran told Levine that he not only was no longer in the starting lineup, he might never play a minute of any game again. Levine's starting spot went instead to Cunningham, the Ithaca native who had tied for the team lead in goals the previous year. "[Moran] started a senior who happened to be a very good player," Levine says. "But by happenstance he dropped the first pass thrown to him. Richie looks at me begrudgingly and growls, 'Get in there.' I go running in thinking to myself, 'I better not fuck this up.'"[20] Levine scored soon after entering the game, then scored again later. By then French had announced his presence with four goals and three assists, and Trenz added two goals and four assists. Cornell won, 14–10, with newcomers French, Levine, Marino, and Trenz accounting for all but one goal, scored by Sanford.[21]

The 1974 team was exhibiting Moran's preferred offensive scheme—one based on the basketball principles of spacing, constant movement, pick-and-rolls, give-and-go's and off-ball movement. "Cornell's lacrosse team has a new look on offense this year," began Joe Glajch's game story for the *Ithaca Journal*, "and from what a crowd of 1,000 at Schoellkopf Field saw on Saturday afternoon, it looks good."[22] "You could see at that time they had a different style of offense," says Mike Farrell, Maryland's three-time all-American defenseman who faced the Big Red in 1974 and 1976. "I think it really was the next chapter of developing offense in the college game. What Richie was doing was more continuity and fluid. It wasn't structured so much, it wasn't set plays like everyone else was running. It was more creating space and seeing what the defense gives you."[23]

Moran and Waldvogel, at least initially, were not at all impressed. Assessing the victory over Adelphi as being less than impressive, they scheduled a conditioning workout for the following day, a Sunday.[24] The coaches did so with an eye toward the next two games on the schedule, against Navy, ranked number 5 by the USILA, and Johns Hopkins, ranked number 3. The Big Red, ranked number 6, was 0–13 all-time against Navy, including the previous year's controversial loss in the rain, and 0–8–1 against the Blue Jays.

Navy and Cornell had won the recruiting battle for the two top high-school attackmen in 1973, Eamon McEneaney and Rochester native Jeff Long. In his career at Irondequoit High, Long finished with 318 points, a record for the state's

Section V that stood for nearly twenty years.[25] As a senior in high school, Long scored 106 points. While in 1974 McEneaney was languishing on the freshman team—"if we'd had Eamon in 1974," Moran would later say, "we would have been invincible"—Long, in Annapolis, had moved into the starting attack.

When the Midshipmen arrived in Ithaca on March 29, they had won all three of their games, and Long was the team's leading scorer, with twelve points. Coach Dick Szlasa's preferred settled offense called on one player to be behind the goal while the other five players ran toward the crease in the hopes of catching a pass and taking a quick shot from close range. With his excellent passing, Long was the ideal Szlasa quarterback. Navy's backup plan for generating goals was to use its superior physical conditioning to play a fast pace and wear down the opposing team. Navy's players were in such good physical shape that Moran, the week of the game, called them "the last superhumans."[26] Still, Cornell entered the game with plenty of confidence. "Our day is due," Sanford told the *Daily Sun*. "I predict we will win by four goals."[27]

In the days leading to the game, Moran's scouting report had been on the bulletin board outside the locker room. The newcomers were facing a Big Five opponent for the first time, but there would be no learning curve, as Moran directed Trenz and French to attack their matchups at will.[28] He told the other four players on offense to move constantly, to make it harder for the Midshipmen to slide, or double-team, Trenz and French.

For the opening face-off at 2 p.m. on Saturday, March 30, 1974, temperatures were in the thirties, complete with gray skies. The Midshipmen ran onto the artificial surface at Schoellkopf Field in blue jerseys, blue shorts, and blue helmets, with many players opting for gray sweatpants instead of shorts to combat the cold weather. Cornell wore white helmets, red jerseys, and red shorts; like Navy, many players chose to wear red sweatpants. The game drew two thousand chilled fans, many bundled up with layers of clothes and huddled under blankets, opting for seats in the Crescent stand, which was in the sunlight. One year earlier Navy and Cornell had combined to score nine goals. In 1974, both with exciting new options on offense, they had eclipsed that mark by the middle of the second quarter, barely twenty minutes into the contest. The game was tied at three, four, five, six, nine, and, after three quarters of play, at 10–10.[29] In the fourth quarter, the Big Red conditioning began to swing the game in its favor; Cornell, in the final quarter, outshot Navy 21–6 and pulled away for a 17–11 victory.

Afterward, Moran made particular mention of his team's superior conditioning, which was quite a claim, given that the opponent was a service academy but also proof that Moran's insistence on full-field, outdoor workouts, even in freezing temperatures, had been beneficial.[30] Newcomers Trenz, French, Levine, and Marino combined to outscore the Midshipmen, twelve goals to eleven. Cornell had struck at the Big Five after a three-year hiatus. Moran had his first victory over Navy. "At game's end," wrote Ira Rosen in the *Cornell Daily Sun*, "Moran ecstatically hugged and kissed his players much like, according to veteran lacrosse fans, the time in 1971 when Cornell won the national championship."[31] In the locker room afterward, Moran asked each player to sign a game ball, congratulating them for their roles in "a history-making game."[32] The ebullient coach had reason to be in a good mood, for he knew something very few in attendance that afternoon did: The natural follow-up to the victory over the Terrapins in 1971 arguably had not even been the biggest Cornell lacrosse news item that day.

Cornell's freshman class, full of talent thanks to Moran's recruiting efforts, included three high-school all-Americans: McEneaney, a two-time honoree from Sewanhaka High on Long Island; attackman Brook Tollman from Hill School in Pottstown, Pennsylvania; and John Reyelt, a defenseman from Scarsdale, New York.[33] Midfielder Brian Lasda had been a standout running back at Tully High outside Syracuse, rushing for 3,766 yards in his career. Five feet, ten inches, 180 pounds, muscular, with long dark hair parted in the middle and a mustache, Lasda was the most intimidating of the recruits, and he arrived in Ithaca having turned down football scholarship offers from Syracuse and Rutgers. The class also featured goalie John Valyo, who the previous year had led his Garden City High team to Long Island's North Shore title.

On October 27, before the varsity scrimmage against Massachusetts, the Cub team lost to Syracuse Lacrosse Club, 14–11. It was a respectable margin for a team of largely eighteen-year-olds who had played together for only a few weeks and was facing a postcollegiate squad. Days later, the *Cornell Daily Sun* gave its verdict. "Freshman Eamon McEneaney has been touted as the best college lacrosse player in the country," wrote Bill Howard in the November 2 editions, "and while that claim may be a bit premature, there is no question—after seeing this thin, red-haired attackman from Sewanhaka HS in the frosh scrimmage last week—that he is going to be an incredible asset to Cornell lacrosse in the future."[34]

McEneaney arrived at Cornell, in the words of one teammate, "a little rough around the edges." "He was basically a street kid," says classmate Dan Mackesey. "But anyone who questions whether Eamon was smart either never met him or didn't know him at all. You can't write as well as he did and be the poet he was without being very intelligent."[35] Stories began circulating about McEneaney's quick smile and quicker temper. "You wouldn't want to challenge him to a fight," says Michael O'Neill, an attackman at Johns Hopkins and longtime friend. "There were stories in Ithaca [from McEneaney's freshman year] about how the football players walked around campus like they owned the place, and they would look at Eamon with his hair down to his shoulders and weighing maybe 150 pounds. And he'd say, 'What the fuck are you looking at? You got a problem?' Then there'd be a fight, and it was over before it began. The poor guy never knew what hit him. By the time people broke it up, Eamon had won. He was tough, fast and wiry strong."[36]

Moran says that McEneaney arrived as a freshman with "a certain cockiness that comes with not being the biggest guy. He was like a James Cagney or a Mickey Rooney. He also had never experienced the sophistication of the students and athletes at Cornell. His high school was a little more rough and tumble, where it was every man for himself; college was a little different." McEneaney lived on campus with roommate Vincent Shanley, a defensemen from Garden City, and to help pay tuition, he washed dishes at the Sigma Alpha Epsilon fraternity house, where he was also given his meals. Things began to change for McEneaney after he took a freshman course in Irish poetry taught by Dr. Phillip Marcus, one of the world's leading scholars on the life of Irish poet William Butler Yeats. The embers of McEneaney's fascination with poetry and Ireland were about to be stoked into flames. "Eamon took that class and really, really liked it," Moran says now. "After his freshman year Dr. Marcus sent him some books to read over the summer, and Eamon read them." McEneaney, as a freshman, was already planning to take as many courses from Marcus as possible.

While McEneaney was navigating the rigors of an Ivy League school, one teammate had spent practically his entire life in the intellectual environment. Mackesey, a freshman goalie whose father held several prominent positions at Cornell, had graduated from Ithaca High. His father, Thomas Mackesey, was at various times at Cornell the dean of the College of Architecture, Art and Planning; the dean of the university's faculty; and at the time his son was looking at colleges, the school's vice president for planning. The elder Mackesey had spent nearly four decades at Cornell and was well known as the man who designed buildings, including the underground campus store, the North Campus dormitories, the Herbert F. Johnson Museum of Art, and Uris Hall.[37] Dan Mackesey was a standout in his own right in town, as a soccer and lacrosse goalie in his senior year at Ithaca High in 1971–72. He applied to Brown, Cornell, and Penn, with plans to play both lacrosse and soccer. He visited Penn and Brown, both of which offered him roughly 50 percent off tuition as the child of an Ivy League employee.[38] He would have received free tuition at Cornell through his father.

Mackesey says now that he was not recruited by the Big Red's lacrosse coaches. "To the best of my recollection nobody [in Cornell lacrosse] ever expressed an interest in me," he says. "I assume the reason Cornell didn't recruit me is because Richie wasn't sure I was good enough."[39] Mackesey also remembered a player on an earlier Cornell lacrosse team whose father was in the university administration. The player received very little playing time; the unhappy father went over

Moran's head to the athletic director, Bob Kane, who had several meetings with Moran about the complaints.[40] Mackesey anticipated some prejudice against faculty kids and thus, during his senior year at Ithaca High, committed to play lacrosse and soccer at Brown.

But Mackesey had also applied to be a Rotary exchange student, a one-year program for recent high-school graduates. He was accepted into the program and, deferring his acceptance to Brown, spent the 1972–73 academic year in Denmark. Mackesey used his time in Denmark to study and play basketball. "I could not have made my high school [basketball] team but over there I was the star," he says with a laugh.[41] And while abroad he changed his mind about his hometown school. Mackesey says his older brothers had mixed experiences during their time at Cornell, and his father had hoped his youngest son would attend a different university. "I started thinking about the cost of college," Mackesey said. "I had free tuition at Cornell through my father. . . . Plus I'd been away from Ithaca and gotten that out of my system."[42] What began was a letter-writing campaign between father and son—the son, in Europe, sending letters via air mail, asking to attend Cornell; the father, in Ithaca, urging him to stick with Brown. "I wrote him a letter saying I really wanted to go to Cornell. I had a great relationship with my father," Mackesey says. "But he sent me a letter back, and I will never forget the first words. It said, 'Dan, I don't know what's gotten into you but it is very unbecoming.'"[43] Eventually the father relented and reinstated his youngest son's application to Cornell. Mackesey again was accepted, this time to the class of 1977. He arrived on campus in the fall of 1973, having matured during his year abroad. By the spring of 1974, Mackesey was with the freshman lacrosse team, splitting time in net with the more heralded Valyo.[44]

Mackesey's Cornell teammates were pleased to have him for more than his prowess as a goalie. He was also arguably the smartest player on the team. He would arrive at Schoellkopf Field for practice wearing glasses and carrying his books, prompting Moran to call him "Professor." Mackesey's teammates took the nickname literally. "Anytime we were having trouble with a class or a paper," says Gary Malm, a midfielder on the 1976 and 1977 teams, "we'd go to Danny and say, 'Can you help us with this?'"[45] Playing in front of the freshman goalies was a defense that included Reyelt, who had spent the fall with the freshman football team playing defensive end at 6'1", 195 pounds; Shanley, an all-County selection on Long Island the previous year; and Jim Scovel, picking up lacrosse for the first time in the fall of 1973 after spending his high-school years in Heidelberg, Germany, where his father was stationed with the US military.[46]

The freshman team's opener came on March 30 at 10:30 in the morning on the artificial turf of Schoellkopf Field, hours before the varsity game against Navy. It was a cold, gray morning, and many on campus may have been sleeping off the previous day's events. From 3 p.m. to 6 p.m. on March 29, the Ivy Room inside Willard Straight Hall had hosted a beer blast, complete with cheap draft beer, free popcorn, and free movies. There were several other happy hours in town, including at the Haunt, at 702 Willow Avenue, roughly a mile off campus and a popular spot for live music, and at the Chapter House, in lower Collegetown, popular with Cornell athletes, where the happy-hour special was a pitcher of beer for ninety-nine cents. That night on campus, the Temple of Zeus coffeehouse, located in the basement of Goldwin Smith Hall and popular among the poets and literary students (it became a favorite hangout of McEneaney), featured folk music from Tracy and Eloise Schwartz of the New Lost City Ramblers. At 10 p.m., the Ivy Room became a dance party lasting until 1 a.m. The university, perhaps suspecting some of the students would be a little worse for wear, instituted "breakfast at midnight" in the Willard Straight Cafeteria, from 11 p.m. to 12:30 a.m.

The next morning it was a sparse crowd that gathered at Schoellkopf Field for the freshman lacrosse team's opener. With first-year coach Bruce Arena on the sideline, McEneaney took the artificial-turf surface wearing jersey number 12 as a starter on attack alongside Taylor Smith and crease attackman Bertram Bertolami. McEneaney quarterbacked the offense, primarily operating behind the goal, with a better view of the other five offensive players. Though the vast majority of college players had switched to plastic sticks—many of Cornell's players had stick heads in red, the school color—McEneaney still was using the large, heavy wooden stick given to him by older brother Blayney ten years earlier. The game began. The Big Red scored first, then four more times for a 5–0 lead at the end of the first quarter. The lead grew to 12–2 at halftime. The final score was 22–6, but even more impressive was McEneaney's performance: He finished with seventeen points, on nine goals and eight assists. By way of comparison, entering the 2021 season, the NCAA record for most points in a varsity game is sixteen, set by Bill Woolford of Air Force in a 24–3 victory over Colorado State in April 1975. As night fell in Ithaca and the Cornell coaches celebrated the Navy victory, they also cast an eye toward the future with McEneaney in the ranks. "We all knew," Arena says now, "that he was going to be great."[47]

The Big Red varsity defeated a nemesis for the first time. A freshman attackman looked ready to be a star. After two lean seasons things were shaping up in Ithaca. The next varsity game, on Tuesday, April 3, came against Syracuse on the chilled Poly-Turf of Schoellkopf Field. The Orange entered having lost its first four games; the Big Red, in the most recent USILA poll, was ranked number 5. After fifteen seconds the Big Red led 1–0. By the end of the first quarter, Cornell was cruising, 9–1, and the starting attack of Levine, French, and Trenz was on the sidelines, their services no longer needed.[48] The previous season Cornell had scored fifteen goals in its first three games. In the first half against Syracuse it scored seventeen. At halftime, their team ahead 17–3, Moran and Waldvogel told the players there would be a practice after the game; they felt a more strenuous workout was needed with the trip to Baltimore three days away.[49] By the time the Syracuse game ended, thirteen players had scored at least once and Cornell won, 27–4. Days after beating Navy for the first time, the Big Red was ready to do the same against Johns Hopkins. "We have to remember that they [Johns Hopkins] may be good," Moran said before leaving for Baltimore, "but we are one of the better teams in the country now too."[50]

In Baltimore on April 6, 1974, cool temperatures, with a strong breeze and bright sun, greeted third-ranked Johns Hopkins and fifth-ranked Cornell. The rest of the sports world was watching the start of the major-league baseball season and especially Hank Aaron's attempt to eclipse Babe Ruth's record for career home runs. In the season opener two days earlier, Aaron had hit his 714th home run, tying the record. His Atlanta Braves were in Cincinnati, to face the Reds in a Saturday night contest.

On the blustery afternoon in Baltimore, six thousand people crammed inside Homewood Field for Cornell's first game in decades at the historic stadium. The marquee matchup was Cornell's Devine against Jack Thomas, the Baltimore native who had scored five goals against the Big Red the previous year. On the other side, Cornell's new-look offense was facing a major test against the well-drilled Blue Jays defense. "Last year I think we were a bit awed at the fact that we were playing a real national power," Moran told the *Ithaca Journal* leading to the game. "This year we know we can play with top-notch schools like Navy and Johns Hopkins, and the key is our mental attitude. The talent of the two teams is just about the same—we just have to convince ourselves we can win."[51]

The Blue Jays had plenty of motivation. They entered the season knowing it would be the twentieth and final year for coach Bob Scott; he was taking a job as the school's athletic director, to be replaced by one-time Johns Hopkins all-American Henry Ciccarone. Soon after the announcement Johns Hopkins fans began wearing "DO IT FOR SCOTTIE" buttons around campus for the coach his players referred to as "Mr. Scott."[52]

The first eighteen minutes went exactly as Moran wanted. Goals by reserve midfielder Bill Haggerty, Levine, and a bounce shot on the grass field by Trenz that eluded Johns Hopkins goalkeeper Mike Godack gave Cornell a 3–0 lead. The Blue Jays battled back, and two goals by Thomas, fourteen seconds apart, tied the game at five late in the second quarter. The Blue Jays scored three more times for an 8–5 halftime lead. In the second half Cornell generated plenty of scoring chances but was undone by uncharacteristic poor shooting. In the fourth quarter Cornell took twenty-two shots and scored on only one. The Blue Jays pulled away for a 13–8 victory, thanks to four goals from Thomas and freshman Richie Hirsch. For the game, Cornell made eight of fifty-four shots (15 percent). French, on crease attack, suffered through a dark day. Though he finished with two goals, he was fed the ball at point-blank range a half dozen other times and misfired every time. The Baltimore establishment must have afforded itself a smirk at Cornell's latest gimmick, the Canadian who shrank on the biggest stage. "Down 8 to 5 at the intermission," wrote John W. Stewart in the *Baltimore Sun*, "the Big Red resembled the gang that couldn't shoot straight in the second half, missing several point-blank opportunities."[53] After the game the *Sun* asked Moran about French's shooting. "He's only a sophomore and is trying to make the switch from the box game to the field game," Moran diplomatically answered.[54]

Joe Finn, archivist for US Lacrosse, was in attendance that day. "I don't know how many shots Mike French took from not that far out and missed," Finn says now. "I don't think he was used to playing field lacrosse. In box lacrosse you're not shooting from very far. But it did not take him long to get adjusted."[55] On paper, 1974 was a year to develop young talent on the varsity. The convincing wins against the Midshipmen and Syracuse made the loss in Baltimore more frustrating. The *Ithaca Journal* noted, after the game, that the Cornell locker room was silent as the players prepared to return to the Finger Lakes region.[56] The first-ever victory over Johns Hopkins would have to wait another year.

Following the loss in Baltimore, the Big Red went on a nine-game winning streak. The most convincing victory came against Brown, on April 27 at Schoellkopf Field. Harlan arranged for the contest to be televised regionally in thirteen markets, one of several lacrosse games that Harlan had arranged to be televised in 1974. (Almost all the other matchups were between Big Five teams.) Lacrosse on television was relatively rare. In the mid-1960s, CBS broadcast one hour of highlights from the Army–Navy game as part of its Summer Sports Spectacular franchise.[57] The 1971 NCAA title game was broadcast by WBAL-TV, the NBC affiliate in Baltimore, but only to that market. Ithaca's WCIC-TV Channel 2, a local cable network, broadcast the 1973 Johns Hopkins–Cornell game on a tape delay and also aired highlights of selected games. The sport's main television exposure came from the Eastern Educational Television Network, later called American Public Television. The network, based in Boston, produced a weekly, one-hour show called *Sports 70's*, funded by a grant from Marine Midland Banks. Several times in 1972 and again in 1973, the show would broadcast week-late highlights from a college lacrosse game. For the Cornell–Brown game in 1974, viewers in markets including Chicago, New York City, Pittsburgh, Raleigh, North Carolina, Knoxville, Tennessee and Washington, DC, saw an impressive showing by French, with seven goals, and Cornell, which defeated the defending Ivy champion, 17–4. The Big Red ended the regular season as Ivy League champions with eleven victories in twelve contests.

Cornell's freshman team was on more of a roller coaster. Following the opening victory over North Country Community College, the Cubs faced a superior Farmingdale Community College squad at Schoellkopf Field on April 6 at 11 a.m., the same day the varsity lost to Johns Hopkins. Just as in Baltimore, it was not a smooth ride. One game earlier, McEneaney had scored seventeen points. This time, his every move attracted a defender. He finished with one goal and no assists and Farmingdale won, 7–4.[58] On April 18 the Big Red traveled to West Point, New York, and defeated the Army JV, 14–5; McEneaney finished with three goals and six assists.[59] Three days later, against Corning Community College on Lower Alumni Field, the final score was 24–2, and McEneaney tallied two goals and six assists.[60]

Next was the showdown with Nassau Community College, four-time defending junior-college champion. The Long Island program generally had more than eighty players try out for only twelve spots—the other twelve spots each year were reserved for returners.[61] Practices were at 5:30 in the morning.[62] The methods clearly worked; its alums dotted college rosters, including Cornell's, with starting goalie Mike Emmerich and, previously, 1971 NCAA title game star Bob Buhmann. "It's our biggest game without a doubt," Arena told the *Cornell Daily Sun* leading to the contest, also adding, in reference to McEneaney's days at Sewanhaka, "a good part of the game depends on Eamon, he has a reputation for not coming through in the big game."[63]

McEneaney, through four freshman games, already had thirty-five points, more than halfway to French's season record of sixty-five. Still, the Farmingdale defense had been able to shut him down, and the talented Nassau team appeared to be an even tougher test. On April 27, the same day that Cornell's varsity defeated Brown, the freshmen played Nassau at 10:30 in the morning on Lower Alumni Field. The Big Red led 6–4 with four minutes to play. Nassau came storming back to tie the game with just thirty seconds remaining, then gained possession following a questionable stalling call on Cornell. Nassau scored the winner with three seconds left for a 7–6 victory.[64] Afterward a frustrated McEneaney challenged one of the Nassau players to a fight; teammates broke it up before it became serious.[65] The loss dropped the freshman team's record to 3–2, and another Long Island squad had shown it was possible to slow down the talented McEneaney.

Three days later, McEneaney gave an interview to the *Cornell Daily Sun*. He was asked about playing for the freshman team in front of sparse crowds when he could have gone to Maryland—which, according to published reports, offered him a full scholarship—and not only played immediately for the varsity but done so for the defending national champions. "There isn't a lot of incentive to win [on the freshman team]. . . . But I'm learning things, too," he said, "like moving without the ball."[66] He added a sentence that must have been music to Moran's ears. "If I didn't like it, I wouldn't be here."[67] Following the Nassau loss the Big Red freshman squad hit its stride, against admittedly lesser competition. On May 1 Cornell defeated Cortland's JV, 12–3, on Lower Alumni Field with McEneaney finishing with four goals and one assist.[68] Through seven games McEneaney had scored fifty-eight points, and French's scoring record was well within striking distance.[69] He claimed the scoring record on May 9 in Geneva, against the Hobart junior varsity team. McEneaney finished with two goals and an incredible twelve assists in a 20–5 victory. After that contest he had amassed seventy-six points, on twenty-six goals and fifty assists.[70] The team's final game, against the Maplewood Lacrosse Club of New Jersey, came on May 11, on Schoellkopf Field. In an 11–1 victory McEneaney finished with one goal and three assists. His eighty points in ten games had shattered the previous record. He and Mackesey shared the team's MVP award.

Cornell's varsity program was selected for the NCAA tournament after a two-year absence, —and without controversy or anxiety. Moran often wrote the phrase "It's Great to Be Here" on top of the chalkboard in the locker room; it was a reminder to the players that regardless of the weather or other circumstances, lacrosse was meant to be fun. On Monday, May 13, the day after the tournament field was released, players entered the locker room and found a different message regarding the NCAA tournament: "It's Nice to Be Back."[71] The tournament still featured eight teams and was run by Bruce Allison, though he was entering his final year in the role. In 1975 the selection committee would be led by Jim "Ace" Adams, the coach at Penn. Cornell was seeded fourth and was set to host number 5 Virginia that weekend. The winner would draw the winner of Rutgers against number 1 Maryland.

But the seedings on the other side of the bracket had a familiar echo for those fighting the Baltimore establishment. Washington and Lee ended the regular season undefeated and ranked number 2, including victories over Big Five members Navy and Virginia. Top-ranked Maryland then lost to Johns Hopkins in the regular-season finale. When the NCAA tournament field was unveiled, the Generals fell from a putative number 1 all the way to number 3—behind Maryland and Johns Hopkins. Generals coach Jack Emmer's reaction sounded a lot like fellow Long Island native Moran earlier in the decade. "You can't crack the lacrosse establishment just by winning," Emmer told the *Washington Post* a couple days after the bracket was revealed. "They can't believe this little school in the Virginia mountains can be any good. . . . We think it was an injustice. . . . We win everything and we go down, not up."[72]

FIGURE 7.2. A field view of a game at Schoellkopf Field between Cornell and Yale in 1974. The Big Red won, 20–4. (Photo courtesy Cornell Athletics)

The University of Virginia, Cornell's first-round opponent, had been undefeated and ranked number 2 in the country until facing the Terrapins on April 13 in College Park. Maryland won, 25–13, in a contest that featured 109 shots and in which Maryland led at halftime by a one-sided score of 17–6.[73] Urso was unstoppable—he scored seven goals, all unassisted. Afterward, when asked how to halt Urso, Virginia coach Glenn Thiel gave a quick answer: "Board up the goal."[74] The twenty-five goals were the most ever given up by the Cavaliers. From there the season unraveled, and the Cavaliers entered the NCAA tournament with a record of six wins and three losses, one of the losses to lower-division Towson State. Virginia's six coaches—Thiel and his five assistants—had scouted Cornell in person on May 11 during its 17–4 victory over host Princeton.[75] They came away impressed with the offense. One year after Cornell's leader had eleven assists and thirty points, the new contributors made the offense unrecognizable. French, despite the poor showing at Homewood Field, entered the NCAA tournament leading the nation in scoring with eighty-four points, on fifty-five goals and twenty-nine assists. Trenz was second on the team, and in the nation, with eighty points, on forty goals and forty assists.[76] The Big Red had particularly destroyed the Ivy League. In 1973 Cornell lost to Brown and needed five overtimes to defeat Penn. One year later: Dartmouth fell by 22–3; Harvard, 20–1; Brown, 17–4; Yale, 20–4; and Princeton, 17–4. Only Penn kept its game close, losing 12–8 in a game in which it employed a stall and held the Big Red to fourteen shots in the first half.[77] Cornell's 108 goals and 181 points in Ivy play were a conference record that stood until 2018.

Cornell's coaches developed their scouting report on Virginia and placed it on the bulletin board outside the locker room at Schoellkopf Field, installed in segments during practice that week. Virginia's starters had plenty of talent, but the team overall had very little depth. And depth is what was needed in facing a Cornell team in very good physical condition. Cornell's game plan was to play up-tempo and try to wear down Virginia. Moran was so certain of his team's advantage in physical conditioning that, the week of the game, he moved practice time as early in the afternoon as possible, given the players' exam schedules, to try and capture the warmest part of the day for a hard workout.[78] The Cavaliers too liked to look for up-tempo when the situation allowed, despite their lack of depth. Of Virginia's philosophy, Moran said, "Fast break like hell and look for unbalanced situations."[79]

On May 18, a perfect sixty-five-degree day at Schoellkopf Field, Cornell and Virginia played a close game for three quarters before the Big Red broke open a close game with seven fourth-quarter goals in a 15–8 victory. The starting attack accounted for thirteen goals, six by French. Next up was a semifinal against defending champions Maryland at Byrd Stadium. One year after Cornell averaged barely more than ten goals per game, it entered the semifinals leading the nation with an average of seventeen goals; Maryland was second with 16.5. The other semifinal featured Johns Hopkins against Washington and Lee. The *Washington Post* wrote of the semifinals, "Two upstarts will challenge the lacrosse establishment today in the semifinal round of the NCAA tournament."[80] The article noted that Cornell, despite having won the inaugural NCAA tournament, was still "considered an outsider."[81]

Maryland and Cornell had not played since the first NCAA title game in 1971. And on May 25, 1974, the Terrapins gained a measure of revenge with a 19–11 victory. Their athleticism, especially in the midfield, was far too much for the Ivy League opponent. Maryland finished with massive advantages in face-offs (24–9), shots (66–30) and groundballs (119–64). Trenz, in his final game in his only varsity season at Cornell, finished with three goals and one assist. French added two goals and two assists. The Big Red concluded the season with twelve wins in fourteen games. The losses came against the two NCAA finalists, Maryland and Johns Hopkins. For a squad written off in the *Baltimore Sun* preseason poll, it had been a memorable year.

French in particular had been a revelation: He finished with sixty-three goals and thirty-one assists, the ninety-four points being both a Cornell school record and the best in the nation that year. French's goal total was an eye-popping amount by any measure but especially at Cornell. By way of comparison, in 1962, just twelve years earlier though during the wooden-stick era, the Big Red had scored sixty-three goals as a team. Trenz added forty-seven goals and forty-four assists. Among the players expected back were French, Levine (twenty-five goals, seventeen assists) and Marino (thirty-one goals, sixteen assists), not to mention McEneaney and Mackesey being called up from the freshman team.

The 1974 title game at Rutgers University pitted, again, Maryland against Johns Hopkins, which advanced with an 11–10 home field win over Washington and Lee. (It was a game in which the Blue Jays trailed 10–7 in the fourth quarter and showed that the W&L coach, Emmer, had been proven correct about his own team's aptitude.)[82] The season arguably was the Baltimore establishment's finest hour. For the second consecutive year, favorite sons Maryland and Johns Hopkins met in the NCAA title game. The Terrapins entered very confident of their chances to defend their title despite having lost to the Blue Jays in the regular season. "People who just read the papers think we were two even teams," Urso told *Sports Illustrated* before the game.[83] "We don't like to hear that. We don't think there's a team that's close to us when we play our best. If we play our game like we did against Cornell, we should win by between seven and 10."[84]

The Blue Jays entered with an offense focused largely around sophomore Franz Wittelsberger. The burly 6'2", 215-pounder from Baltimore's Calvert Hall High enjoyed a divided opinion: He was either a talented, physical attackman or a downright dirty player. He developed his physical style of play from then–Calvert Hall coach Dick Edell, who repeatedly challenged Wittelsberger to initiate contact with defenders. In high school Wittelsberger was a *Baltimore Sun* all-Met linebacker in football—his high-school coach thought he could play football for Penn State—and a two-time honoree in lacrosse.[85] Following his senior year in 1972, Wittelsberger switched his college commitment from Loyola to Johns Hopkins.[86]

Wittelsberger entered the 1974 title game with a team-high thirty-nine goals and added, in the negative column, fourteen penalties in thirteen games. One of his hits, in practice, broke the collarbone of a backup goalie.[87] "We're as afraid of him as the other [teams]," one teammate told the *Evening Sun*.[88] Talented sophomores Urso and Wittelsberger were on center stage before 11,500 fans at Rutgers Stadium in Piscataway, New Jersey. And any raw feelings from the establishment toward driving 175 miles to watch two Baltimore-area teams play in a championship were not helped by a massive traffic jam the morning of the game, on Exit 8A, just before Rutgers University's Exit 9, following a fatal traffic accident.[89] Local media reported that many fans did not arrive at the game until after the first quarter had ended. It was the final game for Scott, whose long career included every accolade and accomplishment except an NCAA tournament title. As James H. Jackson wrote in his account in the *Baltimore Sun*, "The game had just about everything, including a male streaker at halftime."[90]

The Terrapins jumped to a 2–0 lead on goals by Urso and senior Dave Hallock, one of the players that Beardmore had found following the upset victory by the New Jersey all-Stars before the 1970 North–South game. The Blue Jays battled back, and late in the first quarter senior Jack Thomas scored on a long bounce shot to give the Blue Jays a 4–3 lead. Johns Hopkins extended the lead to 14–6 in the third quarter and seemed on the way to giving Scott the perfect going-away gift. Then Wittelsberger's dark side showed up: He knocked star midfielder Roger Tuck unconscious with a vicious hit that was not penalized but so angered one Maryland player on the field that he dropped his gloves and was ready to start a fistfight.[91] Referees broke up the skirmish but the fired-up Terrapins closed to 14–11 early in the fourth quarter. Then Wittelsberger's skilled side reappeared; he and senior Rick Kowalchuck scored consecutive goals for a 16–11 lead that was not threatened. In the final minute the Johns Hopkins band began playing "Amen," made popular by Maryland's basketball fans following a victory. The Blue Jays won, 17–12, and celebrated off the field by throwing Scott into the shower fully clothed.[92] "There's no question about it," Scott said afterward. "This is the biggest win of my career."[93] Several weeks after the championship victory, the Blue Jays embarked on a three-week goodwill tour of California, complete with scrimmages against college and postcollegiate teams. At the start of the tour, Scott officially stepped down, and Ciccarone became head coach.

The 1974 postseason had very much been a parade for the Baltimore establishment. Not only did Johns Hopkins and Maryland play in the championship, but on the small-college level, known as the "National College Division," Baltimore's Towson State won the title with an 18–17 overtime victory over Jerry Schmidt's Hobart Statesmen. Wittelsberger, a first-team all-American, leading goal scorer for the national champions, had two more years of college lacrosse, as did Maryland's trio of Urso, Tuck, and Farrell. On the way up was Cornell, whose rising juniors included French, Levine, and Marino plus, as sophomores, McEneaney and Mackesey. The race to the top of the mountain in college lacrosse was becoming crowded. But there was no question what the establishment expected from the sport's immediate future. At the start of the 1975 season, the *Baltimore Sun* ran its lacrosse preview under the headline, "Area's Domination of Sport Should Continue." The article included the following: "Maryland in general and Baltimore in particular have long been regarded as the hot bed of lacrosse . . . but never has Baltimore dominated the sport more clearly than it did last year."[94]

THE FRENCH CONNECTION

Eamon McEneaney's athletic prowess was such that, entering his sophomore year, he even set off a recruiting battle within Cornell's football programs. The 150-pound football team—its players were not allowed to weigh more than 150 pounds—offered McEneaney, 5'10" and 146 pounds, the chance to play quarterback, his position at Sewanhaka High. The varsity offered him the chance to be a running back–wide receiver hybrid called a wingback. McEneaney nearly did not make it back to Cornell at all. Toward the end of the spring semester of his freshman year, he learned that he would no longer have an on-campus job the following fall. He would have to find another way to help pay tuition. Moran recalls that Lou Schimoler, a close friend, offered McEneaney a job painting his veterinary office in Greenvale, New York, roughly forty-five minutes from the McEneaney home in Elmont. To arrive at work by 7 a.m., Moran recalls that a friend dropped McEneaney off at the Jericho Turnpike, and he hitchhiked the rest of the way. At 11:30 a.m., Dr. Schimoler drove McEneaney to his second job, as a waiter at the New Hyde Park Inn along the Jericho Turnpike. From there McEneaney, without a driver's license or car, would receive a ride home from a coworker, take a quick nap, then leave for his third job, as a bartender at a pub in Elmont. (Moran is a master storyteller and raconteur, and he admits to the occasional embellishment.)

The busy summer meant that McEneaney earned enough money to afford Cornell's tuition, and when he arrived on campus, he opted to play varsity football rather than for the 150-pound team. "I thought we had him," Terry Cullen, the 150-pound coach at the time, says now.[1] McEneaney's brother Kevin later said that the decision to play football was not overly appreciated by the lacrosse coaches, though they did not stand in Eamon's way. The Big Red varsity, coming off a 3–5–1 season under coach Jack Musick, was picked by the *New York Times* to be the best Ivy League team in 1974. McEneaney, extremely competitive, had not won a championship at any level and may have thought this was his chance. Having never played wide receiver, and despite being somewhat undersized for Division I football, McEneaney progressed to the point that before the season opener against Colgate on September 28 at Schoellkopf Field, the *Ithaca Journal* called him "the surprise of fall camp." Against Colgate McEneaney, wearing jersey number 12, made his first catch, a forty-one-yard effort that brought the ball to the Colgate ten-yard line. Afterward he leaped in the air, spiked the ball and began to celebrate, drawing a fifteen-yard penalty.[2] The Big Red won, 40–21, then the following week in Ithaca shut out Bucknell, 24–0.

From there, the Big Red entered Ivy League play, and the season went into a tailspin. Cornell won just one conference game, a 24–0 win over Columbia, and again finished 3–5–1, seventh in the eight-team Ivy League. By the end of the season, McEneaney had moved from reserve wingback to starting flanker. His nineteen receptions for 330 yards were third on the squad, and he led the Big Red in touchdown receptions (four) and yards per catch (17.4). "He had a tremendous change of direction," says Jim Hofher, a teammate and later the head football coach at Cornell. "And he had great hand-eye coordination. But he also had an indomitable spirit. He loved what he was doing, and he played like it. It's exactly who he was as a lacrosse player."[3] Sal Paolantonio graduated from Sewanhaka High two years after McEneaney. He compares the star lacrosse player's football skills to former NFL stars George Sauer, Jr., of the New York Jets and Fred Biletnikoff of the Oakland Raiders. "So quick with soft hands," says Paolantonio, who now covers the pro game for ESPN. "Sinewy, elusive, and great route-running."[4] Still, the football program had seen better days. And roughly one month after the season ended, athletic dean Bob Kane and athletic director Jon Anderson requested Musick's resignation, which he submitted.[5]

On October 19, 1974, while McEneaney and the Cornell football team were in Cambridge, Massachusetts, to face Harvard—a game won by the Crimson, 37–29—the lacrosse team finished its fall workouts with a scrimmage against Cortland State on Schoellkopf Field's artificial turf. On a snowy day and in front of a crowd of only a few hundred people, the contest was tied nine times, including, for the last time, at thirteen. With about one minute to play, junior Bill Marino scored, assisted by French, to secure a 14–13 victory.[6]

The 1975 preseason closely resembled those run by Moran throughout the 1970s. Cornell began preseason workouts on February 3, 1975, inside the Oxley Polo Barns for late-night box lacrosse sessions, held in three one-hour shifts. The first group, usually the freshmen and newcomers, arrived at 10 p.m., standing outside in the cold with two lacrosse goals used for the indoor game, four feet by four feet rather than the six by six used outdoors. As soon as the polo practice was done, the lacrosse players marched inside. Two groups placed the goals in place. The rest shoveled horse manure, remnants of the polo practice, off the playing surface. Moran would then tape plywood over almost the entire face of the goal to act as an ex post facto goalie. In reality he wanted goals to be difficult to score so that the players would continue running. The indoor scrimmages featured twenty-minute halves with a three-minute halftime. The object was not to win but to run. And if Moran or assistant Mike Waldvogel thought the players were not doing enough running, halftime was spent doing push-ups or sit-ups.

The box lacrosse sessions ran three or four times a week, for two or three weeks. From there, Moran moved workouts to the baseball team's Bacon Cage, primarily for one-on-one drills in which players had to navigate a rubber, immovable, ten-inch-high pitcher's mound. The drills in Bacon Cage were held a couple times a week for a week or two, weather permitting. By late February, Moran would move practices outside. The sessions featured a heavy dose of conditioning and then, at least twice a week—usually Tuesday and Wednesday—Moran relied heavily on intrasquad scrimmages. In 1975 the scrimmages gave the returners on defense, including senior Dave Devine, their first chance to face McEneaney, whose freshman team practices in 1974 were held separately from the varsity; he missed the fall workouts while playing football. During the first outdoor Wednesday practice, at the tail end of a scrimmage, the defense had so flustered McEneaney that he threw his wooden stick into the Schoellkopf Field stands in frustration. Moran, after every drill, brought the team into a huddle and asked them if there were any questions or concerns or ideas. This time, he started with a question of his own: "Who wants to go into the stands and get Eamon's stick for him?"

In the preseason Moran also spent a lot of time before the outdoor workouts on Schoellkopf Field's artificial turf at the chalkboard in the locker room, diagramming plays for every conceivable outcome while the players sat and took notes or just absorbed the information. This was particularly true in 1975, given the prominent roles of new varsity players like McEneaney, goalkeeper Dan Mackesey, and face-off specialist Brian Lasda. "Richie was using the chalkboard prepractice and after practice," says Dave Bray, a sophomore midfielder on the 1975 team. "He would draw up what he wanted to work on, then we'd go out on the field and walk through it, then do it at 70 percent speed, then 90 percent speed, then full speed. After practice he would draw it up on the chalkboard again."[7] After every stage Moran asked if there were any questions. If there were none, he would ask the players a specific question about the drill they had just completed; did everyone understand it, was everything clear? The habits of the former high-school teacher never really left.

The Big Red had at least thirty plays, everything from clearing the ball, to "riding" the opposing team, i.e., preventing it from clearing, to extra-man offense and man-down defense, to the settled offense out of numerous formations—2–2–2, 2–3–1, 1–4–1. "Richie wanted to keep the ball hot," Bray says. "Never have the ball in your stick for more than three seconds. Pass and move, pass and move. We were looking for a mathematical advantage, a 2-on-1 or a 3-on-2 on one side of the defense. Even Eamon, as good as he was, never tried to overmonopolize the ball, except once in a while he would take his guy to the cage. But even then he was creating a mathematical advantage. He was just using his speed to do it."[8]

There were defensive talks at the sea-green chalkboard, with Waldvogel scratching the white chalk along Xs and Os and long semicircles or stubby lines. Almost the entire team took part in the defensive sessions; in the 1970s midfielders were relied upon to play both offense and defense. Attackmen McEneaney and French took part as well, McEneaney because he could be counted on, several times a game and almost always out of exuberance, to run across the midfield line and play defense, French because of his role as the team's emergency face-off specialist.

Waldvogel espoused a man-to-man scheme in which a slide, the lacrosse version of a double team, could arrive from either the right or the left, depending on where the offensive player was headed. The defender arriving on the double team was taught to make contact with the offensive player's body first, then his stick if possible, and to keep his head between the player and the goalie. "The second guy always takes the body," Bray says of the defensive rules. "And always keep your head on the inside. If the offensive player spins away from you, it's okay. What I loved about the system, there was always somebody to back you up."[9] The players also learned that their responsibilities included checking the bulletin board outside the locker room every day. The board included everything from scouting reports to daily practice plans to itineraries for upcoming road trips. Such was the regimen that the practice plan for the following day was often posted by the time players left the locker room. (Moran called the bulletin board his team's version of the Bible.) Cornell's coaches and the sports information staff kept track of goals and assists for each player and, for goalies, saves and goals given up. The only statistic available on the board was the number of ground balls for each player, a metric kept by faculty advisor Scotty Johndrew.

The 1975 preseason mirrored many of the others in the 1970s. There was one flourish. The previous year's North–South game had been held in Atlanta, and published reports indicate it had been a financial disaster. Moran, always looking for a chance to enhance Cornell's, and Ithaca's, lacrosse bona fides, pushed to host the 1975 event. The USILA agreed, and in late January Cornell was selected as host for the thirty-fourth annual game, to be held June 14 at Schoellkopf Field. "The all-star game will coincide with Cornell's alumni weekend," Moran said in a press release. "The combination of these two events should make it a memorable weekend for the players, alumni and fans." Moran and Cornell athletic director Bob Kane immediately went to work. By mid-February they had written to President Gerald Ford and New York Governor Hugh Carey, asking each to attend the contest. Neither did, though the White House sent a return letter roughly one month later, thanking Kane and Moran for the invitation. The pair also asked NBC to consider broadcasting the game, an offer refused in a polite return letter from Carl Lindemann, Jr., the vice president of NBC Sports, who noted that the network would be busy with its major-league baseball coverage that day. "As an amusing sidenote," Lindemann added in his letter to Kane and Moran, "I recall attending a reunion weekend at Cornell in 1942 when I was considering transferring from MIT. I can certainly attest to your statement it will be a 'lively, festive, colorful affair.'"[10]

The 1975 season also marked the debut of Cornell's promising attack. To the naked eye the trio looked almost ragtag. One a native of Canada, one Jewish, one in raptures over everything Irish. As plastic sticks flew off the shelves of sporting goods stores, McEneaney was still using a wooden stick; for his sophomore year, his first on Cornell's varsity, he used one purchased from Louis Jacques, a famous stick maker and member of the Onondaga Nation, who lived outside Syracuse. McEneaney and teammate Jake O'Neill had taken a road trip to buy the stick and learn more about lacrosse from Jacques. The bookish Levine took the field wearing heavy, dark glasses. French was one of the few Canadians playing Division I lacrosse, and as a remnant from his days playing box lacrosse, he was considered a very "one-handed" player, meaning he took almost every pass and every shot with his right hand, without developing his off-hand.

The attack unit's public debut was set for Saturday, March 8, 1975, in the first preseason scrimmage, against the Huntington Lacrosse Club of Long Island at Schoellkopf Field. The night before, a heavy snowstorm blanketed Ithaca. The scrimmage was postponed one day, then canceled. [11] The second and final preseason scrimmage, against Army at West Point a week later, was nearly canceled as well following another snowstorm. Army officials moved the scrimmage indoors. No official score was kept, and an estimate in the local media said that Cornell won by about six goals. No other details were made available.[12]

The Big Red, having wrapped up its fitful preseason scrimmage scheduling, entered the year ranked number 3 in the initial USILA poll, behind top-ranked Johns Hopkins and number 2 Maryland.[13] In the *Baltimore Sun* poll Cornell was

FIGURE 8.1.   From left, Mike French, Eamon McEneaney, and Jon Levine were a record-setting attack trio at Cornell in 1975 and 1976. (Photo courtesy Jules Sieburgh)

tied for number 5, with Navy and Virginia, and behind Johns Hopkins, Maryland, Towson State, and Washington and Lee. The season opener was March 22 against Adelphi on Stiles Field in Garden City. In a 16–10 victory McEneaney finished with four goals and five assists, Levine added three goals and one assist, and French finished with two goals and one assist. The game was a promising start. It also showed McEneaney's emotional side when he was benched for nearly an entire quarter after becoming incensed with a referee's questionable call, and Moran worried that his player would be thrown out of the game.[14]

The second game of the year was also on Stiles Field, on March 25 against Massachusetts in a neutral-site contest. The score was the same as the opener—16–10—as was the dominance of the attack unit. McEneaney had four goals and four assists, and French added seven goals and three assists. (Levine was kept quiet and finished with one goal.) The busy first week ended with a contest on March 28, Good Friday, against Franklin and Marshall in Lancaster, Pennsylvania. In a 20–4 rout, French finished with five goals and three assists. McEneaney was held without a goal, though he added seven assists, and Levine scored two goals. In 1974 the Big Red had led the nation in scoring. One year later the offense looked even better.

The national media began to notice. *Sports Illustrated* ran a story on Cornell's offense in its April 7 editions. Titled "The French Connection," a play on the 1971 crime-thriller movie by the same name that had won an Oscar for best picture, the article noted that the game against Franklin and Marshall featured "123 spectators and five dogs." "There are more legitimate contenders for the NCAA title this year than ever before," wrote Joe Marshall. "Hopkins, Maryland, Navy, even possibly Washington & Lee. . . . So is Cornell." He concluded the article: "In this year's jumbled lacrosse picture, McEneaney-to-French may well prove the most direct route to a national championship."[15]

The attack trio was starting to show its near-perfect balance. "To this day that attack unit remains almost the perfect complement of players and talents," says Dom Starsia, an assistant at Brown in 1975 and 1976, who later won four NCAA titles as head coach at Virginia. "Jon Levine was the lefty, didn't really have to carry the ball. Smart and could finish. Michael French was dynamite. So big and strong." Starsia, a defenseman at Brown, played against McEneaney in later years in postcollegiate club games and recalls their on-field chats. "Eamon was tough as nails," he says now. "You'd go up to him before or during a club game and do like you did with the rest of the guys. 'Hey, how you doing? Good to see you.' And he'd be like, 'Get out of my face.' He was a hard-ass player, boy. And what a great athlete."[16] Most of the opposing scouting reports and column inches in the newspapers were devoted to McEneaney and French. Among Cornell's players, Levine was just as appreciated. "One thing about Jonathan Levine," says Bray. "He was always where he was supposed to be. When you had the ball, you knew exactly where he'd be."[17]

Respect was harder to find from some corners of the Baltimore establishment. Following the first three games Cornell was set to face Navy on April 5 in Annapolis. In the week leading to the game, coach Dick Szlasa told the *Baltimore Sun* that Cornell was not deserving of its current number 2 ranking and "shouldn't make the playoffs because of their easy schedule."[18]

Cornell learned of the remarks, which found a prominent spot on Moran's bulletin board. Against the Midshipmen, French finished with five goals and two assists, Levine scored four goals, and McEneaney added one goal and four assists in a 16–7 victory. The Big Red put the game away with a 9–0 run in the second half. Defensively, senior goalie Joe D'Amelio finished with seventeen saves. "Navy is a very good lacrosse team," Moran told the *Sun* afterward, "but our kids just wanted to prove that we are as good as everybody is saying we are."[19] A bad afternoon for Navy was made worse when starting goalie Bill Mueller, a junior, was forced to leave the game in the second quarter. He had been felled after being hit hard in the ankle by a shot from French and did not return. The prognosis was for him to miss several games, but he was expected back in the lineup before the end of the season.

Moran had beefed up Cornell's schedule with an eye toward impressing the NCAA tournament selection committee. The ultimate test would come April 19, when Cornell was set to face Johns Hopkins at Schoellkopf Field. One week before the big game, with the Big Red and Blue Jays both undefeated, Cornell traveled to Providence to face Brown. In the stands that afternoon was Johns Hopkins assistant coach Willie Scroggs, in town to scout the Big Red. Scroggs was free because the Blue Jays had a rare bye week, or a week without a scheduled game, and Baltimore certainly was paying heed to the Big Red.

Traffic was lighter than Scroggs expected, and he arrived ninety minutes early. Soon after he settled into his seat on the gray, chilly Saturday, he noticed a young man wearing black cleats, knee-high white socks with red trimming, and the red game shorts with white piping of the Cornell lacrosse team. The young man was running laps around the worn grass field, just inside the waist-high chain link fence separating spectators from the playing field. Scroggs initially thought it was a player rehabbing an injury in the hour or so before the game started.

Then he looked closer and noticed the long, bushy red hair and skinny legs. It was McEneaney. "I couldn't believe it. He must've run two miles," Scroggs says now. "What an athlete."[20] Showing no signs of fatigue from his pregame workout, McEneaney finished with three goals and three assists in a 17–12 victory. When Moran and Waldvogel sensed their star attackman was a little too keyed up for a game, even after his morning runs, they would place McEneaney as a wing on face-offs—an extreme rarity for an attackman, the equivalent of letting a point guard take a jump ball in basketball—to let him run off some energy before settling into the contest.[21] McEneaney, literally, had energy to burn.

The week of April 19 arrived, culminating in the contest between undefeated Cornell, ranked number 2 in the USILA poll, against undefeated Johns Hopkins, ranked number 1. The 2 p.m. contest was the first game in a doubleheader, with the second game, at 4:30 p.m., pitting the Cornell freshman team, also undefeated, against the Army freshmen, or plebes. French and McEneaney entered the game as the two leading scorers in the nation.[22] Moran, expecting a long week of practice, had given his team a rare gift—a day off on Monday, April 14. After that, the buildup began in earnest. On Thursday, April 17, the on-campus *Cornell Chronicle* featured a full page of lacrosse information, complete with an explanation of its rules, equipment, and penalties. The *Baltimore Sun* sent a young reporter named Philip Hersh to Ithaca to profile McEneaney for Friday's papers. If the *Baltimore Sun* story was not enough proof that the lacrosse establishment had noticed the goings-on in Ithaca, a quote from Johns Hopkins coach Henry

Ciccarone was. When asked about McEneaney, Ciccarone replied, "Eamon is supposed to be the best attackman ever to come out of Long Island. I've never seen him play, but they tell me he's the 'Superman of Lacrosse.'"[23]

April 19 arrived clear and windy, with temperatures in the sixties.[24] The front page of the *Ithaca Journal* that day featured a story about the rise in products geared toward the 1976 bicentennial. In the sports section columnist Kenny Van Sickle predicted a 14–12 Cornell victory. The *Baltimore Sun* began its preview of the lacrosse game in Ithaca: "In the good old days of lacrosse, no team would have challenged Johns Hopkins University unless its lineup was replete with Baltimore area stickers. Times have changed. Today the Blue Jays risk their No. 1 standing against a Cornell ten that has not a single Baltimore prep school product in the starting lineup."[25]

Inside Schoellkopf Field, the middle of the Crescent stands, sections EF and EG, were filled nearly to the point of overflowing, part of a crowd of twelve thousand spectators, the largest ever to see a lacrosse game in Ithaca.[26] Johns Hopkins

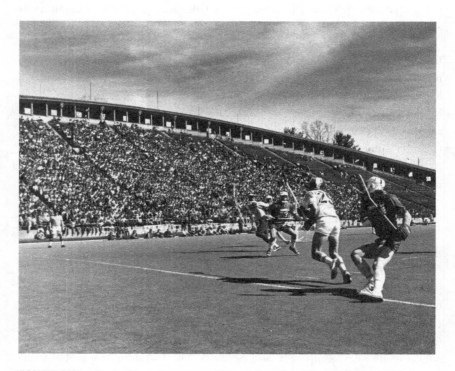

FIGURE 8.2. Cornell lacrosse moved into Schoellkopf Field for the 1972 season and by 1975 was attracting massive crowds. (Photo courtesy Cornell Athletics)

wore its light-blue jerseys with black trim and black helmets with alternating white-and-light-blue stickers. Cornell wore all white—jerseys, shorts, and helmets. At 2 p.m., the two starting goalies stood across from each other, shook hands, and moved to their position's side of the field, ready to start the game. The Blue Jays dispatched junior Jim Moorhead to guard McEneaney. Their paths had crossed before. Moorhead, a graduate of powerful Towson High outside Baltimore, had been on the team in 1971 that faced Sewanhaka when McEneaney was a sophomore. Towson won, 4–3, with McEneaney finishing with one goal and two assists.[27]

In goal was a sophomore from Baltimore named Kevin Mahon, nicknamed "Elf" for his 5'11", 150-pound frame—roughly the same size as McEneaney, who was not considered, in any fashion, an elf. Mahon was inserted into the starting lineup as a freshman in 1974, midway through Bob Scott's final season. With his lightning-quick hands and instincts born from playing top-notch competition at Loyola High, Mahon helped the Blue Jays win their final six games, including the NCAA final over Maryland. Added to the Blue Jays' 4–0 start in 1975, Mahon entered Schoellkopf Field having won all ten games in which he was the starter. Moran's army of scouts had seen the goalie play in person five times. The verdict: The sophomore's rabbit-quick hands made going high a very low percentage look. The scouting report called for Cornell to shoot low.[28]

Less than three minutes into the game, McEneaney scored on a low shot to tie the game at one and send a huge cheer through the vast crowd hoping to see the Big Red's first victory in the series. By the end of the first quarter, Johns Hopkins led 3–1; at halftime the Blue Jays led 7–4, and Mahon had made thirteen saves. The Blue Jays had left the door open with ten seconds remaining in the first half. Wittelsberger, who scored three first-half goals, was ruled to have been using an illegal stick, yet another penalty and more fodder for his detractors. The stick was thrown out of the game, and Wittelsberger was given a three-minute nonreleasable penalty that carried over to the second half.[29] The best offense in college lacrosse would have six attackers to five for the Blue Jays for a good part of the third quarter. But Johns Hopkins won the opening face-off and went into the stall that had helped it stay close to Maryland in the 1973 NCAA title game. The frustrated Big Red offense did not have a chance on extra-man offense before the penalty expired. When Cornell did shoot, it came up with no goals in the third quarter thanks to Mahon, who made five more saves. The Blue Jays led 9–4 at the start of the fourth, then extended it to 15–6 in what became a 16–9 victory.

D'Amelio finished with eight saves, and the Blue Jays, sensing that he was struggling, borrowed from Cornell's up-tempo style to create fast-break chances for Wittelsberger, who finished with six goals, and freshman Michael O'Neill, who added five on only five shots.[30] The *Ithaca Journal* noted that it looked as if the pair "could score at will."[31] But Elf was the big story. Mahon finished with twenty-four saves, and Cornell was left to lament that its fifty-nine shots had resulted in so few goals. Mahon was so commanding that, as the game ended, the spectators, many rooting for Cornell, gave him a standing ovation.[32] After the game Moran closed the locker room to reporters for thirty minutes while he and Waldvogel spoke to the players. "Anytime we get 60 shots, we should get 15 or 16 goals out of it," Moran said upon emerging. "You can't say enough about the kid in the cage. We did a lot of things that were wrong in not following patterns we planned, especially in the first half."[33] He also came away impressed with the Blue Jays. "It's still early in the season," he said. "I hope."[34]

Cornell freshman midfielder Bob Henrickson watched the game from the stands with his teammates. As the varsity teams left the field, the warm afternoon turned foreboding: A heavy breeze tore through Ithaca, and at Schoellkopf Field discarded papers and hot dog wrappers whipped around the stadium. The freshman team had a game of its own against the Army freshman. "That was the saddest of games. We felt like we could have helped [the varsity]," Henrickson says now. "After the game it had gotten dark and windy. There were three people in the stands, and two of them were my parents. We just had no interest in playing."[35] Still, the Big Red freshmen won, 18–3, to improve their record to five victories in as many games.[36] With all of Cornell feeling that the lacrosse future had arrived with French-Levine-McEneaney, less solace was to be had from the freshman team's success.

Following the loss to the Blue Jays, the Big Red varsity defeated Yale (15–3) and Penn (14–6) and entered the contest against Harvard, on May 7 at Schoellkopf Field, in first place in the Ivy League. Harvard chartered a DC-9 airplane and flew to Ithaca for the Wednesday afternoon game.[37] The team arrived in Ithaca in the early afternoon, and Moran arranged for them to have a pregame meal at the tony Statler Hotel on campus. Harvard's Jefferson Flanders, a sophomore starting defenseman from the emerging lacrosse power of Montclair High in New Jersey, recalled that it was some of the best food he had tasted in his life; the Harvard players ate copious amounts.[38]

Brown's Jeff Wagner has a similar recollection of a pregame meal at the Statler Hotel the previous year in which Moran himself offered the players second and third helpings from platters of eggs and sausage. Thus sated, likely overly so, Brown lost by thirteen goals. "We were college kids who weren't used to eating food that good. We ate everything in sight. Richie knew exactly what he was doing," Wagner says now.[39] Moran, for his part, smiles and says he has no recollection of trying to slow an opposing team down with a huge pregame meal.[40]

Harvard took the field for the game against Cornell, and Flanders was matched against French. "In high school I had been strong enough to guard the strong guys and just quick enough to guard the quicker guys," Flanders says now. "But with Mike French, he was faster and stronger than I was. I was completely overmatched."[41] French scored three goals in the first quarter alone. Harvard's coaches removed Flanders from the game. "My roommate was on the team," Flanders says, "and I was benched so quickly he thought it was one of the funniest things he'd ever seen."[42] Early in the second quarter French took Flanders's replacement to the goal and scored again. French finished with four goals and three assists in the 17–4 victory.[43] Flanders says the events of the game itself were difficult enough, but something that happened afterward struck him even more: Cornell's players ran wind sprints, as if the midweek Ivy League contest had not given them enough exercise. "If we had played them 100 times [in 1975] they would have beaten us 100 times," Flanders says now. "I cannot envision a scenario where we would have beaten that team."[44]

Cornell's Ivy League schedule finished with a 12–8 victory over Princeton at Schoellkopf Field. McEneaney accumulated four personal fouls, one short of being expelled from the game, or "fouling out."[45] The Big Red ended the regular season ranked number 2 in the USILA poll and very much in the running for a national title. By that point McEneaney was, for the first time, using a plastic stick. His wooden stick had been badly damaged in a 16–5 victory over Syracuse on April 27, a Monday, where McEneaney was held to no goals and one assist. With a game three days later against Cortland State, McEneaney switched to a plastic stick, believed to be a Brine Superlight.

As Cornell's varsity was cementing its place near the top of the sport, the freshman team was making history as well. In its game against Nassau in early April, the Big Red held a one-goal lead when a Nassau midfielder named Craig Jaeger took a hard outside shot with such velocity it ripped through the goal net and kept going toward the end line. Both referees ruled the shot had gone wide instead of into and out of the goal. "Craig was jumping around screaming it had been a goal," says Tom Marino, then a freshman at Cornell and the high-school teammate of Jaeger at Massapequa High, "and we all knew it had been a goal but we kept quiet."[46] The Big Red hung on to win by one goal. Despite not having the overall star power of a French or McEneaney, the Big Red freshman team in 1975 did something neither of those had done—it finished undefeated, with a 10–0 record.

Among the Southern teams Washington and Lee began the 1975 season ranked fourth in the *Baltimore Sun*, with a twenty-seven-game regular-season winning streak. The Generals opened on March 8 at home against Morgan State, the only historically black college and university with a lacrosse program.[47] Published reports said the Bears' budget for lacrosse included money for ten sticks and nothing else.[48] Morgan State's roster was populated with only a handful of players who had played in high school, rounded out with several students and a few members of the school's football team. On a rainy, windy Saturday in Lexington, Morgan State's one-of-a-kind combination of players made history with an 8–7 victory. "They beat us fair and square," remembers Charlie Stieff, a starting midfielder at Washington and Lee, who was a freshman in 1975. "I remember thinking afterward, 'Why the hell did I go here?'"[49]

The Generals rebounded and entered the finale on May 17 against Virginia with nine wins and six losses. The winner of the Washington and Lee–Virginia game was likely to land the eighth and final spot in the NCAA tournament; the loser's season would be over. The spot went to the Generals following a 9–5 victory in Lexington. Hours later in College Park, top-seeded and undefeated Johns Hopkins faced sixth-ranked Maryland. The Terrapins had lost four games, and several starters were either playing through injuries or had been sidelined by them. The *Washington Post* article previewing the game began, "Two years ago, Maryland was snugly and smugly situated at the top of the provincial but competitive world of college lacrosse. The Terrapins were called The Big Red Machine. . . . They were so young and talented they seemed unbeatable for years to come."[50]

"My recollection of that year," says Wilson Phipps, a reserve defenseman and goalie, of 1975, "was how banged up we were."[51] Senior midfielder Doug Radebaugh put it more simply. He told the *Washington Post*, "We were doing things different for a while. We had more of a control game rather than a running game. I don't think we had faith in our young guys. And we weren't cocky anymore. For two years, we never thought about losing, just about how bad we'd win."[52]

To prepare for the Blue Jays, Maryland coach Buddy Beardmore took the team to Salisbury, Maryland, for a few days to relax and recover from their injuries. (It was not the first time Beardmore had used such a tactic. The night before the 1973 NCAA final, sensing his team was too nervous, Beardmore gathered the players in the hotel, said a few words, then delivered several cases of beer, imploring the team to relax. The Terrapins won the title the next day.) A crowd of 10,300 filed into Byrd Stadium on May 17. They included Moran, in town to scout both teams with an eye toward the NCAA tournament. After one quarter the Terrapins led 11–1. The final score was 19–11, but the game was not even that close.[53] Maryland looked as if it were regaining the swagger with which it had played in winning the title in 1973 and advancing to the title game the following year. Just as the tournament was starting, the Terrapins were getting hot.

Despite the loss the Blue Jays retained the number 1 seed for the NCAA tournament and were drawn against Washington and Lee. Cornell, with fourteen wins in fifteen games, earned the number 2 seed and a first-round game against Rutgers (seven wins, five losses) in Ithaca. The other matchups were Maryland against Hofstra, and Navy against Penn. It would not have escaped the notice of Moran and his players that Cornell's side of the bracket featured Rutgers, Navy, and Penn, each of which the Big Red had defeated in the regular season by at least eight goals.

Johns Hopkins may have felt overconfident as well: It was 10–0 all-time against the Generals. There were signs that W&L was rounding into form. For one, the loss to Morgan State was not nearly as suspect as it might have looked in March. The Bears ended the regular season with ten wins in thirteen games and were selected for the NCAA Division II tournament. On May 17, the same day that Maryland routed Johns Hopkins, the Bears lost a first-round game to Washington College, 17–8, to end their historic season.[54]

Preparing for the Blue Jays, Washington and Lee coach Jack Emmer believed that his team was more fleet of foot. So he charged his attackmen and midfielders to pressure the Blue Jays and make it harder for them to clear the ball from defense to offense. He recruited a face-off specialist from the student body, a good athlete from Montpelier, Vermont, named Ken Miller, who had never played lacrosse but was blessed with quick hands. He was set to take the majority of the face-offs in the first round.[55]

The biggest roster move came in goal. Freshman Charlie Brown, a Long Island native and two-sport standout, was a defensive back on W&L's football team. In lacrosse he was splitting time between midfield and goalie when Emmer named him the starting goalie toward the end of the season. "Coach kind of made me earn my stripes," Brown said later.[56] In front of the freshman goalie were junior defensemen Rob Lindsey and Tom Keigler; both would finish 1975 as first-team all-Americans, a rarity for one team to have two defensemen so honored. For the NCAA first-round game, neither one was assigned to guard Wittelsberger, clearly the Blue Jays' top offensive threat. Emmer's plan was to let Wittelsberger score as many points as he could while shutting down every other option. Emmer further dipped into his bag of tricks by poaching from the football team a lineman whose beefy stature would at least make Wittelsberger work harder on his mad rushes to the goal.[57]

At the end of the first quarter at Homewood Field, the Generals led 3–1, Miller had won the majority of the face-offs, and Lindsey and Keigler were dominating their matchups against O'Neill and Richie Hirsch, respectively. The defenders entered the huddle between the first and second quarters with a message: If the offense could score just a few more goals, the Generals would win regardless of what Wittelsberger did.[58] Early in the second quarter, still leading 3–1, Brown had possession deep in his own territory when he noticed the Blue Jays had slipped into a ten-man ride, a tactic whereby every Johns Hopkins player was standing in front of a Washington and Lee counterpart, mirroring his every move; essentially, they were trying to make it as hard as possible for the goalie to complete a pass and move the ball upfield. The scheme calls for the goalkeeper to defend an opponent, rather than staying in the goal. Brown, still in possession, looked seventy yards up the field and saw Mahon had strayed out of his goal and was defending one of the W&L attackmen.

The one-time midfielder lofted a long shot toward the Johns Hopkins goal. It bounced once, twice, three times and then trickled into the net. The Generals led 4–1. "And Homewood Field," Brown says, "went completely dead silent."[59] (Brown's shot remains one of the few goals ever scored by a goalie in NCAA tournament history.) Following that shot, the Washington and Lee defense, as promised, took over. Freshman phenom O'Neill did not score a goal. Keigler held Hirsch to two goals. Wittelsberger had a big day against the football lineman, five goals and two assists, but it was not nearly enough just as Emmer had predicted. The Generals led by four goals in the final minute when Stieff, the midfielder, heard one small section of fans inside Homewood Field cheering loudly for the Generals. He looked over and noticed they were wearing blue-and-orange Morgan State gear. He looked closer. It was members of the Bears team, rooting for the squad they had defeated two months earlier.[60]

In Ithaca, Cornell and Rutgers began their quarterfinal about an hour after the other games, to accommodate Cornell's final exams. By halftime, the Big Red held a seven-goal lead, and scores from the other quarterfinals were trickling into Schoellkopf Field. In Annapolis the Midshipmen defeated Penn, 17–6; in College Park, the Terrapins defeated Hofstra, 19–11. When Moran was told that Washington and Lee had beaten Johns Hopkins, he demanded the score not be revealed, worried that it would distract his team.[61] In the fourth quarter, with the Big Red holding a ten-goal lead in what became an 18–5 victory, Moran finally permitted public address announcer Kim Eike to announce "final score, Washington and Lee 11, Johns Hopkins 7." The home crowd cheered the shocking news.[62] The top seed was gone. The number 2 seed, Cornell suddenly was in the driver's seat to win a second national title—and on Baltimore's Homewood Field, site of the NCAA title game.

The next day, on the craggy grass of W&L's Wilson Field, Charlie Brown stood in front of one goal, alone except for a bucket filled with two dozen lacrosse balls. He wanted to recreate his seventy-yard goal from the previous day. Brown launched every ball toward the opposite goal. After a few minutes he stopped, the bucket empty. None of the balls had gone in the goal; he had missed every shot. "I guess it was the Hopkins field was so well groomed," Brown says now. "Most grass fields are really bumpy. That one, the ball bounced true. On our field the ball kept bouncing off to the left or off to the right and just refused to go in the goal."[63]

On May 23, one day after the US House of Representatives approved a proposal for females to attend the Naval Academy starting in the 1976–77 academic year, the Navy lacrosse team traveled to Ithaca to face Cornell. Coach Dick Szlasa opted to fly the team rather than taking a bus, the usual mode of transportation. On board the flight was Mueller, the starting goalie, back in the lineup after being injured in the second quarter of the regular-season loss to Cornell. While the lacrosse world focused on Cornell's 16–7 victory, the Midshipmen found solace in the game having been tied at three when Mueller was injured. The Midshipmen boasted sophomore Jeff Long as their leading scorer and quarterback, twenty-five goals and thirty-two assists, along with a hard-shooting freshman from Long Island named Bob DeSimone, with thirty-three goals and a whopping 160 shots in thirteen games. The defense featured senior Jake Lawlor, from Floral Park, New York, who had been named first-team all-American the previous season and was, with Keigler, the top defenseman in the nation. Lawlor, 6'2", 210 pounds, would guard McEneaney.

The Big Red entered with the players ranked numbers 1 and 2 in the nation in scoring—McEneaney was first, with ninety-four points on thirty goals and sixty-four assists. French was second, two points behind with fifty-nine goals and thirty-three assists. Leading to the semifinal, the *Ithaca Journal* sounded the clarion call. "No one can really imagine," wrote assistant sports editor Fred Yahn, "how the Midshipmen, or anyone, can hold down the scoring of the Big Red once the offense gets rolling."[64] The paper included a large photo of McEneaney coming off the field against Rutgers, wearing Adidas high-top basketball sneakers, white socks pulled halfway up his calves and shaking hands with French, wearing low-cut suede Pumas.

Moran asked that the semifinal be played at 4:30 p.m., after the day's exams were done. The NCAA, knowing Cornell's academic schedule, had offered a Sunday time slot, when no exams would take place. Moran, hosting an NCAA semifinal for the first time, stuck with his original game time. On the morning of May 24, game day, Moran noticed several players were missing from the team breakfast. He was told they were taking final exams. Others ate quickly and raced off to their own exams.[65] The regular-season meeting with Navy had been fairly perfunctory. The semifinal was shaping up to be far more taxing, on several levels.

By late afternoon it had grown blazingly hot and muggy in Ithaca. Temperatures were in the nineties; on the artificial turf at Schoellkopf Field, it reached 112 degrees.[66] A sweaty crowd of twenty-five hundred people settled into their seats, hoping to watch Cornell reach the NCAA title game for the second time in five years. Cornell took the field in its all-white ensemble, and Navy, mindful of the searing temperatures, wore its yellow jerseys with white shorts and blue helmets. Following warmups, before the game had even begun, several players on both teams had splotches of sweat visible through their jerseys.[67]

By the end of the first quarter Navy had taken only nine shots, but five had eluded D'Amelio. At the other end, Lawlor had held McEneaney without a point, and the rest of the Big Red, when able to launch a shot on goal, found Mueller equal to the task. The quarter ended with Navy leading 5–0. Billy Marino and Bray scored early in the second quarter to close the gap to 5–2 when Navy attackman Fred Cook, a senior from Baltimore, took a shot that D'Amelio initially saved. But the goalie lost track of the ball for an instant, and it fell out of his stick and into the goal to give Navy a 6–2 lead.[68] On the sideline Moran stared at defensive coordinator Mike Waldvogel.[69] He wanted to know if a goalie change were in order. Sophomore Dan Mackesey had been practicing well and was ready

FIGURE 8.3.   Navy junior goalie Bill Mueller was injured early in the regular-season meeting against Cornell but was back in the lineup later and made a big difference in the NCAA semifinal. (Photo courtesy Naval Academy Athletics)

to play. Mackesey says now that he was told several times to warm up, and he did as instructed.[70] In the Crescent stands, members of the Cornell freshmen team watched the proceedings in disbelief. "Many in the stadium and more than a few on the Cornell sidelines thought Richie should have pulled goalie Joe D'Amelio," says Keith Reitenbach, a midfielder for the freshman team.[71]

D'Amelio played the entire first half. At halftime Cornell trailed 7–4, and Moran and Waldvogel made two decisions. On offense the coaches decided to use the first midfield of Marino, junior Jake O'Neill, and sophomore Steve Dybus on almost every possession.[72] The tactic had worked four years earlier in West Point, in the first NCAA semifinal in program history. On defense, Waldvogel decided to keep D'Amelio in the game. In the regular-season win over Navy, D'Amelio had made seventeen saves. The coaches believed he would return to that form.

Early in the third quarter Cornell went on a 5–0 run, with goals from Levine, McEneaney (his first of the game), Levine again, Marino, and then French, to take a 9–8 lead with four minutes, thirty-five seconds left in the third quarter. On the Navy sideline, Szlasa considered calling a timeout. On the field he saw Mueller had gathered the defense and was screaming at them to refocus, forget the previous five goals and concentrate on finishing strong. Szlasa decided against stopping the game with a timeout. He would leave it in the hands of his goalie and defense.

On the other sideline, Moran, confident in his team's conditioning, continued to insert his first midfield line into the game. In the ninety-degree heat the workload was taking its toll. The Midshipmen scored a goal to tie the game at nine, then scored again to take the lead, then scored another goal, followed by two more, and early in the fourth quarter, Navy led 13–9. With two minutes left Cornell closed to 14–12 after the irrepressible McEneaney forced a turnover on an attempted clear and passed to French, who scored into an empty net; it was McEneaney's first assist of the day, further testament to the job Lawlor was doing against the nation's leading scorer. Navy won the ensuing face-off, and Cornell junior Ted Marchell, an Ithaca native nicknamed "Tombstone" because his father owned a rock quarry used for tombstones, was called for a one-minute slashing penalty. Two years earlier in an NCAA tournament game against Cortland State, Navy had a lead and a man-advantage late in the fourth quarter and took an ill-advised shot that led to Cortland State's tying goal and Navy's eventual overtime loss. Now the Midshipmen held onto the ball, killing the precious minute, and retained possession. With four seconds left in the game, Cook scored into an empty net to put the finishing touches on a 15–12 victory.

Mueller finished with seventeen saves; Lawlor held McEneaney to one goal and one assist; and Long, so often compared with McEneaney, came out on top with a goal and five assists. The Navy coach afterward was overjoyed. "They played a great game," Szlasa said afterward, "and so did we. We got the breaks and we were still running at the end."[73] Moran spoke in more general terms. "There were so many things going on, so many," he told reporters afterward, "that it was hard to pinpoint a key in this one."[74]

Moran said later that he erred in sticking with the Saturday afternoon start time. "It's a true statement that we lost to Navy, and it definitely was my fault," Moran says now. "We had exams, and we should have played Saturday night or Sunday. . . . We had five or six guys who barely made it for the first quarter. We had so many distractions. I'm not taking anything away from Navy. We just had a lot of distractions, and it was stupid on my part."[75] The coaches also lamented in-game decisions. "I remember it clearly," says Waldvogel now. "I think I should have changed goalies and put Mackesey in. Richie asked me about it, and I said no. [D'Amelio] just wasn't there, he wasn't seeing the ball. Mackesey was ready. But it reached a point where it didn't matter anymore."[76] Mackesey says D'Amelio was playing a solid game—he finished with sixteen saves—and there were a lot of reasons for the loss, not just the goalie. "The deal was," Mackesey says, "I was really hot in making saves but I was not very good outside the cage. Joe was excellent in the clearing game, he moved really well outside the cage and had a lot of poise."[77] There would be many postmortem assessments of that late May afternoon. The clear bottom line was that Cornell finished the season 15–2, with both losses coming, again, to the Big Five. The Big Red had not reached the NCAA final, but there was no doubt it had arrived as a national power.

The NCAA title game, once again, would be in Maryland and feature two teams from that state, both members of the Big Five, following Maryland's 15–5 victory over Washington and Lee in College Park.

On May 31 Maryland and Navy took the field for the fifth NCAA tournament—the first held in Baltimore. Navy kept the game close until Urso scored twice just before halftime. Navy threatened again in the third quarter before Urso again scored a pair of goals to put the game away. In the stands that day was Joe Finn. "It really looked like Urso could score whenever he wanted," Finn says now.[78] Urso finished with five goals and Maryland won, 20–13.

Also in the stands at Homewood Field was two-thirds of the "French Connection." Levine had gone to root for his twin brother, a reserve midfielder with the Terrapins, bringing with him close friend and roommate French. As Maryland began to pull away, Levine and French came to believe that Cornell, not Navy, would have given Maryland a tougher game. "Frenchie and I looked at each other," Levine says now, "and said, 'Oh boy, we really screwed up. We should be out there, we should be out on that field.' . . . We'd made mistakes everywhere that Navy game. Coaching mistakes, player mistakes."[79] The third member of the

French Connection had reached that same conclusion one week earlier. After the loss to Navy, McEneaney "was pretty depressed," older brother Kevin says. "At one point he turned to someone, I think Jake O'Neill, and told him, 'Cornell will never lose another game as long as I'm playing here.'"[80] Moran says McEneaney said the same thing to him, as they walked off the field and into a silent locker room.

The 1975 season had ended, but Schoellkopf Field still was hosting the North–South college all-star game, held one week after Maryland's victory over Navy. The all-star players began arriving on Wednesday, June 11, and they received a warm reception. "Richie was a hero in Ithaca," says Bryan Matthews, a goalkeeper for the 1975 South team, having played for Washington College in Chestertown, Maryland, "and as we found out, he was more or less the mayor. He arranged a parade through town, had us riding in convertibles, people lining the streets."[81] The game was scheduled the same weekend as Cornell's reunions, and coupled with perfect weather, meant a North–South record crowd of seventy-seven hundred settled into Schoellkopf Field for the 2 p.m. start, with the Crescent stands bathed in sunlight. The North roster included Devine and D'Amelio. Never one to miss a fundraising opportunity, Moran delegated other Cornell players to sell sun visors to attendees, at a dollar each, with proceeds going toward the team's spring break trip to Baltimore in 1976. Moran also sold commemorative T-shirts, at six dollars each, out of the lacrosse team's offices in Teagle Hall.

Maryland's Doug Radebaugh won the opening face-off and scored in the first ten seconds. By the end of the first quarter, the teams had combined for thirteen goals, seven for the North. At halftime the game was tied at twelve, and the teams had combined for sixty-two shots. The goalkeepers played on a rotational basis, and for the second half, D'Amelio (North) and Virginia's Rodney Rullman (South) entered the game. They could do little to stop the offensive onslaught. At the start of the fourth quarter, the North led 19–18, and the game passed the three-hour mark. In the final four minutes the North led 23–21 when Bert Fett of UMBC and then Radebaugh scored to tie the game at twenty-three and send it to overtime.

In the press box Moran, wearing a short-sleeved oxford shirt and dark tie, decided to let the teams play overtime using the NCAA rules of two four-minute sessions, after which the contest would enter sudden death. In the first four-minute session the North scored for a 24–23 lead; in the second, Radebaugh scored his sixth goal to the game at twenty-four. It went to a third overtime, this one sudden death. Neither team scored. Finally, in the fourth overtime, as the contest neared the four-hour mark, David White, a midfielder from Brown University, scored the winner for the North team in a 25–24 victory. The game lasted three hours, forty-seven minutes. "This game," wrote the *Ithaca Journal* in Monday's editions, "had SCORING." The teams had combined for forty-nine goals and 147 shots. Mike Rinck of Rutgers finished with eight goals, and Hofstra's Phil Marino was named most valuable player after finishing with eight assists. D'Amelio was the winning goalie. He played the entire second half and all the overtimes and finished with twenty-four saves, including one on a breakaway from Radebaugh in sudden death to keep his team in the contest. After the game Moran raced onto the field with a microphone. "It's a shame one of these teams had to lose," he began.

There was a reason that Moran was smiling so soon after the disappointment of the loss in the semifinals. Traditionally, the North and South teams would scrimmage each other in the days before the contest, a way for players who had been away from the sport for a month to reacclimate to lacrosse. (The need was becoming less urgent, given the new postseason tournaments.) A disagreement between the coaching staffs in 1975 meant there would be no pregame scrimmage between North and South. Worried about a game featuring players, some

FIGURE 8.4. Action from the 1975 North–South All-Star game at Schoellkopf Field. The contest featured forty-nine goals, and lasted nearly four hours. (Photo courtesy Cornell Athletics)

of whom had not played a competitive game in about a month, both coaching staffs contacted Terry Cullen, then running a summer league in Ithaca for high-school and college players, about putting together a team to scrimmage the North one day and the South the next. The quickly assembled local team featured players from Cornell, Hobart, and Syracuse. One Cornell player called McEneaney, already at home working on Long Island, and McEneaney traveled back to Ithaca with former Sewanhaka teammate Fran McAleavey, who was a year younger and whose college plans remained undecided. Cullen enlisted Mackesey to play goalie.

The scrimmages, complete with referees, were held inside Schoellkopf Field. Against the top college seniors in the nation, the quickly assembled pickup team, heavily featuring players who would play for Cornell in 1976, won both scrimmages. "Nobody could really cover Eamon," Matthews says now. "And I remember Billy Marino was unstoppable as well." Cullen was more succinct about the scrimmages against North and South: "We kicked the shit out of both of them."

START OF A STREAK

The first official event in every Cornell lacrosse preseason under coach Richie Moran, usually in late January or early February, was a one-mile run, eight laps around the indoor track inside Barton Hall. As the players prepared to reveal whether they had remained in shape during the offseason, and new faces tried to make a good first impression, coaches held the stopwatches that would determine the fastest players. These would be the first indicator of playing time, or bench time, for the upcoming season.

For the 1976 season, Cornell lacrosse had no shortage of fast runners. A junior midfielder named David Bray had been a standout in cross-country and track-and-field at Gowanda High in Versailles, New York. In cross-country, Bray set the school record four times and went undefeated over his final two years on the school's hilly home course. As a sophomore in high school, Bray set Gowanda High's record in the two-mile run (10 minutes 41.1 seconds).[1] He also won several meets in the one-mile run and triple jump. His spring seasons were spent in track-and-field, rather than lacrosse, because Gowanda did not field a team; Bray, who lived on a Native American reservation near Buffalo and was a member of the Seneca Nation, learned the game from playing indoor box lacrosse in the competitive leagues dotting the area.

Also on the 1976 Cornell lacrosse roster was a pair of midfielders who had spent the fall as wide receivers with the football team, senior Bill Marino and sophomore Bob Henrickson. The two labored through a fall campaign in which the Big Red won once in nine games and finished bottom of the Ivy League. No matter the lackluster results on the football field, it was rare for a lacrosse team to have two athletes good enough to also play Division I football—and in Marino's case to be a starter.

Another promising athlete was sophomore Keith Reitenbach, from Central High in Binghamton, New York. He grew up in Baltimore, where his father was a professor at Towson State University, and began playing lacrosse at the age of six. In eighth grade his father's job took the family to Binghamton. "I vividly remember talking to the guidance counselor in junior high," Reitenbach says. "He said, 'Well, Keith, it looks like you have good grades. What else do you like to do?' And I said, 'I play soccer, basketball, and lacrosse.' And the guidance counselor nodded his head and said, 'Well, we have basketball.'"[2] In lieu of lacrosse or soccer, Reitenbach began running, where he was co-captain of the cross-country team for four years and did two years of track-and-field. As a junior, however, he finally helped convince Central High to field a lacrosse team.

Reitenbach arrived in Barton Hall like the rest of his teammates, ready to impress Moran and assistant Mike Waldvogel. The mile run began, players jostling for position. After six of eight laps Reitenbach was toward the front with several others and began thinking that either he or Bray would finish first. "I was determined to be one of the leaders if not the winner," Reitenbach says. "We had a few other guys who had running experience and were serious about being out in front."[3] As the final lap began, Reitenbach and Bray remained at the front. In the final two hundred yards, however, Reitenbach saw someone pass him. It was not Bray but a small, lithe teammate with shoulder-length red hair. Seconds later the timed one-mile run was over. Eamon McEneaney had won. "He raced past all of us and finished first," Reitenbach says. "Like he was saying, 'Guys, you're not going to win this.' He was a cigarette smoker, too. But with his energy level, a mile was nothing."[4]

It was a glimpse of how seriously McEneaney, yet to win a championship at any level, was treating his vow not to lose another lacrosse game at Cornell, a journey that began unexpectedly when he took part in the successful scrimmages against the North and South all-Stars the previous spring.[5] McEneaney also opted out of playing football in the fall, despite having led the team the previous season in touchdown receptions (four) and yards per catch (17.4) and having been slated as a starting flanker, or wide receiver.[6] The football team was under first-year coach George Seifert, a transplant from the West Coast, whose ties to California included his uncanny resemblance to the actor George Hamilton. Hired on January 27, 1975, Seifert convened his first preseason practice on August 28. Roughly one week later, on September 9, Seifert and Terry Cullen were standing outside Schoellkopf Field when McEneaney approached. Speaking in his rapid-fire style, McEneaney said he would not be playing football in the fall, apologized, then walked away, a sequence that took maybe ten seconds. "George looked at me," Cullen says, "and said, 'Does that happen a lot around here?' And I said, 'No, that's Eamon, he's kind of a special case.'"[7] (The *Ithaca Journal* reported that McEneaney had left to focus on lacrosse.)

McEneaney was back on Schoellkopf Field's artificial turf on October 25, 1975, for the lacrosse team's lone fall scrimmage against Cortland State. The previous season the Dragons had won the NCAA Division II title with a 12–11 victory over Hobart and, for the 1976 season, welcomed back twenty-one letter-winners. Cornell, even without the two football players and junior Dan Mackesey, who spent the fall as the starting goalie for Cornell's soccer team, won handily, 19–10. Senior Mike French finished with four goals and four assists, and McEneaney added two goals and three assists.[8] There were no questions about the offense, which returned this lineup on attack: McEneaney, the second-leading scorer in the nation the previous year with ninety-six points (thirty-one goals, sixty-five assists); French, who had led the nation with ninety-seven points (sixty-three goals, thirty-four assists); senior Jonathan Levine (fifty goals); and midfielder Marino (thirty goals). Arriving from the previous year's undefeated freshman team were Henrickson, slated immediately for a spot on the first midfield, and Tom Marino, Billy's younger brother, immediately penciled into the second line.

The defense, by contrast, was far from settled. So much so that in the fall Moran and assistant Mike Waldvogel summoned an offensive midfielder named Chris Kane, fresh off scoring seven goals for the freshman team, into their offices in Teagle Hall. Waldvogel presented Kane with a defenseman's longstick and asked him to consider changing positions. They believed Kane, tall and rangy at 6'2", 175 pounds, could make an impact on defense with his background in basketball and his athletic ability. The defense needed a dominant player.

Kane was introduced to lacrosse as an eighth grader by a sibling—in this case his sister Joan, three years older, who played for Schreiber High in Port Jefferson, New York.[9] "I had no choice," he says. "My sister needed someone to play catch with."[10] Kane's athletic prowess—he was a three-sport athlete—came from the distaff side of his family. His mother had been a standout basketball player at Notre Dame Academy, an all-girls Catholic school on Staten Island.[11] Kane found lacrosse to his liking, to a certain extent. In high school he moved from soccer in the fall to basketball in the winter to lacrosse in the spring to swimming in the summer, with finality—once the season ended, he did not touch his lacrosse stick or a basketball or soccer ball or swimming goggles until the next year.[12] By his senior year he was a solid basketball player, being recruited by Division III schools, and in lacrosse he was a midfielder with good speed but playing for a team with very little talent. In his junior year Kane scored a goal against McEneaney's Sewanhaka High, the only highlight in a 16–1 loss. "They just destroyed us. I saw Sewanhaka," Kane says, "and said, 'This game can be played without the ball being on the ground all the time?'"[13]

Kane applied to four colleges. He was not admitted to any, though Cornell at least put him on the wait list. His father followed up the wait-list designation with almost daily calls to the lacrosse office. Kane was eventually admitted to Cornell's agriculture school, or "ag school," as an agriculture economics major. Like many of his college teammates, Kane says his family could afford some but not all of Cornell's tuition. So he was given a grant-in-aid job on campus.[14] For him, it meant working as a dishwasher and waiter at the Sigma Nu fraternity house. The ag school was at the very tip of the campus atop East Hill; Sigma Nu was at the very bottom, on the slope leading to downtown Ithaca. Every day Kane would do his work for the fraternity in the morning, wolf down a quick meal courtesy of the Sigma Nu chef, walk uphill to the very top of the campus for classes, walk back down to serve lunch, eat a quick lunch himself in the kitchen, then back up the hill for more classes before taking part in lacrosse drills and one last visit to the Sigma Nu house to serve dinner before being given a final meal himself. Walking Cornell's deep hillsides was a workout onto itself.

Though Kane calls Cornell "the greatest experience of my life," his freshman year was difficult. Unable to afford the university's meal plan, he remembers being so underfed that at times he stole food wherever he could find it. "I'm not proud of it," he said later. "The Long Island guys were blue-collar guys. Our team had Long Island guys who literally were hungry. And I know because I was one of them."[15] Schoolwork was similarly tough. "I couldn't compete academically," he says. "My goal was to get a C and move on. We called it, 'Get the hook and get out.'"[16]

Early in his sophomore year things were looking up. He had made enough money in the summer as a lifeguard to afford Cornell's meal plan. His photo for his cafeteria ID card showed Kane, in the instant the camera took the picture, pulling apart his mouth as wide as possible with his hands. "Three good laughs a day," he says when asked the reaction from cashiers who verified his ID card.[17] Now, he was in his coaches' office, being asked to change positions. "I had looked around and seen some of the midfielders we had," Kane says. "I told the coaches, 'I'm going to get off the sidelines less than the cheerleaders if I stick with midfield. If you want me to play defense I'll do it.'"[18]

The second starting defenseman going into the 1976 season had been a high-school teammate of McEneaney, one year younger. Frank Muehleman's decision for college came down to Cornell, Penn, Hofstra, and Division III Williams College; he gained admission to all four. What brought him to Ithaca was that, like teammate Gary Malm, he had received a New York State Regents scholarship that would greatly supplement his tuition but only if he chose an in-state school. (The

FIGURE 9.1. Chris Kane went from an offensive midfielder who scored seven goals for the Cornell freshmen in 1975 to a Hall of Fame defenseman. (Photo courtesy Larry Baum)

scholarship dropped Cornell's tuition to roughly $2,000 per year.)[19] "I was able to afford the whole college experience," he says, "if I stayed in New York state."[20]

Muehleman's nickname among the coaches was "Patience Muehleman," for his tendency to use his 6'1", 190-pound frame to lean on an opposing player while not throwing any checks. Instead, he waited for the opponent to make the first move before countering. He was one of two mechanical engineering majors on the team—reserve midfielder Bob Mathisen was the other—and on road trips the pair sat toward the front of the bus, overhead lights on, doing schoolwork. Muehleman says he nearly left the team several times because of the academic workload. He stayed because of Moran. "He made lacrosse fun," Muehleman says. "Winning was fun too, of course, but if it weren't for Richie I'm not sure I would have stuck around lacrosse."[21]

The third starter was found almost entirely by luck, even by the haphazard standards of 1970s recruiting. Bob Katz's family owned a chain of restaurants in the Baltimore area and sent their son to the tony Park School. Joe Finn, US Lacrosse historian, who has followed Maryland high-school and college lacrosse for decades, says Katz was not recruited by many colleges. Park School was in the Maryland Scholastic Association but in the 'B', or lower, conference. "Park had some very good players," says Finn. "But they mostly went to Division III schools. There were a lot of people who were skeptical if Katz could play at the Division I level."[22]

One of those people, it turns out, was Katz himself, who was encouraged by Moran to apply. Katz selected Cornell to attend its famed hotel administration program and decided to try out for the freshman squad as a walk-on. During tryouts he told teammates he was not sure he would make the team. He did, but Waldvogel and Moran treated him as a long-term project. The coaches insisted he drop weight, and then they changed how he ran, converting him from a "short stepper" into a more natural, longer stride.[23] The coaches weren't planning on his playing a major role in 1976 until senior Ted Marchell, the third starter, strong and rugged at 6', 190 pounds, with shoulder-length hair cut evenly across the back, making him resemble the comic book character Prince Valiant, was sidelined several weeks after suffering an injury in a preseason scrimmage.

As the Big Red plotted its course behind the scenes, another entity, away from the lacrosse field, also placed the Baltimore establishment in its sights.

Since their inception in 1970, the production and sales of plastic sticks had been dominated by STX, located in South Baltimore. For the 1976 season, in western Massachusetts, William and Peter Brine, heading the main competitor of STX, had made a major discovery: Their sources at the DuPont labs in Delaware brought out a plastic composite called Zytel, used primarily in skateboards and men's combs. It was the plastic the Brines had been searching more than a decade for. Finally, the Brine brothers had what they wanted, and for the upcoming season they released the seminal Superlight II stick.[24] "Brine did not have a good stick in 1972," says Jeff Wagner, a face-off specialist for Brown in the early 1970s who later worked for Brine. "It was big, and it was heavy. STX had the best sticks until the Superlight and Superlight II. The Superlight II was the best stick.

It was the lightest stick, and it was much stronger than anything else available. . . . I don't think DuPont cared about lacrosse at all. I think they did Brine a favor by supplying 1,000 pounds of Zytel. It was thinner, lighter, and stronger, and [Brine] figured it out before STX could get their hands on it."[25]

Wagner graduated from Brown in 1973, then spent one year driving a moving truck across the country. What initially was lucrative work took a downturn with the energy crisis of 1973, which led to raised gasoline prices and in some areas, no available gas at all. Wagner left the trucking job in his native Baltimore and moved to Boston because college teammate Bob Scalise had been named head lacrosse coach at Harvard and needed an assistant. Wagner took the job; to supplement his income, he worked as a bouncer at Swinger II nightclub on Route 9 in Framingham, Massachusetts. "People were going into the bathroom and smoking pot," Wagner says, "and one of my jobs was to clear them out of there. I had to hold my breath before going in or I would have been stoned by the first hour."[26]

A job at Brine opened after Bob Shaw, the all-American midfielder at Cornell in the early 1970s, left to attend graduate school. Wagner was hired. His primary duty for the spring of 1976, once he was done coaching Harvard's game, was to take a giant duffel bag of Brine Superlight II sticks in a van to the airport closest to wherever Harvard was playing and fly to his native Baltimore. "I was the Baltimore guy," he says now. "My job was to go to Baltimore and give away hundreds of sticks to every prep school and college that played lacrosse. I had to go where they were going. If they were in a bar drinking beer, I was drinking beer. If they were outside smoking weed, I was smoking with them."[27] Wagner suddenly found himself on the front lines of the battle between Brine and STX. "It was very much north against south," Wagner says now. The Brine sticks caught the Baltimore establishment's attention. "Don't quote me on this," says one Baltimore native associated with STX, still wary decades later, "but the Superlight II was a great stick head."

One other addition to the 1976 lacrosse scene was freshmen on the varsity squad. The Ivy League had voted to disband the mandatory freshman lacrosse team, though Cornell and several other conference programs kept a junior varsity, or "B" team. Only about half a dozen freshmen made Cornell's 1976 varsity roster, including Reiley McDonald, from Gilman School in Baltimore, slated for a spot on a reserve midfield line, and a pair of goalies, John Griffin from Baldwin, New York, and Robert Jackson, from Ithaca, who were Mackesey's backups.

In the middle of March, the USILA released its 1976 preseason rankings. The Big Red was third, behind Johns Hopkins and top-ranked Maryland. Giving the Terrapins the top spot was more than a nod to their having won the championship the previous year. The Terrapins also had back a wealth of talent. Says Wilson

Phipps, "1976 was the best Maryland team." The defenseman and goalie for the Terrapins adds, "We were better than in '75. . . . We were loaded."[28]

Senior midfielder Frank Urso's college career to that point had been a litany of awards. He had scored the winning goal in an NCAA title game (freshman year); was named first-team all-American (freshman, sophomore, and junior); had played on the US National team, which won a world championship in the summer of 1974 in Australia; and was nearing the scoring record for the school's midfielders despite only playing half or one-third of the game, given coach Buddy Beardmore's stated intent to use a lot of midfielders to try and run the opposition into the ground.

Urso, a native of Brentwood, New York, on Long Island, was in junior high, preparing for a track and field practice one spring afternoon when a friend suggested he try out for lacrosse instead. "And I looked at him," Urso says, "and said, 'What's lacrosse?'"[29] By his senior year of high school, Urso led both the football and lacrosse teams to undefeated seasons. A muscular 5'10", 180 pounds, Urso was a highly coveted all-state running back; published reports say he was recruited by Pitt, Penn State, and Ohio State. In lacrosse that year he scored 130 points, sixty-one goals and sixty-nine assists, incredibly high totals for a midfielder. Massapequa High's Michael O'Neill had seen Urso up close and came away impressed. "He had almost a full beard" in high school, O'Neill says now. "By age fourteen, he basically was a grown man."[30]

Urso had decided to play both lacrosse and football in college, which he says made his decision much easier, given that only one school was a standout in both. "Pretty much just Maryland," he says.[31] Maryland gave Urso a half scholarship in each. But just before arriving on campus, he says, he decided to focus on lacrosse, and lacrosse coach Buddy Beardmore, also the freshman football coach, arranged for the football scholarship money to move to lacrosse.[32] Urso turned heads immediately. A few weeks into his Maryland career in 1973 he inspired *Baltimore Sun* columnist Bill Tanton to write a column in which he recounted hearing a young woman, unfamiliar with lacrosse, ask why players don't attack the goal by simply running over their opponents. Tanton's reply: "That's the way Urso plays."

Urso was such a talent that he drew the attention of the National Football League. In 1976 the Green Bay Packers invited him to try out for the team. Urso says he worked out for their scouts inside Byrd Stadium but did not pursue it because he had already signed up to play professional box lacrosse. "The timing was just bad," he said later.[33] That the NFL had noticed the hard-running midfielder spoke volumes about his ability.

The Terrapins boasted more than the star midfielder. Senior Mike Farrell was back on defense, having been named a first-team all-American the previous year. Farrell picked up lacrosse as a junior in high school, unusual given that he came from Baltimore and attended Calvert Hall, one of the top programs in the country. "In the spring I had tried baseball and tennis my freshman and sophomore years and didn't really care for either of them," Farrell says.[34] Tall and wiry strong—he was 6'2", 190 pounds—with exceedingly quick hands, he was convinced by Calvert Hall coach Dick Edell and Doug Radebaugh, Farrell's best friend, to try out for the lacrosse team. Farrell found his way into the starting lineup, and roughly fifteen months after picking up a lacrosse stick for the first time he was named a high-school all-American.

But Farrell had no plans to attend Maryland. Instead, he was committed to play basketball and lacrosse at Bowling Green University, then a Division I program in both sports. Fate intervened one Sunday afternoon in July 1972, just weeks before Farrell was to leave for Ohio. While drinking a beer following a summer league game in Baltimore he casually mentioned to a former high-school team-mate that he thought he was good enough to play at Maryland. The friend was Radebaugh, then the Terrapins' face-off specialist. Before the star defenseman could change his mind, the two drove to Beardmore's house in Severna Park, and Farrell switched his commitment on the spot. As proof of his athletic ability, he also committed to play soccer, meaning Farrell was a rare athlete to commit to play three Division I sports. It was not a gimmick; as a junior in the fall of 1974 he was the Maryland soccer team's starting goalie.[35]

Farrell also became part of an experiment. Beardmore's stated goal was twenty shots a quarter, eighty shots a game. And the new stick technology gave the famous tinkerer a chance to play mad scientist again. Beardmore asked Farrell, and then most of Maryland's other defenders, to affix atop their six-foot shafts a stick head made for midfielders, not defensemen. The defensive stick head was small and narrow, whereas the midfielder, more likely to pass and shoot, had a wider stick head. Farrell still was playing defense, still charged with covering the opposing team's most dangerous offensive threat, but he also had the green light to go upfield and join the offense as needed, with a stick head that would accentu-ate those mad dashes.[36]

Also back was senior Roger Tuck, a midfielder-attackman, 6'1", 190 pounds, who ran the forty-yard dash in 4.7 seconds, a time considered fast by today's standards, let alone nearly fifty years ago.[37] As a senior at Baltimore's Dundalk High, Tuck led the football team in rushing, scoring, interceptions, and punt-ing.[38] Beardmore's recruiting pitch was not fancy. He simply told the Dundalk football coaches, "Just tell Roger we want him really bad."[39] As a senior in high school Tuck also led Dundalk to the county indoor track-and-field title and a second-place finish in lacrosse, and he led Baltimore County in scoring with thirty-seven goals in eleven games.[40] Tuck played freshman football for Maryland as a starting running back before settling on lacrosse.[41]

In the months before the 1976 season, Maryland added to its wealth of talent. Eddie Mullen, an Annapolis native, had been the leading scorer as a sophomore in 1973 on the NCAA champion team. For the other NCAA champions, in 1975, he had scored almost no points after he suffered a season-ending knee injury in the opening game. Incredibly, Mullen says that contest was played on Maryland's Fraternity Row Fields, surrounded by five sorority houses and nine fraternity houses.[42] The grass surface was far more accustomed to hosting the Greek Week Car Demolition and Tug-of-War and intramural flag football than an Atlantic Coast Conference lacrosse game, and Mullen says he was injured on the clumpy grass after trying to make a change-of-direction move against his defenseman, Dave Klarmann.[43] "The rest of the year I basically guarded the bench," Mullen says, "supplying the water and the beer."[44]

His luck was about to turn. A recent NCAA ruling had, for the first time, permitted an extra year of eligibility for athletes in sports other than football. Mullen accepted his extra year. Also on the roster was a group of freshmen that the *Washington Post* said "is the best recruiting crop Beardmore has had at Maryland."[45] Among them was a freshman named Greg Rumpf, from Suffern, New Jersey, a left-handed finisher who had scored seventy-eight goals in his senior year of high school.

The Terrapins were more than talented. They were also intimidating. Tuck and Urso, physically speaking, left opponents stunned. "I was standing next to Frank Urso and Roger Tuck on the field when I was a freshman [in 1975]," says O'Neill, then a starting attackman for Johns Hopkins. "Their wrists were bigger than my biceps."[46] Maryland didn't back down from any challenge. Several players, including Urso and Mullen, were ejected from games for fighting with opponents. "Buddy was more of the military side, if you want to call it that," Mullen says now. "We were lifting weights, we were running long distances, we were doing isometrics. On the flip side, we were kind of hippies. It was the sixties and seventies, and the mindset was more free love, have fun."[47] Indeed, the Terrapins had quite a reputation in lacrosse's small social circles. Stories spread like weeds of upperclass Maryland players asking for, and receiving, permission to drive to preseason scrimmages on their own rather than on the team bus.[48] Beardmore would end Friday practices before a Saturday scrimmage by telling the players what time they needed to be at the opposing school's stadium for warmups, then wouldn't see them again until the next day.[49] An opposing player recalled meeting several Maryland players in the parking lot after one such scrimmage; they were drinking beer around a teammate's car. One Maryland player, a 6'3", 200-pound defenseman, wore a diamond earring and had brought along his girlfriend, a twenty-six-year old stewardess.[50] "I was going to fraternity parties," O'Neill says now. "Those guys were going to the racetrack."[51]

The Terrapins and Big Red were set to hunker down for a season-long game of poker, two top teams eyeing each other from a distance. Then fate upped the ante. On March 16, buried under the *Baltimore Sun*'s National Hockey League and National Basketball Association standings, was an item saying that ABC-TV's seminal *Wide World of Sports* franchise would, for the first time, broadcast extended highlights of the NCAA lacrosse title game. "They are going to tape the game for showing on national television," said Dick Watts, president of the USILA, in the article. "I don't know if they will show it the next day or the next week or what, but they informed me that they will be there."[52] It was to be the sport's first appearance on national television. As one cameraman for the network later said, the broadcast would be a make-or-break moment for the sport.[53]

Cornell's season opener came March 20 against Adelphi, an NCAA tournament participant the previous season. Both the Cornell offense and the weather were in midseason form. The contest was played in unseasonably warm eighty-degree temperatures. In the first twenty-two minutes at Schoellkopf Field, Cornell scored fourteen goals en route to a 24–8 win.[54] From there the Big Red set off for its road trip to Maryland, which included exhibitions against the powerful Mount Washington Wolfpack postcollegiate team and scrimmages against a handful of college teams, including Maryland. Cornell's players recall being excited to eat for several days at the restaurants owned by Katz's family.[55]

The Big Red left Ithaca at 7 a.m. on March 27 and arrived in Baltimore in time to watch Johns Hopkins defeat Towson State, 15–8, at Homewood Field.[56] The next day the Big Red faced the powerful Mount Washington Lacrosse Club, the defending US Club Lacrosse Association champions. The Wolfpack roster was brimming with college all-Americans, all of whom now played as amateurs while pursuing jobs that were almost entirely outside athletics. In the 1960s, facing the best college and postcollegiate teams in the nation, the Wolfpack had won ninety-four games and lost only eight.[57] Though the game was considered an exhibition and would not count in Cornell's won-loss record, it was certain to go a long way toward identifying whether the Big Red was set to send a message to the Baltimore establishment about its intentions, and talent, in 1976.

The Wolfpack featured goalie Dave Creighton, the one-time Hobart standout who had helped thwart Cornell's chances of making the NCAA tournament in 1972. On defense Mount Washington opted to use its best defender, Dennis Townsend, a three-time all-American at Johns Hopkins, on McEneaney.[58] (Funds for the trip had come from the sale of the sun visors and T-shirts by lacrosse players during the previous spring's North–South game. Days after the game, Moran noted in the *Ithaca Journal* that a handful of T-shirts remained and could be purchased in his office inside Teagle Hall.)

In Baltimore the late-March weather cooperated. By the 2 p.m. opening face-off the temperatures had reached seventy degrees, and a crowd of nearly three thousand people swarmed to Mount Washington's Norris Field, essentially a high-school stadium just north of Baltimore, with bleachers that could accommodate roughly one-third that number.[59] Cornell sophomore John Sierra scored the opening goal, off an assist from Levine, two minutes and fifteen seconds into the game. French scored moments later for a 2–0 lead. Cornell led 4–2 at halftime. In the third quarter the game became more comfortable as the Big Red extended the lead against the postcollegiate champions to 10–4. The fourth quarter was a formality; Cornell won, 13–8. French finished with four goals, and Levine added five assists. McEneaney had a quiet day, with no goals and one assist. But the Big Red hadn't needed him. "That was the day," goalkeeper Dan Mackesey says now, "we announced ourselves to Baltimore. That told us—and the lacrosse establishment—we had a really good team."[60]

Two days later, the Cornell team bus drove onto the campus at the University of Maryland for its scrimmage on Denton Field. Maryland's players, noting the field was next to main thoroughfare Route 1, called it "Denton Beach." It was a no-frills environment for a meeting between the top-ranked Terrapins and third-ranked Big Red. Moran and Beardmore decided against a scrimmage that would have simulated a game; instead they opted for a "situational scrimmage"— Cornell defense against Maryland offense at one end, roles reversed at the other in six-on-six and six-on-five set pieces. "I don't think either team wanted to show too much," Kane says. "Neither team wanted to show its hand."[61]

The Big Red went through fairly standard pregame drills—a line of players passing to each other using their right hands, then doing the same using their left. At the other end of the field, the Terrapins added something—passes behind-the-back. "I had never seen that before," Henrickson says.[62] The scrimmage began. Maryland's coaches said they wanted to work on their extra-man offense. Cornell agreed and sent out its man-down defense. The whistle blew. Mackesey says he was stunned by Maryland's armada of midfielders, led by Urso and Tuck, all with cannon-like outside shots. The new plastic sticks generated velocity practically impossible years earlier with wooden sticks. "After that scrimmage," Mackesey says, "Richie started calling their midfielders 'The Guns of Navarone.'"[63]

The Big Red defense gave a good showing as well, despite having only five defensemen to Maryland's six offensive players. "We had a complicated rotation for our man-down," Muehleman says. "Afterward Buddy went up to Bones [Waldvogel's nickname] and asked what we were doing. Bones told him, 'Sorry, Buddy, that's our secret sauce.' Buddy was pretty frustrated by that."[64] The Terrapins remember being impressed as well. "It was obvious," Mullen says, "that

Cornell was very, very good."[65] As players from both teams walked off the grass field, Kane says the Cornell players already were looking ahead to the NCAA tournament. "We were all saying, 'We're going to see these guys again.' We knew we were going to see them again," Kane says now. "We just knew it."[66]

The poker game had begun. On April 4, just days after the scrimmage in College Park, Maryland faced Mount Washington and handed the club champions another rare defeat, this one by an 11–9 final score. The same day in Amherst, Massachusetts, Cornell scored four goals in the first two minutes and thirty-five seconds en route to a 20–9 victory. The fast start was a boon on several levels, not least because the students at U-Mass, thanks to a paucity of stands at the stadium, were famous for lining the sidelines while drinking beer and heckling the opposing team.[67] The fast start had rendered the students relatively quiet.

Maryland upped the ante: On April 10, against the University of Maryland Baltimore County, it made eleven of fifteen shots in the third quarter, an unheard-of 73 percent shooting percentage, on the way to a 19–7 victory. On the same day on Schoellkopf Field, the Big Red hosted Dartmouth. In the first sixteen minutes Cornell scored ten goals en route to a 26–6 victory.[68] The remarkable performances—and further evidence of the widening gap between the eventual NCAA finalists and the rest of the sport—were repeated on April 17. In College Park the Terrapins and Virginia went to overtime, tied at fifteen. The sport's extra session consisted of two four-minute periods; if the game was still tied, only then would it go into sudden death. In the initial eight minutes the Terrapins turned frightening: They took nineteen shots, scoring on eight, while not giving up any shots at all, leading to a final score that will never be equaled, a 24–15 overtime victory.[69]

The same day, the Big Red was back in Baltimore to face Johns Hopkins. And French was showing signs that he was ready for a much different performance from his visit in 1974, when he scored two goals but missed a half-dozen other chances from inside five yards. At one of the practices that week, held on Lower Alumni Field's grass surface to prepare for the grass of Homewood Field, Mackesey peppered the starting attack about the skill of Blue Jays goalkeeper Kevin Mahon. "Danny kept saying, 'He's really good, he's hard to score against,'" Muehleman says now. "'I'm telling you, you're going to have to shoot a different way to beat him. You guys have to be ready.' And finally Frenchie dodges past someone and fires a shot about 110 miles per hour into the top corner of the net. It ripped through the net and kept going down the field. Then he said, 'Hey Danny, you think he can stop that one?' That was one thing about our 1976 team. We had a lot of confidence."[70]

Another adjustment came on defense. Waldvogel, normally meticulously prepared, decided against giving his sophomore starting unit a scouting report on

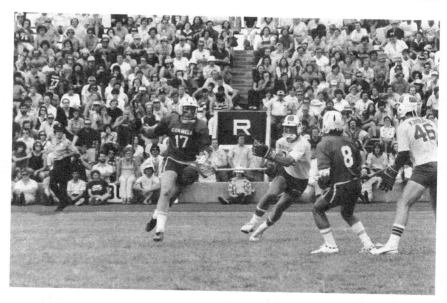

FIGURE 9.2.   Attackman Mike French led the nation in scoring in all three of his years at Cornell. He finished his career with seven goals, on eight shots, in the 1976 NCAA title game. (Photo courtesy Larry Baum)

the Johns Hopkins attack. Instead, he waited until the morning of the game, in the team hotel, to reveal his plan: Rather than playing conservative and trying not to be beaten, the Big Red would play aggressive, in-your-face defense. One year earlier, the *Ithaca Journal* had noted that Franz Wittelsberger and Michael O'Neill looked as if they could score at will against the Big Red, when they combined for eleven goals in a fairly comfortable victory. This time, they would face a far more aggressive scheme.

The bulletin board in Schoellkopf Field housed a little motivation as well. The week of the game, one of Moran's numerous scouts in Maryland had found an article in a local newspaper saying that the game was highly anticipated because "the Big Red seldom plays any of the national powers."[71] Moran still bristles at the accusation, the remnant of years of fruitless attempts to schedule Big Five opponents. Prior to the game, Moran reminded his team that Navy refused to renew the four-year, home-and-home contract that had expired in 1975; Maryland was content to scrimmage Cornell but not play it in the regular season unless the Big Red agreed to three trips to College Park for every one return to Ithaca; Virginia had agreed to play the Big Red in 1970 and 1971 but only in Charlottesville; and Army said it had no room on its schedule, only to add, weeks later, small-college opponent Hobart.[72]

On Saturday, April 17, an overflow crowd of more than eight thousand people filled Homewood Field, basking in the matchup and the warm, eighty-five-degree temperatures.[73] Kane drew O'Neill, and Katz went to guard fellow Baltimore native Wittelsberger, a bulldozer at 6'2", 220 pounds. The better matchup would have been Wittelsberger against Cornell's Tombstone Ted Marchell, 6', 210 pounds. In a game against Dartmouth two years earlier, Marchell had stopped a fast break by legally hitting a Big Green player so hard that the player was separated from the ball and fell to the ground, unconscious, while Marchell picked the ball out of midair and began a fast break. In mid-April 1976, however, Marchell remained sidelined by his injury, though he was expected back in the coming weeks. The third matchup was Muehleman against Johns Hopkins crease attackman Richie Hirsch.

Johns Hopkins jumped to an early lead, thanks to two goals from Wittelsberger, who easily controlled his matchup with Katz.[74] But the Big Red offense provided answers as well. The game was tied at six late in the second quarter when McEneaney escaped senior Jim Moorhead, the Blue Jays' best defender who had held McEneaney in check the previous year and in high school; McEneaney scored unassisted for a 7–6 lead. McEneaney by this point had settled into his role as the team's quarterback, primarily playing behind the goal, going from left to right like a watchdog, looking for a sliver of space to pass the ball to a teammate. He rarely held the ball for long stretches, per Moran's preference. The attackmen on the Big Five teams, like Wittelsberger, O'Neill, and Navy's Jeff Long, were more likely to control the ball on every possession and for long stretches of time.

Cornell scored twice more and took a 9–6 lead at halftime, then led 10–6 early in the third quarter. The Blue Jays closed to 10–7 with eleven minutes, twenty-three seconds left in the third quarter. Then McEneaney and Billy Marino scored for a 12–6 lead. At the other end, the Blue Jays suddenly were struggling to take a good shot, let alone score on Mackesey. In the fourth quarter the suffocating Cornell defense gave up no goals and only three shots, one of which came as the game ended. By then Wittelsberger was on the bench, seething in frustration. He missed his final twelve shots and found his way out of the game after committing two penalties. The young sophomore defenders, seemingly overmatched in the opening minutes, had carried out Waldvogel's plan to the hilt. On offense, French finished with three goals, McEneaney added two goals and three assists, and the Big Red won, 15–7. "Their attack outplayed ours," Johns Hopkins coach Henry Ciccarone said afterward. "No question about that."[75] Cornell's players and Moran repaired to a postgame function hosted by Cornell alums living in Maryland, celebrating the program's first victory over Johns Hopkins. In the USILA rankings released two days later, Cornell was voted number 1, the Terrapins dropping to second.

One other story line emerged from the victory in Baltimore. Mackesey, by his own admission, was struggling. The Big Red was averaging twenty-two goals per game, but after a series of subpar performances, Mackesey had been pulled from the 15–7 victory over Rutgers in early April. Mackesey, then and now, did not offer any excuses for his subpar play. But Moran believed he knew the reason: Mackesey's father was dying of cancer.

His illness did not stop Thomas Mackesey from attending games. One of Mackesey's older brothers owned a Winnebago. He would drive from his home in Baltimore, pick up the father in Ithaca, and bring him onto the track that ringed the playing surface at Schoellkopf Field, out of harm's way but close enough for the father to watch from the front seat.[76] Upon leaving the locker room before the game, the players would first pass by the vehicle and yell to the passenger window, "We're going to win this one for you, Mr. Mackesey."[77] Dan Mackesey, with his father in attendance in Baltimore—Mackesey's brother logging extra miles on the round-trip—had made twelve saves against the Blue Jays. As the game ended, and his teammates ran to celebrate the first-ever victory over the Blue Jays, Mackesey says he dropped to the ground and lay on his back on the Homewood Field grass, basking in the historic victory with his ill father in attendance. "It was like tennis players after they win a big match," he says now. "I just wanted to soak it all in."[78]

The regular season ended in early May with Cornell and Maryland both undefeated. Kane was out for the year with a shoulder injury suffered against Penn in late April. While the Big Red would miss his speed on defense, Marchell had returned to health enough to reenter the starting lineup, giving the unit a more rugged look. Cornell won the Ivy League title, though it struggled in its final regular-season game, a 10–7 victory over Brown at Schoellkopf Field in which a senior midfielder named Peter Bensley finished with four goals, at least two on blistering outside shots that beat Mackesey. Maryland won the Atlantic Coast Conference championship going away. Both had won a conference title. The far more important NCAA tournament awaited.

For the postseason, Maryland was named the top seed, and Cornell was second. Among the other teams in the postseason was first-year participant Massachusetts. The Minutemen, like Moran at Cornell, had unearthed a pipeline from Long Island; the coach at Nassau Community College, Mike Candel, had graduated from U-Mass, and in 1976 the Minutemen had four Nassau alums receiving regular playing time.[79]

The first-round games featured Brown against Maryland, Massachusetts against Johns Hopkins, Navy against newcomer North Carolina, and Washington and Lee traveling to Ithaca to face the Big Red. The previous year the Generals had sprung a huge upset on the Blue Jays; back were defensemen Tom Keigler and Rob Lindsey, first-team all-Americans the previous year. On Tuesday, May 18, as the Generals boarded their flight to Ithaca, leaving behind temperatures of were sixty-four degrees, though the previous day it had reached seventy-eight. The Generals left the Shenandoah Valley in good spirits. "Everyone was thinking about what happened the year before," says W&L's Charlie Stieff, a starting midfielder, "where no one thought we could beat Hopkins. So we were saying, 'Let's rock Cornell.'"[80]

The Washington and Lee players disembarked at Tompkins County Airport, greeted by freezing temperatures and a whipping wind. Stieff still recalls looking with horror at piles of snow along the runway. "We were saying, 'There's still snow up here?'"[81] The Generals shivered through a walk-through practice on Schoellkopf Field's artificial turf, then went to dinner at a nearby diner. A handful of Cornell players, including McEneaney and Kane, were living in an off-campus house, dubbed the "Magic Castle," in the nearby hamlet of Varna. After practice on May 18, two other housemates, Tom Marino and Sierra, stopped by the same diner as the W&L team for a takeout dinner. Marino recognized several W&L players who were, like him, from Long Island. "Those guys looked freezing and miserable," Marino says now. "They did not want to be in Ithaca."[82]

The following day, game day, temperatures briefly hit sixty degrees before, as evening descended, dipping to the thirty-degree range, with freezing rain and an even stronger wind. Because it was Cornell's exam time, the school banned sporting events before 5 p.m. The Cornell–Washington and Lee game started at 5:15 p.m. and would end after dark, with even colder temperatures expected. Washington and Lee's players weren't the only ones expecting—and dressed for—warmer weather. The referees arrived wearing only shorts and wound up with teeth chattering before the first face-off. Moran found them each a pair of sweatpants—red, with "Cornell Lacrosse" printed on one thigh. "The Washington and Lee coaches didn't think much of that," Moran says now.[83]

As the Generals shivered their way through pregame drills, the Big Red stayed in its warm locker room longer than usual. When they left they did not take the field immediately. Instead the players snaked to the five entrances at the Crescent side of the stadium, the same ones used by the fans, who given the weather were in short supply. As the Washington and Lee players began to wonder where their opponents were, the Cornell players came racing down the stadium steps, yelling and screaming at the top of their lungs. "It was quite an entrance," says Jay Sindler, a starting midfielder for the Generals. "They came streaming out of the stadium entrances, yelling like it was Custer's last stand."[84] Once they took the field, Cornell's players went through line drills as close to midfield as they were allowed and yelled things like "What a beautiful day!" loud enough for the southern team to hear. They even borrowed Moran's tagline, "It's great to be here!"

By the time the teams took the field for the opening face-off, the other quarter-finals had ended. Maryland had jumped to a 9–1 lead over Brown, the same team that Cornell had barely defeated the previous week, en route to a 17–8 victory. Navy's Bill Mueller, the hero of the previous year's semifinal in Ithaca, led the way for a 13–9 victory over North Carolina. And Johns Hopkins defeated Massachu-setts, 11–9, meaning the winner in Ithaca would face the Blue Jays on Saturday, May 20. As the game ended in Baltimore, the Johns Hopkins band began playing "Give My Regards to Broadway," the tune of which doubles as Cornell's "Give My Regards to Davy" fight song. The Blue Jays were not expecting to face Washington and Lee for a third consecutive year.

In chilly Ithaca, the game began before a sparse crowd of fifteen hundred, the numbers held down by the raw weather. Washington and Lee's Keigler and Lind-sey guarded McEneaney and French respectively.[85] But in the early going Wash-ington and Lee's offense was not able to generate much against Cornell's defense and Mackesey. Sindler took a shot that hit the goalpost and bounced out. At the end of the first quarter, no member of the French Connection had registered a point, but Cornell led, 4–0.

By the middle of the second quarter, it was 6–0 after goals from Levine and French. At halftime it was 8–0, the Generals having failed to beat Mackesey on any of their twelve shots. Inside the visitor's locker room at Schoellkopf Field, one of Cornell's trainers was tending to an injured Washington and Lee player. The Generals were trailing and as dusk descended, heavy rain, biting wind, and hint of snow had made the waning afternoon even more miserable. Coach Jack Emmer, no stranger to Central New York weather, tried to lift his team's spirits as he mentioned going back out for the second half and pretending the score was 0–0. The Generals were too dispirited and cold to buy into the motivational trick. The trainer later told the Cornell contingent that one of the Washington and Lee players, under his breath, muttered, "Do we *have* to go back out there?"[86]

The second half began, and Cornell's defense and Mackesey continued to dominate. With the Big Red focusing on the defensive game, there was only one goal in the third quarter, scored by Cornell midfielder Albin Haglund. In the fourth quarter, with his team leading 9–0, Moran substituted liberally on offense but kept Mackesey and the starting defense—Katz, Muehleman, and Marchell—in the contest. The Big Red reserves kept scoring; Washington and Lee did not. The final score was 14–0, Cornell's first shutout since 1942 and, to this day, the only shutout in NCAA tournament history. "I've got to give all the credit to Cornell. They've got great shooters and a great team," Emmer said after the game.[87] Word of the shutout spread quickly in lacrosse's small circles. "We couldn't believe that had happened," says Tom Myrick, a starting midfielder at Johns Hopkins in 1976. "Nobody had ever heard of a shutout before between any two teams, much less two top Division I teams." Kiegler and Lindsey had again won their matchups, as the French Connection sputtered. The key to the victory had been the defense and Cornell's midfield depth, with reserve Bob Mitchell, an Ithaca native, leading the way with three goals, the same number as McEneaney, French, and Levine combined.

On Thursday, the day after the victory over Washington and Lee, and with an eye on the semifinal in Ithaca in forty-eight hours, local radio station WVBR asked if one of the Cornell players was available for a live on-air interview at 4 p.m. Because the interview conflicted with the start of practice, Moran offered them Kane, the injured starting defenseman. The interview would be live, and Cornell's players, gathered at the field house, for once took the requisite "Frampton Comes Alive" off the turntable to hear Kane.

The radio interview began as normal, the players, still in the locker room, about to begin practice, laughing and joking at their injured teammate's introduction. Then came a question about the upcoming game against Johns Hopkins. It would have been easy for Kane to go into cliché mode. But giving anodyne answers was not Kane's style. "I had been at Cornell a year and a half and no one wanted to talk to me," he said later. "And now someone wanted to listen? I couldn't believe it. They were going to have to pry that microphone out of my hands."[88]

From the innocuous question Kane proceeded, to the players' surprise and the coaches' horror, to reveal the entire scouting report for Saturday's semifinal. He began by taking a shot at one of his teammates. French, like many Canadian players, tended to be heavily one-handed and rarely handled the ball with his off-hand. Kane revealed this to the audience, adding "Frenchie wouldn't put his stick in his left hand if you held a gun to his head."[89] He also revealed Cornell's plans for a ten-man ride, a full-court press of a defense, against the Blue Jays; how the Big Red would defend the Blue Jays' talented midfielders; and other parts of the top-secret game plan. The more Kane spoke, the quieter the locker room became. As the interview wore on and Kane became more loquacious, players remember Moran's face turning ash-white before he became angry—very angry. "It was very over the top," Muehleman says now. "Chris was talking about how good we were and all the things we do that made us good. Whenever newspapers were writing about us, Richie hated when people did stuff like that."[90]

The team went out to practice with the visit from the Blue Jays in two days, knowing their coach was very unhappy.

Later that evening, interview and practice over, Kane bounded into his Psi Upsilon fraternity house all smiles. "I thought I had crushed it. I thought I was the next Howard Stern," he says. "I thought I had found my calling."[91] He was greeted by a fraternity brother—Jimmy DeNicola, a reserve midfielder. "Oh man," Kane recalls DeNicola saying, "'Richie is going to fucking kill you! He is really pissed you gave away the scouting report.' I went from elation to shitting in my pants in about a half second."[92] There was no chance the radio station's signal would be heard in Baltimore. But Johns Hopkins, like Moran, was famous for having scouts up and down the mid-Atlantic. Had any of those scouts been listening to the interview, or were they perhaps told about it afterward? The Big Red had no idea, and thanks to the compressed NCAA tournament schedule— three games in eleven days—they had little time to alter the game plan that Kane had revealed over the airwaves.

The next day, Friday, was the final practice before the semifinal. The players changed quietly in the locker room, awaiting Kane's arrival and Moran's reaction. The coaches changed their clothes for practice in utter and complete silence. The players followed suit. "We were all waiting," Muehleman says, "for Chris to arrive and for Richie to climb all over him."

Finally the door swung open. The first thing the players noticed was that it was Kane. The second thing they noticed was his outfit. He was wearing a velvet smoking jacket; he had a cigarette in a long cigarette holder, an ascot around his neck, sunglasses, and a small notebook. He proceeded to walk to the middle of the locker room and announce in the loudest voice possible, "Anyone who wants an autograph, the line starts here!" As Kane says now, "The place went nuts."[93] Players say it was the first and only time they ever saw Moran speechless. Eventually even he smiled and then laughed hard with Waldvogel. It was possible that Johns Hopkins knew the scouting report, but it might not matter—the Big Red was that good.

Saturday arrived, and if the Blue Jays had learned about the scouting report, they did not play like it. At halftime the Big Red led, 4–0, the defense pitching another shutout. In ninety minutes of NCAA tournament action against two of the top teams in the sport, Cornell had not given up a goal. Midway through the third quarter Cornell extended its lead to 7–0 when Johns Hopkins finally scored, a goal by Joe Garavante; Mackesey later recalled that it came after Garavante's defender had slipped, leaving the midfielder wide open.[94] It was the first goal the Big Red had given up in ninety-eight minutes and forty-two seconds of NCAA tournament play.

By this point, despite the large deficit, Johns Hopkins coach Henry Ciccarone continued to use a stalling offense. The Big Red extended the lead to 11–1 early in the fourth quarter before the substitutes took over. The final score was 13–5, and the powerful Baltimore squad had been limited to twenty-three shots, less than half what they normally took. The Big Red had entered the previous month hav-

FIGURE 9.3. Cornell and Johns Hopkins had more than a few battles in the 1970s, including here, in the 1976 NCAA semifinals at Schoellkopf Field. Cornell won the game, 13–5. (Photo courtesy Larry Baum)

ing never beaten the Blue Jays. In a matter of weeks, it had turned the trick twice. Cornell's defense was so strong that a writer from the *Syracuse Post-Standard* wrote, "Getting at Mackesey is like trying to get near the Berlin Wall without a tunnel."

Cornell had advanced to the title game. The dream matchup, and rematch of the inaugural title game, was halfway complete. Maryland's semifinal against Navy was scheduled for Sunday in College Park. Only two ticket windows at Byrd Stadium were open, not nearly enough for the overflow crowd attempting to see the game. Published reports say much of the crowd of ten thousand missed the game's early stages. Those in attendance included Moran, Waldvogel, and even Mackesey, who had driven down from Ithaca with a friend for another look at the Terrapins. In a rematch of the 1975 NCAA final, the Terrapins jumped to an 11–1 lead en route to a 22–11 victory. Mullen led the way with seven goals and five assists. As dominant as Cornell had looked against the Blue Jays, Maryland arguably looked even better against the Midshipmen. Maryland had just defeated one of its biggest rivals but its thoughts turned almost immediately to Cornell. In his postgame remarks to the media, Urso recalled the scrimmage of two months earlier. "You could feel the teams wanting to go at each other," he told reporters. "Now we are finally going to get a chance."

FROM BROWN STADIUM

The first public prediction of a Cornell–Maryland NCAA final was written more than one month before the game itself. "College lacrosse appears headed for a Cornell–Maryland national championship game," wrote Bill Tanton in the *Evening Sun* on April 27.[1] It was not a bold prediction, but Tanton was the print authority in the world of Baltimore lacrosse. Weeks later, the *Ithaca Journal* only half-jokingly said the season should have been stopped in mid-April so Maryland and Cornell could have emulated professional sports.[2] Cornell and Maryland "may have wanted a best-of-seven series way back in April, to determine who was the better team," wrote assistant sports editor Fred Yahn. "While the other college teams would have hollered, perhaps that's the way it should have been settled this year."[3]

The Big Red and the Terrapins embodied the yin and yang of the sport: North against South, New York against Maryland, and upstart against establishment. Each boasted a once-in-a-lifetime talent, Urso and McEneaney, athletic enough to draw the interest of the National Football League. (McEneaney caught the eye of the New York Jets in the fall of 1976 and was given a tryout months later.) Each also had a high-placed supporter. Finn has followed the sport for more than five decades. He has high praise for many of the 1970s players including McEneaney but reserves his highest accolade for the Maryland midfielder. "Frank Urso," Finn says, "was the best player I've ever seen."[4] Buck Briggs, a member of Cornell's class of 1976 and longtime lawyer in professional sports, has similarly high praise for McEneaney. "With Eamon, something special could happen at any time," Briggs says. "He was a magical guy. He was capable either through skill or through his being absolutely relentless.... With him holding the ball behind the goal, trotting back and forth, then he would leap in the air almost like a fawn and when he hit the ground he was running full speed. It was just 'woosh!' Full acceleration. He was a joy to watch because he was energy and enthusiasm personified. When he had the ball behind the goal, everyone in Schoellkopf would lean forward in our seats because we knew something magic was coming."[5] Now, McEneaney and Urso were going to meet for the only time as college players. Cornell and Maryland had played once previously in Urso's career, the 1974 NCAA semifinals, the year McEneaney was marooned on the freshman team.

Urso and his teammates arrived in Providence for the title game on Wednesday, May 26, via commercial airplane. A handful of Maryland players went out on the town that night with Mike Evans, a senior midfielder on the Brown lacrosse team, who was high-school friends with Urso. Cornell arrived by bus late Thursday afternoon and went to its hotel in the town neighboring Providence, the Cranston Hilton Inn, about four miles from the stadium.[6] Waiting to greet them were their NCAA hosts, former Brown players Jeff Wagner and Dom Starsia. Wagner was in Boston working for Brine, the lacrosse equipment manufacturing company. Starsia, then an assistant at Brown, was, as an NCAA-designated host, allowed to see the Big Red up close: how the team practiced, how it prepared for games. He still remembers the players emerging from the bus brimming with confidence. "I loved their swagger," Starsia says. "Just everything about them.... It was the first time I was really up close watching a team of that caliber. I was an assistant at Brown and never would have been allowed into Cornell's practice. But as the host coach I was allowed, and they let me watch up close. I remember Mike Waldvogel, I'd never seen a guy warm up a goalie like that, shooting the ball as hard as he did. It just exposed me to a whole different level of what college lacrosse was capable of."[7] Wagner agreed: "It was what big-time lacrosse should look like."[8]

Two-thirds of the French Connection—French and Levine—were not on the bus, nor were Billy Marino and a couple other seniors. They had received permission to remain in Ithaca for Friday morning's graduation ceremony, then arrived in Providence in the afternoon via a private plane, the flight arranged by a friend of Moran.[9] Wagner picked them up at the airport and drove them to the team hotel and to a practice session at Brown Stadium. After Cornell's final practice and the team's return to the Cranston Hilton, several players sat at the hotel pool and relaxed. Mackesey and Waldvogel were headed in the opposite direction. They walked through the lobby, Mackesey carrying his lacrosse gear, Waldvogel carrying a stick and a bag of lacrosse balls. They took a courtesy car and were driven twelve minutes to the stadium. Waiting for them was Peter Bensley, the Brown midfielder who had scored four goals against Cornell in the regular season meeting. Bensley's excellent outside shot resembled those of the Maryland midfielders, and Waldvogel had arranged for him to take dozens of shots on Mackesey in one last bit of preparation. "He had tremendous whip in his stick and it was hard to read his shot," Mackesey says now.[10] Around the goalie, assistant coach and soon-to-be Brown graduate, the workers from ABC's *Wide World of Sports* assembled the equipment for the following day's broadcast, including cameras on top of the press box and in both end zones and a raised platform and table constructed near the sideline for announcers Frank Gifford and Gene Corrigan.

In the stands, Brown coach Cliff Stevenson surveyed the scene with a reporter from *Sports Illustrated*. Stevenson had faced both Maryland and Cornell in the month of May, and he had a unique perspective. "This could be," Stevenson told the writer, "the greatest lacrosse game of all time. I've been coaching 26 years and these are the two best teams I've ever seen."[11] Newspapers picked up on the theme. The headline in Saturday's *Ithaca Journal* was "Perfect Matchup? It's Red vs. Terps."

At 8:45 in the morning on Saturday, May 29, 1976, Tad Barrows left his parents' house on Alumni Avenue in East Providence and walked to the top of the street. On normal mornings he kept going straight, right onto the campus of Moses Brown School, where Barrows was a senior. This time, once he reached the Moses Brown football stadium Barrows turned left, onto Morris Avenue, and began walking north. It was warm and bright, the start of what was forecast to reach the low seventies, sunny, a glorious early-summer New England day. Barrows, wearing a red T-shirt, khaki pants, and sneakers and carrying his lacrosse gear, walked along Morris Avenue, a mostly residential area. Barrows traveled under the shade of trees, the sound of a solitary lawnmower to his left, a few children laughing in their front yards to his right, then farther along the creak of a rocking chair as an unshaven man sat on his front porch, sipped his coffee, and read the account of the Red Sox's 7–2 loss to the visiting Baltimore Orioles the previous night. Barrows walked along Morris Avenue for ten minutes before reaching Sessions Avenue and turning right, into another residential area with fewer trees and three-story apartment buildings, red-brick buildings interspersed with slate-gray ones, replacing the single-family homes. After a few minutes, on the left, the horizon became totally clear, because Barrows had reached his destination, the gray concrete of Brown Stadium. It was 9 a.m. He was right on time.

Barrows walked down a well-worn grass path into the stadium, past the giant beige concrete triangle of the main stands and down onto the grass playing surface. About a dozen other teens were waiting, along with the TV crew from *Wide World of Sports*. Barrows changed into his lacrosse uniform—plain white helmet, dark blue Moses Brown jersey and shorts, lacrosse stick with a navy-blue plastic head, and beige lacrosse gloves. Then he walked onto the field. Earlier that week, producers from ABC had asked the head coach at Moses Brown to round up twenty high-school players to demonstrate the rules of lacrosse as a precursor to the extended highlights of the Cornell–Maryland game, airing in the middle of June. It was the first time the sport had been broadcast on national television, and the show's producers believed that many who tuned in would need a primer.

Moses Brown coach Wayne Curtis phoned Barrows, then several teammates. The ABC request had been made for Memorial Day weekend, and Curtis found several of his players would be out of town. He then dipped into the programs at nearby Providence Country Day and LaSalle Academy, the other two schools fielding lacrosse teams in 1976 in a city with a population of 968,000 people. By 9 a.m. on May 29, it was clear that Curtis's efforts had fallen short: About sixteen teenagers assembled inside Brown Stadium, not the twenty that had been requested. The ABC producers said they would make it work.

Because Rhode Island's youth leagues and summer leagues were virtually nonexistent, Barrows says he knew only his teammates from Moses Brown but none of the other players. Curtis gathered the uniforms and distributed them to the players. He outfitted ten players in Moses Brown's blue uniform, enough for a full team, then pulled out white jerseys, black shorts, and red helmets loaned by an athletic outfitter. These he gave to the remaining half-dozen teens. The uniforms did not belong to any school—they did match the red-and-black color scheme of Providence Country Day and two nearby boarding schools, St. George's and Portsmouth Abbey—but at least it would look to the TV audience that two different teams were taking part.

ABC asked Barrows, at 6', 190 pounds, to stand still, in full uniform, while a camera panned up his body to show a typical lacrosse player's equipment, and color analyst Corrigan provided a voice-over narration telling the audience about the gloves, stick, and helmet. From there, Barrows and a teen wearing the opposing team's uniform were asked to simulate a face-off, then penalties (Barrows stood still while the player, whom he didn't know, was allowed to hit him in the head repeatedly while demonstrating a slashing penalty). The group of sixteen was asked to play a loose scrimmage at half speed to show the basic patterns of play. They were moved to the goal at the Taft Avenue side of the stadium because university facilities managers were watering the grass surface in front of the goal at the other end.

After the half-speed, five-minute scrimmage, the ABC producers thanked the teens and sent them on their way. The morning would prove beneficial to the *Wide World of Sports* audience and also to the TV crew in Providence, many of whom had never seen the sport. There was such concern over the speed of the passing and shooting, even in the light scrimmage, that as the teens left the stadium, one of the producers approached Barrows. *Wide World of Sports* had received permission to have a handheld camera operator in the fifteen yards between the Maryland and Cornell benches on the sideline, almost exactly at midfield. "He said, 'How would you like to protect our camera man on the sideline?'" Barrows says. "And I looked at him and said, 'Of course I would.'" It meant that Barrows, a senior in high school, would have a better vantage point for the battle of unbeaten teams than anyone in the stands, better than Gifford and Corrigan, better even than the Maryland and Cornell coaches. The ABC official produced a sideline pass and gave it to Barrows, adding that, for his day's work, Barrows would be given fifty dollars. "And I thought, fifty bucks!" Barrows said. "That's a lot of beer money."

Around noon on May 29, 1976, Fred Yahn of the *Ithaca Journal* arrived at the media parking lot next to Brown Stadium. Before heading inside, he decided to take a stroll around the parking lots, to gauge the pregame mood. The temperatures were hovering around seventy degrees, and cars were parked on the grass fields adjacent to the stadium. Everywhere Yahn looked he saw plastic lacrosse sticks bobbing in the air as children and adults threw lacrosse balls back and forth. Those who did not bring sticks flung Frisbees to and fro. Music filled the air, primarily the Allman Brothers band, their Southern rock chords joined by the hiss of pop-top beer cans being opened. Slight breezes sifted the smells of freshly cut grass and the smoke from portable barbeques, while lifting the Frisbees a little higher into the cloudless sky. "It was a day that started out like a day at Watkins Glen," Yahn wrote in Monday's paper, "for a Summer Jam, or a grand prix."[12] From there Yahn made his way inside the ancient stadium, built in 1923. Brown Stadium featured, on the Sessions Avenue side, one set of stands, made of beige concrete, rising like a giant triangle. (This was the entrance that Barrows had used hours earlier.) The other side of the stadium had a half dozen small bleachers, several rows tall, all adjacent to each other. A black cinder track with white lanes separated the stands from the playing surface. The press box was at the very top of the triangle, and the stadium had no elevator. Yahn trudged the seemingly endless steps to his spot for the day inside the press box, which was open air and narrow like a train car.

Outside the stadium the party continued. It was a holiday weekend, the weather was perfect, and Cornell and Maryland were both undefeated. Several Big Red fans wore white T-shirts with red piping along the sleeves and neck and the image of a lacrosse player wearing number 17, French's number, under the words "Numero Uno, Cornell '76," a play on the "Arnold Is Numero Uno" shirt worn by bodybuilder Arnold Schwarzenegger the day he won the Mr. Olympia

FIGURE 10.1.   Cornell fans show their spirit at Brown Stadium. One estimate said three thousand Cornell students attended the 1976 title game between the Big Red and Maryland in Providence. (Photo courtesy Larry Baum)

contest in 1975. Fans also brought hand-painted signs, including one placed at the top row of the stadium, courtesy of McEneaney's fraternity brothers in Sigma Alpha Epsilon: "Flamin' Eamon Is #1! Go Big Red!" Another was drawn in the puffy, all lowercase letters popular in the 1970s, and it included both a dig at Maryland and a nod to *Wide World of Sports*: "big red ivy poisons the 'twerps! simple as abc." The mood, especially among Cornell fans, was ecstatic. "We all got caught up in it," says Jim Hofher, a freshman in 1976 who drove with friends to the game that morning from his parents' house in Connecticut. "When your school is playing for a national title, it's a big deal."

At 1 p.m., as Barrows flashed his ABC credential and walked onto the sidelines with his lacrosse stick, the teams took the field for warm-ups, each receiving a smattering of applause from their fans who had already made their way into the stadium. Cornell coach Richie Moran stayed inside the tiny visitor's locker room, writing calmly on the chalkboard his beloved slogans: "Be Yourself!" "Groundballs!" "Stay Down on the Farm." Players later said they had never seen him so calm before a game. When Moran took the field, he was collared by the TV producers, as was Cornell star attackman Mike French, Maryland coach Buddy Beardmore, and Maryland star midfielder Frank Urso. They were asked general questions; their sound bites would be inserted into the footage for the rebroadcast.

Both teams had their game plans ready. Beardmore, whose strategy for the 1971 NCAA title game against Cornell had come under fierce scrutiny, made another set of hard decisions. Farrell, the best defender in college lacrosse, would guard McEneaney. Junior Mark Bethmann drew French, and freshman Randy Ratliff guarded Levine. The Terrapins wanted Farrell to focus entirely on McEneaney and not help either of the other two defensemen. In lacrosse terms, Farrell was "on an island"—he was alone with McEneaney and not expected to provide help to the other two defenders.

Bethmann, at 6'2", 190 pounds, had almost the same physical characteristics as French. But Maryland would not have seen any other Canadian attackmen that season—Dave Huntley, the freshman standout at Johns Hopkins from Toronto, played midfield. Nor did Maryland have any way of simulating French's unique moves, which included one-handed scoop shots, behind-the-back shots, and shots with his shoulders perpendicular to the goal, because no one on the Terrapins roster was from Canada or had a box lacrosse background. French could be physical as well—Muehleman recalled during practice, having sore thumbs from trying to push French out of position once he got the ball near the goal. Whoever guarded French was in for a long afternoon. Ratliff was an excellent athlete, an all-state quarterback at Hereford High outside Baltimore and also a standout in high school track-and-field.[13] His assignment was to worry about Levine, who rarely carried the ball and whose intelligent off-ball movement gave defenses trouble. It seemed an odd decision not to have the more athletic Ratliff on the player who would control the ball more, French. Ratliff was in the lineup because sophomore George Miller, a New Jersey native, missed the game with a sinus infection.

Cornell's game plan was simple: Make Urso, Roger Tuck, and the other talented midfielders play as much defense as possible to try and wear them down and keep the ball out of their sticks. The Big Red would continue to push the ball in transition for fast-break opportunities, but if the fast break was not available, the Big Red was more than happy to slow the game and try and run Maryland's midfielders into the ground with Moran's nonstop "circulation" motion offense. During his pregame interview with ABC's Frank Gifford, Moran lamented the weather was not 110 degrees because it would have made Urso and Tuck more vulnerable to fatigue.

On defense, senior Ted Marchell drew Eddie Mullen, Maryland's leading scorer with thirty-one goals and thirty assists; Frank Muehleman drew senior Bert Caswell, second on the team in goals with twenty-seven; and Bobby Katz guarded freshman John Lamon, an Annapolis native with seven goals and nine

FIGURE 10.2.   Cornell's starting defense, from left, goalkeeper Dan Mackesey and close defensemen Frank Muehleman, Bobby Katz, and Ted Marchell, helped hold opponents scoreless in the 1976 NCAA tournament for more than ninety-eight minutes. (Photo courtesy Jules Sieburgh)

assists, suddenly thrust into a starting role because of an injury. Maryland's midfield depth was such that Urso (twenty-three goals, eighteen assists) and Tuck (twenty-four goals, eleven assists), both just days from being named first-team all-American, played on different lines. Urso was on the first line, joined by face-off specialist Bob Ott and freshman Terry Kimball. Tuck was placed on the second unit with senior Bob Brenton and freshman Lance Kohler. When Urso was in the game, he would be guarded either by sophomore Bob Henrickson or junior Gary Malm. Had Kane been healthy it is possible he would have played defensive midfield. (The designated longstick defensive midfielder would not become popularized for another couple of years.) Instead, Kane was on the sideline, wearing his red, number 42 jersey and khaki pants, with his right arm in a sling, a remnant of his shoulder injury from the previous month.

About 1:40 p.m. the teams went back into the locker rooms, then took the field for a last, quick warm-up. Maryland took the field for the game in white jerseys with the player's last name on the back, red shorts, and red-and-white paneled helmets. Cornell emerged from underneath the stadium, where their small locker room was located, in red jerseys, red shorts, and plain white helmets. Every player on the field was using a plastic stick head. In the minutes before the game started, the stadium becoming more full, the noise starting to grow, Cornell's Jon Levine caught a commotion on the sideline out of the corner of his eye. He looked more closely and saw his mother was trying to talk her way onto the field. Taube Levine had one son on each team—Jon with Cornell, twin brother Harman with Maryland. "She asked me where she should sit," Jon Levine says. "I said, 'Ma, what are you doing here?!' Then I said, 'Go sit in the Cornell section.' She asked why and I said, 'Because we're going to win, that's why.'"[14]

Three captains from each team met at midfield with referees Dave Brody, Pat Dawson, and Ron O'Leary. All three Cornell players were wearing their helmets, ready for action. Two Maryland captains held their helmets on their hips, exposing their long hair to the warm afternoon and soft breeze. By this time the stadium was nearly full. A crowd of 11,954 people, including hundreds of Cornell students, jammed inside. Barrows, who had attended dozens of Brown sporting events growing up, recalled thinking that the stadium was as full and as loud as he had ever seen. At the base of the triangle-shaped stands, seated on the platform at a long wooden table, sat Gifford, a former star with the NFL's New York Giants and famed for his work on *Monday Night Football,* and Corrigan. Both wore mustard-yellow blazers with a black patch, reading ABC's *Wide World of Sports* on the left breast. As the game was about to begin, the crowd filling the stands behind him, Gifford stood and prepared to deliver his on-camera introduction, one or two sentences telling the audience about the action set to unfold. He spoke into the gray camera, the side of which featured a white circular sticker with lowercase letters "abc," the *a* in red, *b* in blue, and *c* in green.

Holding the camera was a man wearing a purple shirt, blue jeans, and a floppy denim hat, the man Barrows was charged using his lacrosse stick to protect from errant passes. The script read: "From Brown Stadium, Brown University, in Providence, Rhode Island, today it's the sixth NCAA lacrosse championship." On the first take Gifford began, "From—what's the name of the stadium again?" On the second take Gifford said the stadium correctly but misspoke a few words later, then misspoke again on the third and fourth takes. On the fifth take, Gifford began, "Welcome to Providence Stadium in Brown, Rhode Island." On the sixth take, Gifford got the introduction correct, then sat down. The cameraman turned his attention to the field, Barrows trailing behind.

Soon it was time for the opening face-off, Maryland's Ott, a Montclair, New Jersey, native, against Henrickson. Following a scramble, the ball popped in the air, and Henrickson controlled it. The Cornell fans, seated behind the bench in the area closest to Sessions Street and Elmgrove Avenue, roared. But the Big Red turned the ball over; the Terrapins cleared the ball, then caught a break—Cornell's Katz was called for a tripping penalty, and Maryland had an extra offensive player for up to thirty seconds. In the scrimmage between the teams in March in College Park, Maryland's extra-man offense never figured out Cornell's man-down defense, and Waldvogel had declined to give Beardmore any insights. Suddenly, roughly one minute into the title game, the two units were head-to-head again.

Cornell's man-down unit was two short-stick defenders—a rotation of junior Dave Bray and seniors Robert Mitchell, Albin Haglund, and Jake O'Neill—and three longsticks, usually Muehleman, Katz, and Marchell, with junior Vinny Shanley entering if the penalty were on one of the starters, as it was in this case. Waldvogel's complicated rotation consisted of sometimes calling for the defender on the crease, or the area right in front of the goal, to slide to the open player, which the offense invariably found because of its extra player. Other times Waldvogel wanted the defender on the wing to run at and harass the open player. Because Maryland had such strong outside shooters, for the NCAA title game, Waldvogel called for slides to come from the crease. Leaving that area open for a possible point-blank shot was preferable to letting the Maryland midfielders have an open shot, even from fifteen yards. Waldvogel had hedged his bet by having Mackesey face the hard outside shots of Bensley the previous day.

On its first extra-man possession, Maryland passed the ball around in a circle, then tried, as Waldvogel had hoped, to feed the ball onto the crease rather than uncorking an outside shot. A Cornell defender tipped the ball, and it went right to Mackesey. The Big Red cleared. Waldvogel's unit had won an early, crucial skirmish.

A few minutes later, with Cornell in possession, French drove the ball, caught Bethmann leaning the wrong way, and used an inside roll to score from point-blank range. The fans sitting near the goal at the opposite end of the stadium, both behind Cornell's bench and across from the team bench, rose to their feet and roared. The NCAA title game was being played in a Northern site, and the team from the north was the clear favorite. Later, Maryland freshman Barry Mitchell easily beat his defender and scored from close range to tie the game at one, with cheers coming mostly from behind the Maryland bench. The first quarter ended tied at one, and Cornell looked a little jittery; as Yahn later noted, the team "had been a nervous loser in the 1974 and 1975 semifinals."[15] Only Mackesey, with six saves, and the man-down defense, which had not given up a goal in three extra-man chances, seemed up to the task.

Early in the second quarter, French scored again, this time on an assist from McEneaney, for a 2–1 lead. French's two goals had come on only three shots. Bethmann was holding his own in six-on-six offense, but French and his unusual shooting angles and techniques were causing major problems on unsettled situations, especially on fast breaks. Such was the dilemma facing Cornell's opponents in 1976—French would lead the nation in scoring three consecutive years, but judging by their actions opposing coaches feared McEneaney more. There were just too many risks to contain.

The Big Red still led 2–1 when Tuck chased a loose ball near the sideline and took a hard, clean hit from Marchell. "Tombstone Ted" had left Tuck, the one-time football recruit and one of the toughest players in lacrosse, with a bad chest and shoulder injury; Tuck headed to the sideline, gasping for breath.

Trailing 2–1 in the second quarter, the Terrapins went on a roll. Urso scored using his off-hand after gaining a step on Henrickson to tie the game at two; freshman Lance Kohler scored on a one-time shot off a feed from Mullen for a 3–2 lead; Lamon scored on a beautiful shot while falling to the ground to make it 4–2, then assisted Caswell for a tic-tac-toe fast break goal and a 5–2 lead. It became 6–2 after Mullen converted a perfect feed from Brenton, a transfer from the Air Force Academy. Then it was 7–2 after junior Bert Olsen dodged three defenders and put a close shot over Mackesey's shoulder with seven minutes and twenty-six seconds left in the first half. Tuck, following the hit from Marchell, continued to play but his running was slower and his breathing visibly labored. It appeared the Terrapins would have their offense clicking even with Tuck not at his best.

The Terrapins had reason to be confident. The spurt included a score from each of the three main midfield lines, a particular point of emphasis for Beardmore. The whole College Park squad was hot. Olsen punctuated the move for a five-goal lead by celebrating with teammates, then turning around and screaming in the Cornell defenders' faces. The Big Red was showing signs of frustration. After the fifth goal Katz had slammed his stick to the ground. After the seventh, Moran, sensing the game was getting away from his team, called timeout. The huddle during the break was typical for the fiery coach. He began by barking about how poorly the team was playing, venting his considerable frustration at having fallen behind his alma mater, one of the Big Five. Moran then moved onto the positive—a lot of time was left, Maryland couldn't possibly continue playing so well, and Cornell was the better team anyway. "He'd start a timeout by coming in pretty strong," Bray says. "He'd cut you down a little bit, then build you back up. He never left you on a negative note. He always sent us back out feeling positive."[16]

By this time, Maryland's players, eyeing a third NCAA title in four years, had become talkative. Cornell players recall being called "country bumpkins" and told to "go back to upstate New York," among other things.[17] McEneaney wasn't above a little trash talk himself. One teammate recalls a running conversation between McEneaney and Farrell, with McEneaney yelling out loud every time he was going to take Farrell to the goal, saying that for a first-team all-American Farrell wasn't all that good. "He was driving Mike crazy," Muehleman says.[18] (Farrell says he has no recollection of McEneaney's running commentary.)[19] With the game threatening to get out of hand, Cornell steadied itself and made it to halftime without any further damage—other than trailing by five goals to one of the best teams of all time. Mackesey had made twelve saves, and the man-down defense had not given up a goal in five opportunities. Very little else was going Cornell's way.

At halftime Vincent Paterno, covering the game for the *Diamondback*, the Maryland student newspaper, sat in the narrow press box and listened to the conversations of the writers around him. All seemed confident that Maryland would win. "The numero uno T-shirts Cornell fans wore," he would write in the June 3 editions, "looked as apropos as a McGovern-Eagleton button."

Underneath the main set of stands, Moran went to work. He had been offered the large locker room in the basement of Marvel Gym across the street—the one used by visiting football teams. In a nod to the Big Red's underdog status, Moran opted instead for the tiny visitors' locker room underneath the main set of stands at Brown Stadium. (Maryland, as the higher seed, was given the Brown football team's home locker room.) With little ventilation, the air inside was heavy and still; Bray recalled thinking back to his childhood and being inside a silo. While players sipped Coca Cola, the preferred halftime energy drink, from wax cups, Moran went to the lime-green chalkboard and described two plays he wanted to run in the second half, the white *X*s and *O*s and arrows chalked alongside the usual litany of phrases the coach had calmly written ninety minutes before the game.

Moran also reminded the team of all the work it had done, all the mile, two-mile, and three-mile runs up and down the hilly campus in Ithaca even amid snow and ice (called "sweat hog runs") and all the practices in frigid Ithaca's early spring weather; the late nights in the polo barns playing box lacrosse games while much of the rest of the campus was sleeping or studying. "I think that's why he gave every [workout] a name," Muehleman says now. "So he could refer to it when he needed to use it as motivation, reminding us of the sweat hog runs.

'You guys have worked your ass off, nobody has worked harder than you, now go out and take this game.'"[20] Moran also took a shot at Beardmore, his close friend, saying Beardmore used to carry Moran's sticks to and from practice when the two were teammates at Maryland. It wasn't true but it was meant to give the Cornell players a boost, a little levity.[21] Moran's audience, in the stifling heat, shifted nervously. Despite Moran's effusiveness, they were unsure. Levine, scoreless in the first half, slipped on a different pair of cleats. "I was just trying anything to bring a little luck," he says now.[22] Muehleman recalled his days at Sewanhaka High with McEneaney, on teams that cruised through the regular season only to fall in the playoffs. "This is just like high school," Muehleman thought at halftime. "We're going to get all the way and then lose again."[23]

McEneaney, the ultracompetitive athlete, carried with him a burden: On the morning of May 29, 1976, he had yet to win a championship at any level, in any sport.[24] Whenever his lacrosse teammates wanted to tease the ultracompetitive attackman, the cudgel they most often used was to remind him of that fact.[25] That Cornell was losing to Maryland would have been particularly galling to McEneaney. Three years earlier he had told Beardmore that rather than accepting a full scholarship to Maryland, he would attend Cornell, working several summer jobs to do so, and would win a national title. What McEneaney remembered most about the moment was Beardmore's laughter.

Moran remained at the chalkboard, collecting his thoughts. The tiny room was steamy and silent. Then a voice broke through, high-pitched, with a Long Island accent. It was McEneaney. "It was unusual," Mackesey said later, "because Eamon didn't normally talk much at halftime. But he became pretty animated in that locker room."[26] McEneaney began calmly, almost like a professor conducting a class. "What are we going to do about this, guys?" Without waiting for an answer he continued, words flying at a rapid pace. If the players had stared at the ground for Moran's words, they looked up to hear their teammate, the Ivy League Player of the Year, the all-American attackman and starting wide receiver who worked three summer jobs to afford Cornell when he could have been in the more spacious home team locker room, playing for Maryland and receiving free tuition, with at least one NCAA championship wristwatch already in his possession. McEneaney continued speaking, his teammates slowly nodding their heads, when he reached his crescendo: "The team that wins this game," he roared, "is the team that loves each other more. And we love each other more than Maryland."

"After hearing him," Malm says, "we were ready to tear the locker room door down to take the field."[27] Moran, with his own motivational speech at the ready, quickly decided to say nothing. He simply waved the team onto the field. Moran later said that the people in the stands seeing Cornell emerge so early might have thought the coach had dismissed the players because he was angry. "That wasn't the case," he says now. "I just didn't need to say anything more after what Eamon said."[28]

Kim Eike, the team's public-address announcer and statistician, spent the game sitting at the wooden scorer's table between the two benches, Maryland on his left, Cornell on his right. At halftime he had stayed on the field to escape the suffocating confines of the tiny locker room. As the Cornell players began warming up for the second half, throwing the ball loosely in groups of twos and threes, Eike walked onto the field and approached midfielder Steve Dybus. Eike suggested Cornell was in significant trouble. "Don't worry," Dybus replied. "'We've got this.'"[29]

The third quarter began. Cornell won the opening face-off, made a quick pass to McEneaney, who fired a laser of a pass to French, who deposited a shot past Reed for a goal. The sequence had taken seventeen seconds. Three-quarters of the ancient stadium erupted in approval.

French had converted a perfect feed from McEneaney on a fast break to cut the deficit to 7–3; the goal clearly calmed the team's nerves. Maryland countered with a score, only for Cornell to go into overdrive. In the third quarter alone French scored two goals and added two assists, and Levine finally broke out of his Providence slump with an unassisted goal late in the third quarter. Malm, one of the team's best defensive midfielders, took a close shot that Maryland's Jake Reed initially saved, but Reed lost control of the ball, and the rebound went back to Malm, who quickly scooped it up and scored to close the deficit to 9–8. (It was Malm's third goal of the year.)

The Big Red became more aggressive on fast breaks and went to more running and cutting when McEneaney held the ball behind Maryland's goal. As the quarter ended, the score was Maryland 9, Cornell 8, and the Cornell fans behind the team bench rose to their feet and cheered. Maryland had the lead, but the Big Red had something perhaps more important: momentum. The *Ithaca Journal* later said that Cornell had played the best third quarter of Moran's tenure. By that point the Big Red had been called for eight penalties, but none had resulted in a Maryland goal, thanks to Waldvogel's well-drilled man-down unit.

Something else was happening—Maryland's midfield, as Moran predicted, was starting to tire. In the third quarter Dybus, from Farmingdale, New York, so small and quick he could be confused with McEneaney on game films, forced a turnover by knocking the much bigger and stronger Urso out of bounds. Early in the fourth quarter Mitchell, the Ithaca native and reserve midfielder who was the hero of the win over W&L, stopped a fast break from the far more heralded Tuck, whose running was still hampered, by catching him from behind and deftly knocking the ball from his stick.

The Terrapins stemmed the tide briefly with a goal by Mullen, assisted by Urso, for a 10–8 lead early in the fourth quarter. Moran, knowing the Big Red needed to regain momentum, called the play that had worked all day: an isolation move for French. The Canadian attackman raced past Bethmann and, when he reached the middle of the restraining box, fired a low shot that eluded Reed to make it a one-goal game: 10–9. It was French's sixth shot. Five had been goals. For the fourth quarter the Big Red offense was shooting at the goal at the end of Brown Stadium, where most of their fans were seated. Barrows, on the sideline between the teams, remembers the ninth Cornell goal; the noise that followed was deafening.

The Big Red still trailed by a goal when, on its ensuing possession, French drove the ball toward the middle of the restraining box. Given the success he had enjoyed to that point, he drew the attention of almost every Maryland defender. Billy Marino made a backdoor cut and French, with only one hand on his stick, tossed a pinpoint pass to Marino, who was wide open in front of the goal. Marino shot the ball past Reed, to tie the game at ten. Around nine minutes remained. The red-clad fans behind Cornell's bench roared while on the field Moran turned to them and began pumping his fist. On the *Wide World of Sports* broadcast, Corrigan said the only other player he had ever seen execute a one-handed pass was NFL Hall of Famer Jim Brown, during his lacrosse playing days in the 1950s at Syracuse. The game still was tied when French gained possession and backed his defender toward the goal. Again he drew attention from the Maryland defense. This time French, his back still to the goal, tossed a behind-the-back, no-look pass to Levine, who caught it in front of the goal, took two steps to improve his shooting angle, and scored. The Big Red led, 11–10, and French and Levine had executed the very same move they had used in the opening game for the freshman team in 1973, in sudden death overtime against Farmingdale Community College.

Now it was Beardmore who was forced to call a timeout as Cornell's fans rose to their feet shouting, "Let's go Red!" Beardmore gathered the team in a loose huddle. "It's your ballgame," he told them, straining to be heard above the Cornell partisans. "If you play smart lacrosse. For 15, 16 minutes you haven't played good, smart lacrosse. Let's see if we can get it back."[30] Having seen French riddle his defense for five goals and two assists, before the Terrapins retook the field, Beardmore switched that assignment and told Ratliff to guard the Canadian.

But French was not the only Big Red player hurting Maryland. Junior Brian Lasda, the one-time football recruit, was dominating face-offs, so much so that Maryland benched its other face-off specialists and as a desperation move began using its best player, Urso. Leading 11–10, Lasda won the ensuing face-off, and the ball went again to French, guarded by Ratliff. French began running from the left wing into the middle of the offensive box, fifteen yards from the goal. Ratliff ran with him stride for stride, staying on French's hip, as defenders are taught. Almost midstride, French uncorked a sidearm shot, a seemingly nonchalant effort, something seen often in box lacrosse but rarely in the outdoor version. The ball eluded a surprised Reed and went into the goal. Cornell led 12–10 with about five minutes to play. It was French's seventh shot; six had been goals. The Cornell fans exchanged high-fives, the players on the bench screaming and jumping. Maryland gained possession and, with little more than three minutes to play, the Big Red was called for its tenth penalty. Maryland went on extra-man offense. To that point the unit had been on the field nine times without scoring on any of them. In desperation Maryland turned to brute force—Urso's ten-yard blast from the left wing, on a sidearm right-handed shot, eluded Mackesey to make the score 12–11 with exactly three minutes remaining.

The teams battled back and forth from there, but neither was able to score. Cornell still led by a goal with fifteen seconds left when Urso gained possession and made a desperate run into the middle of the defense. From the scorer's table a horn sounded, but play on the field continued. The Cornell defenders forced Urso away from the middle of the restraining box and into less advantageous real estate to his left. Urso took an off-balance, off-hand shot that was saved by Mackesey. The rebound remained on the grass, neither team gaining possession, until a Cornell defender kicked it nearly to midfield. Seven seconds remained, then six seconds. The Cornell fans, sensing victory, were standing and chanting, "We're number one!" Dozens of Cornell students, seated on the side opposite the team benches, inched onto the black cinder track, ready to storm the field.

Suddenly, the referees blew their whistles. Everything on the field stopped. The fans, who had been standing and screaming, remained standing but stopped cheering. Eike, at the official scorer's table, was one of the few people among the coaches, players, ABC-TV camera operators, announcers Frank Gifford and Gene Corrigan, and nearly twelve thousand fans who knew what was going on. "Some idiot at the scorer's table blew the horn to stop the game," Eike says now. "And that idiot was me."[31]

In the final seconds, as it became apparent that Urso's mad dash would be fruitless, Maryland's assistant coaches began screaming that Cornell had too many players on the field and was also offside. Either penalty would have stopped the game once the ball hit the ground—as it had done after Mackesey saved Urso's shot—and given Maryland an extra-man opportunity. Eike, hearing the Maryland coaches to his left screaming at him about a penalty, blew the sideline horn, essentially a Marine signal boat horn, to signify there should be a stoppage in play.

Though the scoreboard clock read "0:00," the universal sign indicating the game was over, the referees indicated that the game had not officially ended. Instead they walked toward the scorer's table, placed between both team benches, while a bitter back-and-forth between Maryland's coaches and Moran added even more heat to the early-summer afternoon. "Relax! Relax!" yelled one of the referees to both sidelines. Then the main referee turned to Eike and the team manager from Maryland, not sure which one had initiated the stoppage in play. "What was the horn for?"[32]

"I've tried to block it completely out of my mind," Eike says now. "But I think it was something where they [Maryland] thought Cornell had gone offside and wanted me to stop the game. I thought it was a reasonable thing to do, though Lord knows I was the only one who thought that."[33] Barrows was standing mere feet from the scene, next to the cameraman stationed between the team benches, who was filming the action. Barrows looked at Eike during his explanation, then turned around to see that the referees' faces had turned ashen. "The refs looked at each other," Barrows says, "then looked at [Eike], and said, 'Son, you can't blow the horn for that. You can only blow the horn for an illegal substitution.'" The three referees gathered in a huddle, and Barrows eavesdropped on the conversation. "They were saying," he says, "'Oh, shit, what do we do now?'"

As the packed stadium sat bewildered, the scene on the field was chaos. Urso, with his hands behind his back to appear less threatening, approached each of the referees. "I had the ball, don't forget, I had the ball," he repeated to each of them. "I kept telling them, 'When the horn sounded, I had the ball.'"[34] At the scorer's table Moran, his face red in anger, shouted the game should be over; time had expired. Beardmore wanted the game to resume with time left on the clock, so his team could have one last desperate chance. After several minutes the referees emerged from their huddle. They pointed at midfield, asked for six seconds to be put back on the clock. There would be one face-off at midfield. Urso crouched to take it against Henrickson. Then came another whistle. One referee went between the two players and picked up the ball, then went back into a huddle with the other two officials.

They emerged minutes later and walked to the scorer's table. They requested six seconds to be put back on the clock, then pointed to a spot on the field about thirty-five yards from the Cornell goal and said the game would resume with Urso in possession. Moran was enraged, his arguments so heated some of his spittle accidentally landed on Barrows. By then, officials from the NCAA had arrived on the scene, and Moran told them he was playing the game under protest. Moran also berated the referee assigned to the sideline closest to the Cornell bench, as did McEneaney, who was pulled away by a teammate before he could be assessed an unsportsmanlike conduct penalty.

Moran, mastering himself and realizing the game was not over, turned to Waldvogel to plot the last passage of defensive play. To that point Urso had scored two goals but one came on extra-man offense; the efforts of Malm, Henrickson, and others had kept him relatively quiet. For the final possession Waldvogel suggested Urso be covered by Henrickson. Moran agreed. The sophomore from Long Island whose first lacrosse stick as a teen was, by his request, the same model he had seen Urso use, was inserted into the game to guard one of the only players in the sport's history to be named a four-time, first-team all-American.[35] Before Henrickson took the field a still clearly agitated Moran told him if it became necessary he should simply tackle Urso. It would be a penalty but not enough time remained for Maryland to have a serious chance on extra-man. Henrickson took the field knowing that behind him was Mackesey, who to that point had made twenty-seven saves. Joining Henrickson was the starting defense—Muehleman, Marchell, and Katz, plus senior midfielders Albin Haglund and Mitchell. (Incredibly, three of the seven—Mackesey, Marchell, and Mitchell—had been in the same class at Boynton Junior High on North Cayuga Street in Ithaca.)

On the other sideline Beardmore, the riverboat gambler, rolled the dice once more. He inserted into the lineup the starting attack—Caswell, Mullen, and Lamon. To this he added both of his first-team all-American midfielders, Urso and Tuck. The sixth player was left-handed freshman Greg Rumpf, nominally a third-line midfielder. Rumpf took the field having scored nine goals all year.

Finally, after a lengthy delay—"it wasn't thirty minutes," Barrows says, "but it wasn't five minutes either"—play resumed. Urso, beginning thirty-five yards from the cage and just outside the restraining box, ran with the ball. Henrickson let him have a slip of free space, believing it preferable to give up a long shot from Urso, on the run and not the more dangerous shot with his feet set, and facing the best goalie in college lacrosse. Henrickson had not counted on a teammate thinking trouble was afoot. Cornell's Mitchell had a choice: Stay with his man, Rumpf, or leave Rumpf open to try and stop Urso with a double-team. Mitchell decided that Urso was more of a threat, and he began running toward the white number 21 jersey.

Urso says he expected Cornell to try and get the ball out of his stick as soon as possible, and he was looking to pass all along. When the Cornell defense moved, Urso struck: He passed to the lefty freshman Rumpf, left wide open by Mitchell's gamble. Rumpf received the ball, with time only to turn toward the goal and shoot. He did. The ball eluded Mackesey and went into the goal to tie the game at twelve. One second remained. "He beat me near post," Mackesey says. "Cardinal sin for a goalie."[36] As several Maryland players stormed the field to celebrate, Urso sank to his knees for a moment, then emerged leaping in the air and pumping his first.

On the Cornell side, Moran angrily pointed his finger in the face of one of the referees, then had to pull McEneaney away from confronting the same referee. The game was headed to overtime, for two four-minute sessions and then, if still tied, to sudden death. Years later, Mackesey says he saw Mitchell at a reunion. Mitchell went over to the goalie and said without preamble, "I never should have slid to Urso."[37]

In overtime, after thirty-four seconds had elapsed, Maryland scored first, a goal by freshman Terry Kimball, assisted by Lamon, for a 13–12 lead. At least one Cornell player on the sideline was devastated. "I thought the game was over," Bray says now. "I still didn't really know the rules for the outdoor game." When the game restarted with a face-off, Bray was stunned. "I thought to myself, 'How did Richie pull *that* off?'"[38] Less than one minute later, the Big Red had a fast break, and Billy Marino drew the defense and passed to Henrickson, who converted a close shot off a perfect pass to tie the game. The Big Red regained possession, and Marino dodged from the left wing and converted a close shot past Reed. The Big Red led, 14–13, with about a minute left in the first half of overtime. That was the score at the end of the first four-minute session. The Cornell players gathered in a huddle on the field around Moran. "At that point," Levine says now, "we got serious." In the second session the teams traded possession without further scores. Little more than one minute remained when Levine was free from about twelve yards in the middle of the restraining box. He unleashed a shot, then absorbed a crunching, legal hit to the midsection by one of the frustrated Maryland defenders as the ball left his stick. The shot eluded Reed, and the Big Red had extended the lead to 15–13. The Cornell faithful in the stands began to celebrate again, and several students returned to the black cinder track surrounding the field, ready to storm the grass field if the Big Red could hold on.

With thirty seconds to play, his team trailing 15–13, Urso had the ball deep in Maryland's territory when all three Cornell attackman—the French Connection—swarmed him, bearing witness once again to the group's ability to do more than score points. McEneaney emerged with the ball, the elusive championship now quite literally in his grasp. But McEneaney, rather than running out the clock, began a sprint toward the Maryland goalkeeper. To that point McEneaney had been held quiet, statistically speaking, by Farrell; he had no goals and two assists. Here was his chance at redemption, to secure and even punctuate his first championship with a goal, before nearly twelve thousand fans and a national TV audience.

Three weeks later, when people tuned into *Wide World of Sports* and saw the lacrosse highlights sandwiched between a report from the third round of the US Open golf tournament in Duluth, Georgia, and the World Cliff Diving Championships in Acapulco, Mexico, they did not see McEneaney score.[39] Nor did the crowd in attendance that day. At the last instant McEneaney flipped a pass to French, running just behind him. French caught the ball and scored past Reed for a 16–13 lead with nine seconds to play. It was French's eighth shot of the warm, early-summer afternoon. Seven had been goals.[40] Later, amid the celebrations, someone asked McEneaney why he hadn't shot the ball himself. Here he revealed his gap-toothed, waif-like grin. "Nah," he replied. "It was Frenchie's day."[41]

Seconds later the game ended, Cornell 16, Maryland 13. McEneaney and Muehleman, Sewanhaka High teammates who had endured their share of disappointment on the big stage, made eye contact from fifty yards away, sprinted to each other and embraced near midfield. Moran turned and hugged trainer Rick LaFrance, while the Cornell players threw their sticks and gloves and helmets into the air as if it were a graduation ceremony. On the other sideline, several Maryland players sat with their heads in their hands as parents and friends made their way slowly onto the field to console them.

Moran, the ambassador for lacrosse, basked in victory over his alma mater, the referees, and the Baltimore establishment, all while knowing the game would be, for those who tuned into *Wide World of Sports* later that summer, the best possible advertisement for the sport. He was in such a good mood that he even forgave Kane for his loquacious radio interview the previous week. The smiling coach approached Kane and began with one of his favorite phrases, which could be employed as a compliment, insult, and everything in between. "Big boy," Moran said. "That locker room stunt really set the table. It broke the ice and helped us laugh and relax."[42]

If the moment was sweet relief for McEneaney, and vindication for Moran, for Mackesey it was bittersweet. He had finished with twenty-eight saves, a school record that would stand for more than a decade. But his father, who had spent almost his entire professional life at Cornell and had sent four sons there, was not in attendance. On the morning of May 2, Thomas Mackesey, battling cancer, slipped into a coma. Cornell was set to play Yale at Schoellkopf Field that afternoon, and the family insisted that Dan Mackesey take part, mindful both of Cornell's undefeated season and how much the elder Mackesey had enjoyed watching the season's games from the front seat of the Winnebago.

Dan and the rest of the family, all except his mother, left the house on North Cayuga Street and headed to Schoellkopf Field for the game, while his mother continued her bedside vigil.[43] On a perfect, sunny, seventy-degree day, the first quarter ended with the Big Red leading 9–0. It extended the lead to 14–0 before Mackesey gave up a goal with twenty-two seconds left in the first half.[44] At halftime, the victory secured—Cornell won, 19–5—Mackesey returned to his father's bedside. Two hours later Thomas Mackesey died. He was sixty-seven years old.

FIGURE 10.3.   The thrill of victory: Cornell coach Richie Moran hugs trainer Rick LaFrance as the players celebrate their 16–13 overtime victory over Maryland in the 1976 title game at Brown Stadium. Extended highlights were later broadcast on ABC's seminal *Wide World of Sports*. (Photo courtesy Larry Baum)

Moran had lost his father when he was a sophomore at Maryland and never forgot the support he received from his own coaches. As ever, Moran paid it forward. In the spring of 1976, in the locker room before practice, while "Frampton Comes Alive" was blaring and players were laughing and joking, Moran would whisper encouragement to his starting goalie, asking how he was doing, how he was feeling, how was his mother doing, and his brothers. On May 5, a memorial service was held at Cornell's Sage Chapel. Mackesey recalls looking out at the full house and seeing Moran, Waldvogel, and every lacrosse player wearing jackets and ties. It was an ordeal, one that united Moran and Mackesey. "Richie was important to me during that period. He knew what I was going through," Mackesey says now. "He was like a second father to me at the time. He was always checking on me to make sure I was okay."[45] After the championship was won, as the early-summer afternoon turned to evening, the NCAA mandated there be an on-field awards ceremony. Every Cornell player was to receive a handshake from an NCAA official, a championship medal, and a handshake from Moran. The sweaty, smiling conveyor belt moved quickly, and on a team of free spirits it was the studious Mackesey who broke ranks. He politely greeted the NCAA official, received his medal, shook Moran's hand, then gave his coach a quick kiss on the cheek.[46]

By then the Maryland players were either still in the locker room or in the parking lot, staring glumly at their beers and tailgate food.[47] Tuck, first-team all-American midfielder who, in his final game, finished without a goal or assist, was not in either location. He had been taken to the hospital, where it was determined that he had played the final two-plus quarters of his final college game with a fractured scapular—or broken shoulder. When the all-American teams were announced the next day, Cornell had ten honorees—three attackmen, four midfielders, two defensemen, and Mackesey. Maryland boasted eight. Both teams had beaten the Mount Washington Lacrosse Club, which would win the post-collegiate club championship. Cornell had also beaten Hobart, which won the NCAA Division II title that year. "It was a clash of the titans," Levine says of the title game against Maryland. "They had a great team but somebody had to win."[48] Mullen's reaction was more simple: "Losing that game sucked."[49]

Cornell's team bus pulled out of Brown University and headed toward Bloomfield, Connecticut, where the parents of the girlfriend of one of Cornell's players were hosting a party. The house included a swimming pool, and as Mackesey remembers, every room in the house had a television, an extreme rarity in the 1970s. As the bus pulled away, Kane stood up and asked a question. "Anyone who has never lost a college game, please stand up," he said, his voice rising amid the catcalls. "If anyone on this bus is 26–0, please stand up now." The sophomores on the team had gone 10–0 and 16–0, respectively. The freshmen, finally eligible for varsity, also had yet to lose a game. As their older teammates shouted good-natured protests and insults, roughly half the players on the bus slowly got to their feet.[50]

The controversy in the final stages of regulation in the 1976 title game led to changes from the NCAA. Starting in 1977, the college sports governing body placed officials not associated with either team at the scorer's table, alongside the scorekeepers from the respective schools. Only the NCAA officials have access to the Marine signal horn that can stop play. Barrows, the unlikely eyewitness to history, made history of a different sort a few weeks after the 1976 title game, when he was named a high-school all-American, the first Moses Brown School player to receive the honor. Barrows played four years of football and lacrosse at Brown University. As a senior in the spring of 1980, the Bears entered the regular-season finale against Cornell with a lot on the line: the winner would claim the Ivy League title and a berth in the NCAA tournament. The loser's season would end. Barrows also was three goals from tying the Brown single-game record for goals in a season. The game at Schoellkopf Field went to overtime tied at 9, and

Cornell won, 10–9. Barrows scored two goals, leaving him one short of the record and one short of a berth in the NCAA tournament. His college career was over. After the postgame handshakes, the first person to greet Barrows was Moran. The Cornell coach grabbed Barrows's shoulder, looked him in the eye, and told him what a strong game he had played.

Weeks after the 1976 championship game, Marchell wrote a three-page letter to his teammates who would return for the 1977 season, exhorting them to repeat as champions. Marchell's brother found a copy of the letter in November 2014, days after Ted had died suddenly at the age of sixty-two. Marchell's memorial service was held inside Immaculate Conception Catholic Church in Ithaca. Amid the beige walls and gothic arches, his brother's eulogy included an excerpt from that letter, specifically the section toward the end, about what had separated Cornell from Maryland on that glorious early-summer New England afternoon in the bicentennial year. "I tried to break down our success formula to the very basics," Ted Marchell had written, "and I think that I came up with our championship formula. We were a team that loved lacrosse, loved to win, but most of all, we loved each other. That may sound a little heavy, but when you think about it thats [*sic*] what it was all about. Richie always said it was the team with the most heart that would win, and he was never more right. Eamon said it best during the championship game. . . . 'You know why we are a better team than Maryland, it is because we love each other.'"

FLAMIN' EAMON

In the 1976 playoffs, for the first time, a team from Maryland failed to win either NCAA title. Instead, both championships went to the Finger Lakes region, thanks to Cornell's victory in Providence and the title won by Hobart on the Division II level. Hobart won its title with only one Maryland native on its twenty-six-man roster; Cornell had three. The Baltimore establishment noticed both the trend, and that it had begun around the time of the first NCAA tournament, in 1971. "Hobart is loaded with players from upstate New York," wrote James H. Jackson in the *Baltimore Sun* soon after the Division I title game, "where the game of lacrosse has flourished in the past five years. In addition to an excellent high school program, the upstate New York area also now has junior and midget leagues and is instituting summer leagues in order to get more talented players. Maryland and Long Island for the past 25 years have been the areas that sent most players to major colleges, but now the upstate New York is competing almost on a par with these two areas."[1]

The article also made mention of the youth leagues starting in New England. In Rhode Island it was called "mini lacrosse," founded by Wayne Curtis, the head coach at Moses Brown. It may have been a coincidence, but Curtis started the league in the summer of 1976, just after the NCAA title game was played in Providence.[2] The sport was growing, and the new plastic sticks were at least part of the reason. "The plastic sticks changed the game mostly because little kids could learn it far easier," says Jeff Wagner, who played at Brown in the 1970s and later worked for Boston-based Brine Sporting Goods, which produced lacrosse equipment. "The sticks also became far easier to find and to buy. With wood sticks you were looking for the perfect stick with the perfect weight. With plastic sticks they were all perfect. In the 1970s in Columbus, Ohio, we had a huge youth group playing lacrosse. If we'd had to depend on wood sticks, that league would never have developed. I defy you to think of another sport where a change in technology had such a big difference."[3]

Further evidence of the sport's growth came from the NCAA itself. The *Official Lacrosse Guide*, the publication released by the governing body every year, included a section on the game at the high-school level, complete with a directory of every high-school program and its record the previous spring. For the 1969 season, the guide listed 189 high-school programs. By 1977, the number had jumped to 413.

Lacrosse's growth spurt was felt at Cornell, but the program's 1976 success was rare good news in what was becoming a troubling era for the Big Red athletic department. On July 1, 1976, athletic director Bob Kane's thirty-seven-year tenure at the university ended when he left his alma mater and home town to take a job with the US Olympic Committee. As he told the *Ithaca Journal* a few days before leaving Cornell, "The final five years were a struggle." The previous two had been particularly trying. In 1974, citing a lack of funds, Cornell cut four sports—squash, sailing, riflery, and skiing.[4] In the fall of 1975, under first-year coach George Seifert, the football team won once in eight games and dealt with several players who left the program, including expected starting wide receiver Eamon McEneaney. In the winter and spring of 1976, the final six months of Kane's tenure, three coaches resigned suddenly; two, the fencing coach and the men's soccer coach, both at one time extremely successful, directed their frustration at the Cornell group of faculty, students, and staff that originated in 1970 to have a stronger, more unified voice on campus-related issues. The coaches "pointed an accusatory finger at the University Senate," wrote the *Ithaca Journal*, "saying it was unsympathetic to the needs of intercollegiate athletics, and unknowledgeable about the role of athletics at the university."

This was exacerbated by financial woes in the athletic department. Cornell's athletics' deficits "continued to soar in 1975," wrote the *Ithaca Journal*, "and sports that didn't have rich alumni backers suffered."[5] It put into context Moran's creativity in raising funds, from enlisting the Harlem Globetrotters to play in Barton Hall in November 1970, to cleaning Schoellkopf Field with his players the day after home football games—lacrosse players on the football team were exempted—and selling T-shirts and sun visors at the 1975 North–South All-Star lacrosse game at Schoellkopf Field. For the 1977 season Moran had already figured out his fundraiser. He ordered dozens of twenty-four-ounce, white ceramic mugs with the Cornell University logo, the words "The Perfect Season," the 1976 season results, and the last names of every player on the roster, written in script italics.

Richard D. Schultz, Kane's replacement as athletic director, would not take over until July. He had been hired nearly three months earlier, on April 8, 1976, the day after Cornell defeated Rutgers in lacrosse. Schultz was coming from the University of Iowa, where he was an athletic administrator after having been, at different times, the Hawkeyes' baseball coach and basketball coach. In Ithaca he was introduced at a news conference at the West Lounge of Cornell's Statler Inn. He said his first order of business was to create "a positive image for Cornell athletics." Schultz was charged with overseeing a department with twenty-two men's varsity sports, eighteen women's varsity sports, and a budget of $2.1 million. Schultz's oldest child was enrolled at Cornell as a graduate student, so the new hire knew something about the school. He was not as familiar with its second most popular sport, behind men's hockey. "He knew nothing about lacrosse," says Terry Cullen, then Cornell's 150-pound football coach. "I think he thought it was sort of strange, how everyone knew each other in lacrosse." Moran says he got along with Schultz well, in large part because Schultz, unlike many other athletic administrators, had previously been a coach and understood the pressures of the position.

The Cornell athletic department was struggling, but outside Ithaca, college lacrosse programs were stealing ideas from Moran. In College Park the Terrapins' recruiting class arriving on campus in the fall of 1977 included a pair of freshmen from Windsor, Ontario, each of whom had exceled in box lacrosse.[6] Ron and Wayne Martinello, twin brothers, were the program's first recruits from Canada. Johns Hopkins had its own contributor from Canada, sophomore midfielder Dave Huntley. The Baltimore establishment was dipping into Richie Moran's playbook. The evolution of Cornell's plan was evident.

In the summer of 1976, fresh from winning his first championship in Providence, McEneaney went back to Long Island and again found work that would help him pay Cornell's tuition. (Much of his work in the summer came at the properties in Manhattan where his father worked; one summer, the youngest McEneaney operated a freight elevator.) In mid-August McEneaney decided to play football one last time. He arrived in Ithaca, tried out for and made the team, and for the season opener, earned a spot as a starting wide receiver. In the opening game, against Colgate on September 25, McEneaney finished with ten receptions—one short of a school record—for 112 yards in a 25–20 loss. The following week the Big Red traveled to Piscataway, New Jersey, to face Rutgers. Attending that October 2 game was New York Jets assistant coach Joe Gardi, in town to scout two players from Rutgers. That afternoon McEneaney finished with nine receptions for 114 yards and two touchdowns. The Scarlet Knights won, 21–14, but it was McEneaney who had landed on the Jets' radar. "He hadn't trained or anything,"

Gary Malm says now. "He just showed up and was playing. That's how good an athlete he was."[7]

The Big Red football team again struggled, winning only twice in nine games. But McEneaney thrived. He led the team with thirty-five receptions for 383 yards and caught the only three touchdown passes that Cornell threw that season. Lacrosse teammate Bob Henrickson, the other starting wide receiver, led Cornell with a 14.7 yards-per-reception average. A junior-college transfer named Craig Jaeger, from Nassau Community College, was a reserve running back in football and was also set to be a midfielder for the Big Red lacrosse team. And Dan Mackesey, like McEneaney a returning first-team all-American in lacrosse, missed the fall workouts while being the starting goalkeeper for Cornell's soccer team, which reached the NCAA tournament before losing in the first round to Hartwick, 1–0.

In lacrosse, McEneaney, Mackesey, and senior Gary Malm, who had been on campus only one year following his transfer from Nassau Community College, were voted captains. Malm was the only one around the team in the fall. He was the best defensive midfielder and would be the main short-stick defender on the man-down unit. Malm, 6'2", 185 pounds, had been a standout football quarterback and safety at West Islip High on Long Island. He was recruited by several Division I football programs and as a senior in 1973 took an official visit to an Atlantic Coast Conference school as a football recruit. He was joined by more than two dozen standouts from Long Island.

What he found was an alcohol binge of a weekend. The recruits were taken to a bar. One of the upperclassmen not only brought his Labrador dog to the bar, he poured it a beer and everyone cheered as the dog jumped onto the bar and began to drink it.[8] Later, back in the dormitory, the players took turns seeing who could leave the biggest dent in the front door using only their shoulder. "I returned home," Malm says now, "and told my mom, 'Ma, I don't think college football is for me.'"[9] Malm enrolled at Nassau Community College to play lacrosse. Later he took a recruiting trip to Johns Hopkins and met with then-coach Bob Scott but did not select the Blue Jays for an unusual reason. "I wasn't sure I was good enough to play there," he says now.[10] Instead he chose Cornell, partly because his uncle was an alum and because he had received a Regents scholarship to help lower his tuition at schools in New York state. But mostly he was drawn by Moran, the Long Island native. "There was such a connection between Long Island and Cornell and Richie Moran," Malm says now. "Most of the great players [on Long Island] weren't thinking of going anywhere but Cornell."[11]

That was true for Moran's top two newcomers in 1977. Steve Page was a speedy attackman-midfielder from Levittown, New York, and Farmingdale Community College; and Jaeger was a sturdy midfielder from Massapequa, New York, and Nassau Community College, where he had been a two-time all-American and

FIGURE 11.0. Tom Marino celebrates his clinching goal against Johns Hopkins in 1977. Marino was in his first year as a starter on attack. (Photo courtesy Larry Baum)

two-time most valuable player in the junior-college national title game. It was Jaeger who, two years earlier, after his shot ripped through the net in the game against Cornell's freshmen, screamed in vain when referees ruled the shot had gone wide. Cornell won by a goal. "We all knew it had gone in," says Keith Reitenbach, who as a junior in 1977 had been on the field that day.

Cornell's starting attack was set to look very different. The previous two years, the French Connection had clearly defined roles. Mike French was physical, sometimes drawing attention before passing to an open teammate, sometimes taking a no-look or behind-the-back shot from any angle, and he had led the nation in scoring all three years he was eligible for varsity competition. Jon Levine, often left open because of attention paid to McEnaney and French, was unerringly accurate from the wing, and understood off-ball movement to perfection, knowing exactly where to find pockets of open space; he finished his senior year with fifty goals.

In 1977 the starting attack was comprised of small, speedy, athletic players. Junior Tom Marino, 5'8", 160 pounds, was the team's best shooter and was moving from midfield, where he had played primarily on the second line. Junior John Sierra, 5'11", 170 pounds, was a rare four-sport athlete at Hempstead High on Long Island, having played football, soccer, wrestling, and lacrosse. He scored ten goals in the undefeated 1976 season as a reserve midfielder. McEneaney was set to continue working behind the goal, as he had with French and Levine, and the longtime Moran maxim of having the best offensive player be in possession when play restarts following shots that are wide but backed up by the offense, again meant that McEneaney would be starting most possessions with the ball in his stick.

Without French, Levine, and Billy Marino, a first-team all-American midfielder from the previous year, McEneaney would be called on to control the ball more, to initiate the offense, looking for open teammates while protecting his stick from the checks of defensemen. Sometimes, while scanning the field, McEneaney looked like a tango dancer, hopping three steps one way with his back to the defender to protect his stick, then three steps in the other direction, while waiting for a teammate to pop open even for a second or two.

With his remarkable speed—one teammate said McEneaney ran the forty-yard dash in 4.7 seconds, and was especially fast in the ten-yard shuttle run—McEneaney could have created shots for himself almost at will. And there were times he would use his speed to race from the area behind the goal to right in front of the crease, the three-foot circle around the goal into which offensive players are not allowed to set foot; if they do, it is an infraction, and the opposing team gains possession. But the close shots in the 1970s were not the boondoggle they would appear. The lacrosse stick heads had almost no pocket; the slightest touch from a defender could dislodge the ball easily. McEneaney often moved right to the top of the crease, so close to the open goal he could have reached out and almost touched it, with a goal seemingly certain to follow, only for a nudge from a desperate, less-skilled defender to make the slightest contact with McEneaney's stick to knock the ball to the ground or in the air, just as McEneaney was poised to put the ball into the goal. It could lead to frantic passages of play, with some of the best players in the sport's history struggling to gain control of the ball. Out of context, they would have looked like newcomers to the sport. When Moran was asked to describe McEneaney to someone who had never seen him play, the comparison his coach most often used was to say that McEneaney was the lacrosse version of Fran Tarkenton, then one of the NFL's top quarterbacks for the Minnesota Vikings, known for his scrambling and his ability to improvise successful plays, all while avoiding much larger defenders. (Tarkenton, like McEneaney, also wore jersey number 10.)

Team statistician Kim Eike likened McEneaney to another pro athlete, hockey great Wayne Gretzky, because both passed not to where a player was but to where the player was supposed to be.[12] In three years on the Sewanhaka varsity, McEneaney accumulated 152 career assists. As a sophomore at Cornell, he finished with sixty-five, followed by sixty-one as a junior. When Moran watched McEneaney

FIGURE 11.1. "Lacrosse Superman," read one headline regarding Eamon McEneaney, shown taking part in a ten-man ride in searing heat during the 1977 title game against Johns Hopkins. As a senior that year, McEneaney led the Big Red in assists, points, and penalties. (Photo courtesy Larry Baum)

on the lacrosse field, he was constantly reminded of a line attributed to UCLA basketball coach John Wooden, who won ten NCAA titles: A good player makes himself better, a great player makes those around him better. And as the final seconds of the previous year's NCAA title game showed, when McEneaney passed up a certain goal to let French take the shot instead, McEneaney had no interest in his own scoring totals. He just wanted to win.

The starting midfield featured Jaeger, Henrickson, and senior Dave Bray, the latest in a long line of Cornell players who had not played lacrosse for their high school. In Bray's case, Gowanda High, forty miles south of Buffalo, did not offer the sport. Instead, Bray played box lacrosse, popular among the Native American tribes in New York and Canada (Bray was a member of the Seneca Nation). In box lacrosse he learned how to take a scoop shot— a shot that resembles the motion of throwing shoveled snow over one's shoulder, often successful because the goalie was not expecting the shot from such a low angle. Bray also had tremendous speed, as shown by his work with Gowanda High's cross-country and track-and-field teams. In box lacrosse he used his speed and stamina on isolation moves, where he took his defender twenty yards from the goal, then raced toward the goal for a shot or to draw a slide and then pass to an open teammate. Bray, as a sixteen-year-old, was so good in box lacrosse that he was playing in the Senior B league, against grown men. Bray's nickname was "Smiley," partly for his disposition, partly because he had lost several front teeth in an incident during a high-school basketball game.

As a senior at Gowanda High, Bray applied to Cornell but appeared ready to attend Cobleskill Community College, forty-five miles west of Albany, having been drawn by the school's excellent cross-country and lacrosse programs. He planned to study there for two years, then decide which four-year school to attend, if any. An excellent student, Bray also applied to Cornell, at the behest of family members; when he was accepted, his older brothers told him it was a once in a lifetime opportunity. Bray arrived in Ithaca in the fall of 1973 and was living on the North Campus, while the recruited lacrosse players lived on the West Campus. On the first day of tryouts with the freshman team, he was charged with playing defense in a drill. A player ran toward him and Bray, not having faced the situation in box lacrosse, stood still, debating what his move should be. He remained stationary, still deliberating, when the player blew past him and scored a goal. On offense, Bray learned that the Cornell coaches had forbidden the scoop shot. "Richie was a percentages guy," Bray says now. "He thought it was too risky. He probably didn't realize I was doing this shot at home."

But Bray had two distinct advantages. One, his excellent distance running meant he almost always finished near the front of the pack on Moran's "sweat hog" preseason runs around Cornell's campus. (As a junior and senior, Bray sometimes finished more than one minute ahead of his next-fastest teammate, though McEneaney often finished first in the runs as well.) And, while Bray was new to outdoor lacrosse, he was at least facing opponents roughly his own age. "Playing college ball was pretty easy," Bray says, "because you didn't get hit as hard as you did against the men."

Like Cornell's previous box players, Bray had excellent stick skills. After missing much of his freshman year with an injury, and being buried on the depth chart as a sophomore, as a junior in 1976, Bray found a spot on the man-down defense and was inserted into games when Cornell was protecting a lead, when Moran wanted his best stick handlers on the field to retain possession and run out the clock. After growing up using wooden sticks in box lacrosse, Bray says he quickly learned to use a plastic stick, thanks to French, who taught him that weaving leather strings, rather than nylon ones, into the plastic head would make the stick more closely resemble the ones used in box lacrosse.

Off the field, Bray joined midfielder and classmate Brian Lasda in pledging the Sigma Alpha Epsilon fraternity, where McEneaney was working as a dishwasher and later lived in the house in a room available for very low monthly rent. Bray found he could balance lacrosse, academics, and fraternity life if, immediately after practice and dinner, he went to a study carrel in Uris Library until 11 p.m. Then he returned to the SAE house to play cards, listen to music, and hang out. "It was a struggle," Bray says now. "I struggled to balance it all."[13]

Lasda, set to be a primary face-off specialist in 1977, came to Cornell from Tully High School outside Syracuse. He had rushed for nearly thirty-eight hundred yards as a high school running back and received football scholarship offers from Syracuse and Rutgers; he also drew attention from the football staff at Cornell. Lasda's mother and brother were medical professionals, and they convinced him that the offer from Cornell was too good to pass up. Lasda arrived in Ithaca in 1973 ready to play football in the fall and lacrosse in the spring. But he was also intrigued by the entreaty he received from the SAE fraternity. "We were invited to a rush event at 10 o'clock on a Saturday morning," Lasda says now. "I walked in the house and every single brother was still asleep. I thought, this is the place for me." Pledging SAE, he found, was fairly perfunctory, far easier than the secretive, sometimes punishing pledging done by other fraternities on campus, and the process by which the fraternity selected inductees was even more smooth. "It was almost the antithesis of Greek life," Lasda says. "The joke was that SAE stood for 'Somebody, Anybody, Everybody.'"[14] Lasda and Bray had many friends in common back home, and both also got along famously with McEneaney. "My family is from Latvia and I am very proud of that," Lasda says now. "Eamon was a middle-class Irish guy, and he was really proud of that upbringing. So we had similar backgrounds." Bray and McEneaney bonded over their mutual love of wooden sticks and McEneaney's repeated questions about the Native American perspective on lacrosse.

Lasda says that his freshman year was "a lot of partying," and he soon grew disenchanted with football, whose coaches were not enamored of his long hair, and whose practices were more regimented than Lasda would have liked. In the spring of 1974, Lasda wasn't enjoying freshman lacrosse either, struggling to earn playing time. Then, on a trip to Geneva to play the Hobart freshmen, starting face-off man Bray suffered a knee injury. "Bruce [Arena] leaned over and looked down the line of faces and asked, 'Lasda, you ever taken a face-off?' And I said, 'Shit yeah, I have.' I still recall the smirk on his face." Lasda, in fact, had never taken a face-off, but he figured it was his best chance to get into a game.

FIGURE 11.2. Brian Lasda, right, turned down football scholarship offers from Rutgers and Syracuse to attend Cornell. His work on face-offs was crucial in the 1976 title game. (Photo courtesy Larry Baum)

For the face-off one player from each team crouches at midfield, with the ball placed between them. Twenty yards away, on both the left and right wing, are two other players, one from each team. When the referee blows the whistle, the two players at midfield try to win possession, with their teammates joining from the wings to try and scoop any loose ball that pops out. The face-off takes place at the start of every quarter, at the start of overtime, and after every goal, unless one team is serving a penalty.

In a sport that can exhibit grace, finesse, and speed, the face-off is more grunt work, something of a dark art. But it is vitally important. A team with a good face-off specialist can earn several more possessions each game than its opponent, something almost completely unique to lacrosse among other sports, where possessions are distributed almost equally. Moreover, winning three or four (or more) face-offs in a row can lead to the scoring spurts for which lacrosse is known. A three- or four-goal deficit, even in the final minutes of the fourth quarter, is not at all insurmountable if the team in arrears has a good face-off specialist. The Cornell coaches identified Lasda because of his strength, quickness, and low center of gravity, all of which help in winning face-offs.

Against the Hobart freshmen, Lasda entered the game and, relying on his strong lower body and quick hands, helped the Big Red to a 19–2 victory. Soon, he was learning the tricks of taking face-offs from Arena, who had excelled in the craft. "If taking face-offs hadn't happened," Lasda says, "I'm absolutely positive I would not have stayed on the team. I just didn't have the stick skills." With Lasda's low center of gravity—he was 5'11", 210 pounds—and strong legs and upper body, he was perfectly suited for the role. As much as Moran wished he could have had McEneaney on the varsity attack in 1974, Lasda arguably would have helped even more, given Cornell's struggles on face-offs that year, a weakness exacerbated in the NCAA semifinal loss to Maryland in which the Big Red won only nine of thirty-three face-offs. As a junior in 1976, Lasda's work was vitally important in several games, including the comeback wins over Johns Hopkins in the regular season and against Maryland in the NCAA championship.

Had Lasda left the lacrosse program, he would not have been the only casualty from the class of 1977. For numerous reasons, some academic, some injury, some related to disenchantment over a lack of playing time, the freshmen who arrived in Ithaca in the fall of 1973 had, by the spring of 1977, been whittled down to Bray, Lasda, McEneaney, Mackesey, and the transfer Malm. (Also on the 1977 roster was Vincent Shanley, a reserve defenseman, who arrived in the fall of 1973 as McEneaney's roommate, played on the freshman team, then left school for a year before returning in the fall of 1975 as a sophomore.)

The 1977 starting defense was back intact, with juniors Chris Kane and Frank Muehleman alongside Baltimore native Bob Katz; in goal was Mackesey. Kane was healthy after missing the final half dozen games in 1976 with a shoulder injury suffered in a victory over Penn. He was so confident of his ability that he openly told teammates his stated goal in 1977 was "double donuts"—hold his opponent to no goals, and no assists.

Cornell entered its season opener ranked number two in both the USILA and *Baltimore Sun* polls, with Maryland holding the number one spot in both rankings. In Ithaca optimism was high. In March the *Cornell Daily Sun* sent a reporter to interview Moran. The reporter asked about the upcoming season and how Moran planned to replace French, Levine, and Billy Marino, along with starting defenseman Ted Marchell. The article noted that Moran went through the personnel losses, and the expected starting lineup for the 1977 season, and he never stopped smiling. "That grin makes you wonder," stated the article in the March 30 editions, "what the smiling Irishman has up his sleeve for this season."

Others around the sport had the same feeling. "You just don't bet against Eamon McEneaney in his senior year," says Michael O'Neill, who was entering his junior season at Johns Hopkins in 1977. "You just don't."

Cornell was set to open the season on Wednesday, March 23, 1977, against Hobart at Schoellkopf Field, a rare clash of the returning Division I champion against the returning Division II champion. Unlike in other sports, lacrosse often featured competitive games between teams from different classifications. In 1976, for instance, Hobart had defeated Syracuse, 18–15, its fifth consecutive victory in the series. Hobart had even won the services of attackman Terry Corcoran, a two-time high-school all-American at Corning East, fifty-six miles east of Geneva, who had also been heavily recruited by Moran and was playing at Hobart after spending three semesters at the US Naval Academy. In the days leading to the Hobart–Cornell showdown, however, it snowed six inches in the Finger Lakes region. On Tuesday, March 22, the night before the opener, the snow and rain returned. This time the roads iced over completely. Moran and Schmidt, grudgingly, believed it was unsafe for fans and referees to travel to Ithaca, and the game was postponed.

The Big Red instead opened its season against Adelphi on March 27 in Garden City. Cornell outshot the Panthers from Long Island in the first half, 29–6, and held them scoreless for more than fifty-six minutes in a convincing 16–2 victory.[15] The winning streak was seventeen games. The next day Cornell played an exhibition against the Long Island Athletic Club postcollege team in Garden City, New York. LIAC's roster included Levine and several other one-time college all-Americans. Though it did not count in the won-loss record, Cornell continued its winning ways with a 12–11 victory.[16] Cornell returned to Ithaca for a week of practice, then traveled to Amherst, Massachusetts, where it defeated the University of Massachusetts, 17–9; McEneaney finished with five goals and four assists. The only downside was Mackesey, who was removed from the game after struggling in the first three quarters.[17]

From Amherst, the Big Red departed for its spring break trip to Maryland for a series of scrimmages and an exhibition against Mount Washington. The trip to Maryland was meaningful for Moran, so long the outsider to the Baltimore establishment. "Since 1969," began the *Ithaca Journal*'s preview of the Mount Washington exhibition, "ever since the Long Islander Moran has been head man at Cornell—he's verbally battled with the Baltimore-Washington media, trying to convince them that the Big Red Brand of Lacrosse is the nation's best.... What more does Moran have to do to prove Cornell is not a fluke? Will Maryland-Baltimore sportswriters ever be convinced? Probably not, even if Cornell wins by a fair-sized margin tonight."[18] Coming to Baltimore and College Park ranked second, with two NCAA trophies on display back in his office in Teagle Hall, Moran was looking for the respect that should come with success.

The exhibition with Mount Washington was played on a rainy night in Baltimore, but five thousand fans flocked to Baltimore's Norris Field. Among the crowd was almost every member of the Johns Hopkins team—and all of its coaches, getting a look at the squad it would face in Ithaca in mid-April. The Big Red jumped to a 4–0 lead before the postcollegiate team made a comeback and closed to one goal in the final minute, when Marino scored with forty-six seconds left, to secure a 14–12 victory. [19] The Ivy League team had once again defeated what was essentially a postcollegiate all-star squad. On April 6, the day after beating Mount Washington, Cornell scrimmaged Maryland in College Park, the teams ranked numbers one and two in both polls. It was a half-field situational workout, just as the year before. One published report joked that receiving updates from the scrimmage would be "like finding news of sled dog races in Nome."[20] It was held out of the sight of fans, and the media was shut out. The lacrosse world still expected a Maryland–Cornell rematch in the championship game, but there was no word on the proceedings in College Park. When asked for details of the closed scrimmage, the talkative Moran turned taciturn. "Everything went well," he noted wryly to the *Ithaca Journal*. Immediately following the scrimmage in College Park, Cornell's players returned to Ithaca, arriving by bus at 4:30 in the morning.[21]

On April 9 the Big Red played its first home game. Rutgers entered having won four of five games and ranked number twelve in the nation. Cornell started slowly on the chilly, thirty-five-degree afternoon before taking a seven-goal lead, at which point Moran began substituting liberally in a 15–10 victory.[22] The only downside again was Mackesey, who was removed after struggling to make saves. Cornell was 3–0 against college competition, its winning streak at nineteen, when Johns Hopkins arrived in Ithaca for a regular-season showdown on April 16. In the *Baltimore Sun* poll, Cornell was ranked number one and Johns Hopkins was ranked second. Maryland had moved to third despite being undefeated, at least in part because Cornell and Johns Hopkins looked better, but also on April 9 Maryland had needed overtime to defeat lightly regarded UMBC, 13–12.

For the visit of Johns Hopkins, Cornell officials were expecting a large crowd. The athletic department sold tickets the day before the game, a rarity for a regular-season lacrosse contest. School officials also made game-day tickets easier to purchase by staffing more ticket booths than usual. Interest in the game was intense. The *Ithaca Journal* noted that the 2 p.m. start time was ideal for fans who wanted to see Hobart, undefeated and top-ranked in Division II, battle host Ithaca College at 11 a.m. on the South Hill campus. "Should be just enough time," assistant sports editor Fred Yahn noted, "for lacrosse freaks to lunch in between, buy their sixpacks and head for Schoellkopf."[23] Norm Jollow, columnist for the *Geneva Times*, called April 16 Ithaca's "Super Saturday."[24]

The night before the game, former Cornell star Bob Rule was the guest on a private plane belonging to a man with a dark, distinctive handlebar mustache and his beautiful blonde wife. The man was artist LeRoy Neiman, and his sports-centric paintings were very much in vogue in the 1970s. Neiman and Rule had met through a mutual friend months earlier at a party in Neiman's Manhattan apartment inside the Hotel des Artistes on West 67th Street. (Rule says at one end of the apartment was a life-size portrait of Secretariat, at the other a giant painting of Arnold Schwarzenegger naked.) Rule, once again, tried out his famous luck. "I went up to him and said, 'Mr. Neiman, have you ever seen a lacrosse game?'" Rule says. Neiman, a native of Minnesota who spent most of his professional life in New York City, said he had not but had always wanted to see one. Rule looked at Cornell's 1977 regular-season schedule, which featured only three home Saturday contests and one Sunday game. He rolled the dice on Ithaca's fickle weather and invited Neiman to the mid-April showdown with Johns Hopkins. Neiman agreed. The itinerary included a formal party Friday night at the Sigma Phi Epsilon fraternity and the Cornell–Johns Hopkins lacrosse game on Saturday afternoon; then Neiman was to deliver a lecture to a Sigma Phi group on Saturday night, followed by another party.

Johns Hopkins arrived in Ithaca with a 5–0 record and ranked second in the *Sun* and USILA polls. Like Cornell through much of the 1970s, it boasted an uncommonly talented Canadian player. Sophomore midfielder Dave Huntley had not actually been recruited by the Blue Jays. Growing up in Rexdale, Ontario, he knew about the outdoor version of the game popular in the United States and wrote letters to three schools, along with a college application, asking for a chance to try out for the lacrosse team. The schools were Brown, Washington and Lee, and Johns Hopkins.[25] Huntley had his heart set on Johns Hopkins, but coach Henry Ciccarone misplaced the letter and application and never responded or brought it to the admissions office.[26]

In the summer of 1975, a team from Catonsville, Maryland, a suburb of Baltimore, went to Toronto for a series of box lacrosse games, including one against Huntley's team. Huntley starred in the games and drew the attention of the Catonsville contingent. They asked whether he had considered playing in the United States. He answered that he had always dreamed of playing for Johns Hopkins but had not heard back from either admissions or the coaching staff. ("I figured I would have gone to school and worked in Canada," Huntley later told the *Evening Sun*, sounding like Mike French eyeing the job at the General Motors plant in his hometown prior to receiving his acceptance letter to Cornell.)[27] After a nudge from the Catonsville coach, Huntley's paperwork made its way through the proper channels, and he was a late addition to the Johns Hopkins freshman class in the fall of 1975.[28]

Like many Canadian players, Huntley had an unusual sidearm delivery on his outside shots; it was very hard for goalies to read. He added something to his shot that made it even harder to stop. During the 1977 season, a local TV station in Baltimore arranged for two Baltimore City police officers to attend a Johns Hopkins practice and, using their speed gun normally reserved for clocking traffic speeders, stand behind the goal and measure how fast each player could shoot the ball. The hardest shot belonged to Huntley, at ninety-three miles per hour. "We had no idea how much Dave could help us," Ciccarone told the *Sun*.[29] Huntley, as a sophomore, was moving between the first and second midfield lines, sometimes playing alongside junior Bob DeSimone, a Long Island native and transfer from Navy who, like Huntley, had a hard outside shot.

The night before the Johns Hopkins game, students at Cornell had their choice of on-campus festivities. There were competing happy hours, one at the Thirsty Bear Tavern on the North Campus, named for the turn-of-the-century Cornell football mascot, a live bear named Touchdown, who would climb the goalposts after games. The other happy hour was at the Pub in the Noyes Center, on the West Campus, popular with younger students because employees did not always ask for proof that customers were at least eighteen years old. At 8 p.m., the Temple of Zeus Coffeehouse, in the basement of Goldwin Smith Hall, offered free admission for a reading of Seneca's *The Trojan Women*. Off campus, the State Theater, 109 West State Street, was showing "Rocky," at 7:10 p.m. and 9:20 p.m., followed by a special Pink Floyd concert movie at 11:30 p.m. The Ithaca Theater, three blocks farther down West State Street, was showing the Paul Newman movie *Slapshot* at 7:30 p.m. and 9:45 p.m., while students with a car could have driven to the movie theater at Triphammer Mall, four miles west of Schoellkopf Field, to see *Taxi Driver* at 9:30 p.m. On TV that night, Channel 3, the local ABC affiliate, offered the network's Friday night lineup of *Sanford and Son* at 8 p.m., *Chico and the Man* at 8:30, *The Rockford Files* at 9, and *Quincy* at 10.

The following day, April 16, was clear and warm, with temperatures in the mid-seventies. The *Ithaca Journal*, in its weekend forecast, used the headline "Ideal Spring Weather." By the 2 p.m. start, a crowd of fifteen thousand people filed into Schoellkopf Field. The Crescent seating bowl was filled to its highest point, with people cascading several sections below into the seats with a less advantageous view. Some fans even sat on the field itself, at the base of the Crescent stands, while others stood on the rubber track separating the playing field from the stands. Most fans wore light jackets, and a large contingent of Johns Hopkins fans sat in the Crescent, on the side opposite the team's bench, wearing light-blue shirts and jackets. Among those watching the game from the stands, in the press box side of the stadium opposite the Crescent, was Schmidt and the Hobart players, fresh from an 18–4 victory over Ithaca College. The *Ithaca Journal* later said that the Cornell–Johns Hopkins game might have been the largest crowd ever to see a lacrosse game in Ithaca.

The Friday event at the Sigma Phi house went well, and Saturday morning Rule went back to the house to collect Neiman and his wife and bring them to Schoellkopf Field. Neiman, wearing a beige suit, pink oxford shirt, white sweater, and white panama hat, and his wife, in a dress, white sunhat, and heels, initially set up in the area between the two benches, on the sideline opposite the Crescent stands. Moran recalls thinking it was a dangerous place for a world-famous artist and his wife, so he prevailed upon them to move to the end of the Cornell bench, still with a good vantage point.

Cornell took the field in red jerseys, red shorts, and white helmets. Johns Hopkins wore light blue jerseys, white shorts, and black, white, and light-blue

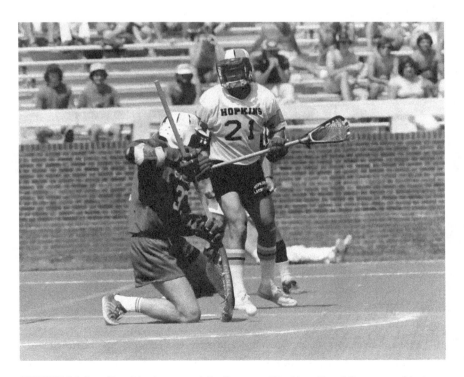

FIGURE 11.3. Dan Mackesey, originally committed to attend Brown, making a save against Johns Hopkins in the 1977 title game (the ball is at the attackman's foot). Cornell won all twenty-nine games in which he was the starting goalie. (Photo courtesy Larry Baum)

FIGURE 11.4. Artist LeRoy Neiman attended the 1977 Johns Hopkins–Cornell game at Schoellkopf Field and later painted a depiction of the game. (Photo courtesy Jules Sieburgh)

checkerboard helmets. As the game was about to start, a tall, thin player wearing the light-blue number 44 jersey stood next to McEneaney. The Johns Hopkins coaches had decided to use freshman Mark Greenberg, from the Baltimore suburb of Pikesville, 6'3", 180 pounds, on the best player in college lacrosse.

Johns Hopkins won the opening face-off. The ball went to Huntley, about fifteen yards from the goal in the middle of the restraining box. He unleashed his sidearm shot, and it whizzed past Mackesey and into the goal. The Blue Jays led, 1–0. On the next possession, the ball went again to Huntley, again fifteen yards in the middle of the restraining box. He unleashed another sidearm shot, and it again eluded Mackesey and went into the goal. Less than three minutes had elapsed, and the Blue Jays led 2–0. "We were in a state of shock," Moran said afterward.[30] The Blue Jays scored again to lead 3–0 at the end of the first quarter. They had extended the lead to 7–1 with about forty-five seconds left before halftime when Jaeger scored to cut the deficit to 7–2 at halftime, the same score by which Maryland had led in the NCAA title game the previous season. Cornell's winning streak, at nineteen, was in jeopardy.

In the locker room Waldvogel and Moran ripped up the scouting report and made changes on the fly. They moved Kane and Muehlemann to the midfield to defend Huntley and DeSimone. Having a defenseman at midfield, called a "longstick midfielder," is now done at every level of the sport. In the 1970s it was unusual; the regular midfielders played both offense and defense without specialization. "We told the defense that it would have to cut off those long shots," Moran said after the game. "That isn't our normal game. But we had to take it away from Hopkins."[31] The coaches also altered the clearing and riding schemes to become more up-tempo and aggressive.[32] On offense, they asked McEneaney and his attack mates to forget the scouting report and play more aggressively.[33] The smaller, quicker, more athletic attack unit was charged with going to a full-court press to make it difficult for the Blue Jays to clear the ball from defense to offense.

While Moran and Waldvogel plotted their changes in the locker room, on the sideline Rule went to check on Neiman and his wife. Neiman, smoking a cigar, had pulled out a giant sketchpad and was drawing sketches of some of the action he had seen in the first half, in front of the goal where he was seated.

In the third quarter the Blue Jays held an 8–5 lead when a shot from Huntley again beat Mackesey but hit the top crossbar, bounced straight down, and agonizingly for Johns Hopkins, rolled away from the goal instead of rolling into it.[34] Marino, playing defense, picked up the loose ball, raced the other way, and scored on a fast break to cut the deficit to 8–6.[35] The crowd, "sitting in stunned silence," as the *Ithaca Journal* noted, then "roared with approval."[36] By the end of the quarter, the game was tied at eight following goals from Henrickson and McEneaney, who had escaped the shackles of Greenberg for his first goal. In the fourth quarter the game was tied at nine and ten when, with approximately ten minutes remaining, Page scored a goal, assisted by Bray, to give the Big Red an 11–10 lead. The teams battled back and forth, but the Big Red still led by a goal when Marino scored again, assisted by Henrickson, for a 12–10 lead with one minute and forty-nine seconds to play. It was Marino's fifth goal of the game. O'Neill, high-school teammate of Marino at Massapequa High, scored for the Blue Jays in the final minute, and senior co-captain Bob Maimone won the ensuing face-off, but the Blue Jays did not take another shot. Cornell's winning streak reached twenty. As the game ended, hundreds of fans stormed the field to celebrate with the players. Moran later likened it to fans storming a basketball court after a signature victory.

Johns Hopkins had entered the 1976 season having never lost to Cornell in nine games. Suddenly the Blue Jays had lost three in a row, all under coach Henry

Ciccarone. Head coach of the Blue Jays was almost certainly the most high-pressure job in the sport. Ciccarone's predecessors had won national titles by the wheelbarrow; not for nothing had *Sports Illustrated* written two years earlier, "At Johns Hopkins University in Baltimore, national championships in lacrosse are almost as inevitable as final exams."[37] After the loss to Cornell, Ciccarone, asked for comment from the *Baltimore Sun*, muttered only, "They beat us, that's all I can say."[38] Long after the game ended, Mackesey ducked his head into the training room. Ciccarone was sitting alone, staring at the ground. "He still looked so downcast," Mackesey says now. "I felt badly for him. I remember saying something like, 'You really outplayed us today,' or 'We got lucky today.' He was just so bummed. I'll never forget how sad he looked."[39]

At Monday's practice Waldvogel, alarmed by Huntley's fifteen-yard shots that had eluded his all-American goalkeeper, suggested somewhat in jest that Mackesey should have his eyes checked. Mackesey went to an eye doctor. The verdict: Waldvogel had been right. Mackesey needed a new prescription. Mackesey's new glasses and contact lenses arrived later that week, and he noticed an immediate difference. "Suddenly when I was walking around campus," Mackesey says, "I could see trees I hadn't noticed before."[40]

Following the win over Johns Hopkins, Cornell began its Ivy League schedule. An article in the *Cornell Daily Sun* noted what the rest of the league thought of the Big Red, courtesy of an unnamed athletic department official at Dartmouth: "We heard that all Cornell does is pick the score it wants to win by and then scores when it wants to."[41] Still, the Ivy League was showing signs that it was improving in 1977. Penn, under coach Ace Adams, began with a seven-game winning streak, and Princeton boasted a senior named Wick Sollers, a Baltimore native who had been the leading scorer in Ivy League play the previous year, with more points than either French or McEneaney in conference games. Moran said the league in 1977 was the most competitive it had been since his arrival eight years earlier.

On April 24 Penn arrived in Ithaca, having won all seven of its games and ranked number eleven in the USILA poll. The Big Red, undefeated in five games, was ranked number one. On a foggy, rainy Sunday afternoon at Schoellkopf Field, Bray scored in the first minute, assisted by McEneaney; by the end of the first quarter, the Big Red led, 6–1, then 11–4 at halftime. In the third quarter the Cornell defense only gave up six shots, and the Big Red was on its way to a 17–8 victory. Marino finished with five goals and one assist, McEneaney added three goals and two assists, and Kane held Penn leading scorer Peter Hollis to "double donuts." Mackesey, with his new contact lenses, made seven saves in the crucial first quarter to stake the Big Red to its big lead.

Mackesey, McEneaney, and the other seniors were entering their final month at Cornell. McEneaney had grown from a cocky freshman to the senior who said hello to almost everyone he greeted on campus, from fellow students to faculty members to custodians to the workers in the Willard Straight dining hall. McEneaney convinced several teammates to take a class on Shakespeare so they could discuss the great plays. He was in good academic standing, he enjoyed talking and listening to fellow students at Cornell's Arts Quad, and he was one of the few athletes to hang out at the Temple of Zeus coffee house, discussing music and literature. He loved the Northern Ireland musician Van Morrison and urged his teammates to listen to Bruce Springsteen. "He was way ahead of everyone on Springsteen," Lasda says now. "I told him no, I prefer my Southern rock. I probably should have listened to Eamon on that one." McEneaney also loved Bob Dylan and sometimes modeled the poems he wrote after song lyrics from Dylan. "Eamon was a very deep guy," Michael O'Neill says now. "He was well read. He loved reading, and he read everything. And he was writing poetry and music." But McEneaney was also feeling pressure to end his college career on a high note. In the latter stages of the 1977 season, Lasda says, McEneaney opened up to him about the pressure he was feeling. "He was always trying to calm himself down," Lasda says. "He knew he had to be the quarterback of the offense, not just the initiator. He felt he had to do more than just dodge from behind."[42] And at times, that pressure could spill out.

On Wednesday, April 27, a game against Yale in New Haven did not appear to be a troubling contest for the Big Red. The Elis entered, having won just once in five Ivy League games. Before a crowd of several hundred people on a rainy afternoon, Cornell started slowly and trailed, 2–1, in the second quarter before rebounding for a 14–2 win. In the locker room afterward, McEneaney accused a teammate of being lazy on the field and grabbed the player by the neck. Teammates quickly broke up the skirmish, but they noted how serious McEneaney had become about winning a title in his final season. "He was so passionate," Reitenbach says of McEneaney. "In 1977 it was almost like he was playing with a fury."[43]

After some of McEneaney's antics, Moran would talk to his star attackman and ask him to tone down some of his attitude, and McEneaney almost always apologized later for his outbursts. Famously, he did not spare the coaches from his ire when he thought they were wrong. Earlier in his career, Waldvogel was in charge of an early-season practice in the polo barn while Moran was out of town at a coaching clinic. During the workout Waldvogel made a request of the players, and McEneaney, then a sophomore, shouted an expletive at him. Waldvogel asked if there was a problem, and McEneaney repeated the expletive. Waldvogel kicked him out of practice and said he was off the team unless and until he apologized. McEneaney left.

The next day Moran returned and asked how practice had gone. "I said, 'It went okay. I kicked Eamon off the team,'" Waldvogel says. "Richie asked what he had done. I explained what happened and told him Eamon was acting like an asshole and a big-timer, and I won't take that. Richie said he agreed."[44] Later that day McEneaney went to the lacrosse offices at Teagle Hall and apologized to Waldvogel. "I said, 'Eamon, you're an asshole sometimes,'" Waldvogel says. "He said, 'I know, I know.' He didn't mean anything by it. He was a great player and a great teammate. Sometimes back then his intensity got the better of him."[45]

In the 1977 season, as the playoffs drew close, Moran began one practice by saying he wanted the team to work on some new plays. McEneaney protested. "We were in the huddle, and Eamon kept saying, 'Why do we need this stuff?'" Lasda says. "'What we are doing is working. Let's just stick with it.'" Says Malm, "Mac was tough. But you have to remember he did not ask anything of anyone else that he was not willing to do himself. He was a hard-ass on guys about conditioning, but Eamon was the first guy to finish our one-mile runs. He was the first guy to finish sprints. He was first in line for drills."[46]

After Yale, the Big Red traveled back to Ithaca; one day later the team was on the road again, this time to Hanover, New Hampshire, to face Dartmouth on April 30. The Big Red broke open a close game midway through the second quarter for a 23–6 victory. Cornell's final regular-season home game came May 7 against Princeton. The winning streak had reached twenty-four games, and the Big Red was on the verge of another Ivy League title, its eighth in nine seasons. Princeton entered Schoellkopf Field ranked number fourteen, thanks mostly to the attack duo of Sollers and Dave Tickner. Sollers again was near the top of scoring leaders in the Ivy League, as was Tickner.

The weather was warm and sunny, and a crowd of seven thousand watched the proceedings inside Schoellkopf Field. By now Mackesey was becoming more familiar with his new contact lenses, and it showed, especially on two shots from Sollers. "I was usually pretty critical of myself," Sollers says. "But two shots in the first half were about as good as I could have done. The first one was headed for the top corner. Mackesey saved it with his left elbow. Then I was coming around from behind the goal and shot it off-stick [to the side away from Mackesey's lacrosse stick], and he kicked it away with his foot. I thought, this guy is just too good."[47] Sollers also remembers McEneaney. "He looked like a leprechaun with no front teeth," Sollers says. "He was so slightly built. And he'd be jawing with our defensemen the whole time. He and I would go at it, yelling at each other across the field too. But he was so good. He was just an extraordinary, extraordinary talent. We took it on the chin from them." Cornell won, 17–8, McEneaney finishing with four goals and three assists.[48]

Cornell's winning streak had reached twenty-five games. Afterward, the players learned that their road game against Cortland State, scheduled for Tuesday afternoon, May 10, had been canceled. The Red Dragons had made the NCAA Division II tournament and were set to face C.W. Post on May 11; they asked to postpone the game against Cornell. Moran, sensing that his team was starting to hit its high notes, was more than happy to bypass the road trip against a team the Big Red had beaten by nine goals in the fall.[49] Given the Midas touch of Cornell lacrosse in the 1970s, it is perhaps no surprise that the weekend was a memorable one. The night after Cornell's victory over Princeton, the Grateful Dead band played a sold-out show at Barton Hall, just down Campus Road from Schoellkopf Field. "The Grateful Dead performed thousands of concerts," began an Associated Press story on the fortieth anniversary of the concert in 2017, "none acclaimed quite like their May 8, 1977, show at a Cornell University field house on a freakishly snowy night."[50] A half dozen lacrosse players attended.[51]

Cornell entered the 1977 NCAA tournament with a 10–0 record and the number one overall seed. In the first round Cornell was drawn into a May 18 quarterfinal against Massachusetts at Schoellkopf Field. Moran worried that his players, in the midst of final exams, were overlooking the Minutemen, not least because the regular-season game had been a perfunctory victory on the road. In the rematch in the NCAA tournament, the game was tied at five late in the first quarter before Cornell eventually pulled away for a 17–13 victory. McEneaney and Marino led the way offensively—each had three goals and four assists. The Big Red had reached the semifinals, with one last home game for McEneaney, Mackesey, and the rest of the seniors. They would face Navy, which defeated Penn, 14–12, in a quarterfinal at Franklin Field. The Midshipmen entered the semifinal with nine wins and four losses and was set to play Army in its regular-season finale on June 4, one week after the NCAA title game. It would be the final showdown between McEneaney and Long, the two best high-school attackmen in the nation in 1973, each leading their team in scoring as seniors. Their teams had met twice in the postseason, each winning once. This time the attackman on the losing end would also end his college career.

On Thursday, May 19, two days before the semifinal, Waldvogel and Moran posted the scouting report on the bulletin board outside the Schoellkopf Field locker room. Two things stood out: Navy's starting goalkeeper, a sophomore from Towson named Jeff Johnson, had a tendency, after making a save, to run the ball upfield himself rather than passing to a defenseman. This drew the attention of McEneaney and Marino, who excelled in the riding game— the lacrosse equivalent of a full-court press in basketball. (Sierra, the third starter when the season began, had since moved to the midfield, replaced on attack by Page.) The other item of note was that Navy's defense was susceptible to backdoor cuts, where a player without possession runs quickly toward the midfield area, then breaks sharply back toward the goal, to receive a pass for a wide-open shot from close range. McEneaney was certain to draw a lot of attention from Navy, so his teammates were expecting lots of opportunities to make those backdoor cuts against the distracted defense.

Not on the bulletin board, but known to at least a handful of Cornell players, was the animus between Moran and Navy coach Dick Szlasa. Moran was still unhappy that Szlasa had discontinued the home-and-home series between the teams, started by Szlasa's predecessor at Navy, Bill Bilderback. Mackesey had received a first-hand glimpse of the raw feelings at the previous year's all-American banquet, in the ballroom at Martin's West Hotel outside Baltimore. That night Szlasa and his wife struck up a conversation with Mackesey. "They could not believe I had good things to say about Richie," Mackesey says. "That really stuck in my mind. Dick Szlasa could not stand him." Moran felt pretty much the same about Szlasa.

The semifinal on May 21 brought Szlasa, Navy, and ninety-degree heat to Ithaca, and the sweltering temperatures did not die down even with a 5 p.m. start time to accommodate exams and with the Cornell facilities management crew using hoses to water down the artificial turf in an effort to make it slightly less scorching. The field turned dark green when watered; as the Poly-Turf dried in the sun, it went back to its lime-green color. A crowd of more than ten thousand filled the stands, a group of spectators the *Ithaca Journal* described as "sun-drenched and beer guzzling."[52] Cornell did its pregame introduction of the starting lineup in the usual order—attack, midfield, defense, and then goalie, then any captain not in the starting lineup, then its coaches. McEneaney and Mackesey, for the final time, ran onto the Poly-Turf of Schoellkopf Field as members of the Cornell lacrosse team.

Navy had the opening possession and took a quick shot in transition that Mackesey saved. The Big Red initially had trouble clearing the ball against the swarming Midshipmen, and Katz, under pressure, passed to McEneaney, who was standing near the midfield line. As soon as McEneaney touched the ball, the Navy defenders ended their pressure and ran into their defensive zone. McEneaney had touched the ball once, forty-five yards from the goal, and the Midshipmen looked petrified. McEneaney entered the game with the lowest scoring totals of his career, thirty-three goals and twenty-eight assists, partly because of the three games that had been canceled. Still, Navy was under no misapprehension about his talent.

Seconds later, McEneaney drew a double team and spotted Jaeger's backdoor cut. The midfielder was wide open. McEneaney fired a quick pass that Jaeger steered into the goal from six yards away; then Jaeger punctuated the move by screaming in Johnson's face. Cornell scored again thirty seconds later, with Page feeding Marino for a goal and a 2–0 lead. The score was still 2–0 late in the first quarter when the Midshipmen were attempting a clear. As McEneaney and Marino relentlessly pursued the ball, the Navy defender passed to the only open player, Johnson. The goalie's instincts told him to try to run the ball upfield himself, as he had done countless times during the season. But none of those self-clears had come with McEneaney on the field. As McEneaney closed in on him, Johnson tried a spin move to elude him. Johnson lost his footing briefly on the wet turf and left his stick up in the air, as if it were an umbrella in the rain. McEneaney left his feet and, perpendicular to the ground, leaped over Johnson, knocked the ball from his stick, landed on his feet like a cat, collected the ball, and deposited it into an empty net for a 3–0 lead. "The crowd went berserk on that one," recounted Fred Yahn in Monday's *Ithaca Journal*.[53] "That was the only time," Moran says, "that the [Navy] goalie tried to clear the ball himself." McEneaney, the player once called the "Lacrosse Superman" had, in his final home game, almost literally shown why the moniker was an accurate one.

McEneaney's ride and goal began a fifty-three-second stretch where the Big Red scored three more times. By the end of the first quarter, Cornell led 9–1. The *Baltimore Sun* writer covering the game caught a glimpse of the NCAA official observer's notes at the end of the first quarter. "Cornell very smart," the official had written. "Navy very ragged."[54] The lead expanded to 13–2 at halftime.[55] The Midshipmen brought four goalies to Ithaca and used all four. Johnson, the starter, was removed in the third quarter after finishing with five saves and giving up sixteen goals. About 7 p.m. on May 21, 1977, the Big Red was putting the final touches on a 22–6 demolition that could have been much worse: Seven Cornell shots hit goalposts and bounced out.[56] McEneaney, in his final game at Schoellkopf Field, finished with five goals and five assists. "I didn't think Navy's defense was anything," Marino said afterward. "They didn't seem to want to play. They weren't hustling. I got three [goals] on easy backdoor plays."[57] Cornell's players left the field slowly, basking in the victory. Given the unusual 5 p.m. start time, McEneaney, Mackesey, and their teammates literally walked into the sunset with the fans chanting, "We're number one!"[58]

On the other side of the bracket, second-seeded Johns Hopkins won its quarterfinal over North Carolina, 16–9, despite an incredible twenty-seven saves from North Carolina goalie Larry Myers. (As Myers left the field, Ciccarone stopped what he was doing and shook the surprised goalie's hand.) The semifinal was against number three Maryland; an overflow crowd of eleven thousand people squeezed into sweltering Homewood Field. In the regular-season meeting, Johns Hopkins had upended Maryland, 21–20.

In the semifinal, the Blue Jays continued where they had left off. They scored on ten of their first sixteen shots, an incredible .625 percent, en route to a 22–12 victory.[59] This was the most goals Maryland had ever given up. Ciccarone basked in the victory but already had one eye on the rematch with Cornell. "You never expect a game like this," Ciccarone told reporters afterward. "When it comes you sure love it. But I'd sure like to play just like this for one more game."[60]

Cornell began its two-day bus trip to Charlottesville for the NCAA title game on Wednesday, May 25, in the early afternoon.[61] The team stopped in Baltimore, held a practice, and spent the night at the Hilltop Motor Inn before departing for Charlottesville. On May 26 in the late morning, the bus pulled into the team hotel, the Sheraton Motor Inn at the Shadwell exit of Interstate 64, where it intersected with Route 250, on the east side of town. The Sheraton was a red-brick, two-story, L-shaped building whose amenities in 1977 included, according to a travel brochure, "wall-to-wall carpeting, air conditioning, color TV, direct dial phones and FM music."[62] It also featured a lounge area and restaurant. Many of the rooms featured orange carpeting and floor-to-ceiling exterior windows that overlooked the hotel swimming pool. The most distinctive trait may have been the giant red S with its bright background that was illuminated at dark, serving as a beacon to tired drivers looking for a place to pull over for the night.

When Cornell arrived on May 26, the hotel swimming pool would have been inviting, as temperatures had drawn close to one hundred degrees. The Cornell contingent received confirmation of something it had first heard earlier in the week: The forecast in Charlottesville was for the oppressive heat to remain in the Virginia piedmont through the weekend.[63] Absorbing the news, Waldvogel and Moran went to work on implementing the scouting report.

The Big Red players were concerned enough about the heat that, before leaving Ithaca, a reserve midfielder named Bob Mathisen approached Mackesey, the team captain he knew best. Coaches had selected Mathisen one of twenty-seven players eligible to play in the championship. The team could travel with as many players as it wanted, and those players could be involved in practices and warm-ups, but the NCAA capped the participants for each game at twenty-seven. Mathisen, who had yet to score a goal in the 1977 season, said his roster spot should go to defenseman Paul Sadowski, with a nod to Sadowski's ability to be a fresh defender, whereas the Big Red had plenty of depth at midfield; Sadowski's fresh legs would be more important, Mathisen reasoned, than his own. Mackesey answered by saying it had been the coach's decision and to trust that Moran and Waldvogel knew what was best.

The focus of Cornell's defensive practice that week, in Ithaca and then Baltimore, was to deny any space for Huntley (thirty-one goals), DeSimone (eighteen goals), or a freshman from Charlottesville named Wayne Davis (nine goals as a reserve) to unleash their wicked outside shots.[64] Since their meeting in mid-April, Moran's scouts in the Baltimore area had attended three Johns Hopkins games.[65] Nothing in their detailed reports made Moran change his initial strategy: Push the tempo for the first twenty minutes and make the talented but methodical Blue Jays play catch-up. Moran continued to believe his team was more athletic and in better shape physically, thanks to all the preseason runs around Cornell's hilly campus.

Moran stuck with the plan even with a forecast that did not seem conducive to playing up-tempo at all, let alone for twenty minutes.[66] The Cornell players certainly did not balk at the plan to play up-tempo in unfriendly conditions. "The Baltimore media liked to call us robots," Mackesey says, "because Richie would tell us to do something, and we'd do it immediately."[67] If the Blue Jays withstood the early barrage, the Big Red was in major trouble. But Cornell entered with a twenty-eight-game winning streak, and its players were not about to question their fiery coach.

On Thursday afternoon Cornell held a light practice on a field next to Scott Stadium. Per NCAA rules, the title game participants were allowed only one workout each inside the venue hosting the title game; both teams decided to be elsewhere on Thursday and inside Scott Stadium on Friday.[68] Scott Stadium, capacity twenty-eight thousand, was a Southern collegiate jewel. Tall green trees surrounded the outside, as did an esplanade where fans could mingle during breaks in the action. The main scoreboard was seated atop a grassy hill at the north end of the field that sloped down into the stadium; people could watch the game while seated on picnic blankets. The south end also had a sloping grass hill and a remarkable view of lush Monticello Mountain in the distance. The stadium featured circular seating on both sides, with row after row of silver aluminum bleachers, and a small brick wall lined the playing surface. Both teams practiced inside the stadium on Friday afternoon. Cornell went first, about 4 p.m. Also inside were workers from ABC, sweating through the stifling heat to set up cameras and equipment to film the following day's game as part of a highlights package to be aired later in the summer. ABC had added a wrinkle not part of the previous year's broadcast: Each member of the Cornell and Johns Hopkins starting lineups would introduce himself, sharing his class year and his hometown, similar to what the network did with its college football broadcasts.

Practice began. Among the items on the agenda were shooting drills, where Waldvogel and Moran would direct the Cornell players to practice shooting low, which was the scouting report on Johns Hopkins goalie Kevin Mahon. The players would also work on ground balls, something of an obsession for Moran, especially when playing away from Schoellkopf Field; he wanted to see how the surface would play compared to his home stadium's Poly-Turf. First, Waldvogel led the starting offense and scout-team defense—essentially the reserve defenders who mimic the upcoming opponent—to one side of the baking Astroturf. On the other side went the starting defense and scout-team offense, watched by Moran. Waldvogel wanted the offense to run a new extra-man play installed just for Johns Hopkins. McEneaney began with the ball. Moran once said of his star attackman, "He is sky high for a Saturday game by Monday and he's about five feet off the ground when game time rolls around."[69]

Waldvogel's whistle blew, and the constant-motion offense ramped up. As his teammates made their moves on the extra-man set, McEneaney passed the ball to where the player cutting down the middle of the field was supposed to be. The player had turned the wrong way, however, and the pass sailed harmlessly through the air and onto the other side of the field. A turnover. McEneaney glared in the player's direction and yelled a quick message that he should wake up.

The players reset themselves and tried again. The whistle pierced the heavy afternoon air. Again McEneaney passed to where the cutter was supposed to be. Again the player had turned the wrong way, and the pass cut through the air, fell to the turf, and rolled out of bounds. This time McEneaney went wild. He raced over to the offending player and took a swing at him. Surprised teammates intervened. Once order was restored, Waldvogel kicked McEneaney out of practice. Moran says he caught the incident from the corner of his eye; by the time he turned his full attention to it, the first thing he noticed was Waldvogel's ashen face.[70] McEneaney, one of the best players in Cornell history, left the field. "Mike was sort of in shock," Moran says now. "I certainly wasn't going to chase after [McEneaney]. That's for sure."[71]

Moran says now he was plotting to play the title game without his star player. "We were a balanced team," he says. "We would have been okay without him. . . . You don't expect something like that to happen, but knowing his personality before games it wasn't a surprise. He was a perfectionist."[72] McEneaney's competitive streak had shown itself at the worst possible time, and he had pushed Waldvogel too far. Still, Moran kept his wits about him; the final fifteen minutes of the final practice of the season were spent on ground balls, and Moran, relieved, noted that Scott Stadium's Astroturf was almost identical to the surface at Schoellkopf Field. Ground balls in the title game would not look any different from what his players had seen for months.

After practice, an ABC producer reminded Moran of the pregame introductions. Moran sent out nine players, with only two starting attackmen. Bray took the producers' request about hometown so literally that he identified himself as hailing from the "Cattaraugus Indian Reservation." (When *Wide World of Sports* aired the highlights later that summer, Bray said the name's inclusion on a national TV broadcast became a point of pride among those in the Seneca Nation.) When the producers asked who would fill the third spot on attack, Moran said that decision would be made before the game and that player would be available to add as a "drop-in." Practice, mercifully, was over, and the players and coaches boarded their bus to return to the Sheraton Inn. McEneaney was not on board the bus. When they returned to the Sheraton Inn, there was no sign of him there either.

Johns Hopkins took the steamy hot artificial turf for its final practice of the 1977 season after Cornell left. The Blue Jays entered, having won eleven of twelve games, the only loss to Cornell by one goal. They had their array of star power: Huntley, with the rocket of a sidearm lefty shot, entered with a team-high thirty-one goals; O'Neill, a shoo-in as a first-team all-American, smart and tough and a tremendously accurate passer, was right behind in goals, with thirty, and thirty-three assists (roughly the same numbers as McEneaney's thirty-eight goals and thirty-three assists); and senior face-off specialist Bob Maimone, who entered with more than one hundred ground balls.

The coaching staff featured Ciccarone, a hard-living Annapolis native who had played lacrosse and football at Johns Hopkins. The head coach was famous among his players for late-night poker games and for being brutally honest. ("He didn't suffer fools well," was O'Neill's assessment.) Assistant Willie Scroggs was a one-time Johns Hopkins football-lacrosse standout now in charge of the lacrosse team's defense. Also on the staff was Townsend, the Baltimore native and Mount Washington defenseman who had shut down McEneaney in the previous year's Mount Washington–Cornell exhibition. It was a Baltimore establishment team, from top to bottom.

Though the Blue Jays would not have known about the fracas involving McEneaney on the Scott Stadium Astroturf, little else about the Big Red escaped their notice. The two programs in the 1970s were engaged in lacrosse's cold war; Johns Hopkins and Cornell watched each other's every move. At many games there was a scout for one team or the other lurking in the stands, observing, taking notes, trying to find the one flaw, the one "tell" in gambling parlance that could turn a moment, a game, a season. Moran habitually read the *Baltimore Sun,* scanning the statistics and reading between the lines of the reports to find some edge on the Blue Jays. Scroggs took it one step further. Tucked away in the drawer of his desk at the Newton White Athletic Center on the Baltimore campus was a secret strategic instrument. These were the days before coach's films became de rigueur as a method for preparing scouting reports. But the Blue Jays, under the weight of expectations from a rabid and knowledgeable fan base, had to know the strengths and weaknesses of every opponent.

So Scroggs improvised. As team trainers went through mounds of white athletic tape, Scroggs would collect the discarded wooden tape rolls. He created a makeshift lacrosse field, the cylinders acting as one-inch-tall players, miniature warriors he used to simulate the opposing team's favored offensive sets and plays—and how the Johns Hopkins defense should respond. For his players Scroggs took a heavy black pen and drew the jersey number and a name or nickname on each. Mark Greenberg, a starting defenseman, later elected to the Hall of Fame, still knows exactly where he keeps his athletic-tape chess piece, with "44" and, in tiny letters, "GREENBERG" on the back.[73]

"It was like a piece to a board game," Greenberg says. Using nearly two dozen tape rolls, Scroggs would create three teams: His own; a generic group of six cylinders for use with any opponent's offensive personnel; and a third group, names and numbers written carefully in red ink. More than forty years later Scroggs closes his eyes and recalls the corresponding numbers and names perfectly. "Ten was McEneaney," he says now. "Twenty-four was Henrickson. Twenty-three was Sierra. Fifteen was one of the Marinos."[74]

The red ink could have belonged to Maryland, the Blue Jays' biggest rival. But the names were Cornell's. Whenever outdoor practice was impossible because of rain or snow, or if the team had a little extra time following a weight-lifting session, Scroggs would pull out the game pieces and diagram the latest trick that Cornell had revealed to him or that one of the scouts had seen during their most recent games in person. "We didn't have them for any other [opposing] players," Scroggs says now. "Only Cornell's."[75] The Blue Jays, the sport's most successful program, the program with the sport's Hall of Fame on its campus, had trained its sights on the Big Red.

Johns Hopkins had watched enough film of Cornell to have formulated a plan for McEneaney. "McEneaney is a water bug type player," senior defender Mike Sheedy told the *Evening Sun*. "In our first game he tried to go to the goal in the opening minutes of the game to get the quick score, but after a while he just tried to draw people towards him. He does telegraph some of his moves, we saw that in the films. The best thing to do against him is to stick with him and try to hit his hand when he goes for the pass."[76] Sheedy added something about the Blue Jays' near-constant rotation of defensemen—all but Greenberg often found their way onto the bench for a breather—and the expected warm temperatures. "McEneaney runs the entire game," he said. "We'll be fresh and they will be tired." Ironically, Moran had been saying the very same thing about Cornell's stamina and depth against the lack of it from the Blue Jays. After their final practice Johns Hopkins posed by position group for the ABC cameras before leaving sweltering Scott Stadium.

After their practice and the bus ride back to the hotel, Cornell's players settled down to their team dinner at the Sheraton Motor Inn. There still was no sign of McEneaney, and Moran recalls that the players were eating their dinner quietly.[77] Finally McEneaney walked into the room. The players and coaches ignored him. He could have walked out again, but instead he went to Moran and whispered in his ear. Moran looked up from his meal in surprise. "I said, 'Are you still part of this team?'" Moran says. "He looked at me in amazement. Then he said, 'I want to apologize.'"[78] McEneaney proceeded to apologize to the coaches, players, particularly the teammate he had taken a swing at. "He said it was a stupid thing to do," Moran says, "and it was." McEneaney then walked out of the room. Just before he reached the exit, however, Moran called to him. "You better have something to eat," he said.[79] Apology accepted.

Game day, May 28, began boiling hot. Temperatures again were expected to exceed ninety degrees.[80] About 8 a.m. Kim Eike, the team statistician and a Cornell alumnus who was set to leave Ithaca in a few weeks to begin graduate school in Michigan, settled down at the swimming pool with a cold drink and the newspaper. He unfolded the paper and began reading. From the corner of his eye he saw someone wearing a T-shirt, shorts, and running shoes headed out of the hotel. Then he noticed the bushy, blonde-red hair. It was McEneaney. "I remember thinking," Eike says now, "I am *not* going to tell Richie about this. He would have gone nuts."[81]

McEneaney left the Sheraton Motor Inn and turned right, went down a winding asphalt road, and began to run along the grass-and-dirt shoulder of Richmond Road, also known as Route 250. Trucks would have sped past him, their breeze feeling good on the roasting morning. He ran roughly three miles before returning to the hotel. "Eamon ran several miles that morning to clear his head," brother Kevin McEneaney says now. "His anxiety must have been getting to him."[82]

McEneaney returned from his run in time for a shower and a quick lunch. But he had one last piece of business to which to attend. McEneaney was famous for going up to every player before the game, looking him in the eye, and asking, "Are you ready?" To Muehleman, his teammate in high school and college, it was always, "Mules, are you ready?" Meaning, are you ready to play, to give your all for your teammates and for Moran and for Cornell? This time, however, before his final game at Cornell, McEneaney had a different message. He gathered the four other seniors and repeated a mantra to them. "He kept saying something over and over," Malm says now. "He kept saying, 'Today, Cornell won't be denied. Cornell won't be denied.'"[83] With that, the Big Red boarded their bus and drove roughly eight miles to Scott Stadium.

Facilities staff at the University of Virginia, unlike their counterparts at Cornell, did not water the Astroturf to keep it cool. A photographer from the *Ithaca Journal*, in town to work the championship game, says he remembers how hot the playing surface was. "It was a hot, humid, uncomfortable day," says Larry Baum.[84] Baum had seen his share of lacrosse dating from his undergraduate days at Cornell in the late 1960s. And he was expecting the worst: The undefeated Big Red had reached the title game with an up-tempo offense and this, patently, was not the weather for constant fast breaks. "I thought, 'This is going to be a slow game,'" Baum says now.[85]

Cornell's players took the field for warm-ups, and the playing surface was so hot the plastic soles of the high-top leather basketball shoes they wore stuck to the turf.[86] Moran later estimated the temperature on the turf was 110 degrees.[87] As pregame drills began, roughly an hour before the 2 p.m. start, almost all the players on both teams wore the bare minimum acceptable clothing: for Cornell, that meant red uniform shorts and white T-shirts rolled up to their armpits, to expose their midriffs, the only way to catch any vagrant breezes; Johns Hopkins players in their black shorts and also wore their gray T-shirts rolled up to the armpits. Only four Cornell players were in full uniform. Three were the goalies who were facing shots from Waldvogel, in red polo shirt and khaki shorts. The fourth was McEneaney, already in his red jersey with the white number ten on the back, in his full uniform, ready to go. (The superstitious Moran took the field as always, in white polo shirt, black slacks, and black turf shoes.)

McEneaney took time away from warm-ups to be filmed by *Wide World of Sports* for the introduction he had missed the previous day, giving his name, class year, and hometown. He also answered a quick question about how his senior year had gone so far. Soon the players went back into the locker room and reemerged in their game uniforms. Cornell's attackmen and midfielders passed the ball to each other near the midfield line; the defensemen threw the ball to each other in back of the goal, in the end zone that read "VIRGINIA" in white capital letters, a remnant from the stadium's main tenant, the football team.

The crowd of 11,340, another record for the NCAA title game, filed into the stadium. Despite the heat, the seating area behind the team benches was almost completely full. On the opposite side were a smattering of fans and then large swaths of unoccupied aluminum benches. The soaring temperatures made the aluminum bleachers a veritable frying pan. "I walked out of there," says Dave Spivey, a member of the Johns Hopkins class of 1980 who attended the game, "with the worst damn sunburn of my life." The grassy area around the main scoreboard, in the direct sun, was completely empty, fans opting instead to watch from the shade of clusters of nearby trees—a worse view but at least out of the sun.

Spivey, like the majority of the crowd with the much shorter drive from Baltimore, was rooting for the Blue Jays. Baum, an amateur pilot, recalls renting a plane and flying to Charlottesville from Ithaca with friends. Dozens of other Cornell fans had arrived Saturday morning via an airplane chartered for the event. They would arrive back at Tompkins Regional Airport that night.[88] The fans brought hand-painted signs reading "BIG RED LACROSSE IS #1!" "Cornell '77: Once Is Never Enough," and the ubiquitous six-foot-by six-foot red flag with a simple giant white C in the middle.

Fans were already seeking shade; players on both teams were dressed in the bare minimum; and McEneaney, having already run three miles that day, spent the final minutes before the opening face-off running around the field holding two sticks above his head, as if celebrating a victory.[89] Looking in the stands, he spotted his nephew, Howard Wulforst, Jr., age twelve, who had been driven to the game by Peter Watkins, a McEneaney cousin from New Jersey. McEneaney motioned for Wulforst to come onto the field before turning his attention back to something Moran was saying. A security guard was standing behind the Cornell team bench, checking for credentials. Those without were sent to the stands. Watkins told the preteen to tell the security guard there was a fight in the bathroom, and when the security guard left, he could sneak onto the field.

Wulforst told the security guard about the phantom fight; the guard thanked him, and sprinted toward the men's room. Wulforst then snuck onto the field and greeted his uncle.

In the final minute before the game began, Moran let loose his shrill whistle, and the players gathered around him and Waldvogel in the corner of the north end zone. Amid a backdrop of trees and green-brown grass, beneath the large stadium scoreboard and the American flag, hanging limp on the heavy afternoon, the Big Red held their final pregame huddle of the 1977 season, the final one ever for McEneaney and Mackesey in Cornell red. The two stood amid their teammates, all of them loose and confident, winners of twenty-eight consecutive games, ready to take the field one last time. After a few words, Moran released the players. Loose limbed, with heads high, they raced onto the Astroturf and ran forty yards to the Cornell bench as the fans in red stood and cheered. Moran stayed behind, watching from the end zone. He later likened the scene to watching a pack of horses on the loose, telling one TV reporter, "It gave me chills."

Both teams stood at attention for the national anthem, staring at the flag behind the main scoreboard at the north end of the stadium. Cornell's players lined up in single file along the sideline; the Johns Hopkins players clumped around each other in a circle. Most of the fans in the stands were dressed for a day at the beach, with sun hats and lots of bare skin. Once the anthem ended, the players went back

FIGURE 11.5. Cornell's players take the field for the 1977 NCAA title game in Charlottesville. Coach Richie Moran later compared the scene to wild horses running free. "It gave me chills," he said. (Photo courtesy Cornell Athletics)

to the bench for their final instructions. Almost all of the Cornell players gathered in a circle around Moran. McEneaney was an exception. Instead, he went around the huddle until he found the player he had confronted the previous day in practice. McEneaney greeted him, looked him in the eye, then lightly, affectionately, tapped him on the helmet three times. McEneaney then made his way to Kane and gave a similar greeting while Kane affixed a red bandana to his head, to keep his long dark hair out of his eyes. Then it was time for the captains to head to the midfield to meet each other and talk with the referees. When the meeting ended, both starting lineups of ten players took the field, each standing in a line facing the other team, a decades-old tradition in lacrosse. The two starting goalies, Mahon and Mackesey, ran to each other and shook hands. The game, finally, was ready to begin.

Maimone won the advantage on the opening face-off. As he sent the ball to a teammate from the midfield line, a puff of white chalk flew into the air. The Blue Jays worked the ball to O'Neill— in a pregame article Mackesey said that O'Neill controlled the ball 80 percent of the time that Johns Hopkins had possession. O'Neill, despite close attention from Kane, spotted a sophomore midfielder named Joe Garavante wide open for a point-blank shot. Garavante, a starter who had scored ten goals in 1977, collected the pass, but at the crucial moment he lost his balance and shot wide. A minute later another chance fell to Garavante; from a low angle on the wing, he shot directly into Mackesey's stick. Meantime, Cornell was looking for fast breaks at every opportunity, just as Moran had planned. Hen-

FIGURE 11.6.   Cornell coach Richie Moran stands at attention for the national anthem before the 1977 NCAA title game. Also pictured are Frank Muehleman (37), and Craig Jaeger (8). (Photo courtesy Larry Baum)

rickson led one break and passed to a wide-open McEneaney standing roughly five yards from the goal, with an apparent open shot. But the ball tipped off the top of McEneaney's stick and went out of bounds. McEneaney stared at the ground and screamed at himself. Another time the Big Red, off a broken clear, had a three-on-two, the numerical advantage upon which Moran based his offense. Marino, in possession, passed to McEneaney on his left. McEneaney shot low, just as the scouting report directed. Mahon read it perfectly and made an easy save.

So eager was Cornell to play up-tempo that another early fast break was led by defenseman Kane. He nearly took a shot on goal before deciding to pass to McEneaney; the ball was tipped and controlled instead by Johns Hopkins defender Curt Ahrendsen, a sophomore from Rochester, New York. A fourth fast break began following an errant pass by the Blue Jays. The ball went to Page, who appeared to have a breakaway, but just as he readied to shoot from eight yards, Greenberg knocked the ball from his stick and out of harm's way. The boiling heat would not slow down Cornell. The Big Red, perhaps because of the hot weather, was doing all the little things wrong.

After six minutes, the game still scoreless, McEneaney took the ball and went behind the goal. Greenberg, who towered over him at 6'3", went with him. In the regular season, Greenberg had held McEneaney to one goal and two assists, and he entered the title game with confidence. On the Astroturf in Charlottesville, McEneaney ran at half speed toward the goal. Greenberg, with a perfectly timed check from his light-brown wooden stick shaft and black plastic head, dislodged the ball. McEneaney scrambled to collect it. Challenge accepted. In the stands Buck Briggs, who had attended Cornell lacrosse games for years, knew what was coming next. "It was a great check, but it was also a mistake," he says. "Because he had made Eamon angry."[90]

McEneaney, still in possession, made the same move, trotting at half speed with Greenberg watching closely. This time McEneaney burst from half speed to full speed in an instant. Greenberg had the far longer stride and longer stick, but he was left in the attackman's wake. Freshman Wayne Davis, the Charlottesville native and second-line offensive midfielder, was within five yards of McEneaney but did not slide to stop the move, perhaps fearful that McEneaney would find an open man for a pass and easy shot. McEneaney continued unimpeded to the goal; he shot the ball from just outside the crease, depositing it lightly and easily over Mahon's left shoulder. The Blue Jays had known McEneaney would go to the goal early; with their best defender on him, still the move had resulted in a goal.

On the ensuing possession McEneaney again was behind the goal with the ball in his light-brown stick with the red stick head. He went into his half-speed jog, then fired a perfect pass to Page, cutting toward the goal. Page touched the ball past Mahon and into the net for a 2–0 lead, then leaped with both arms in the air before hugging McEneaney.

Still trailing by two goals, the Blue Jays gained possession following a save and clear by Mahon. Starting attackmen Richie Hirsch and Frank Cutrone each took a point-blank shot; Mackesey deflected both. Later in the quarter O'Neill passed to Huntley for an eight-yard shot from the left wing. The Canadian uncorked one of his trademark sidearm left-handed shots. In the regular-season meeting, two of those shots had eluded Mackesey and gone into the goal, and a third had hit the crossbar and bounced away. This time, with his new contact lenses, Mackesey made the save. "'Hot Rod' Huntley was our best shooter," Myrick says now. "He had a high, hard shot from eight yards. When he let it go, we just assumed that's in. We had seen him take that shot dozens of times, and it always was a goal. But Mackesey saved it. And on the sideline we all looked at each other and said, 'This could be a long day.'"[91]

At the other end of the field, Mahon stopped but did not control a tough bounce shot from eight yards from Jaeger. The loose ball spilled in front of the goal, and Henrickson collected it. Seconds later he fired a perfect twenty-yard pass to Jaeger, again standing about eight yards from the goal. This time Jaeger's bounce shot went past Mahon and into the goal for a 3–0 lead. Two minutes remained in the first quarter. The Blue Jays called time-out.

In lacrosse both teams' benches are on the same side of the field, just as in basketball and hockey (and unlike football). So as Johns Hopkins called time-out, Cornell's offensive players had to pass the Johns Hopkins bench to reach their own. The Blue Jays players and coaches were just starting to assemble on the sideline when McEneaney, en route to the Cornell bench, appeared to say something to someone from Johns Hopkins. A Johns Hopkins coach responded. Within seconds, the entire Johns Hopkins team surrounded McEneaney and two Cornell teammates. Both groups began screaming at each other, pushing and shoving. Moran and Cornell's players raced toward the scuffle. Moran made a beeline for Ciccarone, and the two began shoving each other and screaming, each one red in the face. The skirmish ended without further incident, nor were any penalties called.

During the timeout that followed, Wulforst joined the team huddle and made eye contact with McEneaney, who smiled at him. Wulforst gave a quick "hello" to his uncle while Moran was discussing strategy, and a Cornell player told Wulforst to be quiet, "rightfully so," Wulforst says. McEneaney informed the player that Wulforst was his nephew and his guest, and the player apologized. From there, Wulforst stood behind the bench, offering water bottles to the players as they came off the field and trying to look as official as he could.

The game resumed. The Big Red won the ensuing face-off after the skirmish, and the ball went to McEneaney behind the goal. He raced past Greenberg again, his point-blank bounce shot eluding Mahon for a 4–0 lead. Johns Hopkins followed that with a penalty, and seconds later, working their new man-up play, the Big Red led 5–0, after Henrickson threw another perfect fifteen-yard crossfield pass that Marino caught and shot from point-blank range. The first quarter ended with Cornell in command, the Cornell fans behind the team's bench standing and cheering.

The second quarter began. McEneaney was called for a penalty while chasing and then fouling Mahon during a Johns Hopkins clear. (1977 was the first year that Cornell kept individual penalty totals, and the foul on Mahon was McEneaney's sixteenth of the year, a team high.) The Blue Jays, on extra-man offense, worked the ball to the left wing for a wide-open shot from Hirsch, the three-year starter. He aimed for the top of the goal; Mackesey met the ball and guided it over the goalpost. The Blue Jays retained possession, their player being closest to the ball when it crossed the end line and, still with the man advantage, worked the ball to O'Neill for an open eight-yard shot from the right wing. Against the best player on the Johns Hopkins roster, Mackesey again made a save. One year after making a school-record twenty-eight saves in the NCAA title game, Mackesey arguably looked even better. "It can easily be said," Fred Yahn wrote in his report for the *Ithaca Journal*, "that [Mackesey in the first half] took away five goals from the Jays."

At this point the Blue Jays became frustrated and sloppy. A dropped pass led to a fast break for Cornell. McEneaney received the ball ten yards from the goal. He paused, readied to shoot, then instead passed to sophomore Reiley McDonald, a little-used, third-line midfielder, wide open in front of the goal. McDonald collected the pass and shot an instant later high into the goal, the lacrosse version of a layup. The Big Red led 6–0. That was the score when McEneaney again collected the ball on the right wing, seven yards from the goal. He squared to the goal and looked for all the world as if he were going to shoot the ball, only at the last second to pass instead to a cutting Marino, who guided the ball into the net for a 7–0 lead midway through the second quarter. Another fast break culminated with Henrickson collecting a pass from McEneaney and scoring on a bounce shot from fifteen yards. The score was 8–0, still in the second quarter.

It was after that goal, midway through the second quarter, that McEneaney raised both arms in the air in triumph, "Cornell" and "10" on his chest like a lacrosse superman. Baum captured the moment; the photo led the *Ithaca Journal* sports section coverage from the game. McEneaney himself scored again on another point-blank shot. The score was 9–0, the Big Red out in front, just as Moran wanted. Now it was time to see whether the Blue Jays could play catch-up.

Johns Hopkins finally scored, Cutrone from point-blank, Hirsch on the assist, though Mackesey argued to referees that Cutrone had stepped inside the goal crease before shooting and the goal should have been disallowed. Johns Hopkins brought with it to Charlottesville the small cannon that it fired after each goal at Homewood Field. As the cannon discharged for the first time, the Cornell fans cheered derisively.[92]

There was no sense that the tide might turn for the Blue Jays because soon after, on another Cornell breakaway, Mathisen, inserted into the game with his fourth midfield line, scored past Mahon, then leaped into the arms of McEneaney. The player who, days earlier, suggested he should not be on the game day roster had just given Cornell a 10–1 lead. It was his first goal of the year. That was the score when halftime arrived.

"That game is something I will never forget," Greenberg says now. "The game was lost pretty quickly. We just did not show up. No ifs, ands, or buts about it. We got crushed. It was the worst feeling in the world. I tell people to this day it was the longest day of lacrosse in my life. It felt like the game was never going to end, like we were never going to get off that field."[93] In the Johns Hopkins locker room, Ciccarone told his players they would need another 7–1 or 7–2 run, similar to what they had done in the first half of the regular-season meeting in Ithaca. That day, however, Mackesey and McEneaney were not playing their final college games.

In the Cornell locker room a season of destiny was in its final act. "That year was a cruising year," Bray says. "We were good, and we knew we were good. I just remember our games mostly being straightforward. We had that confidence from the previous year, and as an athlete, once you have that confidence you're hard to beat. Lots of times [in 1977] we were just cruising." Says Muehleman, "The Maryland game [in the 1976 championship] was the breakthrough for us. I remember being much more excited for that game. In '77 I remember talking to the guy I was covering while our offense had the ball." At halftime Moran revisited his stated goal of playing up-tempo for the first twenty minutes and decided to keep the pressure on. No need to change a successful plan, and Cornell was receiving more energy from their success than was being sapped by the sun.

The second half began; the Big Red, by plan, poured it on. Huntley took two of his sidearm shots from the middle of the restraining box; Mackesey saved both. One loose ball fell to DeSimone from the middle of the box, about eighteen yards from the goal. His long, low shot was easily saved by Mackesey. The Big Red extended its lead to 13–1 when Johns Hopkins sophomore Scott Baugher scored a goal late in the third quarter to cut the deficit to 13–2. The Blue Jays were so dispirited that rather than shake any teammates' hands after the goal, Baugher just went directly back to the sideline.

FIGURE 11.7. The lead photo in the *Ithaca Journal* after the 1977 title game showed Eamon McEneaney in the moment after a Cornell goal. Since his death in the terror attacks of September 11, 2001, Cornell has placed a "10" in the scoreboard at every practice in his honor. (Photo courtesy Larry Baum)

FIGURE 11.8. Away from the field, Eamon McEneaney, shown as a senior at Cornell in 1977, was kind, funny, and loved everything Irish, including poetry and music. "He was a very deep guy," said one friend. (Photo courtesy Larry Baum)

By the end of the third quarter, the Big Red led 14–3. They scored the open-ing goal of the fourth quarter as well McEneaney assisting junior George Lau to make the score 15–3. The assist was McEneaney's final point; fittingly it went to a Sewanhaka High alumnus, one year younger. As Moran waved his substitutes into the game, McEneaney left the field for the final time, with three goals and five assists. McEneaney spent the final minutes of his college career sitting on the sideline, enjoying his team's 16–8 victory, literally basking in the Virginia sun. One family picture shows him smiling, helmet still on, still wearing his puffy red Brine L35 lacrosse gloves with "Mac" written on them, stick in one hand, white towel around his neck, and his arm around Wulforst, whose smile is even bigger than McEneaney's.[94] McEneaney had played twenty-nine games follow-ing his promise never to lose a game at Cornell again. The Big Red had won all twenty-nine. In the title game Marino added three goals, and Mackesey made thirteen saves while giving up three goals through three-plus quarters. Mackesey joined the varsity as a sophomore in 1975 and was a backup who appeared in ten games that year, then started every game as a junior and senior. In all thirty-nine contests in which he appeared, Cornell won.

McEneaney finished his senior season with seventy-nine points, forty-one goals, and thirty-eight assists, the third-best total in the nation. (Larry Stor-rier from Syracuse and Mickey Menna from Massachusetts each had eighty-four points.) In his final season McEneaney led the Big Red in points, assists, and penalties, was second in goals, and third in ground balls, with seventy-one. Mackesey finished with a 5.2 goals-against average, and a .642 save percentage.

The Big Red, in 1976 and 1977, also went undefeated in scrimmages against postcollegiate teams and other college teams. It would be hard to imagine a bet-ter ending than the triumph at Scott Stadium. Days earlier, soon after the team arrived in Charlottesville, McEneaney had given an interview to a writer from *Sports Illustrated* in town to cover the game. McEneaney looked back on his career and his relationship with his coach. "I love Richie," McEneaney said. "I love him because he made me a winner, and that's what I wanted to be."[95]

As the Cornell bus pulled out of Charlottesville, Kane repeated his line from the previous year in Providence. "Would anyone on this bus," he said, "who has never lost a college game please stand up?" This time all but four seniors stood. (Malm, a transfer in 1976, would have made five, but he was not on the bus. Instead, he was driving from Charlottesville directly to Long Island where he was scheduled to begin his job as a bartender at the Kismet Inn in Kismet, New York, in two days.) Nearly every player on the bus was undefeated, and they were feeling invincible. The *Ithaca Journal* noted that while Mackesey, McEneaney, and Malm were seniors, expected back were second-leading scorer

Marino, starting midfielders Jaeger and Henrickson, and the entire starting defense, plus top reserve Vincent Shanley.

On the other bus, headed to Baltimore, the Johns Hopkins contingent was chastened. "They [Cornell] did nothing we hadn't expected," Ciccarone told reporters after the game. "But I did feel that we could have come back, even when it was 6–0. They just never gave us a chance to get back." Says Myrick, a Johns Hopkins team captain in 1977, "We beat Maryland by ten goals in the semifinals. That was our blood rival. We hated each other. I'll never forget the celebration afterward. We couldn't imagine anything better than that. We kind of forgot there was another game to be played the following week."[96]

McEneaney and Mackesey had one last game together. Those two and Bray had been selected for the North–South game, held June 5 at the University of Maryland–Baltimore County in Catonsville. It was another departure for the sport, its once-showcase game being played in the Baltimore area but not at Homewood Field. Sollers, the Princeton attackman, was also playing for the North. He recalled the Thursday before the North–South game when the players were to arrive in Catonsville, have lunch, and then begin practice with their ceremonial teams. When the players gathered in the university cafeteria, there was no sign of McEneaney.

Finally the redhead arrived, wearing a smile and toting a six-pack of beer. "He walked in and said, 'What's up, guys!'" Sollers says. "What a character."[97] The North–South game was one of the first big events at UMBC's stadium, located on the southeast corner of the campus, almost hidden amid a backdrop of trees and small hills. Following a cookout for players and coaches on Thursday night, and partly to drum up support for the game, UMBC sports information director Dan O'Connell arranged for both head coaches—Ciccarone, coaching the South, and Tom Hayes of Rutgers, a close friend of Moran and Sewanhaka alumnus who was coaching the North—to be interviewed on a local radio show. O'Connell also brought a handful of players, including McEneaney, to be interviewed in the show's makeshift studio, the lobby of the Hilton Hotel on Reisterstown Road near campus. "Eamon was great for that," O'Connell says now. "He was a natural. I could see that he loved the spotlight. He was a confident kid, and he loved joking around."[98] At practice the next day, O'Connell watched as McEneaney threw behind-the-back passes as accurately as those he threw using the normal motion. The teams gathered again for the All-American banquet on Friday night at the UMBC dining hall. Moran was given the Morris Touchstone award, as the Division I coach of the year. McEneaney was named the 1977 player of the year, and the most valuable player of the NCAA tournament. Mackesey was named the best goalie of 1977, and junior Chris Kane won the award for best defenseman.

The game was played the next day, a warm, sticky Saturday afternoon. Five thousand people crammed into the one-year-old stadium. Both McEneaney and

FIGURE 11.9. Cornell's Eamon McEneaney, one of the best players in the sport's history, spent the final moments of his college career on the sideline with his twelve year-old nephew, who had snuck onto the field by distracting a security guard. (Photo courtesy Howard Wulforst)

FIGURE 11.10. Cornell coach Richie Moran and, from left, Bob Mathisen, Pat Avery, and team captain Gary Malm, celebrate following the 16–8 victory over Johns Hopkins in the 1977 title game in Charlottesville. (Photo courtesy Larry Baum)

Mackesey were in the starting lineup, bringing with them, one last time, their uncanny knack for being on the winning side in a lacrosse game. The South, with a roster full of all-Americans, many of them Baltimore natives, opened the game with four quick shots. Mackesey saved all of them. By tradition, each goalie plays only one half, so Mackesey departed at halftime with the North leading, 12–4. The South rallied and closed to 17–15 with about three minutes remaining. The South defense forced a wild shot from a North player, but McEneaney was closest to the end line when it went out of bounds, so his team retained possession. The South sent defender John Pirro from Roanoke College and Mahon to double-team McEneaney. When the game restarted, McEneaney raced to the sliver of space that Pirro and Mahon had left between them, ran to the front of the goal, and scored into the empty net, his final goal as a college player. The North held on to win, 20–15. McEneaney finished with two goals and two assists, Mackesey with seven saves. Afterward, Sollers brought two local high-school students he had befriended through tennis lessons into the victorious locker room. The teens walked in slowly and nervously. McEneaney spotted them immediately and gave them a welcome by spraying them with champagne, just as he was doing with those who had played for the North. "They didn't really know anyone," Sollers says now, "and Eamon wanted them to feel like they were part of the team."[99]

THAT-A-WAY IN PISCATAWAY

On Saturday, July 16, 1977, *Wide World of Sports* aired its highlights from the Johns Hopkins–Cornell lacrosse championship game, along with highlights from the Firecracker 400 stock car race at Daytona International Speedway and the women's masters surfing championship from Oahu, Hawaii. Lacrosse was given roughly thirteen minutes of the ninety-minute broadcast. The show ended at 6:30 p.m. At that point, the book finally closed on the 1977 college lacrosse season. For Johns Hopkins the book had closed much sooner. A writer from *Sports Illustrated* had captured Johns Hopkins star attackman Michael O'Neill in the final moments of the championship game in Charlottesville, sitting on the bench as reserves from both teams took over. Cornell led 16–3 before the Blue Jays scored the final five goals against Cornell's backups. "They're just better than us," O'Neill said on the sideline, partly to the reporter and partly to himself. "But I don't think they're that much better. This is embarrassing. Come on clock, run down."[1]

O'Neill entered the 1978 season as the best attackman in college lacrosse. Like Eamon McEneaney, best attackman the previous year, O'Neill had been named first-team all-American as a sophomore and junior. The second-youngest of eleven children, O'Neill was, like McEneaney, a Long Island native who had been introduced to the sport by an older brother.

O'Neill attended Massapequa High, where his classmates included Tom Marino, his best friend since kindergarten. Massapequa High's lacrosse coach was a gym teacher who was not well versed in the sport; he did not know how to throw and catch with a lacrosse stick, so he warmed up goalies by throwing

FIGURE 12.1. Michael O'Neill entered his senior year at Johns Hopkins having been a two-time, first-team all-American, but he had yet to win an NCAA title. "O'Neill was on a mission," said one teammate. (Photo courtesy Johns Hopkins Athletics)

the ball with his hand as if he were a baseball pitcher. By the time Marino and O'Neill were seniors in 1974, they were both being heavily recruited by colleges, and the pair said openly that they planned on attending the same school. Among the suitors was Navy. Coach Dick Szlasa arrived at the guidance counselor's office at Massapequa High to deliver his recruiting pitch, accompanied by two Navy officers in full uniform. Szlasa began by showing O'Neill and Marino pictures of the campus in Annapolis and what life would be like on the lacrosse team and at the academy. At one point he showed a picture of a fighter jet, then turned to O'Neill and said, "Can't you see yourself flying this?" O'Neill looked at the coach in disbelief. "You're fucking nuts," he replied. The pair crossed Navy off their list.

By the spring of 1974, O'Neill and Marino had narrowed the choices down to Cornell and Johns Hopkins. Both gained admission at Johns Hopkins and were given scholarship money to cover the cost of tuition. Marino was also admitted at Cornell; O'Neill was placed on the wait list. In the interim O'Neill went on a recruiting trip to Johns Hopkins, where, on March 23, 1974, he took in a 19–6 victory over Yale at Homewood Field. After the game he went into the Newton White Athletic Center to meet with Henry Ciccarone, then an assistant but already tabbed as the replacement for Bob Scott, who was in his final year. Ciccarone asked O'Neill what he thought of the game. "I was the tenth of eleven kids," O'Neill says now. "I was pretty cocky. Chic asked me what I thought and I said, 'I think I could play for you guys right now.'" By this point O'Neill still had not heard from Cornell. "It was getting to be February and March, and I hadn't heard shit," he says. "I just figured I didn't get in."[2] O'Neill accepted the scholarship from Johns Hopkins. Marino, with an older brother at Cornell and a budding friendship with McEneaney, accepted the offer from Cornell, complete with financial aid.

Massapequa finished with a 14–7 record, and O'Neill was named high-school all-American. In the fall of 1974, he enrolled at Johns Hopkins. O'Neill was in for a learning experience, on and off the field. At 10 a.m. on Saturday mornings in the fall, O'Neill was awakened at his fraternity house by assistant coach Dennis Townsend, a former star defenseman at Johns Hopkins currently playing for Mount Washington. (The initiation was similar to Glen Mueller's waking up Mike French in the fall of 1972—"I was usually pretty groggy from having had a few beers the previous night," French says—and taking him to play pickup basketball and learn Moran's motion offense.)

O'Neill and Townsend would head to a local park and play one-on-one lacrosse. O'Neill received one point for every goal; Townsend would earn one point every time he dislodged the ball from O'Neill's stick and gained possession himself. The games would go to thirty. The early games were no contest. "He used to strip the ball from me easily," O'Neill says. "I didn't like getting the ball taken, and I was cursing and throwing my stick to the ground. But he was breaking things down for me geometrically. He was saying, 'If the guy is giving you something on the outside, don't always try to take him inside.'" Townsend also was teaching O'Neill about taking angles, about protecting his lacrosse stick, about being patient. O'Neill likened it to learning how to play offense by approaching it like wrestling. "He was teaching me how to play attack," O'Neill says, "rather than how to be an athlete playing attack."[3]

For the season opener in the spring of 1975 against Virginia—Ciccarone's first game as head coach, O'Neill's first game as a freshman–O'Neill was in the starting lineup on attack. He finished with four goals, including the winning goal in overtime. He remained in the starting lineup throughout the season, including the 16–9 victory over Cornell at Schoellkopf Field in mid-April. On the bus ride home, the driver pulled over at the first shopping mall outside Ithaca, and each player was given fifteen dollars for food. O'Neill says that most of the players got a quick bite at Burger King, then went to a liquor store and used their remaining money for beer. "Everyone on the bus ride home was playing cards, smoking," O'Neill says now. (Cornell's bus trips following games had a similar look, depending on which coaches were on board. "If Richie was on board," Gary Malm says now, "we almost never drank. If it was Bones or Scotty Anderson," he adds with a smile, "we might have had a little to drink."[4]) O'Neill finished the 1975 season with thirty-six goals and fourteen assists, though the Blue Jays lost in the first round of the NCAA tournament to Washington and Lee.

The following fall O'Neill and Townsend resumed their one-on-one games. Townsend still won, but the scores were becoming closer. That spring O'Neill finished with identical statistics to his freshman year—thirty-six goals and fourteen assists—and the Blue Jays reached the 1976 NCAA semifinals before losing to Cornell. O'Neill was named first-team all-American. As a junior O'Neill began to beat Townsend in the one-on-one fall contests. In the spring he finished with thirty-one goals and thirty-four assists, was named first-team all-American and attackman of the year. But the loss in the 1977 title game had been humiliating— so much so that O'Neill, one of 120 players invited on consecutive weekends in July to try out for the US national team, decided not to go at all. He remained on Long Island all summer, held a summer job, and played pickup basketball. He did not pick up his lacrosse stick for weeks. "I was so pissed off with my performance and the whole scene," he says. "I didn't pick up my stick until the first fall practice senior year."[5]

O'Neill entered his senior year having failed to win an NCAA title—his stated goal when arriving at Johns Hopkins in the fall of 1974. He had one last chance. In 1978 the Blue Jays had plenty of returning talent. Like O'Neill, junior midfielder Dave Huntley had been named first-team all-American in 1977, following a season in which he finished with thirty-two goals. Also back was senior midfielder Bob DeSimone, coming off a season-long shooting slump. In 1977 he led the Blue Jays with 114 shots, and scored only eighteen goals (15.7 percent). Another player may have been cowed by the lack of success. DeSimone was not. He was well known among his teammates for not lacking confidence in his shooting. "He could go zero-for-April, and he'd just keep shooting," Leroy Katz says. "It didn't bother him a bit. He'd always say, 'When you're hot, you're hot. When you're not, keep shooting.'"[6] The midfield also had returning junior Steve Wey, from Calvert Hall, considered the team's toughest player. "He'd knock your head off in practice," says O'Neill, "then apologize, and help you pick it up." Wey, 5'11", 190 pounds, was set for a spot on the starting midfield alongside DeSimone and Huntley. The recruiting class included a 5'10", 160-pound redhead from Baltimore named Ned Radebaugh. At Calvert Hall he had played midfield and scored twenty-four goals as a senior. But his biggest contribution was giving the Cardinals the ball, repeatedly, by winning face-offs, and his prowess had been a main reason that Calvert Hall won the prestigious Maryland Scholastic Association "A" Conference title that spring. At Calvert Hall's graduation ceremony, when Radebaugh's named was called to receive his diploma, one of the Christian Brothers, the order that founded the school, leaned over to lacrosse coach Mike Thomas and said, "There goes your lacrosse team."

But the fulcrum at Johns Hopkins in the spring of 1978 would be O'Neill, and his teammates picked up on it. On the silent bus ride home from Charlottesville to Baltimore following the NCAA title game in 1977, the only sound was O'Neill visiting every single player who was set to return the next season. He stopped by their seats on the bus, quietly telling them what had happened in Charlottesville would not happen again, that they should be ready, starting in the fall, for a much better end of the season. O'Neill's teammates listened. In the preseason of 1978, when the players gathered to vote for team captains, the only player who received the requisite number was O'Neill. For the first time since 1952, Johns Hopkins would enter the lacrosse season with one captain.

In 1978 Cornell was without the incomparable McEneaney and Mackesey. McEneaney remained in Ithaca, finishing his undergraduate degree and living with Malm in a two-bedroom house on Route 79, just outside Collegetown. McEneaney was also helping to coach the Cornell "B" team and briefly worked with the Syracuse varsity program as well. McEneaney's tryout with the New York Jets over the summer had not gone as planned. The night before the tryouts, held on the campus at Hofstra, McEneaney sliced his hand open while shucking clams. The next day he was fielding punts with his hand heavily wrapped when he noticed that Jets coach Joe Walton was continuously watching another part of the practice field. Joe Gardi, a Jets assistant coach and friend of Moran from their time together at the University of Maryland, later recounted that McEneaney walked up to Walton and said, "Why did you ask me to tryout if you aren't going to watch me?" Moran recalls McEneaney was offered a spot on the Jets' taxi squad, a group of players who would practice with the team but were not likely to play in games unless there were injuries or suspensions. Many athletes would have jumped at the chance to have their foot in the door of an NFL franchise. McEneaney decided instead to return to Ithaca and finish his degree.

Mackesey was in Charlottesville, in his first year of law school at the University of Virginia and helping the lacrosse team that spring. Mackesey's roommate was Jim Graham, a former midfielder from Yale, who had assisted the lone goal that Mackesey gave up to the Elis on May 2, 1976, the day Mackesey's father died. (On May 2, 1980, when Mackesey was in his third year of law school, he went on the first date with the woman he would marry. At their wedding, Graham was the best man.)

But almost every other main contributor from Cornell's undefeated 1977 team was in place for 1978. Marino was back after having scored a team-high forty-six goals the previous year. Marino was bright and personable; he spent one year with his on-campus job as a tour guide for prospective Cornell students and their parents. He spent his senior year playing lacrosse, finishing his degree in business, and bartending at both the Haunt and Simeon's, popular bars in the three-year-old Ithaca Commons, just down the hill from Cornell. Also back were seniors and starting midfielders Bob Henrickson (eighteen goals, twelve assists, team-high ninety-three ground balls in 1977) and Craig Jaeger (sixteen goals, ten assists, seventy-nine ground balls), and senior Steve Page, who had moved into the starting attack unit the previous year and finished with twenty-one goals.

Henrickson grew up in Burbank, California, where his sports of choice were baseball, skateboarding, and riding bicycles.[7] His father's job in sales moved the family to Long Island, and they settled in Manhasset. Henrickson's father drove past the local high school on his daily commute. And he had some sobering news for his son, then in fifth grade. "He said there didn't look like there was much baseball," Henrickson says. "But they had that sport where it looked like they were playing with butterfly nets."[8] Bob Henrickson was a good athlete, and he found lacrosse, and especially midfield, to his liking. "You got to play defense, offense, take face-offs," he says. "It was the perfect position."[9]

Henrickson had a strong interest in becoming a veterinarian and chose Cornell over Penn, Virginia, and Maryland. His father and Moran became close friends, so much so that Moran often visited the Henrickson family home on Mill Spring Road in the Strathmore neighborhood of Manhasset. One night a few weeks after the 1976 title game, Moran stopped by the Henrickson home as Henrickson's mother was folding laundry. Her son had mistakenly taken his red lacrosse game shorts home with him from Providence, rather than returning them to the school, as required. In the middle of a sentence, Moran spied the red game shorts, stopped talking, grabbed the contraband with a quick "I'll take those," then resumed his story.

The entire starting defense returned as well. Frank Muehleman, Bobby Katz, and Chris Kane would be playing together for a third consecutive year. The previous season Cornell had given up fewer than six goals a game. Mackesey's replacement was set to be junior John Griffin, from Baldwin High on Long Island, who had been the top reserve in 1976 and 1977.

Cornell picked three captains—Kane, Marino, and Henrickson. On the surface the 1978 captains were a perfect combination—one each from attack, midfield, and defense. But the frighteningly competitive McEneaney was gone, and the Big Red did not have a leader to fill that void. "None of us were really yellers and screamers," Henrickson says. "We didn't really have a 'get-in-line' guy, though

FIGURE 12.2. Cornell midfielder Bob Henrickson moves upfield in the 1978 semifinals against Navy. The two lines of eye black on his face began as a mistake by a trainer in the first game of his varsity career. (Photo courtesy Larry Baum)

I guess Chris came closest. We were captains more for our playing ability than our leadership qualities. And down the stretch that might have been an issue."[10] Johns Hopkins had no such reservations about its choice as captain.

Among Cornell's reserves one player in particular was intriguing: defenseman Pat Avery, a sophomore from Hartford, Connecticut, who had played in eleven games in 1977. Avery was the first African American player at Cornell in recent memory, followed closely by midfielder Sam Edwards, a freshman in 1978 from Jamaica, New York. Avery, 6'2", 215 pounds, had arrived at Cornell as a two-sport recruit, defensive end in football, defender in lacrosse, but he left the football program as a sophomore and focused on lacrosse. Edwards, 5'4", 126 pounds, was a standout wrestler at Eastern Military Academy in Cold Spring Harbor, New York, and was set to spend his freshman season in 1978 with the Cornell "B" lacrosse team after spending the winter with Cornell's varsity wrestling squad.

African American players on the whole were enjoying more prominence. The 1978 official NCAA lacrosse guide featured, on its cover, Morgan State senior Joe "Flaky" Fowlkes, a midfielder who had scored forty-two goals the previous year and sixty-one as a sophomore in 1976, with that total leading the entire NCAA Division II.

The magazine had been published annually, first by Spalding Sporting Goods, since the 1920s, and Fowlkes was the first African American player ever pictured on the cover. (The 1977 edition had featured McEneaney on the cover.) "I think it was a good thing for the game," Morgan State coach Sheldon Freed told the *Baltimore Sun* in February 1978, "and a good thing for our squad. What we need is recognition to get the great athletes at Morgan interested in lacrosse."[11] Freed said that Morgan State had gone from eighteen players in 1977 to thirty-three for 1978, and he attributed the publicity from Fowlkes's appearance on the magazine cover as the main reason. Fowlkes had grown up in Baltimore and began playing lacrosse at Walbrook High, northwest of the city. At Morgan State he was also a standout cornerback in football, and his school record of fifteen interceptions in one season stood for several decades. In lacrosse Fowlkes entered the 1978 season having been twice named honorable mention all-American and had led the Bears in ground balls three consecutive years. Fowlkes clearly was one of the best players in the sport.

In 1977 the Maryland Scholastic Association "C" Conference title had been won by Southwestern High, which featured an almost entirely African American roster. Also in 1977 an African American senior at Annapolis High named Sid Abernethy was named a high-school all-American, and he chose to follow his older brother to the US Naval Academy. For the 1978 season Sid Abernethy was slated to be a reserve attackman for the Midshipmen. On Long Island more than half the players on the Hempstead High team were African American. (Hempstead had finished with seven wins in seventeen games in 1977.) "There were definitely some [African American] players on Hempstead High's team we were very interested in," Moran says. "When it came down to it, financial aid became very difficult for black and white players." A handful of Hempstead High's African American players wound up playing at Rutgers for Tom Hayes, a close friend of Moran and a fellow graduate of Sewanhaka High. In the 1970s Moran only landed two players from Hempstead High: Sierra and a reserve mid-fielder named Brian Conroy, a transfer from Nassau Community College, who suited up for the Big Red in 1977 and 1978.

The sport was showing signs of change geographically as well. Cornell and Hobart had swept NCAA lacrosse championships in consecutive seasons, shutting out Maryland. "Is losing our lacrosse supremacy," asked columnist Alan Goldstein in the *Baltimore Sun* soon after the 1977 season, "as traumatic as Linus losing his security blanket? Have we given the game back to the uncivilized tribes of New York?" Goldstein sought comment from Bob Scott, former coach at Johns Hopkins. "The game is spreading everywhere," Scott was quoted as saying in the column. "New Jersey has become a real hotbed. Who would have ever believed a school from Jersey would beat Gilman? But it happened this year," he said, referring to Montclair High's 8–4 victory over Gilman in the first game of a double-header, also featuring Navy's 12–9 victory over Princeton, on April 9, 1977, at Princeton's Palmer Stadium. Later in the column Scott stopped short of saying that Cornell was on its way to a dynasty. "The [youth leagues] in our area are getting better and better coaching," Scott was quoted in the article. "Baltimore started with three youth teams [in 1959]. Now there are 55 or 60."[12]

Cornell's seniors entered the spring of 1978 having never lost a game or scrimmage in their careers. They were 10–0 on the freshman team, 16–0 and 13–0 in their first two years on varsity; they won single fall scrimmages in 1975, 1976, and 1977, won all three of their games against postcollege club competition, and all three of its preseason scrimmages. The unofficial record in all competition was forty-eight wins, zero losses. Against this backdrop, in early February 1978 Cornell held its initial spring practice, the annual one-mile timed run inside Barton Hall, eight laps around the rubberized track. Marino finished in under five minutes. He was eclipsed by Kane, Henrickson, and Sierra, all of whom finished in the 4:30 to 4:40 range.[13] Senior Keith Reitenbach, set to play both offensive midfield and longstick defensive midfield, finished in under five minutes as well. There would be no letdown in Ithaca.

In Baltimore, Johns Hopkins held its first practice on Homewood Field on February 18. When asked about his team's chances, coach Henry Ciccarone said laconically, "We'll be competitive."[14] Johns Hopkins was set to pin its hopes on O'Neill. Three local products would play important roles as well. Sophomore Mark Greenberg, a native of the Baltimore suburb of Pikesville, was back as the number one defenseman. Making his way up the depth chart was a sophomore goalkeeper from Boys' Latin School named Mike Federico. In high school he had been a backup for three years. Finally given the job as a senior in 1976, Federico excelled and was named a high-school all-American in leading the Lakers to the MSA "A" championship game. By 1978, entering his sophomore year at Johns Hopkins, Federico had grown to be 6'1", 170 pounds, marrying catlike quickness with toughness both on the field and in the weight room. He was also considered the best athlete on the Johns Hopkins lacrosse team and surprised teammates in pickup basketball games with his ability to dunk the basketball. "Mike was small in high school," said Ridge Warfield, then coach at Boys' Latin, "but even then, we knew he would have all-American ability when he matured."[15] Federico's transformation was so startling that he was set to be the starter for Johns Hopkins ahead of a junior named Howie Nichlas who for two years at Boys' Latin had started ahead of Federico.[16]

The third Baltimore native set for a large role was sophomore Leroy Katz. He had grown up as one of eight siblings in a lower-middle-class family in Reisterstown, Maryland, a Baltimore suburb. "My parents," Katz says now, "didn't have two nickels to rub together." In the seventh grade Katz, following in his older brother's footsteps, received a scholarship to attend McDonogh School in Owings Mills as a boarding student. It was there, in the eighth grade, he learned how to throw and catch a lacrosse ball with a wooden stick, on the school's parking lots, with his two best friends as his tutors. Katz made McDonogh's varsity as a sophomore, and the three-year stint in the Maryland Scholastic Association was an even greater learning experience: the Eagles played thirty MSA games and lost all of them.

Despite the losses Katz drew the attention of colleges, and he narrowed his list to Virginia, Johns Hopkins, and Yale. On his official visit to Virginia, he noticed that the players spoke almost exclusively of having fun and never placed any emphasis on winning games. He took Virginia off his list. The final two schools, Yale and Johns Hopkins, were set to play in the season opener in 1976 in Baltimore. Coaches from both programs invited Katz to attend, Johns Hopkins sending him two tickets to the game, Yale sending him a pass for entry into an alumni function afterward. That afternoon, the Blue Jays jumped to a 6–0 lead en route to a 19–6 victory. "I loved Yale and I loved coach Bob McHenry," Katz says, "but I said there is no way I am spending another four years playing games like I had done in high school." With that, Katz committed to Johns Hopkins.[17]

The first team meeting every fall with Johns Hopkins coach Henry Ciccarone and the players was held in a meeting room inside the Newton White Athletic Center. In the fall of 1976, Katz, a freshman, listened as Ciccarone gave the traditional opening speech of the season, some version of which he used every year. "He said, 'Listen, lacrosse is fun, but it's only fun if you're winning,'" Katz recalls. "'And we're here to win a national championship. Anyone here for any other reason, you might as well hit the door now.'" From there, the players went onto the grass practice fields for their first fall workout. Ciccarone's speech was music to Katz's ears, but not everyone was sold. The 1976–77 opening practice began with a lap around the field, then the players would run to the sideline and gather around Ciccarone and the assistants. One player took the field with the team, joined in the lap around the field, ran toward the coaches on the sideline, then kept going, past the coaches and into the locker room. By the time practice ended, the player had cleared out his locker and was gone.[18]

The workouts in the fall of 1976 culminated with a scrimmage against UMBC, one the Blue Jays won easily. Katz recalls celebrating on the sideline, only to be approached by Ciccarone. "He said, 'Leroy, don't celebrate. You need to learn this is the expectation around here,'" Katz recalls. Ciccarone was no less intense on the sideline. After every Johns Hopkins goal, while the spectators in the stands cheered, Ciccarone would walk up and down the sideline repeating the phrase, "Next goal!

Next goal!" The goal that had just been scored made the spectators happy, but Ciccarone had already moved on. It was time to focus on how to score again.

In the fall of 1977, the crushing afternoon in Charlottesville still on his mind, Ciccarone added a wrinkle to his traditional opening speech, saying there would be no talk of the 1977 title game. It was time to move on.

And at the first practice of the spring, on February 18, 1978, Ciccarone took aim at the defending champions, who would visit Homewood Field on April 15. "Cornell plays Dartmouth before our game and has nothing to worry about after us," Ciccarone said, taking a shot at the Big Red's schedule.[19] The two-time defending champions were not above wielding a few verbal brickbats of their own. From his office inside Schoellkopf House, Cornell sports information director Dave Wohlhueter mentioned in his 1978 preseason release, mailed to newspapers and television stations around the mid-Atlantic "Moran, whose toughest foe in the past two years has been the weatherman."[20] It was true that one opponent that Moran's remarkable team could not completely overcome was Mother Nature. Cornell again was set to escape frigid Ithaca for spring break in mid-March 1978. It was headed to Baltimore for a week of practices, scrimmages against two postcollegiate teams, and what was now a traditional exhibition against the Mount Washington Lacrosse Club, the three-time defending postcollegiate national champions.

Cornell began the season ranked number one in the USILA poll, with the Big Five in its wake. Johns Hopkins was ranked second, Maryland third, Navy fourth, Virginia fifth, and Army tenth. Spring break arrived on March 17, accompanied by a snowstorm in Maryland. Moran was informed that there was more snow in Baltimore than Ithaca, and so the team stayed put, practicing on dry and clear Schoellkopf Field.[21] Cornell finally hit the road on Sunday, two days behind schedule. The team practiced Monday and Tuesday on Mount Washington's Norris Field outside Baltimore.[22] On Wednesday night, despite significant mud on Norris Field's grass surface, the contest between two-time defending NCAA champion Cornell and the Wolfpack went ahead after a one-day delay. The *Baltimore Sun*'s James H. Jackson began his preview story, "In recent years, few have played the ancient game of lacrosse better than the Cornell University teams coached by Richie Moran."[23] Jackson ended the story, "Lacrosse was first played by the [Native Americans], and later refined by Baltimore area colleges. Collegiate lacrosse has traditionally been dominated by the University of Maryland, Johns Hopkins, Navy, the U.S. Military Academy, Washington College, Towson State University, and Virginia. Until the last two years, that is, when Hobart and Cornell, both upstate New York colleges, won national titles."[24]

On Wednesday, March 22, 1978, Cornell and Mount Washington, the two-time defending NCAA Division I champion and three-time defending club champion, took the field. The game was tied at eight at halftime.[25] Less than a minute into the second half, Ned Gerber, along with senior Bob Katz the only Baltimore natives in the starting lineup, scored to give the Big Red the lead.[26] Three more goals followed. The Big Red kept the pace the entire second half and won going away, 18–12. Midfielders Henrickson and Sierra led the way with four goals each, and Jaeger won his head-to-head matchup on face-offs with Doug Radebaugh, the 1975 NCAA midfielder of the year at Maryland. Both Griffin and junior Bob Jackson, an Ithaca native, played in goal, with Griffin earning the starting nod. The Mount Washington coach, having lost to Cornell for a third consecutive year, was impressed. "They are a better team this year than last year," said Gene Fusting. "They are playing better team lacrosse."[27]

The Big Red returned to Ithaca and prepared to face another team that had won a championship the previous year, NCAA Division II champion Hobart. The 1977 contest had been canceled because of snow. In Geneva, New York, Hobart's coaches questioned how hard Cornell had tried to reschedule the contest. When asked by a local paper whether Cornell had "ducked" the game against Hobart, Schmidt, well past his brief episode of cooperation with Moran, replied, "That would be the general consensus."[28]

Cornell entered with a thirty-game winning streak, the Statesmen a twenty-game streak. Each was the top-ranked team in its respective NCAA classification. Moran told the *Finger Lakes Times* beforehand that the game had the potential to be "one of the finest games ever seen in Upstate New York."[29] The *Ithaca Journal* headline on the day of the contest was "At Last, Cornell vs. Hobart." The game was set to start on Wednesday, March 28, at 3 p.m. Slate-gray skies greeted the teams during their warm-ups: Cornell in its red jerseys, red shorts, and white helmets; Hobart in creamsicle-orange jerseys, white shorts, and white helmets. Hobart enlisted eight buses to bring students to Ithaca—an impressive total given that the school's enrollment was 1,050.[30] Many of the Hobart fans had gathered earlier at the Twin Oaks bar in Geneva, a small, white-frame building at 271 Pulteney Street, at the intersection of Pulteney and Hamilton streets, walking distance from campus, for a few beers before the roughly one-hour bus ride down Route 96A. When the Hobart students arrived in Ithaca, most of them had painted their faces and bared their chests despite the cool temperatures and dark conditions.[31]

A crowd of 10,500 descended on Schoellkopf Field, a very impressive total for a midweek matinee game. Cornell officials had sold tickets the day before the game, the only contest for which they would do so in 1978. The roads leading to Schoellkopf Field, already choked, it being a weekday afternoon with classes in session, became snarled. Parking spaces on the narrow streets around Schoellkopf Field were scarce, and many walked at least a quarter mile to get to the stadium. A light drizzle fell on the field as the teams took the field for the opening face-off.

Though Kane had been voted the Division I defenseman of the year the previous year, the job of guarding senior Terry Corcoran fell to Muehleman, who would receive help from constant slides.[32]

Hobart's defensive scheme, under assistant coach Dave Urick, was aggressive. The Statesmen constantly sent double-teams, the lacrosse equivalent of a blitz in football, toward the player with the ball. If he handled the pressure, there would be an open teammate to be found for a good shot; but Hobart found few opponents who could handle the onslaught. Schmidt, as the plastic lacrosse sticks began to take hold in the mid-1970s, borrowed a page from former Navy coach Bill Bilderback and recruited Hobart's football players to the lacrosse team, even though they had never played the sport before. "The plastic stick was allowing good athletes to pick up the sport in high school and immediately become impact players," Corcoran says. "Baltimore and Long Island weren't the only lacrosse hotbeds anymore, upstate [New York] players were appearing on college rosters everywhere." The Statesmen took the field on March 28 with fifteen natives of central New York on the roster, the Big Red with six.

Overlooking the artificial turf and looking out on the hills rising to the east of the Ithaca campus, writers from *Sports Illustrated*, the Associated Press, and numerous outlets in upstate New York settled into their seats in the three-level concrete press box opposite the Crescent. Seven years after the start of the NCAA tournament, the preeminent game in college lacrosse was between two schools in the Finger Lakes region, with barely a half-dozen Baltimore natives combined on the two rosters. (In his article for *Sports Illustrated*, Joe Marshall noted the game had been billed "the Super Bowl of lacrosse"; he added, "Baltimore may still be home of the oriole, Blaze Starr and crab cakes, but the capital of lacrosse has moved north to the scenic Finger Lakes region of New York.")[33] The concrete stands below the press box were nearly completely full.

Page scored the opening goal, assisted by Jaeger. By the middle of the second quarter, the Big Red had extended the lead 5–0, with Griffin, starting in goal, having made eight saves. Corcoran was taking shots despite the constant double-teams, and Hobart's high-powered offense was struggling. At halftime the Big Red led 7–2. Schmidt told his team to remain calm, then directed his attention to Corcoran. "I was holding the ball too long, and forcing shots against double-teams," Corcoran says. "I needed to go to the cage, draw the defense, and get the ball out of my stick to a teammate." Schmidt also delivered a message to the whole team: "Anybody who thinks we can't win shouldn't go back out there again."[34] Schmidt later noted, "They all took the field." The third quarter began. Cornell stretched its lead to 8–2 on a goal by junior Reiley McDonald. But in the third quarter Hobart's gambling defense was starting to force turnovers, and Bill Sipperly, a freshman from Suffern, New York, began dominating face-offs. Corcoran was following his coach's directions, drawing a slide and passing the ball rather than trying to beat the double-team on his own. At the end of the third quarter, Corcoran still was without a goal, but the Statesmen had closed the deficit to 10–7.

Early in the fourth quarter Corcoran assisted on a goal by Scott Petosa, a 5'5" sophomore from West Genesee High outside Syracuse, to close the deficit to 10–8. The Statesmen added three more goals, and took an 11–10 lead on a goal by freshman Mark Darcangelo with four minutes, fifteen seconds remaining. The Hobart faithful, many still without shirts in the cool weather, were delirious. Cornell fans sat on their frozen hands, waiting for an opportunity to cheer. Cornell's offense had gone more than eleven minutes without a shot on goal in relinquishing the lead. The thousands of fans rooting for Cornell were silent.

Moran remained confident. After falling behind by a goal, he decided against calling a timeout. "My players knew what they needed to do," he told *Sports Illustrated* later. "Sometimes it takes a traumatic experience to wake them up." Trailing by a goal, and with Sipperly dominating returning first-team all-American Jaeger on face-offs, Moran told Henrickson to take the crucial draw after Darcangelo's goal. If Sipperly won the face-off, Hobart could try to run out the clock without giving up possession, protecting its one-goal lead. Henrickson won the draw. The ball went to Marino behind the goal. Cornell players ran through their off-ball cuts and picks. Marino waited, then spotted Sierra breaking free. His pass connected, and Sierra flicked the ball past goalie Rick Blick to tie the game at eleven with three minutes, thirty-three seconds remaining.[35]

Henrickson won the ensuing face-off. With one minute and forty-eight seconds remaining, Jaeger controlled a loose ball in front of the Hobart goal, spun and scored past Blick for a 12–11 lead, then Page scored with four seconds left to clinch the 13–11 win. Before departing on the team bus back to Geneva, Schmidt swallowed his dislike for Cornell and walked into the home team's locker room to visit Moran and the players. "We want both championships to stay right here in upstate New York," he told them. "These are the two best teams in the country, there's no doubt about that."[36]

On Saturday, April 1, the Big Red hosted Massachusetts. For the 1978 season, Cornell began selling a twelve-page game program at a cost of fifty cents, and it was filled with lineups, statistics, rosters, and a write-up on the 1977 season. The lead story for the U-Mass game was written by Phil Langan of the *Ithaca Journal* and Cornell's Wohlhueter. Under the headline "Central New York—'New' Home of Lacrosse," the story began, "They used to call Baltimore the lacrosse capital of the world. No longer. Central New York is now number one."

The arguable claim was based primarily on Cornell and Hobart. Elsewhere, evidence was not as strong. Colgate had finished the 1977 season with a 5–9 record, including a 31–3 loss to Hobart in Hamilton, New York, a game the

Statesmen led 19–0 at halftime. Nearby Hamilton College had finished with a 3–6 record. Cortland State reached the 1977 NCAA Division II semifinals before losing to UMBC, 17–7. And Syracuse, under Roy Simmons, Jr., went 8–6, but the long series with Cornell was on a two-year hiatus, ostensibly over a disagreement on whether the 1977 game should be played in Syracuse or Ithaca, though several of Cornell's players at the time recall Moran halting the rivalry following a series of incidents in the 1976 contest, won by Cornell, 24–6, and featuring twenty-eight penalties.

At the high school level central New York was making strides. In 1977 New York installed for the first time a high-school state lacrosse tournament. Syracuse's West Genesee finished its regular season undefeated and advanced to the state semifinals at Hofstra following a quarterfinal victory over Ithaca High. In the state semifinals the Wildcats had their thirty-nine-game winning streak snapped by Ward Melville, 16–5, but they bounced back in the consolation game to defeat Suffern and finished with a 23–1 record. Also in central New York, Corning East High finished 17–0 in 1977, but it was a member of New York's Section V, which opted not to send its champion to the New York State Intersection tournament. (Elmont High won the first state title by beating Ward Melville, 12–11, before a crowd of five thousand fans at Hofstra. The MVP of the title game was Jim Zaffuto, an attackman who in 1978 was in the starting lineup at Johns Hopkins.)

In the game program Moran also noted the large number of youth players and teams who would attend Cornell games at Schoellkopf Field. "The rise in popularity for lacrosse in this area since I came here in 1969 is amazing," Moran was quoted as saying. "When we played a game then, you would never see young kids with lacrosse sticks. Now, take a look at them. The success we've had has helped this along, but the action, excitement, and speed involved in the sport are the main reasons it is catching on."

The Massachusetts–Cornell game was played on a cloudy, sixty-degree day, and before six thousand fans, the Big Red ran its winning streak to thirty-two with a 17–7 victory; Marino and Page each scored four goals. The only worry, again, was face-offs; the Big Red barely reached 50 percent, winning fourteen of twenty-seven. Logan's claim about central New York did not seem to be hyperbole. The Big Red continued its winning ways with a 19–12 victory over Dartmouth on April 8 at Schoellkopf Field. Reitenbach scored after eighteen seconds, and the Big Red jumped to leads of 9–1 and 14–5. It was Cornell's thirty-third consecutive victory at the varsity level, tying the all-time record set by Navy from 1964–1967.

Because of the three game cancellations in 1977, Cornell's shot at breaking the college lacrosse record with a thirty-fourth consecutive victory would come on April 15, in Baltimore, against second-ranked Johns Hopkins.

There was a party atmosphere when Cornell arrived on the Johns Hopkins campus on April 15 for the matchup between—according to the most recent USILA poll—the top-ranked Big Red and the second-ranked Blue Jays. The chance to see the undefeated Blue Jays end Cornell's long winning streak and deny it a place in the record books was only part of the festivities. The school was also hosting its annual spring fair. Called "3400 on Stage"—a reference to the school's 3400 N. Charles Street address—the three-day annual event was fairly new but had already become one of the most eagerly anticipated weekends in the school year. The theme that spring was the 1893 World's Columbian Exhibition—a reference to part of the Chicago World's Fair that honored Christopher Columbus.[37] At Johns Hopkins the freshman quad, on the part of campus closest to the stadium, featured a flea market, solar energy exhibits, and kiddie rides.[38] Other attractions included works for sale by several hundred artists from around the East Coast; live music; food trucks; a beer garden; a dog show; a chemistry magic show; and a giant Ferris wheel in honor of the first Ferris wheel built for the 1893 event.[39] All events were free except the nighttime performances, held indoors, from comedian Robert Klein, a two-time host of *Saturday Night Live*.

The campus would have been busy even without the lacrosse game. And the lacrosse game, especially involving Cornell and its chance to break the record for consecutive wins, would have drawn an overflow crowd without the spring fair. Early spring weather in Baltimore is a mixed bag. On this day, temperatures were in the mid-sixties under cloudy skies. Everyone wanted to be outside, and Johns Hopkins was the place to be. Demand for tickets was so high that reports earlier in the week said the game had sold out days in advance. University officials took to local media to say the reports were wrong, that tickets were still available.

One person with tickets to the game was Bill Bilderback, the coach of Navy during its record win streak. Still living in the area, two tickets had come in the mail, a gift from Johns Hopkins athletic director Bob Scott. Bilderback had not coached in several years, but he followed lacrosse closely. The previous year, he had been interviewed by *Baltimore Sun* columnist Bill Tanton on the state of the game since plastic sticks had been introduced. Bilderback's analysis: Lacrosse "is better now than it ever was. The new sticks improved the game, but so did things like little league, fall [college] lacrosse, and the summer leagues run by these Heroes people."[40] On April 15, 1978, Bilderback said he had no plans to use his free tickets and instead would spend the day at his wife's high-school reunion.

He may have been the only person with unused tickets.

Fans walking through campus to Homewood Field for Saturday's game would have been accompanied by music from the Hopkins Swing Band, playing the 2 p.m. time slot at the spring fair on a stage not far from the stadium's permanent bleachers. While the party was in full swing outside Homewood Field, inside the game was serious business. An announced crowd of 12,500 made its way into the stadium, which one published report said had a capacity of ten thousand. People in attendance that afternoon say the attendance was closer to fourteen thousand. Tickets were two dollars for adults, one dollar for students, and no attempt to stop selling tickets appears to have been made, even as the crowd grew larger and larger. "We drew some big crowds," Cornell's Henrickson says now. "Because everyone wanted to see us lose."[41]

FIGURE 12.3. Ned Radebaugh of Johns Hopkins moves against Bob Henrickson of Cornell in the 1978 regular-season meeting. The game drew an estimated fourteen thousand fans to Homewood Field, well above the stadium's capacity of ten thousand. (Photo courtesy Johns Hopkins Athletics)

The boisterous crowds spilled onto Charles Street, usually a busy thorough-fare, and West University Parkway. Though fun for participants, it was a night-mare for residents, and traffic soon stopped completely. Among those stuck in the car and not moving was the scheduled starting pitcher that night for the Baltimore Orioles. Jim Palmer was trying to make his way to Memorial Stadium on 33rd Street, roughly one mile from the Johns Hopkins campus. It was his first start of the 1978 season, and for the occasion he had brought with him his youngest daughter Kelly, aged eleven. Palmer recounted the scene later to the *Baltimore Sun*. He remembered his daughter expressing her excitement at the large throng of people who were going to see her dad pitch that night. "I told her, 'No, sorry dear,'" Palmer replied. "'Those people are all going to Homewood to see the Hopkins–Cornell lacrosse game.'"[42] (Palmer made it to Memorial Stadium in time to throw a two-hitter in a 7–0 victory over the Milwaukee Brewers, though the crowd of 7,532 was far less than had been at Homewood Field.)[43]

As the teams went through their warm-ups, Cornell in red jerseys, red shorts, and plain white helmets, the Blue Jays, in their home white jerseys, black shorts, and light-blue-and-white paneled black helmets, the stadium became more and more crowded. As the opening face-off drew closer, it became obvious that every available seat in the stands at Homewood Field was long gone, and people lined the fence that circled the field four and five deep. People with tickets in the more expensive reserved section of Homewood Field were angered when they arrived to find there was no more room and they'd have to watch the game while stand-ing around the field, surrounded by hundreds of others. Dave Spivey, a Baltimore native, a sophomore at Johns Hopkins, was a defenseman on the junior varsity lacrosse team and working security at Homewood Field; he wore an orange vest and earned ten dollars for his afternoon labor.[44] For more than forty years, he has served as the public-address announcer for home games, so he has seen almost every lacrosse game at Homewood Field in that time. And he adds context to April 15, 1978. "I've never seen Homewood Field so crowded," Spivey says. "And I would not want to see it that crowded again. It was a crawling mass of human-ity."[45] Anyone who stood up to get a hot dog and Coke—being sold for one dollar by the Phi Gamma Delta fraternity—would return and find his seat had been taken, a situation that led to numerous arguments and several near fights.

Then there was the small matter of the game itself. The Blue Jays had lost four in a row to the Big Red and, as Spivey says, "Hopkins fans were getting a little tired of Cornell."[46] The rap on the brand of lacrosse supported by the Baltimore establishment was that it was a bit genteel. There was no trace of that gentility in the overflow crowd. Johns Hopkins fans wanted to see Cornell drubbed. Johns Hopkins sophomore Kevin Kilner, a reserve midfielder who was watching from the sideline in street clothes because of a hand injury, remembers the crowd, which included several hundred Cornell fans. "There was what I would call an 'electric tension' in the stands. Both teams were undefeated, both teams seeing each other for the first time since the '77 title game in Charlottesville," Kilner says. "Back then fans did a lot of tailgating. It was like the crowd at a heavyweight fight, they were drinking and looking for action."

At 2 p.m., the Cornell and Johns Hopkins players went to their respective benches for one final huddle before the start of the game. The teams took the field for the pregame handshake, then went to their respective sides of the field for the opening face-off. Kane had guarded O'Neill in each of the past three meetings over two years. On April 15, 1978, O'Neill stood at his spot on attack, and next to him walked Muehleman. The Cornell coaches, having scouted Johns Hopkins several times already, noticed that O'Neill was staying closer to the crease area than in past years, and they wanted Muehleman to guard him, to allow Kane to cause havoc closer to midfield, where he was more likely to be able to start a fast break if he forced a loose ball. Kane was also better suited to defend the hard-shooting midfielders. On offense, Moran also had a wrinkle ready. Knowing Johns Hopkins had been in attendance when the Big Red midfield dominated play in the win over Mount Washington, and believing the Blue Jays would be expecting the ball to be controlled by Henrickson, Jaeger, Reitenbach, and others, Moran decided to call for the attackmen to take the majority of shots, a big call for starters Marino, Page, and a junior from Baltimore named Ned Gerber, who was playing in his hometown on his twenty-first birthday.

Amid the circus atmosphere the game began. At the end of the first quarter, the game was tied at four; early in the second it was tied at five. At that point Cornell's superior athletes began to take over. In one spurt during the second and third quarters, the speedy Page scored three goals, Henrickson added two goals and one assist, and late in the third quarter Cornell had jumped to a 13–6 lead as the defense put the clamps on O'Neill and company. With about one minute to play, and Cornell leading 16–11, many of the spectators inside overcrowded Homewood Field decided to take their leave and file back onto the congested campus. As fans made their way out of the bustling stadium, walking back through the teeming, sticky campus they would have heard the Red Lion Jazz Band at one end of campus and the Blue Meanies, a Beatles cover band, at the other.[47] For Hopkins fans and the Baltimore establishment, the day had sauntered into disappointment, and the big game against Cornell became just another diversion within the campus festival.

With less than a minute to play Moran called one of his two timeouts. The spot in the record books and the effect in Baltimore was not lost on anyone in Ithaca, as the previous week's Cornell–Dartmouth game program had anticipated. Moran could be forgiven for wanting to bask in the moment: A fifth consecutive victory over the Blue Jays, the NCAA record for consecutive wins, all not only in front of the Baltimore establishment but just steps from the sport's Hall of Fame, where inside stood a mannequin wearing a Cornell lacrosse uniform as emblematic of the defending Division I national champions. It was the pinnacle of vindication. All of it, Moran knew, was being recorded by Cameron Snyder, covering the game for lacrosse's paper of record, the *Baltimore Sun.*

In the final seconds, however, with the victory completely assured, Moran called his second, final, and cruel timeout. He decided to let the Blue Jays marinate in the disappointment of a big loss in front of what remained of the huge crowd. O'Neill was very close with Moran through his older brother, who had played at Cornell and was not inclined to hate the Big Red. The second time-out left even him upset. "In hindsight," O'Neill says, "it was kind of a shitty thing to do."[48] The Johns Hopkins head coach was blind with anger. "Chic was in a fury," says Kilner, "as furious as I'd ever seen him, and he had a bad temper for cheap shots of any kind, unfairness, and kind of crap outside the code of how you competed in sports." When Ciccarone was angry he had no trouble reaching high-enough decibel levels that the players could hear him loud and clear. When he was extremely angry, he spoke quietly and would tell the team to move closer to him so they would be able to hear. During the timeout in the final seconds against Cornell, Ciccarone gathered the team, then told them to move closer, then closer still. He was so angry, players remember now, his words came out with spittle. "Look at the scoreboard," Ciccarone began. "Look at how those motherfuckers do things. We won't win today, but I promise you—*promise you*—these mother-fuckers will *never* beat us again." In the tense post-game handshake, Ciccarone told Moran, "The same people you see on the way up, you also run into them on the way down," leading to a brief argument that coaches quickly ended by separating the two. Once the handshake was done, Federico sprinted off the field, head down, so quickly he nearly ran over two female students who were standing in front of the entrance to the locker room. He had made twelve saves but several other Cornell shots that he thought he should have stopped had, instead, gone past him into the goal. By the time Ciccarone and the players entered the locker room, Federico was fully dressed. As soon as Ciccarone was done with his postgame address, Federico sprinted for the door and left. "He was really upset with how he had played," Katz says now.[49]

Ciccarone then left to conduct postgame interviews. Snyder, from the *Baltimore Sun,* asked Ciccarone about the late Cornell timeouts. "'That was unnecessary,' said Ciccarone, adding a few vivid comments about his coaching counterpart."[50] Moran defended himself, saying he was trying to put more substitutes into the game.[51] Ciccarone, when told of Moran's comments, countered that there had been a dead ball seconds earlier when Moran could have done exactly that.[52]

The timeouts "could make a difference," wrote the *Baltimore Sun*, "when the two teams meet again, as they might, in the [NCAA] playoffs."[53]

While the rest of the team quietly changed, Katz went to the training room below the main stands of Homewood Field for treatment for an ankle injury. While there, he heard a commotion outside; at some point following the post-game interviews, which each coach conducted separately, Ciccarone and Moran had run into each other in the hallway, and another loud argument ensued between the coaches, both former Marines (Ciccarone spent two years in the Marines after high school), their voices bouncing and echoing off the painted cinderblock walls. "I thought they were going to start swinging at each other," Katz says now. The two coaches were separated, again.

For Moran, those were problems for another day. Instead, he focused on the record his team had clinched on the hallowed ground of Homewood Field, home turf of the Baltimore establishment. Moran and Waldvogel's game plan had worked to perfection. Though O'Neill finished with four goals and one assist, Kane wreaked havoc on other parts of the field; DeSimone was known for having one of the hardest shots in the college game, but on April 15, guarded primarily by Kane, he took seventeen shots and made one. Cornell's emphasis on attack and its preferred 2–2–2 motion scheme also paid off when starting attackmen Page and junior Ned Gerber, lesser lights among their considerably talented teammates, combined for nine goals, five from Page.[54] Afterward, reporters made their way to the jubilant visiting team's locker room. Kane, rarely at a loss for words, was asked his thoughts, later published in the *Washington Post*. "I thought we'd blow them out," he said. "We're the best team that ever played the game. No one else [won thirty-four games in a row], did they? Thirty-four, go for more!"[55] Seconds later players threw a joyful Moran into the shower while he was still wearing his lucky black pants and white, short-sleeved Cornell lacrosse shirt.[56]

In the home team locker room, following the run-in with Moran, Ciccarone and his staff temporarily put aside their anger over the timeouts and absorbed the box score, light-purple numbers and letters plastered forever onto white paper. Despite the five-goal defeat, the Blue Jays had outshot the Big Red fifty-six to thirty-eight; had more ground balls, eighty-four to eighty-three; and had won twenty of the game's thirty-seven face-offs. As was the case at Scott Stadium in late May 1977, the difference was that Cornell was far more successful at converting its chances into goals. The Blue Jay machine won the fundamental game but failed to hit the back of the net at a high percentage. At practice on Monday, players noted that Federico had a different energy about him, a different focus. Lacrosse is not a shutout sport, goes an old saying, and even the best goalies and defenses will give up at least a few goals every game. But in the Monday practice, almost nothing got past Federico. He, like O'Neill, seemed focused on doing everything he could to have another shot at Cornell.

Cornell progressed through the rest of the season virtually unscathed. Against Penn on April 22, the Big Red jumped to a 9–2 lead en route to a 15–6 victory. Against Yale on April 26, it jumped to a 9–1 lead en route to a 17–2 victory. On April 29, inside Rutgers Stadium, the Big Red received a scare. Early in the fourth quarter the Scarlet Knights held a 9–8 lead. Marino scored for Cornell to tie the game, but Rutgers gained possession with four minutes to play and had the chance to hold the ball for a final shot. But the referees deemed Rutgers had taken too long to make a substitution, a rarely enforced rule, and called a penalty.[57] The Big Red gained possession and Jaeger scored for a 10–9 lead with three minutes to play; Cornell held on for a one-goal victory. The winning streak, by the narrowest of margins, had reached thirty-nine; including scrimmages and exhibitions, the class of 1978 was now 61–0. "If Cornell is number one," Rutgers coach Tom Hayes sniffed afterward, "then we're number two."[58] One week later the Big Red was back in New Jersey for a game against Princeton. Reitenbach finished with two goals in an 11–7 victory. That night, back in Ithaca after a four-hour bus ride, he decided to eschew the regular rotation of fraternity parties—including at his own ATO house—and head downtown instead. Soon he ran into McEneaney, then coaching the Cornell 'B' team. "He saw me and said, 'Hey kid, how you doing?'" Reitenbach says now. "I said I was good, and he asked how we'd done that day. I said we won. 'Great, that's great, what was the score?'" Reitenbach mentioned the score. "And immediately a cloud fell over his face. He eyes started bulging, and he got his game face on, and he got real close to my face. 'Oh, 11–7, that's great for you, you're a senior, you guys are seniors. What about my guys? What about my 'B' team? Now they got Princeton guys next year who think they can beat Cornell.' Eamon was always competitive, and looking out for his guys."[59]

The Big Red won its final regular-season game with ease, beating Brown, 19–7, at Schoellkopf Field, and entering the NCAA tournament with an 11–0 record and its winning streak at forty. Cornell took the number one seed, and its quarterfinal opponent was a familiar one, with an unlikely year-end story. Washington and Lee ended the regular season ranked number nine, seemingly outside the top eight spots for tournament teams. Moreover, the Generals lost their final regular-season game, to Hofstra. Two-thirds of the starting midfield expected the season was over. "Jay Sindler and I weren't getting along with [coach Jack Emmer] too well," said Charlie Stieff, a senior starting midfielder on the team. "Once we lost to Hofstra we thought okay, the season is over, we don't have to practice anymore."[60] At the end of the regular season, the Generals were ranked number nine in the USILA poll, one spot behind Rutgers. The NCAA tournament seedings exactly matched the USILA poll for spots one through seven. Also on Cornell's side of the bracket was number four Navy, set to host number five Army in the quarterfinals. On the other side of the bracket, number two Johns Hopkins faced number seven Hofstra, and number three Maryland played number six Virginia. For the eighth and final spot in the tournament, and Cornell's quarterfinal opponent, the selection committee tabbed Washington and Lee instead of the eighth-ranked Scarlet Knights.

Coach Hayes was so certain that his team would be selected he had continued to practice after their regular-season finale. In fairness, Rutgers lost head-to-head to Washington and Lee, 11–9. But the decision left Hayes furious. "No one can give me a reason why we're not in the playoffs," he told reporters after the selections were unveiled. "It just never entered our minds we wouldn't be in the playoffs."[61]

So Cornell's quarterfinal opponent, instead of dangerous Rutgers, was disinterested Washington and Lee. As Stieff says of himself and his line mate and friend Sindler, "When we found out we were in the tournament and were playing Cornell, we both knew we had no chance."[62] Would a rematch against Rutgers have given Cornell a wakeup call? Would Rutgers have pulled the upset? One thing is certain: The confident, if not overconfident, Big Red faced a first-round opponent with very little motivation. Indeed, at halftime of the quarterfinal contest on the Schoellkopf Field Poly-Turf on May 17, Cornell led 8–0. To that point, Washington and Lee had played six quarters, or ninety minutes, of NCAA tournament lacrosse against the Big Red and scored zero goals. Washington and Lee finally broke through when John Kemp scored early in the third quarter. It was a rare bright spot in a 12–2 loss.

Afterward, Stieff and another player did not even shower before leaving the stadium and hanging out with friends who attended Cornell. They recall drinking beer for a few hours and being ready to take a twenty-plus hour Greyhound bus back to Lexington, Virginia. At the thought of paying their own way, however, such a long bus ride eventually became less appealing. On a whim, in the wee hours of Wednesday night, they decided to check Tompkins Regional Airport, just a couple miles north of campus, to see if the team's plane might somehow still be on the ground. There, they saw their teammates and Emmer. Finally, a trip to Ithaca provided them with a tiny bit of luck: A mechanical failure had grounded the plane; the Washington and Lee players and coaches had not yet left. Stieff and his teammate, unshowered and not quite sober, snuck back in with the group just as they were about to board a different plane. "Coach Emmer never said anything to us about it," Stieff says now. "And we never said anything to him."[63]

The semifinals pitted Navy against Cornell and Johns Hopkins against Maryland, the same matchups as the previous year. In Ithaca, Cornell jumped to leads of 5–1 and 7–3 en route to a 13–7 victory. The final home game for the 1978 seniors drew ten thousand people. But again, just as in the regular season wins over Johns Hopkins and Rutgers, there were signs of trouble. Navy cut its deficit to 10–7 with about four minutes to play. (The 1978 squad was not burying opponents the way the 1977 team had.) Sierra, Henrickson, and Marino scored the final goals to put the game out of reach. But earlier in the fourth quarter Muehleman had left the game for good with a sprained ankle. Cornell's winning streak had reached forty-two games, the unofficial streak at sixty-four, and it was in the NCAA championship for the third year in a row. Navy left Schoellkopf Field in a hurry. Coach Dick Szlasa gave reporters one comment as he boarded the team bus back to Annapolis. "I'm very proud of the kids," he said. "We were very tight in the beginning and I don't give a damn who wins the national title now that we're out of it. Is that enough?"[64]

Johns Hopkins won its first-round game over Hofstra, 20–8, then defeated Maryland in the semifinals, 17–11. The previous year, after its semifinal victory over Maryland, Ciccarone had told the team over and over, "We made it to the final!" He later said he regretted the words because he believed they conveyed the message that reaching the title game was good enough. One year later Ciccarone's attitude was completely different. He began the week leading to the championship game by telling the players that it was time to teach Cornell a little humility.[65] That was the message on Tuesday and Wednesday as well. On Thursday, before boarding the team bus to Piscataway, Ciccarone had one last motivational trick up his sleeve.

He invited the players into the lobby of the Newton White Athletic Center for his wife's famous cheesecake. But the lobby was also the location of the sport's Hall of Fame. And it included the mannequin dressed in the colors of the defending Division I champion, Cornell. This time the message was far different: We are not the champions. Cornell is.[66] "In the regular season meeting," says Mark Greenberg, a starting defenseman, "we felt we played pretty poorly. We knew if we met Cornell again and played to our potential we'd be able to beat them."[67] From there the Blue Jays boarded the team bus. Ciccarone, superstitious like Moran, insisted on having the same bus driver as for the team's victories that season, so Sylvester Gee drove the team up Route 95 to the Holiday Inn in Edison, at the intersection of US Route 1 and Interstate 287, twelve miles from Rutgers Stadium, complete with the green-and-yellow neon sign outside, a swimming pool, and the Hideaway restaurant. Freshman Brian Goodman, statistician and team trainer, had booked the hotel. He was also in charge of the party at the hotel afterward, should the Blue Jays win. (Cornell stayed at the Somerset Marriott, five miles from the stadium.)

On Friday, May 26, the day before the game, the Johns Hopkins players arrived at Rutgers Stadium for their final practice; Cornell, as the higher seeded team, practiced first. The Johns Hopkins players were walking into the stadium when the Cornell team bus drove past. Cornell's players noticed the Johns Hopkins contingent, and several Big Red players opened the bus windows and began cat-calling the Blue Jays, taunting and teasing them, singing made-up song lyrics to them. The Blue Jays, in response, said nothing. Ciccarone and offensive coor-dinator Joe Cowan waited for the bus to pass, the noise drifting into the warm air, before they turned around to the players. "Cornell thinks they've got it won already," the coaches said. "Remember that." Says Kilner, "Chic was a master at taking any kind of slight and turning it into a competitive edge. He knew how to get us pissed off, and ready to go." Added Greenberg, "We were all business. We were very stoic and quiet. We knew our job was to do one thing—win the game."[68] The writer from *Sports Illustrated* covering the game picked up on the vibe. "Usually a loose and lively bunch," Joe Marshall wrote, "the Blue Jays came to Rutgers displaying all the frivolity of a group of CPAs getting ready to tackle tax returns."[69]

Saturday, May 27, dawned warm and hazy in Piscataway, New Jersey. The day was more comfortable than the previous year's championship, and the grass field more forgiving than the unwatered Astroturf of Charlottesville. Rutgers Stadium was oval-shaped, with off-white concrete stands interspersed with green, grassy hills, and a line of trees peering onto the grass playing surface below. The main scoreboard, bright red and on the south end of the stadium, had as a backdrop a sloping grass hill. Highlights from the game would be shown on a tape-delay basis on NBC's *Sportsworld*, the network's version of ABC's *Wide World of Sports*. The NCAA was also in Piscataway to film official highlights, which would be packaged and made available for purchase.

The Big Red took the field for warm-ups wearing white jerseys, red shorts, and plain white helmets. Henrickson, for the final time, donned the two lines of eye black under each eye, streaking down his face. The eye black had been applied by mistake by distracted trainer Rick LaFrance for the season opener in 1976. After Cornell's 24–8 victory over Adelphi, Moran insisted Henrickson keep the look until the Big Red lost. Forty-three games later, it had yet to happen. "I know people thought it looked kind of cool," Henrickson says, "but it was a total mis-take, and kind of a pain in the neck. It was like makeup. It could take thirty min-utes to remove."[70] Henrickson and Marino, asked to pose for the NCAA cameras, obliged with smiles. The camera crew made its way to the Johns Hopkins bench. The Blue Jays players, in light-blue jerseys, white shorts, and black helmets with alternating light-blue-and-white stickers, had just finished pregame warm-ups. The camera crew asked for a pose from DeSimone, who shook his head "no" and trotted past them and back onto the field. O'Neill, drinking water on the bench, ignored the request completely. The NBC crew did not fare any better. When its producers and camera person approached O'Neill to ask his thoughts on the contest, O'Neill said that having to answer any questions would take his focus off the game; then he walked away.[71]

As the teams finished their warmups, the crowd of 17,500—yet another record for the NCAA title game—settled in. The teams lined up across from each other at midfield; goalies Mike Federico and John Griffin ran toward each other and shook hands. Brown coach Cliff Stevenson, who had faced both teams in a five-day span, said in an interview with the *Baltimore Sun* the day before the game that the goalie matchup would determine the outcome. Griffin had made seventeen saves in the regular season meeting against the Blue Jays, but the Brown coach gave the edge to the sophomore from Baltimore. "I don't think," he said in the story, "there can be a goalie much better than Federico."

O'Neill took his place near the goal at the north end zone. Standing next to him, just as in the regular-season meeting, was Muehleman. This time Muehleman's left leg was wrapped with heavy white tape. His ankle injury from the semifinal had not healed, but he insisted on trying to play through the pain. The game began. Three minutes into the contest Kane was called for slashing, a one-minute penalty. Johns Hopkins worked the ball to DeSimone in the middle of the restraining box. In the regular-season meeting he had been hounded by Kane and scored one goal on eighteen shots. Less than four minutes into the final game of his college career, he had an open shot from fifteen yards and Kane was in the penalty box. DeSimone, nicknamed "Deese" by his teammates, had earned the reputation of aiming the first shot of every game right at the goalkeeper's chest, a ninety-mile-per-hour shot meant to send an intimidating message to the goalie. This time, DeSimone fired his trademark sidearm shot, looking somewhat like Huntley, but was aiming for the corner, not Griffin. The ball sped past Griffin and into the net. The Blue Jays had taken the lead. Minutes later, still in the first quarter, Muehleman was in so much pain that he took himself out of the game, sending a surprised, and not quite ready, Vinny Shanley in his place. The quarter ended with the game tied at two.

By this point, Ciccarone had sent Radebaugh into the game to take a face-off. Radebaugh, Baltimore native and the younger brother of former Maryland standout Doug, was physically overmatched against the Cornell duo of Henrickson and Jaeger, both Cornell football players, both first-team lacrosse all-Americans. But Radebaugh's older brother had faced the pair earlier in the season while playing for Mount Washington. And his younger brother took heed of Doug's scouting report: He would rely on speed moves and not muscle.

Two goals in fifteen seconds, both from Henrickson, gave the Big Red a 4–2 lead less than one minute into the second quarter. Rather than celebrating the sec-

FIGURE 12.4. Coach Richie Moran gathers his players for their final instructions before the 1978 NCAA final at Rutgers Stadium. At back right is assistant coach Bruce Arena, later the head coach for the US men's soccer team. (Photo courtesy Larry Baum)

ond goal, Henrickson simply motioned for his teammates instead to prepare for the ensuing face-off. In response, the Blue Jays made another adjustment—they moved sophomore Scott Baugher, a Long Island native, into the first midfield, to join DeSimone and Huntley. Wey, the previous starter, was a solid defender and exceled on ground balls, but he was not much of a scorer. (He entered the title game with seven goals and four assists.) Baugher, the anchor of the second midfield, had scored twenty-seven goals, many on an outside shot nearly as impressive as Huntley and DeSimone. Soon after Baugher's move, Huntley scored on an eighteen-yard shot to cut the Blue Jays' deficit to 4–3. Less than a minute later, DeSimone scored on a ten-yard shot to tie the game. Thirty seconds after that, Baugher scored on a ten-yard shot, and the Blue Jays led, 5–4, with nine minutes left until halftime.

When Cornell had the ball, Marino, one of the most accurate shooters in the country, was twice open from six yards and shot wide of the goal both times. Marino's shots that were on target were being stopped by Federico. What had been the Blue Jays' curse against Cornell—poor shooting percentages—was now the Big Red's problem.

Late in the first half Marino scored his first goal of the game, from point-blank range off a perfect pass from classmate Keith Reitenbach to tie the game at five.

At the other end, the Johns Hopkins offense was finding more than enough room to generate good looks. Following the early goals on long-range shots, Cornell's usually compact interior defense was forced to expand, all the way out to the top of the restraining box, to try to thwart the outstanding outside shooters. This left more room than usual closer to the goal. With the score tied at five midway through the second quarter, Johns Hopkins gained possession. Senior Joe Devlin, a reserve attackman from Annapolis, made a cut down the middle of the crease and quick-sticked an inch-perfect pass from O'Neill into the goal for a 6–5 lead. In the stands Dave Spivey, his brother, and another friend could hardly believe their eyes. Following the goal by Devlin, Spivey turned to his brother and friend and made a surprising announcement. "I said, 'I think we just won the game,'" Spivey says now. "Hopkins had two great crease attackmen and when the ball was going behind [the goal] Cornell was losing track of one of them. . . . I said, 'If Hopkins can keep breaking the crease like that they'll win.'"[72] The Blue Jays scored again, on an eight-yard shot by Davis with six minutes left in the half, for a 7–5 lead. Neither team scored the rest of the quarter.

In the locker room at halftime, Muehleman asked for, and received, permission to finish the game despite his injury.[73] Moran also approached midfielder Jimmy DeNicola, a little-used senior. DeNicola was told he would take face-offs against Radebaugh, who had won ten of fourteen in the first half. DeNicola was smaller than Henrickson and Jaeger, and Moran thought he might be fast enough to match the slender freshman from Baltimore.

FIGURE 12.5. Mark Greenberg (44) defends Tom Marino in the 1978 NCAA title game. The Blue Jays snapped Cornell's forty-two-game winning streak. (Photo courtesy Larry Baum)

In the Johns Hopkins locker room, junior Curt Ahrendsen, a longstick defender who excelled as a face-off wing, received attention for a shoulder injury he had sustained in the first quarter. Ahrendsen came out of the game only briefly, and even though trainers believed he had separated his shoulder, he went back into the game. At halftime he told the coaches he wanted to play in the second half. Trainers taped his shoulder into place.

The third quarter began, and Radebaugh won yet another face-off, but the Big Red forced a turnover. Within three minutes the Big Red scored on extra-man, senior Steve Page from freshman Ned Gerber, to cut the deficit to 7–6. Radebaugh won the ensuing face-off, and the Blue Jays went back to work. Attackman Jim

FIGURE 12.6.   Cornell's offense found very little room to operate in the 1978 NCAA title game. Here, Mike Sheedy defends first-team all-American Craig Jaeger. (Photo courtesy Larry Baum)

Bidne, a freshman from Baltimore, made another off-ball cut similar to Devine's and scored from point-blank range off a perfect pass from Baugher for an 8–6 lead. Radebaugh won the ensuing face-off, and a frustrated Kane was called for another slashing penalty. Fifteen seconds later sophomore Wayne Davis—like the first-line midfielders, an excellent outside shooter—ripped an eighteen-yard shot past Griffin for a 9–6 lead. A goal by Reitenbach closed the deficit to 9–7 at the start of the fourth quarter.

Radebaugh won the first face-off of the final quarter and got the ball to the attack. O'Neill, with the ball behind the goal, found Bidne on another off-ball cut, and Bidne deposited the ball into the net for a 10–7 lead. That was the score when O'Neill grabbed a loose ball near midfield and suddenly found himself on a fast break with only Griffin to beat. O'Neill ran thirty yards, shot the ball, then fell to the ground as it floated past Griffin. The Blue Jays led by a decisive 11–7. Cornell's winning streak would last another eight minutes, thirty-three seconds, but for all intents and purposes the game was over. "We've been down by two and three goals before [in the fourth quarter] but never four," Henrickson told reporters afterward. "That's when I knew." Moran was at wit's end with Radebaugh, so much so that he even enlisted Marino to take a fourth-quarter face-off. "Richie looked at me and said, 'You go try,'" Marino recalls now.[74] It didn't work—Radebaugh won that one as well. In the end, he won twenty of twenty-two face-offs, including thirteen in a row, and finished with seventeen ground balls. For the most part, Radebaugh had won possession before Cornell's athletic wing players could try to scoop the ground ball.

When the game ended the Blue Jays fans in the stands began singing the "Amen" chorus. The Johns Hopkins players lifted Ciccarone on their shoulders and paraded him around the field. And Marino swallowed the disappointment of his first, and only, college loss to jog to midfield to hug the victorious O'Neill, his best friend since kindergarten. Moran gathered the team in a huddle and did something he had not done in more than three years—spoke to them after a loss. He told them to keep their heads up and to be proud of what they had accomplished.

O'Neill was overjoyed. Two days before the title game he had graduated from Johns Hopkins and then won a national title. "It justified my decision to go to Hopkins," O'Neill says. Federico finished with fourteen saves, many on point-blank shots. The last word belonged to James H. Jackson, who wrote in the *Baltimore Sun* two days after the title game, "To the contrary of some published reports, crabcakes, the Orioles and the national lacrosse championship still reside in Baltimore."

For Cornell, Marino in the title game had gone one for eight shooting; Jaeger went zero for eight. Muehleman held O'Neill in check despite playing with his injury, but Kane was out of sorts: his two one-minute penalties both leading to Johns Hopkins man-up goals. "Me, Hondo, Craig, Sierra, and Kane were the ones who should have delivered," Marino says. "And none of us did. Hondo probably came the closest."[75] Says Muehleman, "I think our whole team went out there too overconfident. We didn't have the same intensity. And Hopkins smoked us."

Afterward in the locker room, Henrickson approached Marino with a question. "I said, 'Hey, Tom, how are we supposed to act after a loss?'" Henrickson says. "I mean, we had never lost a college game before."[76] "I just looked at him," Marino says, "and said, 'I have no idea.'"[77] There were stunned looks all around. Cornell alumnus Buck Briggs had missed the championship game to attend a wedding. The next day he opened the *Boston Globe* and turned to the sports section, to the page with the standings and box scores. He saw the score "Johns Hopkins 13, Cornell 8," and thought it was a misprint. So he flipped the paper to page 68, where he found the game story with this first sentence: "Cornell's record went that-a-way in Piscataway."

Cornell's first loss since the 1975 NCAA semifinal had one common element, Johns Hopkins midfielder DeSimone. On the roasting hot May afternoon at Schoellkopf Field, "Deece" had been a freshman midfielder for the Midshipmen and scored three goals. He transferred to Johns Hopkins following the season. And at Rutgers Stadium in 1978, in the NCAA title game, DeSimone again scored three goals.

The epitaph for the 1978 season at Johns Hopkins goes beyond the national title. Since the Cornell–Johns Hopkins meeting on April 15, 1978, the university has avoided placing the "3400 on Stage" festival, later called "Spring Fair," on the same weekend as a home lacrosse game. The following year Homewood Field also, for the first time, posted an attendance limit of eight thousand to ten thousand spectators. Several times since 1978, the university has stopped selling tickets when capacity is reached.

The rivalry between Johns Hopkins and Cornell in the late 1970s was incredibly fierce. But the rivalry between the coaches cooled after Ciccarone retired in 1983, with three NCAA titles, the same number as Moran. (Also, like Moran, Ciccarone's brusque manners did not endear him to the Baltimore establishment; incredibly, Ciccarone never was named coach of the year.) When Ciccarone was inducted into the sport's Hall of Fame in a ceremony in Baltimore in 1987, Moran was present, and a friend snapped a picture of Moran giving a smiling Ciccarone a playful kiss on the cheek. Months later, in November 1988, Ciccarone suffered a third heart attack, this one fatal. He was fifty years old. Yet Ciccarone's vow in the huddle in the final seconds of the 1978 regular-season game against the Big Red, that the Blue Jays would never again lose to Cornell, has thus far proved prophetic. Entering the 2022 season, the teams have met six times since that bustling afternoon in the 1978 regular season. The Blue Jays have won all six, all while Ciccarone was still alive.

The 1978 NCAA championship had been decided. The North–South game remained. In 1978 Moran again convinced the USILA to have the North–South All-Star game played on the Poly-Turf of Schoellkopf Field. This time, there was a wrinkle: The second New York state high-school lacrosse tournament semifinals and final would be played on the same weekend. On Friday, June 9, the state semifinals would feature Ithaca High against Ward Melville of Long Island at 5 p.m., followed by Rush-Henrietta High of Rochester against Farmingdale of Long Island. On Saturday, June 10, the North–South game would start at 2 p.m., with the high-school title game at 7 p.m.

North–South players began arriving in Ithaca on Wednesday, June 7. That night, Moran arranged for a welcome barbeque dinner at Moakley House, on the Cornell University golf course. Moran emceed the event, asking each player to stand up and give his name, hometown, and lacrosse position. There were so many Long Island natives that Brown senior midfielder Bill Ohlsen, a native of Providence and graduate of Moses Brown School, began his remarks with, "I'm from the other island, Rhode Island." Moran, during his remarks, noted that of the fifty players gathered that night, he had, when they were seniors in high school, recruited forty-eight of them. He landed only three—Marino, Katz, and Muehleman, the representatives from Cornell, who reached the USILA limit of three participants from each school. Kane, Jaeger, and Henrickson sat out because they had made the US national team, set to play in the World Games later that summer in Manchester, England.

On Thursday, June 8, the players were guests at a dinner hosted by local government officials; the players then were guests of honor at a jazz concert in the Ithaca Commons. On Friday, June 9, while the high-school games were played on Schoellkopf Field, a large Cornell contingent was among the guests at the USILA All-American banquet, held at the Holiday Inn on Triphammer Road. Inside the stadium Ithaca High fell to Ward Melville, 16–9, and Farmingdale defeated Rush-Henrietta, 7–4. (Ward Melville won the title with an 8–5 victory over Farmingdale, thanks to five goals from Rich Wehman, committed to play for Navy.) On Saturday, June 10, the North–South game was played in sunny, warm conditions. Johns Hopkins did not send any representatives—its players and coaches were on a three-week tour of California and Hawaii, meeting alumni and playing exhibitions against local club teams. Before a record crowd of seventy-seven hundred people, the North jumped to a 6–0 lead and never looked back in a 19–6 victory. Cornell's participating seniors had been part of sixty-six contests in their college careers—and won sixty-five.

EPILOGUE
End of an Era

The 1970s, a decade full of change in lacrosse, finished with another one: For the 1979 season, the USILA eliminated the face-off after every goal, retaining it only for the start of each quarter. Published reports indicated that the rule was intended to make the pace of play faster. It had the opposite effect. Now, teams were given a dead-ball situation with which to substitute defensive personnel into the game, and Johns Hopkins and Maryland were among the first, with no limit on the number of longsticks allowed on the field, to use five and sometimes six defenders at one time, to match the six offensive players. Other teams followed suit.

Suddenly, defenses had the upper hand, and fans were not thrilled. Eddie Mullen, attackman on the Maryland teams in the mid-1970s, whose stated goals were twenty shots per quarter, eighty shots per game, remembers attending a Maryland game in 1979, and being surprised at the half-field nature of the action. "I thought, what the shit is this?" Mullen says. "It was slow and boring." Cornell featured an ironclad defense in 1979, including senior Jim Buckley and junior Pat Avery, and it won another Ivy League title. The season ended with a 15–6 loss to Virginia in the NCAA quarterfinals in Charlottesville. Johns Hopkins, with five defensive players making all-American teams, plus first-team all-American goalie Mike Federico, won the NCAA title with a 14–9 victory over Maryland at Byrd Stadium. In 1980 the USILA brought back the face-off after every goal, but the longstick defensive midfield position had become a mainstay.

As the 1980s began, *Sports Illustrated* noted that college lacrosse had a new Big Five. Lacrosse "is played by about 130 colleges but dominated by a few—Johns

Hopkins, Maryland, Navy, Virginia, and Cornell," began a story in the March 30, 1981 edition. The story was introducing fans to the burgeoning lacrosse power at the University of North Carolina. Willie Scroggs, former assistant at Johns Hopkins, arrived at the school following the 1978 season, and he found a program that had reached the NCAA tournament twice in its history, losing in the first round both times.

Whether by accident or design, his progression sounded much like Moran's roughly a decade earlier. Where Moran used hometown scouts to find the best players on Long Island, Scroggs, a Baltimore native, landed six of the twelve first-team all-metropolitan lacrosse players in the *Baltimore Sun* in 1980. Scroggs maintained sources throughout Baltimore, and recruited in Long Island and central New York himself. In 1980 the Tar Heels even landed an offensive player from Windsor, Ontario, named Terry Martinello, whose twenty-one goals as a freshman in 1980 were second on the team. In 1981 they landed defenseman Jamie Allen, the MVP of the junior-college national title game the previous year at Nassau Community College, a designation that often led the winner to Ithaca. The Tar Heels, to supplement the lacrosse budget, cleaned the football stadium after home games. The coaches emphasized the importance of practice and of paying attention to details. Scroggs, like Moran, also emphasized the teaching aspect of being a coach.

Then there was the not insignificant matter of motivation. While Moran fought the Baltimore establishment, Scroggs battled indifference on his own campus, where basketball and football were king, lacrosse practice locations were moved to accommodate other sports, and Scroggs often brought the lacrosse uniforms home with him to wash.[1] Scroggs's pragmatic and patient approach was the delicate touch needed, whereas Moran had been dealt, and played, a much different hand. The University of North Carolina entered the spring of 1981 having not won a national championship, in any sport, since men's basketball in 1957. On March 30, 1981, the Tar Heels faced Indiana in the NCAA basketball final in Philadelphia. Scroggs attended the game, which Indiana won, 63–50. The next day Scroggs met the lacrosse team in Baltimore, where it was spending spring break with practices before facing Maryland on April 4. "I told them, basketball lost, now it's our turn to win one," Scroggs says.

North Carolina advanced to the NCAA lacrosse title game and faced three-time defending champion Johns Hopkins on May 30, 1981, at Palmer Stadium on the campus of Princeton University. Before a record crowd of 22,100, North Carolina used a late rally for a 14–13 victory, and another first-time champion had defeated one of the sport's established powers. "All year long our lacrosse program has won over people in the Chapel Hill area," Scroggs said after the game. "Being national champions should mean a lot to the people of North Carolina, probably more than another title would have meant to the people of Baltimore."[2]

North Carolina and Johns Hopkins had entered the 1981 title game undefeated. When a team outside the Big Five and a Big Five member both finished undefeated in 1957 and 1968, the USILA awarded the title only to the Big Five member. On the field, in both 1976 and 1981, the results were different. "Before the NCAA took over," Scroggs says, "we sort of had a feudal system, with little fiefdoms in the sport. Every region had its own way of doing things. The NCAA tournament brought lacrosse into the 20th Century."[3] The Tar Heels repeated as champions in 1982, again with a victory over Johns Hopkins. In 1983 North Carolina was unseated by a Syracuse team with a starting lineup featuring nine players who hailed from within thirty minutes of the school's central New York campus. The Orange won the NCAA title by defeating Johns Hopkins, 17–16, in the championship game at Rutgers Stadium. In the Wingate trophy days, the Big Five had won or shared all but two titles for decades. Suddenly, the winners were programs from the sport's southern and northern outposts. And the Big Five fell on lean times. Two members, Army and Navy, have not won a championship in the NCAA era. Maryland has won three but went forty-three years without an NCAA championship. Virginia went twenty-seven years between NCAA titles, and even Johns Hopkins went eighteen years between NCAA titles and is currently in a fifteen-year championship drought.

Under Moran, Cornell remained a successful program. When he retired after the 1997 season, his teams had won or shared fifteen Ivy League titles in twenty-nine years. But the Big Red has not won an NCAA title since that searingly warm afternoon in May 1977, when Eamon McEneaney and Dan Mackesey walked off the field for the final time in their Cornell careers. There are several reasons for the drought. One, Cornell has gotten close. It reached the NCAA title game under Moran in 1987 and 1988, and under Jeff Tambroni in 2009. The Big Red has reached the sport's Final Four in 2005, 2010, and 2013, and the quarterfinals, most recently in 2016. In 2020 Cornell won its first five games, including a convincing victory over second-ranked Penn State, coached by Tambroni. The Cornell lacrosse alumni email chains and text message groups were busy. "We thought, this is the year," says Keith Reitenbach, a 1978 graduate who later served as an assistant for Moran. But the 2020 season was canceled because of the coronavirus pandemic, and in 2021 the Ivy League, again citing the pandemic, opted not to field lacrosse.

Another reason was a change in admissions in the late 1970s. "The standards were a little different," Moran said later. "The admissions committee was constantly changing, and a lot of times they did not have a real strong interest in athletics. Not that they were biased against athletes, it just wasn't an important feature. Some of our recruits were very good athletes and very good students, and they were rated just as students."[4]

The final reason is that the game itself has expanded well beyond five teams who realistically could win a title, the so-called Big Five. Between 2000 and 2021, the following programs won an NCAA title: Syracuse, Princeton, Virginia, Johns Hopkins, Duke, Loyola University, Denver, North Carolina, Maryland, and Yale. Some familiar names, for sure, but interlopers as well, some of whom did not even field a Division I team in the 1970s. There were a handful of geographic outsiders who reached the title game in that span, including the University of Massachusetts, Notre Dame, and Ohio State. The insular sport that Moran discovered when he took over the Cornell program in 1969 will never return.

Those within the sport believe that Cornell will win a national title again, given the support and interest it receives from alumni. It says something about the program Moran left behind that Johns Hopkins, once a bitter rival, has hired its two most recent coaches from Cornell. And for now, perhaps it is fitting that Cornell's most recent title came from a team piloted by Moran and led by McEneaney, as the two Sewanhaka High alumni are entwined. Both were from large families, McEneaney the youngest of seven, Moran the youngest of eight. McEneaney's death occurred on September 11, 2001, Moran's forty-first wedding anniversary. Every year on September 11, or the weekday closest to the anniversary, the Cornell coaches ask Moran to speak to the current players about McEneaney, and Moran turns the clock back to when he was the coach, asking the players to stand in a circle around the American flag, to sing "God Bless America," to listen and pay respect to those who came before.

When Moran graduated from Sewanhaka High in 1959, his coach, Bill Ritch, who later coached McEneaney, addressed the senior lacrosse players at a graduation dinner; he closed with these words: "Wherever you go, please be a missionary for the sport of lacrosse." If Moran has an epitaph, it may well be that. The public-address announcer for the 1978 season was a student intern with the Cornell sports information department. Years later, Scott Schiller says he doesn't remember many details about the games or any of his trademark phrases for working a lacrosse game. He does, however, remember Moran. "Richie didn't distinguish between player and staff," Schiller says now. "Everyone was part of his team." In 2021 Moran turned eighty-four years old. The coronavirus pandemic was ongoing, so the best way to reach the former coach was via a Zoom call. One night in March 2021 former Cornell football great Ed Marinaro asked Moran to join a call. There, Moran found Marino and more than a dozen former players from the 1970s Johns Hopkins teams. One-time rivals, they had organized the Zoom through Marinaro to wish the former coach happy birthday.

Prior to the pandemic, Moran was a frequent visitor to Cornell's campus. In April 2019, the day after Cornell defeated Princeton in the regular-season finale at Schoellkopf Field, Moran held court for several hours at the Statler Hotel on campus, answering questions, providing memories. As he readied to leave, he noticed a picture of John Glynn, a Cornell lacrosse all-American in 2009 from Long Island, playing in a game against Syracuse. "They should change that picture though," Moran says. "It's from a game we lost."

Moran picked up his car from the valet, then asked the young valet where she was from. When she replied New Jersey, he asked which town, then mentioned a few people he knew from her hometown. Then he drove off, but he will be back because Cornell is such a big part of his life. But Moran is part of Cornell as well. A few years ago, the university endowed the position of lacrosse coach, a practice done in academia. The donors requested that the position permanently retain Moran's name, the Richard R. Moran Endowed Chair. He will be part of Cornell lacrosse forever.

Acknowledgments

The team at Cornell University Press/Three Hills was as formidable and effective as any assembled by Richie Moran in the 1970s. Michael McGandy took the lead on the project, and I am very lucky and grateful he did. Michael played lacrosse in the late 1970s and 1980s—he was one of the leading high-school goal scorers in New Jersey in 1986—and attended a handful of the games mentioned in the book. His memories and suggestions were unerringly helpful, the equivalent of a pass from Eamon McEneaney to a teammate who has come open only for a second and suddenly finds himself with a point-blank shot on goal. Clare Jones was the Bob Henrickson of the project; she did a little bit of everything and made hard tasks look effortless. Jennifer Savran Kelly was as encouraging and help-ful as the Long Island high-school coaches to Moran when he was mining the region for prospects. Copy editor Aimee Anderson made so many good fixes to the manuscript, the equivalent of Mike Waldvogel watching film of opponents to find any weaknesses and correct his own team's missteps.

The Bob Kane of the project, the brainchild, was Julie Greco, a longtime friend and inspiration who put the project in motion years ago. (She also has the expansive vocabulary to match Mr. Kane's.) In reviewing rare coach's film of the 1971 NCAA lacrosse title game, I noticed the first person to handle the trophy postgame was Cornell sports information director Ben Mintz, who handed it to Moran. Jeremy Hartigan is a worthy successor to Ben, all these years later. Jer-emy is smart and hardworking and loves Cornell. For this project he provided a mountain of statistics, stories, photos, and encouragement.

Other sports information directors who helped with this project were Brian Laubscher at Washington and Lee, Stacie Michaud at Navy, Ernie Larossa at Johns Hopkins, Jerry Price at Princeton, Vince Breidis at Virginia, plus Mike Daly and John Svec from the lacrosse coaching staff at Brown, which provided rare game footage from several Cornell–Brown games from the time period in question.

Special thanks to Richie Moran for always giving so generously of his time; one of the rewards of this project was hearing how glowingly even opposing players spoke of Moran. That is the true sign of someone who made a differ-ence. The project took shape in 1999, when the then-lacrosse coach at Centreville High, Gary Malm, provided me with a coach's film on VHS (!) from the 1976 title game. Gary was a resource throughout the book, putting me in contact with former teammates, answering questions especially about Eamon McEneaney, and making the best steak I have ever had in my life. Kevin McEneaney also was invaluable—and a testament to how many people it took to bring this project to life, given that he did not play lacrosse or attend Cornell.

Writing this book was a five-year project that would have proved impossible without significant help. My mother, Marilyn Swezey, is a published author, and she provided inspiration professionally and personally. She is also quite literally my best friend. Mom has written more than a half-dozen books; finally, I am on the scoreboard with one. Siblings Marilyn "Buffy" Swezey, Nicholas Swezey, and Alexandra Slaton provided encouragement and, as through my entire life, more patience than I deserve. My nieces and nephews, William, Charlotte, Beatrice, Robert, and Walker, are bundles of energy and positivity who brightened the days I thought the book would not come to fruition and made the days it looked like a reality even better.

Lastly, thank you to my colleagues at the Eternal Word Television Network (EWTN), for providing prayers and inspiration and encouragement. I felt, and needed, every single prayer. This process brought me closer to Saint Kateri Tekak-witha, the "Lily of the Mohawks," whom I am virtually certain knew of lacrosse. Saint Kateri, pray for us!

Notes

PROLOGUE

1. Keith Reitenbach, interview with the author, January 12, 2021.
2. Larry Baum, photos from May 20, 1978.
3. Chris Kane, interview with the author, January 26, 2021.
4. Frank Muehleman, interview with the author, January 26, 2021.
5. Chris Kane, interview with the author, August 22, 2019.
6. Cornellbigred.com, "Cornell Athletics Facilities," https://cornellbigred.com/facili ties/schoellkopf-field/18.
7. Kenny Van Sickle, "Celebrating 20 Years of Rugs at Schoellkopf," *Ithaca Journal*, May 7, 1991.
8. Kevin McEneaney, interview with the author, October 15, 2019.
9. Keith Reitenbach, interview with the author, January 5, 2021.
10. Bruce Arena, interview with the author, December 30, 2020.
11. Chris Kane, interview with the author, August 22, 2019.
12. Keith Reitenbach, interview with the author, June 18, 2020.
13. Bob Henrickson, interview with the author, October 16, 2019.
14. "A Man with a Secret," *New York Times*, September 27, 2001; Kevin McEneaney, interview with the author, January 9, 2021.
15. McEneaney interview.
16. Gary Malm, interview with the author, August 15, 2019.
17. Barbara O'Neil Mingle, "Remembering Eamon McEneaney: Cornell Lacrosse Legend with a Heart of Gold," *Cornell Spirit*, March 2005.
18. Gary Malm, interview with the author, January 28, 2021.
19. Paul Attner, "Maryland–Cornell Pits Moran vs. Alma Mater," *Washington Post*, June 3, 1971.
20. Richie Moran, interview with the author, April 28, 2019.

1. JUNE 13, 1970

1. Richie Moran, interview with the author, April 29, 2019.
2. Paul Attner, "Lacrosse May Be Fun, but a Hot Item It Isn't," *Washington Post*, May 15, 1976.
3. USILA.org, "USILA North–South Game History."
4. "North South Lacrosse Game to Be Held Here June 13," *Washington and Lee Alumnus*, April 1970.
5. "A Big Surprise," *Washington and Lee Alumnus*, August 1970.
6. "North South Lacrosse Game to Be Held Here June 13."
7. Itinerary from North–South game given to participants, author's collection.
8. "North South Lacrosse Game to Be Held Here June 13."
9. "Things to Do," given to North–South participants, 1970, author's collection.
10. "W&L Hosts All-Star Lacrosse Game," *Staunton Leader*, April 30, 1970.
11. "North South Lacrosse Game to Be Held Here June 13."
12. Charlie Steiff, interview with the author, May 18, 2019.
13. Map of Lexington given to North–South participants in 1970, author's collection.

14. Washington and Lee athletic department release, June 10, 1970.

15. "Lacrosse—Here's How It's Played," *Lexington News-Gazette,* June 10, 1970.

16. John Bartimole, "A Stick in Time Saves Lacrosse," 1986 NCAA lacrosse tournament game program.

17. Tom Groton, interview with the author, March 13, 2020.

18. 1970 North–South game program.

19. Johns Hopkins Lacrosse Record Book, 2020, https://hopkinssports.com/documents/2020/11/6/NEW_MEN_S_RECORD_BOOK_.pdf.

20. David Corrigan, interview with the author, July 16, 2019.

21. 1970 North–South game program.

22. David Corrigan, interview with the author, July 16, 2019.

23. Greg Murphy, interview with the author, May 15, 2019.

24. Richie Moran, interview with the author, April 29, 2019.

25. Harry MacLaughlin, interview with the author, June 3, 2019.

26. Bob Rule, interview with the author, April 2, 2019.

27. Richie Moran, interview with the author, April 29, 2019.

28. Tom Leanos, interview with the author, May 6, 2019.

29. Leanos interview.

30. Leanos interview.

31. Army Men's Lacrosse 2020 Record Book, https://goarmywestpoint.com/documents/2021/1/20/2020_Record_Book.pdf.

32. USILA.org, Composite USILA North–South game rosters.

33. William H. Moore, *A Half Century of Lacrosse* (Baltimore, MD: Lacrosse Foundation, 1973), 42.

34. Moore, *Half-Century.*

35. "Daughter Born Day Father Dies in Battle Zone," *Shamokin* [Pa.] *News-Dispatch,* Aug. 17, 1965.

36. "Princeton Athletes Quit Over U.S. Military Policy," *Philadelphia Inquirer,* May 7, 1970.

37. Peter Lips, interview with the author, February 21, 2020.

38. "Princeton Athletes Quit Over U.S. Military Policy."

39. Peter Lips, interview with the author, May 19, 2019.

40. Lips interview, May 19, 2019.

41. "Dartmouth Teams Cancel Week's Athletic Games," *Rutland Daily Herald,* May 7, 1970.

42. James Wanderstock, "Lacrossemen Whip Brown, 20–6, Seek Loop Clincher at Princeton," *Cornell Daily Sun,* May 10, 1970.

43. Wanderstock, "Lacrossemen."

44. Monty Cottier, "W&L's 1960s: A Retrospection," *Ring-Tum Phi,* January 9, 1970.

45. "Fall Campus Changes Will Be No Less Significant than They Were a Hundred Years Ago under Lee," *Washington and Lee Alumnus,* August 1970.

46. "Fall Campus Changes."

47. 1970 North–South game program.

48. Al Fischer, "Review of the 1970 Lacrosse Season," 1970 North–South game program.

49. Fischer, "Review."

50. Doug Tarring, interview with the author, August 15, 2019.

51. James H. Jackson, "NCAA Group Approves First Stick Title Game in 1971," *Baltimore Sun,* August 20, 1969.

52. "Writer's Widow Asks $100,000 in Damages," *Baltimore Sun,* December 12, 1936.

53. Milton R. Roberts and Alexander M. Weyand, *The Lacrosse Story* (Baltimore, MD: H&A Herman, 1965).

54. "Club Conquers Star Stickmen," *Baltimore Sun*, June 20, 1936

55. "Star Stickmen."

56. 1938 *Official Lacrosse Guide*, Spalding's Athletic Library, American Sports Publishing Company, New York.

57. Joe Finn, interview with the author, September 18, 2019.

58. Bill Reddy, "Keeping Posted," *Syracuse Post-Standard*, May 18, 1957.

59. Tom Harkness, interview with the author, July 19, 2019.

60. Bob Shaw, interview with the author, March 14, 2019.

61. Bill Tanton, "Lacrosse Expecting Final 3-Way Tie," *Baltimore Sun*, May 13, 1970.

62. Bill Free, "County Sets Playoffs," *Baltimore Sun*, May 19, 1970.

63. "Classic Here Wins Many New Lacrosse Fans," *Lexington News-Gazette*, June 17, 1970.

64. "Game Wins New Fans," *Lacrosse Newsletter*, April 1971.

65. "Navy Wins Lacrosse Game," Baltimore *Evening Sun*, May 11, 1971.

66. Harry MacLaughlin, interview with the author, June 3, 2019.

67. MacLaughlin interview.

68. MacLaughlin interview.

69. MacLaughlin interview.

70. Greg Murphy, interview with the author, May 15, 2019.

71. Steve Tober, "Gibbs and Robinson, a Coaching Duo Surpassed by No One," *Montclair Times*, June 19, 2008.

72. Tober, "Gibbs and Robinson."

73. Tober, "Gibbs and Robinson."

2. THE CLIMB BEGINS

1. Bob Kane bio, Cornell University Athletics Hall of Fame, Cornell University athletic relations, https://cornellbigred.com/honors/hall-of-fame/robert-j-kane/321.

2. Kenny Van Sickle, "Robert Kane, Renowned CU Sportsman, Dies," *Ithaca Journal*, June 1, 1992.

3. Van Sickle, "Robert Kane."

4. Van Sickle, "Robert Kane."

5. Mike Lopresti, "Political Blues: Meagher Remembers '80 Boycott as Soviet Troops Leave Afghanistan," *Cincinnati Enquirer*, February 22, 1989.

6. Bob Kane bio.

7. Elli Harkness, interview with the author, July 19, 2019.

8. "Cullen Becomes Cornell Varsity Lacrosse Coach," *Ithaca Journal*, February 7, 1962.

9. Terry Cullen, interview with the author, July 17, 2019.

10. Massachusetts Institute of Technology athletics record book, https://mitathletics.com/sports/2021/4/20/information-excellence-NationalChampions.aspx.

11. Terry Cullen interview, July 17, 2019.

12. "Baltimore U Crushes Hofstra Ten by 20–2," *Baltimore Sun*, April 20, 1961.

13. "Cullen to Coach Varsity Lacrosse Team," *Cornell Daily Sun*, February 7, 1962.

14. "Box Lacrosse Set Saturday," *Ithaca Journal*, March 3, 1965.

15. "Boys' Latin Places 4 on Scholastic Stick Team," *Baltimore Sun*, June 7, 1964.

16. Terry Cullen interview, July 17, 2019.

17. "Cornell Loses in Lacrosse to Maryland," *Ithaca Journal*, April 3, 1965.

18. "Yale Drubs Cornell Stick Team," *Ithaca Journal*, April 9, 1965.

19. "Yale Tops Red Stickmen; Cohen Injured," *Cornell Daily Sun*, April 19, 1965.

20. "Plane Crash Fatal to 3 from Cornell," *Utica Observer*, April 22, 1965.

21. Terry Cullen interview, July 17, 2019.

22. "Plane Crash Kills Three Men from Cornell University," *Ithaca Journal*, April 22, 1965.

23. "Otsego Plane Crash Kills Three from Cornell," *Binghamton Sun-Bulletin*, April 22, 1965.

24. "Plane Crash Kills Three Men."

25. "Plane Crash Kills Three Men."

26. "Plane Crash Kills Three Men."

27. "Plane Crash Fatal to 3."

28. "Plane Crash Fatal to 3."

29. "Otsego Plane Crash."

30. "Plane That Crashed Killing Three Ithacans Was Out of Fuel," *Ithaca Journal*, August 22, 1965.

31. "Plane Crash Kills Three Men."

32. "Plane That Crashed."

33. "Plane That Crashed."

34. "Plane Crash Settlement is $85,000," *Ithaca Journal*, October 19, 1967.

35. Terry Cullen interview, July 17, 2019.

36. Terry Cullen interview, July 17, 2019.

37. Tom Harkness interview with the author, July 17, 2019.

38. NCAA Hockey Tournament Record Book, https://www.ncaa.org/championships/statistics/ncaa-mens-ice-hockey-records-books.

39. Stuart J. McIver, "Wingate Trophy, Lacrosse Title Cup, Missing," *Baltimore Sun*, December 21, 1952.

40. Tom Harkness interview.

41. Bob Fusco, "Alphabet Soup," *Times Record*, March 24, 1953.

42. "RPI Had Many Rooters in NCAA Hockey Final," *Times Record*, March 15, 1954.

43. Tom Harkness interview.

44. Jeremy Hartigan, "Remembering Legendary Big Red Coach Ned Harkness," *Ezra Magazine*, Winter 2009.

45. Terry Cullen, interview with the author, February 14, 2021.

46. "Harkness New Cornell Lacrosse Coach; Cullen Steps Down," *Ithaca Journal*, May 28, 1965.

47. Terry Cullen interview, July 17, 2019.

48. Elli Harkness interview.

49. Tom Harkness interview.

50. Kenny Van Sickle, "Red Stickmen Victorious in Whirlwind Windup," *Ithaca Journal*, April 19, 1966.

51. Kenny Van Sickle, "View of Cornell Lacrosse Win Still Possible," *Ithaca Journal*, May 19, 1966.

52. Jerry Langdon, "Red Lacrossers, Sure of Title Tie, Can Win it All," *Ithaca Journal*, May 23, 1966.

53. Langdon, "Red Lacrossers."

54. Van Sickle, "View of Cornell Lacrosse."

55. Kenny Van Sickle, "Sport Tower," *Ithaca Journal*, May 27, 1966.

56. Dave Rossie, "Harkness Cornell's Expert in Picking Up Sticks," *Press and Sun Bulletin*, May 16, 1966.

57. Malcolm I. Ross, "Stickmen Host Tigers for Ivy League Championship," *Cornell Daily Sun*, May 19, 1967.

58. Terry Cullen interview, February 14, 2021.

59. Jerry Langdon, "Princeton's Finesse Big Difference in Victory over Red for Ivy League," *Ithaca Journal*, May 22, 1967.

60. Terry Cullen interview, February 14, 2021.

61. Terry Cullen interview, February 14, 2021.

62. Langdon, "Princeton's Finesse."

63. Elli Harkness interview.

64. "Cornell Names Lacrosse Aide," *Ithaca Journal*, August 31, 1968.

65. "Cornell Hires Lacrosse Assistant," *Ithaca Journal*, November 2, 1966.

66. *Cornell Daily Sun*, April 8, 1968.

67. Terry Cullen interview, February 14, 2021.

68. "Moran's Highlights," *Ithaca Journal*, December 24, 1976.

69. "Cornell Names Lacrosse Aide."

70. "Moran's Highlights."

71. Richie Moran, interview with the author, April 29, 2019.

72. "Cornell Names Lacrosse Aide."

73. Cornell University campus brochure, 1980–81, author's collection.

74. Campus brochure.

75. Campus brochure.

76. Richie Moran, interview with the author, April 28, 2019.

77. Tom Harkness interview.

78. Tom Harkness interview.

79. Mark Webster, interview with the author, May 15, 2019.

80. List of US Lacrosse Hall of Fame members with year of induction, https://www.usalacrosse.com/roster/hall-fame-inductees.

81. Jerry Langdon, "Harvard Stick Team in Control," *Ithaca Journal*, April 21, 1969.

82. Mickey Fenzel, interview with the author, December 13, 2018.

83. Fenzel interview.

84. George Lowery, "A Campus Takeover That Symbolized an Era of Change," *Cornell Chronicle*, April 16, 2009.

85. Lowery, "Campus Takeover."

86. Lowery, "Campus Takeover."

87. Plaque outside Willard Straight Hall commemorating the events.

88. Fenzel interview.

89. Fenzel interview.

90. Bob Rule, interview with the author, October 18, 2019.

91. Buck Briggs, interview with the author, April 30, 2019.

92. Briggs interview.

93. Moran interview, April 29, 2019.

94. Moran interview, April 29, 2019.

95. Keith Reitenbach, interview with the author, December 30, 2020.

96. Reitenbach interview.

97. Christ Kane, interview with the author, August 22, 2019.

98. Albert R. Fischer, "Cornell's Moran Is Contented," *Baltimore Sun*, May 15, 1970.

99. Fred Yah, "Stickmen Top Orange to Complete Perfect Year," *Ithaca Journal*, May 25, 1970.

100. Yah, "Stickmen Top Orange."

3. BARBARIANS AT THE GATE

1. Paul Kaye, "Stickmen, Nine Seek to Clinch Crowns," *Cornell Daily Sun*, May 14, 1971.

2. Ed Atwater, "Stick Title Game May Replace 'Star Tilt,'" *Evening Sun*, June 14, 1969.

3. Pat Gallagher, interview with the author, August 5, 2019.

4. Peter Carry, "Big Red Votes Itself No. 1," *Sports Illustrated*, June 13, 1971.

5. Bob Rule, interview with the author, April 2, 2019.

6. Dan Mackesey, interview with the author, July 22, 2019.

7. Mickey Fenzel, interview with the author, December 13, 2018.

8. Richie Moran, interview with the author, April 29, 2019.

9. Tom Cafaro, interview with the author, April 7, 2019.

10. Kim Eike, interview with the author, August 19, 2019.

11. Richie Moran, interview with the author, April 28, 2019.

12. Fenzel interview.

13. Moran interview, April 29, 2019.

14. Frank Davis, interview with the author, July 14, 2019.

15. Frank Davis interview.

16. Frank Davis interview.

17. Hannah Davis, interview with the author, July 14, 2019.

18. Bob Shaw, interview with the author, March 16, 2019.

19. Shaw interview.

20. Jules Sieburgh, interview with the author, July 19, 2019.

21. John Burnap, interview with the author, July 30, 2019.

22. Bill Ellis, interview with the author, July 1, 2019.

23. Ellis interview.

24. Jordan Lauterbach, "Bob Buhmann, Triple National Collegiate Lacrosse Title-holder from Seaford, Dies at 65," *Newsday*, December 18, 2014.

25. Buck Briggs, interview with the author, May 2, 2019.

26. Briggs interview.

27. Ira Hochstadt, interview with the author, January 5, 2019.

28. Rule interview.

29. Mike Waldvogel, interview with the author, December 14, 2018.

30. Fenzel interview.

31. "LI Goalie Twins Star for Cornell," *Newsday*, June 9, 1970.

32. Mike Waldvogel, interview with the author, December 14, 2018.

33. Waldvogel interview.

34. Fenzel interview.

35. Hochstadt interview.

36. Hochstadt interview.

37. Dan Connolly, "Globie Show Draws 5,200," *Ithaca Journal*, November 19, 1970.

38. Rule interview.

39. Rule interview; promotional postcard, College Inn, circa 1970, author's collection.

40. Burnap interview.

41. Associated Press, "Southeastern States Get Snow, Ice, Sleet," *High Point Enterprise,* March 26, 1971; "It's a Late Snow—But a Good One," *High Point Enterprise*, March 26, 1971.

42. Bill Ellis, interview with the author, July 2, 2019.

43. "Virginia Biggest Hurdle for Cornell Stickmen?" *Ithaca Journal*, April 1, 1971.

44. "Virginia Biggest Hurdle."

45. Fenzel interview.

46. James H. Jackson, "Yale Surprises Blue Jays," *Baltimore Sun*, March 21, 1971.

47. Fred Yahn, "Cornell Rally Nearly Tops Virginia Lacrossemen," *Ithaca Journal*, April 2, 1971.

48. Tom Duquette, interview with the author, August 27, 2019.

49. John Stewart, "STX branches Out in Seeking to Put Fresh Face on Putter Market," *Baltimore Sun*, June 23, 1991.

50. Wick Sollers, interview with the author, September 5, 2019.

51. Duquette interview.
52. Duquette interview.
53. Duquette interview.
54. Duquette interview.
55. William Ferguson, "The Lacrosse Head," *New York Times Magazine*, June 7, 2013.
56. Duquette interview.
57. Duquette interview.
58. Bucky Gunts, interview with the author, July 31, 2019.
59. "This Week in Sports," *Baltimore Sun*, March 28, 1971.
60. James Jackson, "Strong Cornell Ten Surges to 13–8 Victory Over BAC," *Baltimore Sun*, April 3, 1971.
61. Bill Ellis, interview with the author, February 3, 2021.
62. Advertisement for Bacharach Rasin, *Baltimore Sun*, December 20, 1970.
63. "Virginia Retains Lead in Stick Poll," *Baltimore Sun*, April 4, 1971
64. "Lacrosse Group Picks Allison," *Troy Record*, December 8, 1970.
65. Paul Pinckney, "Allison Takes Command of Dutchmen," *Democrat and Chronicle*, February 27, 1971.
66. Albert R. Fischer, "NCAA Stick Tourney Planned," *Baltimore Sun*, November 5, 1970.
67. "They're Not Going to Like It in Maryland," *Sports Illustrated*, May 4, 1970.
68. "They're Not Going to Like It in Maryland."
69. Joe Finn, interview with the author, October 2, 2019.
70. Bill Tanton, "Southern Lacrosse Gets One More Shot," *Evening Sun*, June 15, 1971.
71. Tanton, "Southern Lacrosse."
72. "They're Not Going to Like It in Baltimore."
73. John B. Forbes, "Hofstra May Get U.S. Title Final," *New York Times*, June 21, 1970; James H. Jackson, "Three Share Stick Title," *Baltimore Sun*, June 13, 1970.
74. Jackson, "Three Share Stick Title."
75. Jackson, "Three Share Stick Title."
76. Jackson, "Three Share Stick Title."
77. Albert R. Fischer, "Army Goalie Fools Navy Scouts," *Baltimore Sun*, June 1, 1969.
78. Jack Chevalier, "Navy, Army May Skip NCAA Stick Tourney," *Baltimore Sun*, May 6, 1971.
79. "Ithacan Plays for Dartmouth," *Ithaca Journal*, May 11, 1971.
80. "Ithacan Plays for Dartmouth."
81. Bill Tanton, "Bildy against NCAA Playoff," *Baltimore Sun*, May 30, 1975.
82. Wilson Phipps, interview with the author, August 13, 2019.
83. Chevalier, "Navy, Army May Skip."
84. Chevalier, "Navy, Army May Skip."
85. Chevalier, "Navy, Army May Skip."
86. Reid Detchon, "Stick Plan Stirs Navy Chief's Ire," *Evening Sun*, May 21, 1971.
87. Rule interview.
88. Shelley Cosgrove, interview with the author, July 21, 2020.
89. Fred Yahn, "Rimmer Prolific as Red Locks Up Ivy Stick Title," *Ithaca Journal*, May 17, 1971.
90. Rule interview.
91. Rule interview.
92. Cosgrove interview.
93. Richie Moran, interview with the author, July 5, 2020.
94. Rule interview.
95. Rule interview.

96. Rule interview.

97. Fred Yahn, "Red Stickers Top Hobart," *Ithaca Journal*, May 19, 1971.

98. Cornell sports information release, May 17, 1971, author's collection.

4. THE FIRST NCAA TOURNAMENT

1. James H. Jackson, "Scheduling Hassle Snags NCAA Lacrosse Tournament," *Baltimore Sun*, May 13, 1971.

2. James H. Jackson, "Confusion Hits Stick Tournament," *Baltimore Sun*, May 17, 1971.

3. Jackson, "Confusion."

4. "Virginia Ten Remains No. 1," *Baltimore Sun*, May 17, 1971.

5. Jack Chevalier, "Tourney Will Change College Stick Values," *Baltimore Sun*, June 7, 1971.

6. Albert R. Fischer, "Eighth Bid in Tourney to Hofstra," *Baltimore Sun*, May 18, 1971.

7. Fischer, "Eighth Bid."

8. Reid Detchon, "Navy Stickers to Hit Terps Next Tuesday," *Evening Sun*, May 18, 1971.

9. Albert R. Fischer, "NCAA Tens Begin Play at 4 Sites," *Baltimore Sun*, May 22, 1971.

10. Chuck Hlava, "Air Force Stickers Rebuild Fast," *Colorado Springs Gazette-Telegraph*, April 18, 1971.

11. James H. Jackson, "Air Force–Terp Stick Clash a 'Homecoming' for Keating," *Baltimore Sun*, May 19, 1971.

12. "Virginia Ten Remains No. 1," *Baltimore Sun*, May 17, 1971.

13. 1971 Air Force lacrosse roster, provided by Air Force Athletics, author's collection.

14. 1971 roster.

15. Jackson, "Air Force-Terp Stick Clash."

16. Tom Cafaro, interview with the author, February 3, 2019.

17. Cafaro interview.

18. Reid Detchon, "Army, Navy at It Again, in Lacrosse Anticlimax," *Evening Sun*, June 5, 1971.

19. Detchon, "Army, Navy."

20. Detchon, "Army, Navy."

21. Tom Duquette, interview with the author, February 3, 2021.

22. Fred Yahn, "Cornell–Army Matched Up; Red Takes Brown," *Ithaca Journal*, May 24, 1971.

23. Bill Ellis, interview with the author, June 25, 2019.

24. Yahn, "Cornell–Army Matched Up."

25. Yahn, "Cornell–Army Matched Up."

26. Yahn, "Cornell–Army Matched Up."

27. Cafaro interview.

28. Cafaro interview.

29. Associated Press, "Nixon Says Peace to Blossom," May 29, 1971.

30. Jeffrey Antevil, "Peace Stirs, Nixon Tells Cadets," *New York Daily News*, May 30, 1971.

31. Fred Yahn, "Tenacious Big Red in NCAA Stick Final," *Ithaca Journal*, June 1, 1971.

32. Fred Yahn, "Red Seeks First Lacrosse Victory Over West Point," *Ithaca Journal*, May 27, 1971.

33. Bob Shaw, interview with the author, March 16, 2019.

34. Bill Ellis, interview with the author, July 15, 2019.

35. Richie Moran, interview with the author, April 29, 2019.

36. Cafaro interview.

37. Yahn, "Tenacious Big Red."

38. Mickey Fenzel, interview with the author, December 13, 2018.

39. Bill Tanton, "Nachlas, Cut as Soph, Hero of Big Terp Win," *Baltimore Sun*, May 31, 1971.

40. Tanton, "Nachlas."

41. Moran interview, April 29, 2019.

42. Moran interview, April 29, 2019.

43. Jane Marcham, "Corson: Help Rebuild Faith of the Public," *Ithaca Journal*, June 7, 1971.

44. Moran interview.

45. Pat Gallagher, interview with the author, August 5, 2019.

46. Dennis Weintraub, "Austere Roosevelt Alive and Well," *Newsday*, September 24, 1969.

47. John Kaestner, interview with the author, February 4, 2019.

48. Kaestner interview, February 4, 2019.

49. Kaestner interview, February 4, 2019.

50. Kaestner interview, February 4, 2019.

51. Kaestner interview, February 4, 2019.

52. Jim Smith, "Jets Set to Defend the Title," *Newsday*, March 25, 1970.

53. Jim Smith, "'Other Guys' Help Elmont Win Semifinal," *Newsday*, May 25, 1970.

54. "McMillen Impressive," *Ithaca Journal*, April 7, 1971.

55. Reid Detchon, "Lacrosse Rematch Better for Navy," *Evening Sun*, May 24, 1971.

56. John Danowski, interview with the author, July 1, 2019.

57. Richie Moran, interview with the author, April 28, 2019.

58. John Kaestner, interview with the author, February 5, 2019.

59. James Jackson, "College Lacrosse Play-Off Pits 2 Maryland Grads," *Baltimore Sun*, June 2, 1971.

60. Jackson, "College Lacrosse."

61. William Boniface, "Canonero 4–5 Pick in Belmont," *Baltimore Sun*, June 6, 1971.

62. Moran interview, April 29, 2019.

63. Bob Shaw, interview with the author, March 16, 2019.

64. "NCAA Stick Final Will Be Televised," *Baltimore Sun*, June 3, 1971.

65. Fred Yahn, "Red Lacrossers Ride Crest of 12-Game Win Streak Into National Title Game," *Ithaca Journal*, June 3, 1971.

66. Gordon S. White, Jr., "Lacrosse to Decide No. 1. . . on the Field," *New York Times*, June 5, 1971.

67. Paul Attner, "'Big 5' Outsider Challenges Maryland," *Washington Post*, June 5, 1971.

68. "Red, Md. to Play Lacrosse on L.I.," *Daily News*, June 5, 1971.

69. Hymy Cohen, "Army Favored over Navy in Lacrosse," *Capital*, June 5, 1971.

70. Danowski interview.

71. Jonathan Levine, interview with the author, August 16, 2019.

72. Tom Leanos, interview with the author, May 7, 2019.

73. NCAA Lacrosse Silver Anniversary booklet, 1995, author's collection.

74. "Biggest Moment for Moran," *Ithaca Journal*, June 7, 1971.

75. Fred Yahn, "Cornell National Lacrosse Champ," *Ithaca Journal*, June 7, 1971; Albert R. Fischer, "Army Ten Whips Maryland," *Baltimore Sun*, May 2, 1971.

76. Danowski interview.

77. Interview with Pat Gallagher, August 5, 2019.

78. Interview with Ira Hochstadt, January 4, 2019.

79. Kaestner interview.

80. Peter Carry, "Big Red Votes Itself No. 1," *Sports Illustrated*, June 10, 1971.

81. James H. Jackson, "Cornell Trips Terps Ten, 12–6," *Baltimore Sun*, June 6, 1971.

82. Carry, "Big Red Votes."

83. Shieh, Joseph. "Former Laxers Remember 1971 NCAA Championship," *Cornell Chronicle*, June 1991.

84. Bob Rule, interview with author, April 3, 2019.

85. "Lacrosse: No. 1," *Ithaca Journal*, June 7, 1971.

86. Peter Carry, interview with author, December 2, 2018.

87. Moran interview, April 29, 2019.

88. Moran interview, April 29, 2019.

89. Moran interview, April 29, 2019.

90. "Cop Killed in Hit-and-Run," LIHerald.com, December 5, 2002.

91. Richard Kucner, "Second Stringer Wraps Up Lacrosse Title," *News American*, June 6, 1971.

92. Buck Briggs, interview with author, April 30, 2019.

93. Bob Rule, interview with author, April 2, 2020.

94. Rule interview, April 2, 2010.

95. Rule interview, April 2, 2010.

5. FALLING SHORT

1. Letter from Robert J. Kane to Bob Buhmann, July 9, 1971. Courtesy of Cornell Sports Information Archives, author's collection.

2. Manny Schiffres, "We're Number One—Finally!" *Cornell Daily Sun*, September 1, 1971.

3. Schiffres, "We're Number One."

4. Bob Fusco, "Alphabet Soup," *Troy Record*, November 20, 1951.

5. "Brooklyn Stickmen Out at Rutgers Drill," *Times Union*, November 14, 1924.

6. "Fall Lacrosse Practice Held," *Poughkeepsie Eagle-News*, September 28, 1926.

7. Kenny Van Sickle, "Harvard Next for Unbeaten Red 11," *Ithaca Journal*, October 11, 1971.

8. Richie Moran, interview with the author, October 9, 2019.

9. Kenny Van Sickle, "Celebrating 20 Years of Rugs at Schoellkopf," *Ithaca Journal*, May 7, 1991.

10. Cornell Lacrosse Newsletter, Spring 1972, author's collection.

11. Bucky Gunts, interview with the author, August 1, 2019.

12. "All M.S.A. Lacrosse Team," *Baltimore Sun*, June 9, 1968.

13. "All M.S.A. Lacrosse."

14. "All M.S.A. Lacrosse."

15. "Red Stick Team Wins Exhibition," *Ithaca Journal*, October 25, 1971.

16. "Red Stick Team."

17. Gunts interview.

18. James H. Jackson, "Army and Navy Meet Today in 'Ordinary' Game," *Baltimore Sun*, June 6, 1971.

19. Steve Soroka, interview with the author, February 13, 2021.

20. Bill Tanton, "Southern Lacrosse Gets One More Shot," *Evening Sun*, June 15, 1971.

21. Jack Chevalier, "Tourney Will Change College Stick Values," *Baltimore Sun*, June 7, 1971.

22. James H. Jackson, "Army, Navy to Use Frosh," *Baltimore Sun*, June 5, 1971.

23. Jackson, "Army, Navy."

24. Peter Carry, "Big Red Votes Itself No. 1," *Sports Illustrated*, June 12, 1971.

25. Joe Finn, interview with the author, September 18, 2019.

26. Finn interview.

27. Finn interview.

28. Tom Duquette, interview with the author, March 6, 2020.

29. "Lacrosse Factory Reopens," *Ottawa Citizen*, June 8, 1968.

30. "Lacrosse Factory Reopens."

31. Finn interview.

32. Tom Myrick, interview with the author, January 10, 2019.

33. John Danowski, interview with the author, July 1, 2019.

34. Danowski interview.

35. Jeff Wagner, interview with the author, August 13, 2019.

36. Frank Davis, interview with the author, February 4, 2019.

37. Davis interview.

38. Eamon J. McEneaney, "The Death of the Wooden Lacrosse Stick," *Lacrosse Magazine*, January–February 1998.

39. Fred Yahn, "Cornell Lacrosse Season to Start," *Ithaca Journal*, March 21, 1972.

40. *New York Times*, April 2, 1972.

41. Gunts interview.

42. Fred Yahn, "Cornell Shows Passwork and Footwork," *Ithaca Journal*, April 21, 1972.

43. Richie Moran, interview with the author, April 29, 2019.

44. Brooks Bradley, interview with the author, September 7, 2019.

45. Bradley interview.

46. Paul Kaye, "Lacrosse Squad Opens Season with Wins at Hofstra, Adelphi," *Cornell Daily Sun*, March 27, 1972.

47. Roy Rifkin, "Frosh Stickmen Key to Cornell's Future Success," *Cornell Daily Sun*, April 3, 1972.

48. Gunts interview.

49. Gunts interview.

50. Gunts interview.

51. Gunts interview.

52. Bill Ellis, interview with the author, June 25, 2019.

53. "Cornell Ten Heads Sun Poll Again," *Baltimore Sun*, March 27, 1972.

54. Fred Yahn, "Cornell Lacrosse No. 1, At Least Until Saturday," *Ithaca Journal*, March 31, 1972.

55. Reid Detchon, "Romp at WC Preps Navy for Terps," *Evening Sun*, March 23, 1972.

56. Fred Yahn, "Navy Stickmen in Rare Visit," *Ithaca Journal*, March 30, 1972.

57. Albert R. Fischer, "Cornell's Moran Is Contented," *Baltimore Sun*, May 19, 1970.

58. Tom Cafaro, interview with the author, February 3, 2019.

59. Steve Soroka, interview with the author, February 13, 2021.

60. James H. Jackson, "Tar Tops 'Hit-Minded' Harvard, 8–3," *Baltimore Sun*, April 8, 1971.

61. Soroka interview.

62. Jackson, "Tar Tops."

63. James H. Jackson, "Local Stick Schedule Lists Four Big Games," *Baltimore Sun*, April 7, 1973.

64. Bill Howard, "An Old Indian Bloodbath Gets a Cornell Revival," *Cornell Daily Sun*, March 31, 1972.

65. "No. 1 Cornell Needs a Goalie," *Press and Sun-Bulletin*, April 2, 1972.

66. Soroka interview.

67. Soroka interview.

68. Soroka interview.

69. Kenny Van Sickle, "Cornell Strong at Finish in 12–9 Defeat to Navy," *Ithaca Journal*, April 3, 1972.

70. "Navy Upsets Cornell," *Capital*, April 3, 1972.

71. "Mids Stun Big Red in Lacrosse," *Evening Capital*, April 3, 1972.

72. "Mids Stun."

73. Fred Yahn, "Evel Knievel at Glen? It's Off (For Now)," *Ithaca Journal*, April 6, 1972.

74. Tom Nugent, "Making a Million the Hard Way," *Detroit Free Press*, March 22, 1972.

75. James H. Jackson, "Virginia Ten Wins Title," *Baltimore Sun*, April 3, 1972.

76. Reid Detchon, "Dream Tilt Was Money Flop, but Stick Fans Were Happy," *Evening Sun*, April 3, 1972.

77. "Cavaliers Ranked No. 1 in Stick Poll," *Baltimore Sun*, April 3, 1972.

78. "1972 Didascaleion," Cortland State yearbook, https://digitalcommons.cortland.edu/didascaleion/54/.

79. "Cortland State 1972 Lacrosse Preview," Cortland State publicity department.

80. Jack Emmer, interview with the author, February 4, 2019; "You're Somebody When You Play Lacrosse at Cortland," *Cortland Standard*, August 28, 1972.

81. 2019 Cortland State football media guide, https://www.cortlandreddragons.com/documents/2019/9/11//2019guidenoscreen.pdf?id=1566.

82. Emmer interview.

83. Reid Detchon, "Cortland in Major Upset," *Evening Sun*, March 31, 1972.

84. Emmer interview.

85. Bill Howard, "Cortland Cancels Lacrosse Game," *Cornell Daily Sun*, April 12, 1972.

86. Howard, "Cortland Cancels."

87. Howard, "Cortland Cancels."

88. Howard, "Cortland Cancels."

89. Howard, "Cortland Cancels."

90. Howard, "Cortland Cancels."

91. Fred Yahn, "Red Lacrossemen Turn Attention to Penn Contest," *Ithaca Journal*, April 12, 1972.

92. Ellis interview.

93. Bill Howard, "Red Lacrossemen Face Cortland," *Cornell Daily Sun*, May 2, 1972.

94. John W. Fox, "6–0 Cornell till Dragons Dine," *Press Sun-Bulletin*, May 3, 1972.

95. Fox, "Dragons Dine."

96. Bill Howard, "Cortland Upends Red Stickmen," *Cornell Daily Sun*, May 3, 1972.

97. Ellis interview.

98. Ellis interview.

99. Fred Yahn, "Red Lacrossers Trampled in Late Cortland Rush," *Ithaca Journal*, May 3, 1972.

100. Fox, "Dragons Dine."

101. Yahn, "Red Lacrossers Trampled."

102. Yahn, "Red Lacrossers Trampled."

103. 1972 *Didascaleion*, Cortland State yearbook.

104. Howard, "Cortland Upends Red Stickmen."

105. Bill Tierney, interview with the author, December 12, 2019.

106. Ellis interview.

107. Fred Yahn, "Hither . . . and Yonder," *Ithaca Journal*, May 6, 1972.

108. Yahn, "Hither . . . and Yonder."

109. "Big Red 10 Certain of Ivy League Tie," *Ithaca Journal*, May 8, 1972.

110. Dave Creighton, interview with the author, February 9, 2019.

111. Creighton interview.

112. "Honors Continue to Pour in for Hobart Stickers," *Geneva Times*, May 31, 1972.

113. List available at wgvarsitylax.com.

114. Joe Marshall, "Statesmen Are Big Shots," *Sports Illustrated*, April 22, 1974.

115. Norm Jollow, "Little Time to Celebrate, Hobart at RIT Today," *Geneva Times*, May 10, 1972.

116. Fred Yahn, "Cornell 'Hurt' by 11–10 Loss to Hobart," *Ithaca Journal*, May 10, 1972.

117. Yahn, "Cornell 'Hurt.'"

118. Yahn, "Cornell 'Hurt.'"

119. Terry Cullen, interview with the author, February 14, 2021.

120. Cullen interview.

121. Jollow, "Little Time."

122. Jollow, "Little Time."

123. Cullen interview.

124. Cullen interview.

125. "Hobart Hall of Famer Don Aleksiewicz Passes," Hobart and William Smith Colleges, June 9, 2014.

126. Reid Detchon, "Lacrosse Draw Favors Cadets," *Evening Sun*, May 15, 1972.

127. Fred Yahn, "Cornell Notches 5th Straight Ivy Lacrosse Title," *Ithaca Journal*, May 15, 1972.

128. Yahn, "Cornell Notches."

129. Yahn, "Cornell Notches."

130. "Terps Replace Hopkins as Top Lacrosse Team," *Baltimore Sun*, May 15, 1972.

131. "Terps Replace Hopkins."

132. Davis interview.

133. Reid Detchon, "Cornell Lacrosse Coach Moran Piqued at Snub by NCAA," *Evening Sun*, May 16, 1972.

134. Detchon, "Moran Piqued."

135. Pat Gallagher, interview with the author, August 5, 2019.

136. Gallagher interview.

137. "Cornell 'Out,'" *Ithaca Journal*, May 15, 1972.

138. Mike Waldvogel, interview with the author, December 16, 2019.

139. "John Fox Column," *Press and Sun-Bulletin*, May 14, 1972.

140. "John Fox Column."

141. Bill Tierney, interview with the author, December 13, 2019.

142. Emmer interview.

143. Tierney interview, December 13, 2019.

144. James H. Jackson, "Cortland Trims Navy in Overtime Thriller," *Baltimore Sun*, May 21, 1972.

145. Hymy Cohen, "A Happy Crowd at Navy," *Capital*, May 22, 1972.

146. 1972 Cortland State roster, https://digitalcommons.cortland.edu/menlacrosse_documents/7/.

147. "Guardian Graham Goal Gold," *Cortland Standard*, May 16, 1974.

148. "You're Somebody When You Play Lacrosse at Cortland," *Cortland Standard*, August 28, 1972.

149. "You're Somebody."

150. "You're Somebody."

151. Cohen, "Happy Crowd."

152. "Supremes to Star at West Point in Sickle Cell Foundation Show," *Herald-News*, May 16, 1972.

153. Emmer interview.

154. Doug Tarring, interview with the author, August 23, 2019.

155. Tarring interview.

156. 1972 *Didascaleion*, Cortland State yearbook.

157. 1972 *Didascaleion*.

158. Tarring interview.
159. Tarring interview.
160. Tarring interview.
161. "Dragon Stickmen Hosting Virginia Saturday," *Cortland Standard*, May 26, 1972.
162. "UVa Defeats Cortland," *News Leader*, May 28, 1972.
163. Rol Randall, "Objections Withdrawn! Ginny's Best," *Cortland Standard*, May 28, 1972.
164. Randall, "Objections Withdrawn!"
165. John W. Fox, "C-State Rout Home-Made," *Press and Sun-Bulletin*, May 28, 1972.
166. Fox, "C-State Rout."
167. Emmer interview.
168. 1972 *Didascaleion*.
169. Emmer interview.
170. Bill Tanton, "Birds a Lot Better Than They're Playing," *Evening Sun*, June 6, 1972.
171. "Stick Playoffs: Both Cornell, Cortland Host," *Ithaca Journal*, May 13, 1974.
172. "You're Somebody."
173. Tarring interview.

6. THE ESTABLISHMENT STRIKES BACK

1. Reid Detchon, "Midfielders Eldredge, Wener Key Cavalier Win," *Baltimore Sun*, June 4, 1972.
2. Bill Tanton, "Birds a Lot Better than They're Playing," *Evening Sun*, June 6, 1972.
3. Jeff Wagner, interview with author, August 13, 2019.
4. Wagner interview, August 13, 2019.
5. Jeff Wagner, interview with author, February 16, 2021.
6. Wagner interview, February 16, 2021.
7. Advertisement in the *Capital*, December 11, 1971.
8. Advertisement in the *Capital*, March 4, 1972.
9. Wagner interview, February 16, 2021.
10. "Navy Lacrosse Coach Resigns," *Daily Times*, June 13, 1972.
11. "Coach Resigns."
12. Wilson Phipps, interview with author, August 14, 2019.
13. Steve Soroka, interview with author, February 13, 2021.
14. Joe Glajch, "Moran Pleased with Red Lacrosse Program," *Ithaca Journal*, March 1, 1973.
15. Advertisement in the *Baltimore Sun*, February 25, 1973.
16. Advertisement in the *Baltimore Sun*, February 25, 1973.
17. Brooks Bradley, interview with author, September 7, 2019.
18. Bradley interview.
19. "Laxmen Top Rutgers," *Cornell Daily Sun*, October 24, 1972.
20. "Red Stickmen Preparing for Tourney," *Ithaca Journal*, March 21, 1973.
21. Glajch, "Moran Pleased."
22. Roy Rifkin, "Stickmen Prep for South," *Cornell Daily Sun*, March 13, 1973.
23. Rifkin, "Stickmen Prep."
24. "Red Stickmen Preparing for Tourney," *Ithaca Journal,* March 21, 1973.
25. Richie Moran, interview with author, April 29, 2019.
26. Moran interview, April 29, 2019.
27. Joe Glacjh, "Trenz Making the Difference," *Ithaca Journal*, April 2, 1974.
28. Tom Marino, interview with author, June 16, 2020.
29. Marino interview.

30. Frank Muehleman, interview with author, August 19, 2019.
31. Buck Briggs, interview with author, May 1, 2019.
32. Mike French, interview with author, July 19, 2019.
33. French interview.
34. French interview.
35. French interview.
36. French interview.
37. Moran interview.
38. French interview.
39. French interview.
40. Jon Levine, interview with author, August 16, 2019.
41. Glen Mueller, interview with author, April 28, 2019.
42. French interview.
43. Levine interview.
44. "Streety, Rhinehart and Deinhardt in the Nassau Showcases," *Press and Sun-Bulletin*, August 22, 1972.
45. "Red Stickmen Lose in Overtime, 7–6," *Ithaca Journal*, March 24, 1973.
46. Bill Free, "W&L, Carling Tens Win," *Baltimore Sun*, March 24, 1973.
47. Free, "W&L."
48. Free, "W&L."
49. "Can Red 10 Stop Navy's Big Guns?" *Ithaca Journal*, March 30, 1973
50. James H. Jackson, "Cornell Protests Winning Navy Goal," *Baltimore Sun*, April 1, 1973.
51. Fred Yahn, "Cornell Loses Stick Opener to Navy, 5–4," *Ithaca Journal*, April 2, 1973.
52. Jackson, "Cornell Protests."
53. Yahn, "Cornell Loses."
54. Yahn, "Cornell Loses."
55. Hymy Cohen, "Navy Stickers Edge Cornell," *Capital*, April 2, 1973
56. James H. Jackson, "Virginia and Hopkins 1–2 in Stick Poll," *Baltimore Sun*, April 2, 1973.
57. Bradley interview.
58. Bradley interview.
59. Dave O'Hara, "Cornellian Wins Boston Marathon," *Associated Press*, April 16, 1973.
60. "Hopkins Ten Takes No. 1 Spot," *Baltimore Sun*, April 16, 1973.
61. Roy Rifkin, "Winless Red Laxers Face Impotent Orange Stickmen," *Cornell Daily Sun*, April 18, 1973.
62. Fred Yahn, "Red Lacrossers Post First Verdict," *Ithaca Journal*, April 19, 1973.
63. "Big Macs Chew Up Sewanhaka Foes," *Daily News*, April 8, 1973.
64. John Smith, "Lacrosse Veteran Soured by Losing," *Newsday*, May 1970.
65. Smith, "Lacrosse Veteran Soured."
66. Ibid Smith, "Lacrosse Veteran Soured."
67. John Danowski, interview with author, July 2, 2019.
68. Frank Muehleman, interview with author, June 19, 2019.
69. Muehleman interview, June 19, 2019.
70. Bill Free, "Sewanhaka Scores Early to Beat Boys' Latin," *Baltimore Sun*, April 2, 1972.
71. Kevin McEneaney, interview with author, September 12, 2019.
72. Joe Glajch, "IHS Stickmen Inexperienced?" *Ithaca Journal*, March 13, 1972.
73. John Danowski, interview with author, July 1, 2019.
74. Sal Paolantonio, interview with author, May 19, 2019.

75. Richie Moran, interview with author, October 9, 2019.

76. Moran interview, October 9, 2019.

77. Associated Press, "Vietnam Settlement Possible Next Week," *Ithaca Journal*, December 2, 1972.

78. Kathleen Bolton, "Coach Moran Remembers Eamon," *Cornell Spirit*, March 2005.

79. "Appointed Director," *Ithaca Journal*, November 20, 1970.

80. "Appointed Director."

81. "Appointed Director."

82. Moran interview, April 29, 2019.

83. Joe Glajch, "Booters Miami Bound," *Ithaca Journal*, December 3, 1972.

84. Bruce Arena, interview with author, December 31, 2020.

85. Peter Kaplan, interview with author, September 7, 2019.

86. Arena interview.

87. Bolton, "Coach Moran Remembers Eamon."

88. Terry Corcoran, interview with author, February 23, 2021.

89. Joe Glajch, "Long Island Lacrossers Win," *Ithaca Journal*, March 31, 1973.

90. Joe Glajch, "IHS Falls to Sewanhaka Stick Experience," *Ithaca Journal*, April 2, 1973.

91. Glajch, "HIS Falls."

92. Glajch, "HIS Falls."

93. Tom Harkness, interview with author, July 21, 2019.

94. Elli Harkness, interview with author, July 21, 2019.

95. Michael O'Neill, interview with author, August 23, 2019.

96. Sal Paolantonio, interview with author, May 19, 2019.

97. Chris Kane, interview with author, August 22, 2019.

98. Kane interview.

99. 1973 *Totem,* Sewanhaka High School.

100. Moran interview, April 29, 2019.

101. Marino interview.

102. Marino interview.

103. Frank Muehleman, interview with author, July 19, 2019.

104. Jay Sindler, interview with author, May 14, 2019.

105. Fred Yahn, "It Took Five Overtimes but Red Ruled," *Ithaca Journal*, April 30, 1973.

106. Yahn, "Five Overtimes."

107. Albert R. Fischer, "Terp Ten Win Stick Title by Edging Jays," *Baltimore Sun*, June 3, 1973.

108. Brian Delaney, "Remembering Eamon McEneaney, Cornell's 'Wild Irish Rose,'" *Lacrosse Magazine*, September 11, 2017.

109. Kim Eike, interview with author, August 28, 2019.

7. ASSEMBLING THE PIECES

1. Bill Gilbert, "Wrong Time, but a Super Game," *Sports Illustrated*, October 8, 1973.

2. Teamusa.uslacrosse.org.

3. James H. Jackson, "College Stick Stars Score 15–11 Victory," *Baltimore Sun*, September 29, 1973.

4. Jackson, "College Stick Stars."

5. Jackson, "College Stick Stars."

6. "Stickers Tab Three," *Ithaca Journal*, September 14, 1973.

7. Gilbert, "Wrong Time."

8. Gilbert, "Wrong Time."

9. Jeff Wagner, interview with author, February 15, 2021.

10. Bob Rule, interview with author, April 3, 2019.

11. Rule interview.

12. Rule interview.

13. Oldschoollaxfreak.com.

14. Oldschoollaxfreak.com.

15. "Stickmen Victorious," *Ithaca Journal*, October 29, 1973

16. Joe Glajch, "Red Stickmen Open March 23," *Ithaca Journal*, March 1, 1974.

17. Peter Kaplan, interview with the author, September 7, 2019.

18. Jennifer Wing, "Dr. Steven Sanford, 64," *Eagle News* online, July 28, 2017, https://www.vtcng.com/news_and_citizen/community/obituaries/dr-steven-sanford/article_4bc80a58-7864-11e7-a5cb-1fd053392b77.html.

19. Jon Levine, interview with the author, August 16, 2019.

20. Levine interview.

21. Cornell Sports Information press release, March 25, 1974.

22. Joe Glajch, "Red Stickmen Beat Adelphi," *Ithaca Journal*, March 25, 1974.

23. Mike Farrell, interview with the author.

24. Glajch, "Stickmen Beat Adelphi."

25. "Irondequoit's Whipple Sets Career Mark," *Democrat and Chronicle*, May 14, 1993

26. Ira Rosen, "Laxmen Entertain Middies," *Cornell Daily Sun*, March 29, 1974.

27. Rosen, "Laxmen Entertain."

28. Kenny Van Sickle, "Red Lacrossers Defeat Middies," *Ithaca Journal*, April 1, 1974.

29. Van Sickle, "Red Lacrossers Defeat Middies."

30. Van Sickle, "Red Lacrossers Defeat Middies."

31. Ira Rosen, "Laxmen Triumph over Navy, 17–11," *Cornell Daily Sun*, April 2, 1974,

32. Rosen, "Laxmen Triumph."

33. "Cornell Lacrosse: 8–3 in 73," *Cornell Daily Sun*, August 29, 1973.

34. Bill Howard, "Injuries, Inconsistency Hamper Red," *Cornell Daily Sun*, November 2, 1973.

35. Dan Mackesey, interview with the author, July 18, 2019.

36. Michael O'Neill, interview with the author, August 23, 2019.

37. "Retired CU Planner Dies at 67," *Ithaca Journal*, May 3, 1976.

38. Dan Mackesey, interview with the author, July 18, 2019.

39. Mackesey interview.

40. Mackesey interview.

41. Mackesey interview.

42. Mackesey interview.

43. Mackesey interview.

44. Bill Howard, "McEneaney Sparks Talented Frosh," *Cornell Daily Sun*, April 30, 1974.

45. Gary Malm, interview with the author, August 15, 2019.

46. Joe Glajch, "Schoolboy Tourney Pays Off," *Ithaca Journal*, March 24, 1974.

47. Bruce Arena, interview with the author, December 30, 2020.

48. Joe Glajch, "Hopkins Next Stop," *Ithaca Journal*, April 4, 1974.

49. Glajch, "Hopkins Next Stop."

50. Glajch, "Hopkins Next Stop."

51. Joe Glajch, "Redmen Go to Grass at Hopkins," *Ithaca Journal*, April 4, 1974.

52. Joe Marshall, "The Jays Take It Back," *Sports Illustrated*, June 10, 1974.

53. Marshall, "Jays Take It Back."

54. Marshall, "Jays Take It Back."

55. Joe Finn, interview with the author, October 16, 2019.

56. "Hopkins Halts Red Lacrossers," *Ithaca Journal*, April 8, 1974.

57. Fred Yahn, "NCAAs Expected Next Year in Lacrosse," *Ithaca Journal*, May 25, 1970.

58. Steve Klein, "McEneaney Neutralized as Frosh Stickmen Lose," *Cornell Daily Sun*, April 15, 1974.

59. "Cornell Frosh 10 Beats Army JVs," *Ithaca Journal*, April 18, 1974.

60. "Frosh Laxmen Beat Corning; Face Nassau on Saturday," *Cornell Daily Sun*, April 25, 1974.

61. Brian Conroy, interview with the author, June 24, 2020.

62. Conroy interview.

63. "Cub Laxmen in Big Match," *Cornell Daily Sun*, April 26, 1974.

64. "Cubs Beaten," *Ithaca Journal*, April 29, 1974.

65. Richie Meade, interview with the author, May 22, 2019.

66. Bill Howard, "McEneaney Sparks Talented Frosh," *Cornell Daily Sun*, April 30, 1974.

67. Howard, "McEneaney Sparks."

68. "Cornell Frosh Now 5–2," *Ithaca Journal*, May 2, 1974.

69. "Frosh Stickmen Crush Cortland," *Cornell Daily Sun*, May 2, 1974.

70. "Red Frosh Stickmen in Romp," *Ithaca Journal*, May 10, 1974.

71. Joe Glajch, "Red Stickmen Get Shot at NCAA Title," *Ithaca Journal*, May 14, 1974.

72. Paul Attner, "Lacrosse Rating Makes W&L Fans Cross," *Washington Post*, May 16, 1974.

73. Kent Baker, "Maryland Routs Virginia Stickmen," *Baltimore Sun*, April 14, 1974.

74. Baker, "Maryland Routs."

75. Joe Glajch, "After Virginia, Cornell Gets Maryland," *Ithaca Journal*, May 20, 1974.

76. Joe Glajch, "Red 10 Ivy Champs," *Ithaca Journal*, May 13, 1974.

77. "Red Stick Team Defeats Penn," *Ithaca Journal*, May 2, 1974.

78. Joe Glajch, "Just Like 1971?" *Ithaca Journal*, May 17, 1974.

79. Glajch, "Just Like 1971?"

80. Paul Attner, "Upstarts Seek Upsets in NCAA Lacrosse," *Washington Post*, May 25, 1974.

81. Attner, "Upstarts Seek Upsets."

82. Marshall, "Jays Take It Back."

83. Marshall, "Jays Take It Back."

84. Marshall, "Jays Take It Back."

85. Bob Ibach, "Thomas Johnson Places 4 on All-Metro Team," *Evening Sun*, December 2, 1971; Bill Tanton, "Jays, Terps Emerge as Lacrosse Cream," *Evening Sun*, April 16, 1973.

86. Bill Free, "Wittelsberger Headed to Johns Hopkins," *Baltimore Sun*, June 5, 1972.

87. Mike Klingaman, "Hopkins Has Own 'Hit Man,'" *Evening Sun*, May 22, 1974.

88. Klingaman, "Hit Man."

89. James H. Jackson, "Hopkins Dethrones Maryland, 17–12, for NCAA Lacrosse Title," *Baltimore Sun*, June 2, 1974.

90. Jackson, "Hopkins Dethrones."

91. Phil Hersh, "Wittelsberger Sticks Goalie," *Evening Sun*, March 24, 1975.

92. Marshall, "Jays Take It Back."

93. Jackson, "Hopkins Dethrones."

94. James H. Jackson, "Area's Domination of Sport Should Continue," *Baltimore Sun*, March 9, 1975.

8. THE FRENCH CONNECTION

1. Terry Cullen, interview with the author, February 14, 2021.
2. John W. Fox, "Big Red 'Veers' Past Colgate, 40–21," *Press and Sun-Bulletin*, September 29, 1974.
3. Jim Hofher, interview with the author, September 4, 2019.
4. Sal Paolantonio, interview with the author, June 3, 2019.
5. Associated Press, "Musick Resigns as Cornell Coach," *New York Times*, December 28, 1974.
6. "Cornell Lacrosse Winner," *Ithaca Journal*, October 21, 1974.
7. David Bray, interview with the author, February 28, 2021.
8. Bray interview.
9. Bray interview.
10. Letter from Carl Lindemann, Jr., to Robert J. Kane, March 30, 1975. Courtesy of Cornell Sports Information Archives.
11. "Lacrosse Canceled," *Ithaca Journal*, March 10, 1975.
12. Joe Glajch, "Lacrosse: Just around the Corner," *Ithaca Journal*, March 17, 1975.
13. "Cornell Third in USILA Poll," *Ithaca Journal*, March 17, 1975.
14. Joe Marshall, "Cornell's Wild Irish Rose," *Sports Illustrated*, June 6, 1977.
15. Joe Marshall, "The French Connection," *Sports Illustrated*, April 7, 1975.
16. Dom Starsia, interview with the author, December 19, 2019.
17. Bray interview.
18. Phil Hersh, "UB Stickmen Sharp in Road Play," *Evening Sun*, April 7, 1975.
19. James H. Jackson, "Cornell Thumps Navy," *Baltimore Sun*, April 6, 1975.
20. Willie Scroggs, interview with the author, May 13, 2019.
21. Mike Waldvogel, interview with the author, December 16, 2018.
22. John W. Fox, "Cornell Lacrosse No. 2 Is No Match for No. 1." *Press and Sun-Bulletin*, April 20, 1975.
23. Phil Hersh, "Cornell Has a 'Lacrosse Superman,'" *Baltimore Sun*, April 18, 1975.
24. Joe Glajch, "Johns Hopkins Impregnable in Showdown, 16–9," *Ithaca Journal*, April 21, 1975.
25. James J. Jackson, "Hopkins, Cornell Tens Play Today," *Baltimore Sun*, April 19, 1975.
26. Jackson, "Hopkins, Cornell Tens."
27. "Towson High Edges Sewanhaka 10, 4–3," *Baltimore Sun*, April 2, 1971.
28. Glajch, "Johns Hopkins Impregnable."
29. Glajch, "Johns Hopkins Impregnable."
30. Glajch, "Johns Hopkins Impregnable."
31. Glajch, "Johns Hopkins Impregnable."
32. Phil Hersh, "Hopkins Even Better than No. 1 Ranking," *Evening Sun*, April 21, 1975.
33. Fox, "Cornell Lacrosse No Match."
34. Hersh, "Hopkins Even Better."
35. Bob Henrickson, interview with the author, October 16, 2019.
36. "Cornell Frosh Win Lacrosse," *Ithaca Journal*, April 21, 1975
37. Jefferson Flanders, interview with the author, September 25, 2018.
38. Flanders interview.
39. Jeff Wagner, interview with the author, December 13, 2018.
40. Richie Moran, interview with the author, April 29, 2019.
41. Flanders interview.
42. Flanders interview.
43. Fred Yahn, "Cornell Stickers Mash Harvard," *Ithaca Journal*, May 8, 1975.

44. Flanders interview.

45. Joe Glajch, "Cornell Lacrossers Win Ivy Title," *Ithaca Journal*, May 12, 1975.

46. Tom Marino, interview with the author, June 16, 2020.

47. Phil Hersh, "Morgan Ready to Join Top 10 of Lacrosse," *Evening Sun*, March 18, 1975.

48. Cameron C. Snyder, "Here Come the Bears in Lacrosse," *Baltimore Sun*, March 21, 1975.

49. Charlie Stieff, interview with the author, May 20, 2019.

50. Attner, "Terrapin Lacrossers Fade."

51. Wilson Phipps, interview with the author, August 14, 2019.

52. Phipps interview.

53. Paul Attner, "Terps Smite Hopkins by 8 in Lacrosse," *Washington Post*, May 18, 1975.

54. Mike Klingaman, "For Morgan State's 1975 Lacrosse Team, Stunning Upset Still Resonates Decades Later," *Baltimore Sun*, October 18, 2018.

55. Cameron C. Snyder, "Navy, Terps Advance, Jays Fall in Tourney," *Baltimore Sun*, May 22, 1975.

56. Charlie Brown, interview with the author, May 17, 2019.

57. Brown interview, May 17, 2019.

58. Brown interview, May 17, 2019.

59. Brown interview, May 17, 2019.

60. Stieff interview.

61. Fred Yahn, "After Rutgers, Cornell Gets Navy," *Ithaca Journal*, May 22, 1975.

62. Yahn, "After Rutgers."

63. Charlie Brown, interview with the author, May 18, 2019.

64. "Red Odds-On Favorite," *Ithaca Journal*, May 23, 1975.

65. Moran interview, April 29, 2019.

66. Cameron C. Snyder, "Terps, Middies Triumph to Gain Lacrosse Final," *Baltimore Sun*, May 25, 1975.

67. Snyder, "Terps, Middies Triumph."

68. Fred Yahn, "Middies Upend Red Stickmen," *Ithaca Journal*, May 26, 1975.

69. Waldvogel interview.

70. Dan Mackesey, interview with the author, August 1, 2019.

71. Keith Reitenbach, interview with the author, June 18, 2020.

72. Ibid.

73. Cameron C. Snyder, "Terps, Middies triumph to gain lacrosse final," *The Baltimore Sun*, May 25, 1975

74. Fred Yahn, "Middies Upend Red Stickmen," *The Ithaca Journal*, May 26, 1975

75. Richie Moran, interview with the author, March 21, 2021.

76. Waldvogel interview.

77. Dan Mackesey, interview with the author, August 1, 2019.

78. Joe Finn, interview with the author, September 18, 2019.

79. Jon Levine, interview with the author, August 14, 2019.

80. Kevin McEneaney, interview with the author, September 12, 2019.

81. Bryan Matthews, interview with the author, February 24, 2021.

9. START OF A STREAK

1. "Gowanda Cindermen Defeat Pioneer, Depew; Bray Breaks 2-Mile Record," *Gowanda News & Observer*, May 27, 1971.

2. "Gowanda Cindermen."

3. "Gowanda Cindermen."

4. "Gowanda Cindermen."

5. Richie Moran, interview with the author, April 12, 2021.

6. Sportsreference.com.

7. Terry Cullen, interview with the author, February 14, 2021.

8. "Stickmen Triumph Twice," *Ithaca Journal*, October 27, 1975.

9. "Port Light," Schreiber High 1971 Yearbook.

10. "Port Light."

11. Cornell sports information release, spring 1978.

12. Cornell sports information release.

13. Chris Kane, interview with the author, August 22, 2019.

14. Kane interview.

15. Kane interview.

16. Kane interview.

17. Kane interview.

18. Kane interview.

19. Gary Malm, interview with the author, September 30, 2019.

20. Frank Muehleman, interview with the author, August 9, 2019.

21. Muehleman interview.

22. Joe Finn, interview with the author, September 18, 2019.

23. Phil Hersh, "Katz Fears No Attack," *Evening Sun*, April 16, 1976.

24. Jeff Wagner, interview with the author, February 16, 2021.

25. Wagner interview, February 16, 2021.

26. Wagner interview, February 16, 2021.

27. Jeff Wagner, interview with the author, February 17, 2021.

28. Wilson Phipps, interview with the author, August 14, 2019.

29. Frank Urso, interview with the author, August 15, 2019.

30. Michael O'Neill, interview with the author, August 23, 2019.

31. Urso interview.

32. Urso interview.

33. Urso interview.

34. Mike Farrell, interview with the author, August 15, 2019.

35. Maryland Men's Soccer Media Guide, https://umterps.com/sports/2018/10/5/digital-media-guide-mens-soccer.aspx.

36. Ed Mullen, interview with the author, August 13, 2019.

37. Mike Klingaman, "Tuck's Luck Gives Owls a Big Hoot," *Baltimore Sun*, April 10, 1972.

38. Bob Ibach, "Thomas Johnson Winds Up as No. 1 Team for 1971," *Evening Sun*, November 29, 1971.

39. Ibach, "Thomas Johnson."

40. Mike Klingaman, "Tuck's Luck"; "Dundalk's Tuck Wins Scoring Title," *Baltimore Sun*, May 30, 1972.

41. "Terp Jayvees Face Bainbridge," *Baltimore Sun*, October 19, 1972.

42. Mullen interview.

43. University of Maryland Fraternity-Sorority Yearbook, 1975.

44. University of Maryland Fraternity-Sorority Yearbook, 1975.

45. Paul Attner, "Maryland Opens in Lacrosse," *Washington Post*, March 15, 1976.

46. O'Neill interview.

47. Mullen interview.

48. O'Neill interview.

49. O'Neill interview.

50. O'Neill interview.

51. O'Neill interview.

52. "ABC Will Televise Lacrosse Title Game," *Baltimore Sun*, March 16, 1976.

53. Joe Marshall, "Big Red Sticks It to the Terps," *Sports Illustrated*, June 7, 1976.

54. Ron Dziengiel, "It Was a Nice Day, Time for Lacrosse," *Ithaca Journal*, March 22, 1976.

55. Kane interview.

56. Fred Yahn, "Cornell's Lacrossers to Meet Top Club Team," *Ithaca Journal*, March 24, 1976

57. Gary Ronberg, "The Old Boys Are Still Best," *Sports Illustrated*, March 31, 1969.

58. Dave Creighton, interview with the author, February 9, 2019.

59. "Cornell's Lacrossers Stop Mt. Washington, 13–8," *Ithaca Journal*, March 28, 1976

60. Dan Mackesey, interview with the author, July 25, 2019.

61. Kane interview.

62. Bob Henrickson, interview with the author, October 16, 2019.

63. Mackesey interview.

64. Muehleman interview.

65. Mullen interview.

66. Kane interview.

67. Keith Reitenbach, interview with the author, June 18, 2020.

68. Fred Yahn, "Cornell Lacrosse Victim No. 4," *Ithaca Journal*, April 12, 1976.

69. Ron Grover, "Maryland Defeats Virginia for [ACC] Title," *Washington Post*, April 18, 1976.

70. Grover, "Maryland Defeats Virginia."

71. Richie Moran, interview with the author, April 29, 2019.

72. Phil Hersh, "Cornell Retorts to Critics of Its Lacrosse Schedule," *Evening Sun*, April 19, 1976.

73. Cameron C. Snyder, "Cornell Ten Trips Hopkins," *Baltimore Sun*, April 18, 1976.

74. Snyder, "Corner Trips Hopkins."

75. Snyder, "Corner Trips Hopkins."

76. Mackesey interview.

77. Mackesey interview.

78. Mackesey interview.

79. Phil Hersh, "A Thesis Pointed UMass toward Big Lacrosse Map," *Evening Sun*, May 18, 1976.

80. Charlie Stieff, interview with the author, May 20, 2019.

81. Stieff interview.

82. Tom Marino, interview with the author, June 16, 2020.

83. Richie Moran, interview with the author, May 13, 2019.

84. Jay Sindler, interview with the author, May 13, 2019.

85. Fred Yahn, "14–0!" *Ithaca Journal*, May 20, 1976.

86. Kim Eike, interview with the author, August 22, 2019.

87. Yahn, "14–0!"

88. Kane interview

89. Kane interview.

90. Muehleman interview.

91. Kane interview.

92. Kane interview.

93. Kane interview.

94. Dan Mackesey, interview with the author, August 1, 2019.

10. FROM BROWN STADIUM

1. Bill Tanton, "Bullets Face Thursday Jinx," *Evening Sun*, April 27, 1976.
2. Fred Yahn, "Cornell Number One," *Ithaca Journal*, May 31, 1976.
3. Yahn, "Cornell Number One."
4. Joe Finn, interview with the author, September 18, 2019.
5. Buck Briggs, interview with the author, April 30, 2019.
6. Keith Reitenbach, interview with the author, January 5, 2021.
7. Dom Starsia interview, with the author, December 13, 2019.
8. Jeff Wagner, interview with the author, December 13, 2019.
9. Mike French, interview with the author, July 22, 2019.
10. French interview.
11. Joe Marshall, "Big Red Sticks It to the Terps," *Sports Illustrated*, June 7, 1976.
12. Fred Yahn, "Cornell, Baby, We're No. 1," *Ithaca Journal*, May 31, 1976.
13. 1976 Maryland Lacrosse Media Guide.
14. Jon Levine, interview with the author, August 14, 2019.
15. Yahn, "Cornell, Baby."
16. Dave Bray, interview with the author, February 28, 2021.
17. Gary Malm, interview with the author, September 30, 2019.
18. Frank Muehleman, interview with the author, August 9, 2019.
19. Mike Farrell, interview with the author, August 15, 2019.
20. Muehleman interview.
21. Dan Mackesey, interview with the author, August 1, 2019.
22. Levine interview.
23. Muehleman interview.
24. Bob Henrickson, interview with the author, October 16, 2019; Richie Moran, interview with the author, July 3, 2019.
25. Richie Moran, interview with the author, April 29, 2019.
26. Mackesey interview, August 1, 2019.
27. Malm interview.
28. Moran interview, April 29, 2019.
29. Kim Eike, interview with the author, August 22, 2019.
30. Footage from ABC's *Wide World of Sports*.
31. Eike interview.
32. Eike interview.
33. Eike interview.
34. Frank Urso, interview with the author, August 15, 2019.
35. Henrickson interview.
36. Mackesey interview, August 1, 2019.
37. Mackesey interview, August 1, 2019.
38. Dave Bray, interview with the author, February 22, 2021.
39. Footage from ABC's *Wide World of Sports*.
40. 1976 NCAA lacrosse championship official box score.
41. Malm interview.
42. Chris Kane, interview with the author, August 22, 2019.
43. Mackesey interview, August 2, 2019.
44. Ron Dziengiel, "Our Very Own Big Red Machine Keeps Rolling Along," *Ithaca Journal*, May 3, 1976.
45. Mackesey interview, August 2, 2019.
46. Joe Marshall, "Big Red Sticks It to the Terps," *Sports Illustrated*, June 7, 1976.
47. Ed Mullen, interview with the author, August 13, 2019.
48. Levine interview.

49. Mullen interview.

50. Chris Kane, interview with the author, August 22, 2019.

11. FLAMIN' EAMON

1. James H. Jackson, "Upstate N.Y. Assumes College Lacrosse Leadership, and with Few Maryland-breds," *Baltimore Sun*, June 2, 1976.

2. Provlax.com.

3. Jeff Wagner, interview with the author, February 17, 2021.

4. Dave Newton, "Brighter Days Ahead, Says Kane," *Ithaca Journal*, June 25, 1976.

5. Newton, "Brighter Days."

6. 1977 Maryland Lacrosse Media Guide.

7. 1977 Maryland Lacrosse Media Guide.

8. Gary Malm, interview with the author, September 30, 2019.

9. Malm interview.

10. Malm interview.

11. Malm interview.

12. Kim Eike, interview with the author, August 22, 2019.

13. Dave Bray, interview with the author, March 6, 2021.

14. Brian Lasda, interview with the author, March 2, 2021.

15. "Laxers Trounce Long Island Foes," *Cornell Daily Sun*, March 28, 1977.

16. "Laxers Trounce Foes."

17. Cornell Sports Review-Preview, April 4, 1977.

18. "Cornell Lacrossers at Mount Washington," *Ithaca Journal*, April 5, 1977.

19. "Cornell's Lacrossers Trip Mt. Washington," *Ithaca Journal*, April 6, 1977.

20. "Cornell Stickers Stop UMass, *Cornell Daily Sun*, April 3, 1977.

21. Fred Yahn, "Red Lacrossers Eye Rutgers," *Ithaca Journal*, April 7, 1977.

22. David Bilmes, "Stickmen Stay Undefeated with Victory over Rutgers," *Cornell Daily Sun*, April 11, 1977.

23. Fred Yahn, "Red, Hopkins on East Hill; IC vs. Hobart in Morning," *Ithaca Journal*, April 16, 1977.

24. Norm Jollow, "No Reminder," *Geneva Times*, April 18, 1977.

25. Phil Hersh, "Huntley New Surprise for Hopkins," *Evening Sun*, March 19, 1976.

26. Hersh, "Huntley."

27. Hersh, "Huntley."

28. Hersh, "Huntley."

29. Hersh, "Huntley."

30. Cameron C. Snyder, "Cornell Ten Wins over Hopkins," *Baltimore Sun*, April 17, 1977.

31. Snyder, "Cornell Ten Wins"; Steve Grandin, "Laxers Edge Hopkins, 12–11," *Cornell Daily Sun*, April 18, 1977.

32. Steve Grandin, "Laxers Edge Hopkins."

33. Grandin, "Laxers Edge Hopkins."

34. Grandin, "Laxers Edge Hopkins."

35. Grandin, "Laxers Edge Hopkins."

36. Cornell sports information release.

37. Joe Marshall, "He's Put Hop in Hopkins," *Sports Illustrated*, May 12, 1975.

38. Snyder, "Cornell Ten Wins."

39. Dan Mackesey, interview with the author, August 2, 2019.

40. Mackesey interview.

41. Steve Grandin, "Laxmen Head to Dartmouth," *Cornell Daily Sun*, April 29, 1977.

42. Brian Lasda, interview with the author, March 2, 2021.

43. Keith Reitenbach, interview with the author, January 9, 2019.

44. Mike Waldvogel, interview with the author, December 16, 2019.

45. Waldvogel interview.

46. Malm interview.

47. Wick Sollers, interview with the author, September 2, 2019.

48. Fred Yahn, "Cornell Lacrossers Smash Princeton, 15–7," *Ithaca Journal*, May 9, 1977.

49. Yahn, "Cornell Lacrossers Smash."

50. Associated Press, "Legend of 1977 Grateful Dead Show at Cornell Lives on at 40th Anniversary," May 8, 2017.

51. Matt Kinnear, "40 Years Ago: The Crazy Intersection of the Grateful Dead and Cornell Lacrosse," Insidelacrosse.com, https://www.insidelacrosse.com/article/40-years-ago-the-crazy-intersection-of-the-grateful-dead-and-cornell-lacrosse/49473.

52. Kinnear, "40 Years Ago."

53. Fred Yahn, "Cornell to Meet Hopkins in NCAA championship," *Ithaca Journal*, May 23, 1977.

54. Cameron C. Snyder, "Cornell Bombs Navy, 22–6, in NCAA Semifinal," *Baltimore Sun*, May 22, 1977.

55. Cornell sports information release.

56. Cornell sports information release.

57. "Cornell, Jay Stickers Puzzle Each Other," *Evening Sun*, May 23, 1977.

58. Snyder, "Cornell bombs Navy."

59. James H. Jackson, "Blue Jays Stun Terps in Lacrosse," *Baltimore Sun*, May 22, 1977.

60. Paul Attner, "Hopkins Wallops Terrapins," *Washington Post*, May 22, 1977.

61. Cornell sports information release, Spring 1977.

62. "Red's Destination: Charlottesville," *Ithaca Journal*, May 25, 1977.

63. "Red's Destination."

64. Mackesey interview.

65. Reid Detchon, "Cornell, Jays Stickers Puzzle Each Other," *Evening Sun*, May 23, 1977.

66. Cornell sports information press release.

67. Mackesey interview.

68. Yahn, "Cornell, Hopkins Eye Title," *Ithaca Journal*, May 27, 1977.

69. Cornell lacrosse press release.

70. Richie Moran, interview with the author, March 21, 2021.

71. Moran interview.

72. Moran interview.

73. Mark Greenberg, interview with the author, March 7, 2019.

74. Willie Scroggs, interview with the author, May 13, 2019.

75. Scroggs interview.

76. Dutch Snyder, "McEneaney & Co. Test Jays' 'No-Name' Defense," *Evening Sun*, May 27, 1977.

77. Moran interview.

78. Moran interview.

79. Moran interview.

80. Cornell sports information release.

81. Eike interview.

82. Kevin McEneaney, interview with the author, September 12, 2019.

83. Malm interview.

84. Larry Baum, interview with the author, September 5, 2019.

85. Baum interview.

86. Bob Henrickson, interview with the author, October 16, 2019.

87. "Cornell Stays on Top," *Democrat & Chronicle*, May 28, 1977.

88. Yahn, "Cornell, Hopkins Eye Title."

89. "Journal Picks Four 'Coaches of the Year,'" *Ithaca Journal*, December 31, 1977.

90. Buck Briggs, interview with the author, April 30, 2019.

91. Tom Myrick, interview with the author, January 10, 2019.

92. Joe Marshall, "Cornell's Wild Irish Rose," *Sports Illustrated*, June 6, 1977.

93. Greenberg interview.

94. Photo courtesy of Kevin McEneaney.

95. Marshall, "Cornell's Wild Irish Rose."

96. Myrick interview.

97. Sollers interview.

98. Dan O'Connell, interview with the author, May 24, 2021.

99. Sollers interview.

12. THAT-A-WAY IN PISCATAWAY

1. Joe Marshall, "Cornell's Wild Irish Rose," *Sports Illustrated*, June 6, 1977.

2. Michael O'Neill, interview with the author, August 23, 2019.

3. O'Neill interview.

4. Gary Malm, interview with the author, August 15, 2019.

5. O'Neill interview.

6. Leroy Katz, interview with the author, April 3, 2021.

7. Marshall, "Cornell's Wild Irish Rose."

8. Marshall, "Cornell's Wild Irish Rose."

9. Bob Henrickson, interview with the author, October 16, 2019.

10. Henrickson interview.

11. Cameron C. Snyder, "Fowlkes, Freed Upgrade Morgan Lacrosse Program," *Baltimore Sun*, February 3, 1978.

12. Alan Goldstein, "Another Day," *Baltimore Sun*, May 31, 1977.

13. Tom Marino, interview with the author, June 23, 2019.

14. Cameron C. Snyder, "Ciccarone Says Jay Ten Will Be Competitive," *Baltimore Sun*, February 19, 1978.

15. Dutch Snyder, "Goalies Rated Key to Llacrosse Title Game," *Evening Sun*, May 24, 1979.

16. Snyder, "Ciccarone Says."

17. Katz interview.

18. Katz interview.

19. Snyder, "Ciccarone Says."

20. Cornell sports information release.

21. Cornell sports information release.

22. Dutch Snyder, "Look Out, Here Comes Cornell Again," *Evening Sun*, March 23, 1978.

23. James H. Jackson, "No. 1 Cornell Stick Team Visits Wolfpack Tonight," *Baltimore Sun*, March 22, 1978.

24. Jackson, "No. 1 Cornell."

25. Cameron C. Snyder, "Cornell Defeats Wolfpack; Fusting Rates Big Red Better than Last Year," *Baltimore Sun*, March 23, 1978.

26. Snyder, "Cornell Defeats Wolfpack."

27. Snyder, "Cornell Defeats Wolfpack."

28. John Kolomic, "Lacrosse Champions to face off," *Democrat and Chronicle*, March 27, 1978.

29. Norm Jollow, "Moran Sees No. 1 Battle as 'One of the Finest Ever,'" *Finger Lakes Times*, March 27, 1978.

30. Joe Marshall, "Cornell Stayed Down on the Farm," *Sports Illustrated*, April 10, 1978.

31. Norm Jollow, "Statesmen May Start Slowly," *Finger Lakes Times*, March 24, 1978.

32. Marshall, "Cornell Stayed Down."

33. Marshall, "Cornell Stayed Down."

34. Larry Bump, "Cornell Survives Late Hobart Scare," *Democrat and Chronicle*, March 29, 1978.

35. Glen Crevier, "Now Bragging Rights Belong to Cornell," *Ithaca Journal*, March 29, 1978.

36. Norm Jollow, "No Loser," *Finger Lakes Times*, March 29, 1978.

37. "Spring Fair to Liven Homewood Next Week," *Johns Hopkins News-Letter*, April 7, 1978; "Comedian Klein at Hopkins Fair," *Evening Sun*, April 14, 1978.

38. "Spring Fair."

39. "Spring Fair."

40. Bill Tanton, "Lacrosse Better than Ever," *Evening Sun*, June 8, 1977.

41. Henrickson interview.

42. Alan Goldstein, "Palmer's 2-Hitter in '78 Debut Leads 7–0 Romp," *Baltimore Sun*, April 16, 1978.

43. Goldstein, "Palmer's 2-Hitter."

44. Dave Spivey, interview with the author, October 29, 2019.

45. Spivey interview.

46. Spivey interview.

47. Goldstein, "Palmer's 2-Hitter."

48. Snyder, "Cornell Ten Downs."

49. Katz interview.

50. Cameron C. Snyder, "Cornell Ten Downs Jays by 16–11," *Baltimore Sun*, April 16, 1978.

51. Snyder, "Cornell Ten Downs."

52. Snyder, "Cornell Ten Downs."

53. Snyder, "Cornell Ten Downs."

54. John D. Forbes, "Cornell Wins 34th Straight in Lacrosse," *New York Times*, April 16, 1978.

55. Forbes, "Cornell Wins."

56. Mark Asher, "Cornell Belts Hopkins for Record 34th in Row," *Washington Post*, April 16, 1978.

57. "Scarlet Knights Fall Short," *Courier-News*, May 1, 1978.

58. "Scarlet Knights."

59. Keith Reitenbach, interview with the author, January 5, 2021.

60. Charlie Stieff, interview with the author, May 18, 2019.

61. Ken O'Brien, "Rutgers Teams Fails to Earn Postseason Bids," *Central New Jersey Home News*, May 16, 1978.

62. Jay Sindler, interview with the author, May 14, 2019.

63. Stieff interview.

64. Glen Crevier, "It's on to the NCAA Final," *Ithaca Journal*, May 22, 1978.

65. James H. Jackson, "Earlier Loss to Cornell Gave Hopkins Incentive for Championship Game," *Baltimore Sun*, May 29, 1978.

66. Joe Marshall, "The Big Red Ended up Red-Faced," *Sports Illustrated*, June 5, 1978.

67. Mark Greenberg, interview with the author, August 21, 2019.

68. Greenberg interview.

69. Marshall, "Big Red Red-Faced."
70. Henrickson interview.
71. Transcript from *NBC Sportsworld* broadcast.
72. Spivey interview.
73. Frank Muehleman, interview with the author, August 9, 2019.
74. Marino interview.
75. Marino interview.
76. Henrickson interview.
77. Marino interview.

EPILOGUE

1. "New Boy on an Old Block," *Sports Illustrated*, March 30, 1981, https://vault.si.com/vault/1981/03/30/new-boy-on-an-old-block-led-by-coach-willie-scroggs-upstart-north-carolina-is-about-to-crash-and-perhaps-crush-the-sports-elite.
2. Dave Fassett, "Tar Heels Take Lacrosse Crown," *News and Observer*, May 31, 1981.
3. Willie Scroggs, interview with the author, May 13, 2019.
4. Richie Moran, interview with the author, May 29, 2019.

Bibliographic Note

Much of the information for this book came from interviews with more than ninety former players, coaches, administrators, and students, from schools including Army, Brown, Cornell, Cortland State, Duke, Harvard, Hobart, Hofstra, Johns Hopkins, Maryland, Navy, North Carolina, Princeton, Virginia, and Washington and Lee. Texts consulted for this book primarily include the archives of the *Baltimore Sun*, the *Cornell Daily Sun*, and the *Ithaca Journal*. The Cornell sports information department supplied copies of game notes, game programs, and artwork from the 1970s. The sports information offices at Air Force, Army, Brown, Cortland State, Hobart, Hofstra, Johns Hopkins, Maryland, Navy, Virginia, and Washington and Lee also supplied game notes, rosters, and statistics as requested.

Also consulted were videos from three games in the 1971 season, provided by former players. Video footage from 1976–1978 was sparse; it included highlights from a handful of games, with incomplete game action. Brown University's lacrosse coaches provided complete coach's films from two Brown–Cornell games of the 1970s, which proved invaluable. Several editions of *The Official Lacrosse Guide*, published by the NCAA during the 1970s, were purchased online to aid research for the book. Also consulted were the archives of the *Capital Newspapers*, the *New York Times*, and *Sports Illustrated*, among others. Lastly, Larry Baum, a photographer formerly with the *Ithaca Journal*, and Jules Sieburgh, a student at Cornell in the 1970s who attended many lacrosse games, graciously donated their work to be consulted for context and also to be used in the book.

Index